Advance praise for *Onward, Backward!*

If you've got to take your wife and three daughters on a 1,000-mile, seven-week death march--sorry, "family adventure"--across Europe, it helps if you're Ben Voyles: steeped in European history, transparent about the complexities of family dynamics, and burst-out-loud funny as a writer. I'm still not sure I would have traded places with him that summer--my feet ached just reading about the journey--but I'm so grateful that he wrote about the trip. I'll remember it as long as he does.

David Pogue
New York Times columnist
Emmy award-winning
CBS News Sunday Morning corres
Frequent NOVA host

GW00492643

If you like a leisurely travel book with sudden detours and crazy tangents, Bennett Voyles and family make good company on the road to Santiago. Voyles' research is wide and his footnotes deep and delightful, with meditations on everything from saints to bedbugs, and fleeting, indelible images of the pilgrims' progress. I give it five scallop shells.

Mary Norris
Author of *Between You and Me: Confessions of a Comma Queen*, and *Greek to Me: Adventures of the Comma Queen*
Former copy editor at *The New Yorker*

Funny, warm and memorable journey that became a book! I wish I had been there too! And separate thanks for great selection of cultural/historic information cameos! They are so enriching!

Andrey Kurkov
Author of *Death and the Penguin* and *Grey Bees*

I read *Onward Backward!* with much joy and laughter.

Bennett Voyles' travel memoir *Onward, Backward!* joins the other great memoirs of the Camino de Santiago oeuvre, but from an entirely different point of view: with his wife and his three daughters in tow. They travel by both foot and by bike all the way from Le Puy en Velay in France to Santiago de Compostela in Spain. Like all good Camino journeys, Voyles starts his with the crazy idea that he and his wife Cybèle had to take their girls on this epic journey. The only thing is that this "epic journey" happens to coincide when they are all teenagers -- and Parisian teenagers at that!

I also loved all his descriptions of the history along the route. For me as a professional guide, his book will be invaluable, and for any person considering walking or biking the Camino it is a must- read, a great introduction to the reality of the Chemin/Camino/path - which is always equal parts joy, hurt feet, smelly pilgrims, great encounters with locals and good and bad food - and an arrival in Santiago with a happy heart.

A highly recommended read for anyone considering the Camino -- or any other grand adventure -- with their kids.

Sally Bentley
Producer, "Walking the Camino; Six Ways to Santiago,"
Winner of five film festival awards for Best Documentary
Camino Guide with Spanish Steps Tours of Asturias, Spain

Onward, Backward! -or- A Ramble to Santiago by Bennett Voyles is an extraordinary story about an extraordinary family - Voyles and his wife and three daughters trek 1,000 miles across France and Spain. The plot is dramatic on its own, as the family overcomes physical and emotional obstacles with enough drama to satisfy any reader - but the book is also a fascinating historical saga. Along their route we meet delightful characters, some in the current day, others from centuries ago.

Voyles' wit and keen eye are reminiscent of the delightful PBS series, "The Durrells in Corfu" based on the wonderful writings of Gerald Durrell - both are madcap, poignant and wise.

Voyles and his family may not have taken the pilgrimage for religious reasons, but this reader found it to be divinely uplifting.

Patty Dann
Author of *Mermaids* **and**
most recently, *The Wright Sister*

Wonderfully engaging, filled with information, wit, beautiful writing, and tenderness. Don't miss it!

Sheila Kohler
Author of *Open Secrets* **and nine other novels,**
two-time winner of the O. Henry Short Story Prize

I read this funny, engaging, and informative book at a gentle pace, about a chapter a day, at roughly the same speed Bennett Voyles and his family walked and biked the Camino de Santiago one summer holiday that must seem like a century ago now. I'm glad I took my time to savor the journey: Voyles is an evocative writer with a born storyteller's gift for bringing a landscape to life. I could feel the sunshine as I travelled alongside him and his charming family through a world of old stone villages, mysterious sculptures, mercurial innkeepers, cheese, chocolate, donkeys, flat tires and the many adventures they encounter along the way.

Voyles is good on life as it was as well, back when the Camino was the Route 66 of the medieval world, imparting observations about everything from the magical chickens of Santo Domingo de la Calzada to the exploding-dragon / stone-boat origin story of Santiago himself, with plenty of serious scholarship too about the complex religious and political history of the Camino, all of which I found fascinating. I enjoyed every page, particularly Voyles' witty asides, which even in a gray lockdown winter made me laugh out loud.

Bennett Voyles is the wise and wry friend that anyone and everyone would want to go on this remarkable journey with, and his family is delightful company too. I highly recommend.

Ellen McGarrahan
Author, *Two Lies and a Truth:*
A murder, a private investigator, and her search for justice

This is an engaging, entertaining, and historically well-informed account of one international family's adventures along the Camino de Santiago, the famous pilgrim's trail that leads from central France to Santiago de Compostela in northwest Spain. Blisters, bicycles, and breakdowns, both mechanical and personal; graceful prose, good humor and a gentle appreciation for the foibles, irritations, and joys of family life on the road: they are all here. It is the story of a journey, told with sympathy and understanding, but with a clear-eyed realism about the difficulties along the way. I found it a highly rewarding reading experience.

Robert Stacey
Professor of Medieval History
Dean of the College of Arts and Sciences
University of Washington

Voyles' book made me want to do something I never would have contemplated before -- taking a very, very long walk with my family. Like a good ramble, *Onward, Backward!* is full of discoveries and discursions -- many of them very funny.

Robert Armstrong
US finance editor
Financial Times

Equal parts rough travel guide and memoir of one expat family's best/worst summer vacation ever, this charming, wryly humorous ramble through southwestern France and Spain is as packed with arcane-yet-riveting medieval lore as *Foucault's Pendulum*. Voyles› boundless curiosity and keen eye for cultural difference make him a delightful traveling companion on a journey that will resonate with Americans abroad and parents of teenagers. It made me feel like I'd walked the pilgrims› path myself, but without the blisters and sunstroke.

Jordan Mechner
Creator of *Prince of Persia*
and author of *Year 1 in France*

Onward, Backward! is a highly enjoyable read -- a lively mix of family adventure and historical travelogue. Voyles writes with warmth and humor and is a sure-footed guide to the colorful history of the Camino de Santiago. It's a part of Europe I'll never visit again without thinking of medieval pilgrims, mad monks and the obsessive hikers who are still retracing those early journeys. Highly recommended.

Don Durfee
Managing Editor for News Strategy & Operations
Reuters News

A poignant, funny, charming family adventure -- think Laurie Lee with reluctant teenagers -- that will make you ache to walk the Camino de Santiago the second lockdown ends.

Julia Hobsbawm, OBE
Author of the best-selling and award-winning book
The Simplicity Principle

Three hundred thousand people walk the Camino de Santiago each year. You may not ever be one of them. But through Bennett Voyles' engaging and disarming memoir/travelogue, you can journey across 1,500 kilometers of France and Spain, and through half a million years of history, in the company of the author, his intrepid wife and his three reluctantly-along-for-the-trek adolescent daughters. Voyles' irrepressible curiosity enlivens the text with digressions into everything from Roman mythology to New Wave film to the Visigothic alphabet, and his whimsical pencil drawings give the book a homespun feel. Onward, Backward! reminds us that, no matter our age or perspective or path, we're all pilgrims, journeying alone and together for a time that is all too brief.

Anndee Hochman
Author of *Everyday Acts and Small Subversions* **and**
Anatomies: A Novella and Stories
Columnist, The Philadelphia Inquirer

When I finished this, I really felt like I'd been on your ramble with you, so vivid are the day-by-day events that you describe with such enlivening detail, so inviting and beguiling is your persona (serious at times, but never taking yourself too seriously), that this reader felt swept up in an extraordinary adventure. Even now, days after I finished, I still feel myself in your grip.

Bill Nagler
Editor and writer

Bennett Voyles is an engaging, quirky storyteller and a fantastic wrangler of teenagers in this formidable, enviable tale of a long family journey through France and Spain. When we're all looking back on our lives decades from now, we'll wish we had created such memories for our families. What an accomplishment, in living through it so successfully, and writing about it so well!

Tina Kelley
Poet and journalist
Author of *Rise Wildly, Abloom & Awry, Precise,* **and**
The Gospel of Galore

A lifelong fan of long walks and travel memoirs, I knew I had to read Onward, Backward! as soon as I saw that enthusiastic, gently comic title. The book captivated me from first page to last. Here is an unexpected pilgrim who knows how to make everything from obscure French history to the threat of punaises (bed bugs) entertaining. Making the book even more engaging is the presence and occasional journal entries of the author's wife and three reluctant teenage daughters, who complain about the forced march while still clearly enjoying the family adventure. The parents of this "heathen family" are on the verge of having their first daughter leave the nest, adding a poignance to the group undertaking.

Perhaps my favorite part of the memoir, though, is Voyles's line drawings of incidental sights along the Camino de Santiago.

I read this hefty book in a weekend and actually felt regretful when the 1,500 km trip came to an end. Highly recommended.

Elizabeth Judd
Writer and Book Critic

Imagine the challenges, logistical and otherwise, of undertaking a 1500 km family pilgrimage (with not all family members necessarily 100% on board) and you'll get a sense of the fun in reading Onward, Backward! - alternately comic, heroic, and wry, with the daily progress marked by surprising explorations of local histories and cultural curiosities of the Camino route itself.

John McQuaid
Science and environment journalist
Three-time Pulitzer Prize winner
Author of *Tasty: The Art and Science of What We Eat*

What a vicarious treat to travel the Camino de Santiago with Bennett Voyles and his family. The next best thing to being there, he brings alive the countryside, the people, the food, and the blisters – all with great good humor. Along the way, he adds in fascinating history, made even more enjoyable with his wry commentary. This journey reminded me of adventures with my family, and I can't wait to share this book with my sisters.

Maria Burton
Filmmaker with Five Sisters Productions
Director of films including *Manna From Heaven* **and** *A Sort of Homecoming*

I relished every word, every drawing, every footnote. The writing is fluid and easy and perfectly balanced between Voyles's account of his family's day-to-day experiences on the Camino and digressions into anything that piques his curiosity: monks and nuns and saints and sinners, kings and queens, farmers and dogs, lions and chickens, religious wars, religious tolerance, ancient history, current politics, agriculture, Roman road-building techniques, Spanish food, Basque proverbs, etc. etc. etc. Voyles is both extremely erudite and also humble enough to do a prodigious amount of research: the bibliography is 18 pages long! The book packs in at 430 pages, but my interest never flagged.

Sally Tittmann
Artist

Bennett Voyles embarks on the Camino de Santiago with his wife Cybèle and their three wary daughters (aged 16, 13 and 11) because he likes walking and thought the journey would be fun. The result is an account that rambles across the centuries, offering a wry look at the quirks of present-day life along the trail and a meditation on the role of mythmaking in history.

Voyles is an idiosyncratic guide, his curiosity leading him into the corners of the past with a historian's sweep of significance and a reporter's eye for the telling detail. His day job as a business writer gives him a sharp understanding of just how much the profit motive underlies sacred devotion.

His account also shows how the Camino de Santiago is woven into the foundational myths of both France and Spain. In France, schoolchildren are force-fed the medieval epic of the Song of Roland, who was killed at Roncevaux Pass in the Pyrenees – supposedly fighting the Moors for Charlemagne– and whose heroism was used to "puff up national pride."

In Spain, the apostle Saint James, or Santiago, has been at the heart of the country's jealous assertion of its Christian identity, ever since King Alfonso the Great made him patron saint around 900. The legend of the Moor-slayer grew to the point that a Baroque poet estimated that Santiago had personally killed "11,015,000 and some odd Moors."

If all this sounds rather grim, it isn't. Voyles leavens his account of Europe's bloodletting over religion and power with meanderings into such oddities as the population of boars in French forests, the origins of foie gras, Roman goldmining and the rather gruesome discovery that half a million years ago early humans practiced "gastronomic cannibalism."

His lightest notes, accompanied by his whimsical drawings, touch on the present-day trail, peopled by pilgrims all wearing the same kit purchased at the giant French sporting goods chain Decathlon. Voyles' musing on his host countries hit the humorist´s mark: Could it be that French schoolkids learn so much about préhistoire because the French are fascinated with places they imagine lack rules?

It seems fitting that Voyles chooses Don Quixote (downloaded as an audio book) to accompany his walking and he admits to a certain kinship with the would-be knight errant born of "trudging down a dusty road in a silly hat on a pointless quest." Silly hat, yes. Pointless quest, far from it.

Elisabeth Malkin
Freelance journalist
Former *New York Times* reporter for Mexico

Onward, Backward!

-or-

A Ramble to Santiago

Being a True Account of
a Heathen Family's 1,500-kilometer pilgrimage
to Santiago de Compostela, together with
many *Interesting Stories* and *Occasionally Useful Facts*
pertaining to **Life** along that ancient and popular **Way.**

Written, illustrated, and carefully combobulated

By Bennett Voyles

Dämmerungskollektiv
Berlin

Dämmerungskollektiv

Berlin, Germany

9783982258010 EPUB

9783982258003 Print

For Cybèle

Table of Contents

A reflective pilgrim on the road to Santiago always makes a double journey when he tries to collect his memories —the backward journey through Time and the forward journey through Space.

Walter Starkie
The Road to Santiago: Pilgrims of St. James

Preface

In which a whim takes root.

I first read about the Camino de Santiago in a *New York Times* travel story 12 or 13 years before we tried it. I know it was long enough ago that my wife, Cybèle, asked me whether I thought we could do it with strollers. In any case, after we read that story, walking the Way of Saint James was an idea that took root and eventually grew into a low-grade obsession.

A thousand-year-old pilgrimage trail might seem like an unlikely thing to capture the imagination of a couple of secular Manhattanites, but we each had our reasons.

To begin with, I liked to walk.

Like most Americans, I grew up in a place where most of the walking we did was from the house to the car or the parking lot to the store. The one exception, because we lived on the Oregon coast, was an occasional stroll down the cold, windy beach. This had its points—when I was little, I liked balancing on the logs that washed up all over the beach or playing Lewis and Clark with my best friend, the conveniently named Mike Clark, and when I was older, it was a great place for a bout of adolescent self-pity—but otherwise I hardly ever went there. The Pacific is beautiful but the water is freezing, you can only walk in two directions—either up or down, like a sentry on a very long wall— and either way, the view mostly reinforced my feeling that I lived on the Edge of the World.

I really contracted the habit of walking when I went back east to college, on the opposite coast, at Yale University. I would go out for a few hours every Saturday afternoon—longer if the weather was good, but again along a narrow track (mostly because New Haven, Connecticut, in the 1980s was a dangerous city), up Yale's Hillhouse Avenue, then out St. Ronan Street to the Hamden Reservoir, and occasionally, the top of East Rock, which had a view of the campus, the city, and Long Island Sound. I kept up this routine after graduation, when I took a job as a reporter about an hour inland, at *The Middletown Press*, making my way along the Connecticut River in Haddam or the fields outside the village of Portland, but here too, there were limits. A young man on foot was an object of suspicion in those little towns, even if the young man in question was a mild-mannered reporter with no viable alter ego.

Then I moved to New York City, which was much better for walking. For one thing, I didn't have any old ladies peering at me over their hedges as I ambled by. For another, there were many more things to see—all the buildings and the parks, but also the odd shop window, too many used books, and snatches of bizarre conversations that came up so often I started packing one of the reporter's notebooks I'd filched from the *Press*. And best of all, I found some company: Cybèle, the best walker I've ever known. Our first dates usually started out with a walk, and my solitary constitutionals became all-day conversations that stretched from brunch to midnight, winding through squares and streets and galleries. Even after our daughters came along, our walks continued, but turned now into Saturday saunters over to the story hour in Central Park, and eventually, Monday morning dashes to P.S. 87, the William Tecumseh Sherman School, on West 78th Street.

The Camino appealed to me for a second reason as well: I had majored in English and in history, mostly medieval (because the medievalists were all brilliant, funny, and told the best stories). Ever since those studies, part of me still *longen ... to goon on pilgrimages*.

I also may as well admit that in the best medieval tradition, I thought it would be fun. Most people are drawn to the Camino as an opportunity for introspection and renewal, but to me it sounded like the mother of all road trips, Route 66 on the Rioja—a thousand-year-old circus with a thousand-mile midway.

Cybèle liked the idea of the Camino too, but for somewhat different reasons. First, we would really be all together all day long—she hated vacations where everyone spent their days separately and met only at dinner. Second, her workaholic husband would have to take an actual break to get to our next destination, and not just work at a different desk in a different room. Third, we would be outside all day.

This last feature attracted her most. Cybèle had grown up in New York and Paris, but she had always spent every minute she could outside. Nor had motherhood slowed her down. Even when our three daughters were small, even in the worst weather, my huckleberry friend was always happiest outdoors. If you ever saw her striding down Columbus Avenue behind our double stroller—the two younger girls sitting side by side; the oldest clinging to the rigging behind them, athwart a running board we called the pirate step—you would have noticed a certain glint in her eye that always made me think of Mongols on horseback. For Cybèle, the Camino sounded less like a holiday than the way she was meant to live.[1]

---

1   Left to her own devices, she might have turned into a nomad. Once or twice, I even saw her nurse *en route*.

October 2011

In which various obstacles hinder us.

But circumstances prevented us from exorcising this particular obsession for a long time: the girls were little; I had only two or three weeks off a year; and we lived in New York, a long way from northern Spain.

Eventually, the obstacles began to fall away. The girls got bigger. The dotcoms that ate my thirties collapsed, and I parlayed a night school MBA and a short stint with the Economist Intelligence Unit into a career of sorts as a freelance business writer, writing for trade magazines, big companies, and business schools. My work became incredibly portable; I still couldn't take much time off, but I could take off (and did: in 2006, we moved to Paris). We were also living in the age of universal Wi-Fi, and it was now possible to work almost as well on a hillside as at home—at least theoretically.

Then the fates started to trip us up again. One year, Cybèle developed a stress fracture. Another summer, I had a similar injury. A third year, I twisted my ankle. A fourth year, Cybèle had had an ankle problem too: a skin cancer whose removal laid her up for a month. And besides our ailments, we had pilgrimages back to the States that were not to be missed if we didn't want to be excommunicated from our families.

Finally, in late 2011, I began to think we might have an opportunity: Cybèle and I were simultaneously ambulatory, our families had made no claims on the upcoming summer, and the girls had no plans.

The girls were also good walkers now. For years, they had walked 20 minutes to and from school every day, lugging backpacks big as anvils, and in any case, with Cybèle for a mother, they had never stayed off their feet for long.

But at the same time as hiking the Camino began to feel more possible, it had also begun to feel more urgent. Cybèle and I weren't so young anymore. Our daughters were growing up fast—soon, they would have their own plans, which would probably not involve us. With our 50s just around the corner and our daughters out the door very soon, it really did seem that there would be no time like the present for this trip, or more precisely, no time but the present. Before we went our separate ways, I wanted to end our family adventures with something audacious, and a 1,500-kilometer trek across France and Spain fit the bill.

November 2011

In which we hatch a plot to ruin our children's summer.

Cybèle and I began conspiring in earnest in November. A four-day test run she had made in October with her friend Caroline had gone well—Cybèle at least had come back glowing—but the idea seemed crazy enough that we kept it to ourselves until we worked out our plan. When your children, your parents, and most of your friends are saner than you are, you can't be too careful.

We each had our own worries about the project. Marginally more rational than I am, Cybèle worried about selling the girls on the idea. I didn't; I assumed there would be moaning. I worried about the distance.

From the French point of view, the *chemin de Compostelle* (at least the most popular route, the *Via Podiensis*) begins at Le Puy-en-Velay in south-central France and runs to Saint-Jean-Pied-de-Port, on the near side of the Pyrenees. At that point, it meets the trailhead of the *Camino francés* (the French Way), which climbs over the Roncesvalles Pass and then runs almost the whole breadth of northern Spain, to Saint James's tomb in Santiago de Compostela. Taken altogether, the two trails add up to 1,516 kilometers. No matter how Cybèle divided the stages, there wouldn't be time to walk both legs. Even if we left as soon as school ended and returned the day before the *rentrée* (back to school – one of my favorite French words), she couldn't get the mileage to work out.

"Maybe we can do just the first half this summer?" Cybèle asked, reasonably enough. "The girls would really like it if we spent a few weeks at the beach. Or maybe we can plan on the French Camino and then just go as far as we can on the Spanish?"

I kept shaking my head no. My feeling was that if we planned an epic, we had to do the whole thing. Not doing the whole thing would be like watching half a movie, writing half a book, or leading an expedition to the North Pole that stopped at Montreal. It might be a nice trip but it would still be just a trip.[2]

Then one day I had an idea: bicycles! People often made the pilgrimage on bicycles. We would walk from Le Puy-en-Velay to Saint-Jean-Pied-de-Port and over the Pyrenees to Pamplona, where we could rent bicycles. That way, we could finish the whole thing, and still have one and a half or maybe even two whole days before school started! My finger slid across the map from Le Puy, over three dark mountain ranges, and on to Santiago. No problem.

---

2   For the record, this is nonsense. You can start in Lapland if you like, but at least according to the Catholic Church, if you manage the last 100 kilometers to Santiago in some nonmotorized way, you have officially "done" the Camino.

I wonder how many disasters have started with a finger on a map. *Invade Russia? How hard could it be?*

PARIS

FRANCE

Bordeaux

Garonne River

Aubrac

Conques

Le Puy-en-Velay

SAINT-
Jean-
Pied-
de-
Pont

Cahors

Espalion

Lot River

The MIDI

Canal du Midi

The Pyrenees

AIN

MEDITERRANNEAN

December 2011

In which our daughters hear the most dreadful news.

We made our announcement at dinner, a week or two before Christmas.

Our girls glanced at each other. They didn't like the sound of this.

"You'll love it," their mother said brightly. "We'll take the train to Le Puy, walk five weeks, whip through Spain on bikes the last two weeks, and get back in time for school."

Silence.

"It will be fun," she said again.

Sure, they thought.

She went on dictating the rest of the brochure: the walking itself would not be hard. The 20–27 kilometers a day she had planned would probably only take the morning, so they would have the afternoon free to swim or read or do whatever they liked. While they walked, they could listen to music, or even books on their iPods. And we would be walking through gorgeous landscapes— with castles, cathedrals, beautiful old villages—

She was on a roll—I sometimes think it's a shame she went into art instead of sales.

 "Just imagine, we'll be walking over the Pyrenees into Spain!" Cybèle said, with that familiar glint in her eye that always put them on their guard. "Right over the mountains! It will be an adventure!"

I winced, the way you do when a skater misses her triple axel. The judges were not going to like this—the "A word" always made them bristle.

They looked at each other: *1,500 kilometers? They can't be serious.* And then: *Oh, but of course they are. You know them. They never joke about trips.*

Their mother might make it sound like we would be the Von Trapps gamboling over the Alps in three-part harmony, but they knew better. They were no longer taken in by what they called *mommaganda*. They remembered the night they had to sleep on the deck of the ferry to Palermo, and the night in Egypt at the Horus House—the hotel where Thea found a giant cockroach on her pillow, like a six-legged chocolate, a place Dad insisted was not a brothel, even though the doors in the hall slammed open and shut all night. And that time on the Trans-Siberian Railway when Dad had somehow screwed up the codes on both their ATM cards at a convenience store in Ulan-Ude and they had to live on instant soup and oatmeal for two days until the train reached Vladivostok.

As for the idea that the Camino would be a mobile beach vacation, they knew from experience that their mother was either being delusional or out-and-out lying. They had visited cathedrals, mosques, and monkey-god temples. They had toured coal mines and kremlins, car factories and concentration camps. They had seen cacti and catacombs, wild horses and wild flowers. But as for relaxing beaches, that kind of holiday had been limited mostly to visits with their grandparents—rare intervals when Mom and Dad had tried to pass for normal. Whatever happened this summer, it was unlikely to involve anything most people would consider relaxing.

With respect to the Camino in particular, they may have also remembered the minor detail that by the third day of their mother's four-day trial run in October, Caroline's feet had started to bother her and Mom had to carry half her pack.

All in all, where Cybèle and I envisioned a chance for the family to grow closer and a metaphor that would give us all a sense of possibility—after all, if you can walk a thousand miles, what can't you do?—the girls saw the theft of their holiday and outright sadism, the Trans-Siberian all over again, but this time without the train, a Bataan Death March of summer vacations.[3]

Over the next few weeks, Cybèle kept trying to stoke their enthusiasm, but didn't make much progress.

One night at dinner, Masha, our 15-year-old (10th grade), told us she had talked to a girl at school whose family had started the walk only to quit the second day, when she and her brother had staged a sit-down strike on the trail.

"What happens if we just stop?" asked Thea. As the youngest, she was always the quickest to seize on precedent. Although she was only 11 (6th grade), she had my vote for most likely to go to law school.

Charlotte, 13 (8th grade), looked up, interested again in the conversation.

I stayed calm and shrugged. After six years in France, I could almost do the Gallic shrug: "You'll get hungry, then cold. But you sing well. Maybe people will give you some change—"

As an alternative, Thea and Masha suggested that we rent a house near a lake or by the sea and take some day hikes. Wouldn't that make more sense than walking the whole day before collapsing at some smelly hostel, then getting up in the morning and doing the same thing all over again? Then we wouldn't have to rent bikes either. And wouldn't that be easier for your work, Dad?

Cybèle countered with an intense salvo of pictures of the lovely summer out on the Camino: the amazing scenery, the long, lazy

---

3   They were right to be wary. Even in the old days, not everyone had a great time. In 1520, travel writer Andrew Borde advised friends against making the pilgrimage to Santiago overland. He wrote that he would prefer to murder them himself at home than have them die out on that trail. "I had rather to go five times out of England to Rome – and so I have – than one to go from Orleans to Compostel . . . by water it is no pain, but by land it is the greatest journey that an Englishman may go." Chaucer, however, wrote a poem about the grimness of making the pilgrimage by ship, so I'm not sure the sea voyage was always much fun either; the poem's main subjects are seasickness and the smell of the cabin:

> For when that we shall go to bedde,
> The pumpe was nygh oure beddes hede;
> A man were as good to be dede
> As smell therof the stynk.

afternoons—

Throughout the whole barrage, Charlotte said nothing. When it came to discussing the Camino, Charlotte never said anything. Her silence rattled me much more than her sisters' protests, and I asked her about it one night as I tucked her in.

"What's the point?" she asked. "You're going to do what you want anyway, whatever we say."

I found this funny and repeated it to Cybèle, but she didn't laugh. She had higher aspirations for parenthood than I did; she liked to think of us as flexible parents who listen to our kids.

"Don't worry," I told her. I remembered plenty of family projects growing up—houses torn down, decks added on, hedges ripped out—that I hadn't cared for at the time but in retrospect were among the most vivid and in certain respects even happiest of my childhood memories. Whatever the Club Med or Disney World posters suggest, happy, in my experience, always tends to be more of an accident than a destination.

As usual, Cybèle didn't let my philosophizing deflect her. "They really might mutiny," she whispered.

"Don't worry," I said, "it'll work out. Things always work out."

A day or two later, I stepped off a curb and sprained my ankle.

January 2012
Wherein we organize the expedition.

Our preparations began in January.

The biggest I made was to lose weight. Obesity is an occupational hazard when you work at home that is probably trebled if you live in Paris, and I had gained steadily over the six years since we had moved into our apartment on rue Cambronne—slowly when I was walking, more quickly during a hobbling period like the one I was going through now—and at this point I needed to lose about 40 pounds of excess baggage before we made the hike or face utter humiliation on the first hot day.

An earlier attempt with a Japanese diet book called *Sayonara, Mr. Fatty* hadn't worked out so well, so now I decided to try the South Beach Diet. This regimen also made me fairly grumpy to be around but it did have the advantage of actually working. You should try it sometime—but only if you need to lose a lot of weight in a hurry and really, really like eggs.

Cybèle, meanwhile, kept thinking about how she could make the expedition more tolerable to the girls. Ice cream breaks would get stale quickly, and they were too old now for *I Spy* and *Statues*. Really, the only thing that might work, she concluded, would be if a few other people joined us. We all tended to be on better behavior with witnesses. Maybe Carson and Leen, our old friends and frequent traveling companions, would be interested.[4] They were New Yorkers; if they came, maybe they could bring along Lola, Masha's old friend, a girl she had known since West Side Montessori—?[5] Leen and Carson did not know Lola, but as they lived three blocks away from each other on the Upper West Side, it wouldn't be much trouble to arrange. And there was Della, our Canadian friend from Cybèle's French class, and her youngest daughter Enya, who sometimes took the after-school art classes Cybèle taught in our apartment. Maybe, if our girls were walking with kids their age, who were there voluntarily, it would be a lot tougher for ours to classify the expedition as child abuse.

So Cybèle put her persuasive skills to work on our friends, with better effect—Della and Enya decided to join us for the first five days; Carson, Leen, and Lola for the first two weeks. By then, maybe we would have gained enough momentum that we could manage the remaining month and a half on our own.

---

4 Very old friends: Cybèle and Leen met at Yale in the early 80s, when Leen was the first deaf law student at Yale Law School and Cybèle was the first deaf undergraduate, and they had been fast friends ever since.

5 Not long before, Lola's father had sent me an old picture of Lola and Masha sitting at a little table at the school, both aged four: Lola drawing intently, Masha in her tiara staring dreamily into space. Neither had changed much since then, aside from the fact that Masha didn't wear tiaras much anymore as far as I knew and now wrote her imaginings down.

One morning in March, my ankle operational again and our friends all signed up, I started making the calls for the French side(Cybèle is a better linguist than I am, but because of her deafness, I always get the telephone duty)—34 bookings in all, one for every night in France. Many pilgrims stop wherever they happen to find themselves, but with eight of us (Della wanted to book her own rooms), Cybèle and I didn't want to take any chances.[6]

Most of the hostels were mom-and-pop operations—a surprising number didn't even have email—and the reservation process was a little old-fashioned. Some places wanted deposits, but rather than take credit card numbers, they asked that I send them a check—which was a tricky business for me. The hosts often had long French names with silent letters that had to be spelled out, the amounts of the checks all varied, and French numbers can be surprisingly treacherous—92, for instance, is *quatre-vingt douze*—literally, four 20s and a 12. Occasionally, these checks were for 30 or 40 euros but more often they were for odd amounts—11.72, say, for reasons I never understood.

The further down my list we got, the more rural the walk seemed to become. Once I heard cows in the background. The booking itself became easier too: my French is not good, but farther south, the accent turns to more of a slow singsong—like the American South in that way—and I could follow more easily.

South of the Pyrenees, I began to have a harder time again. The Spanish clerks often sounded like they were having trouble hearing me over the noise of a restaurant kitchen. On the bright side, they didn't have this check system—which was lucky, because despite the common currency, French checks aren't good in Spain. Instead, the people at the *albergues* often just took our

---

6   This is the cheapest way to organize the hike, but far from the only way. The Camino is a big enough business that a number of specialized travel agencies have formed that will take care of all these details for you. There are also tour operators who will lead you in a group, companies that will haul your luggage from hotel to hotel, and agencies that will rent you bicycles, horses, or mules. No one has reinvented the business that developed in the Middle Ages of hiring someone to do the walking for you too, but I am sure it is only a matter of time. Someone out there is probably testing an all-terrain Roomba as we speak.

name. I liked the informality, but I worried about whether they had actually written anything down. The fact that I had to make most of the reservations in Spanish didn't reassure me either—the average Zorro movie *hablas* more *espagnole* than I have in my repertoire.

We also started buying hiking equipment. We needed everything: backpacks, hiking boots, hiking socks, and quick-dry clothes. We also needed bedding (at most of the hostels where we were staying, you had to bring your own towel and sleeping bag—or "sleep sack" in hostelese—a body bag with an opening at one end).

We found almost all this gear in two places. The first was a big box store that everyone in France loves, a chain called Decathlon, which is a little like Target if Target were devoted entirely to sporting goods and camping equipment. It's one of the few cheap stores in France, and it's always crowded with people buying sneakers and polar fleece.

The Decathlon we went to most often was in an enormous basement not far from the Madeleine. Ironically, given their outdoor theme, Decathlons are always about as pastoral as a bomb shelter. They never have any windows or even daylight—at the Madeleine outlet you can walk straight in from the Métro.

The girls hated this place, and never found anything there almost on principle. They had always tended to be much more stylish than either Cybèle or me and defended their outfits fiercely. Masha was the most vociferous. Normally, she was a very sweet girl, but when it came to clothes, she had the soul of a diva. At three years old, she would roll her eyeballs when I suggested an outfit, and at six we often got into trouble with her teachers for letting her go to school in the dead of winter in princess dresses, no tights, and ruby slippers—but you try telling Maria Callas she can't do something. Ten years later, she had grown somewhat more reasonable, and announced in advance that she would only wear a small leather backpack, leather hiking boots, a tiny tank top, and jean shorts. Thea said she would not wear anything from Decathlon, period. And as usual, Charlotte said nothing.

On the other hand, Cybèle and I liked the place. Cheap is always appreciated when you're multiplying by five, and the store had most of what we needed: aluminum canteens, rain jackets that could be packed in a pouch, light fleece cardigans with extra-strong zippers, tiny rubbery camp towels that looked like something Santa's elves would take to the beach in the offseason. I also picked up a pair of shorts, and a pair of pants with many pockets and zip-off legs—I had always wanted an excuse to buy pants with zip-off legs. I found water-resistant T-shirts too, most in horrible Day-Glo colors whose only virtue was that they would make search and rescue easier. Not elegant but for three euros instead of thirty, I could live with it.

After some hesitation, we splurged on silk sleeping bag liners. This was my proudest new possession. The silk sacks were soft and very light—only 200 grams, as opposed to the kilo or so of the conventional cotton sleep sack—and their very possession made me feel more professional, as if we were outfitting ourselves for a real expedition. *Commodore Voyles (far left) pictured in anorak of his own devising.*

Our second stop was at a more upscale store called *Au Vieux Campeur* – "At The Old Camper"— for our backpacks and boots.[7] Au Vieux Campeur is an odd outlet because it is located in and around Boulevard Saint-Germain, some of the most expensive real estate in Paris. Rather than build a big box on the edge of town, generations of old campers have slowly expanded into 30 smallish shops, each specialized in something different. This might sound charming—the company's marketers call it "a village"—but it gets old quickly: when you go in and ask for something, they invariably direct you to another store two blocks up, three blocks right, on the far side of the street.

First, we went to the backpack store and bought our packs. Cybèle had wanted us to get good-quality packs that would not glue to our backs on hot days. Then we went to the boot store next door, where they sold only heavy-duty hiking boots, the kind

---

7   Decathlon has perfectly good packs and boots too, but we did not want to take any chances because ours had to last at least 700 kilometers.

you see on Swiss travel posters. As we weren't planning to scale any glaciers, we asked the clerk if they had any lighter-weight walking shoes. She directed us to the running shoe store, but once we got there, the clerks frowned when Cybèle told them what we were doing and sent us back to the serious hiking boot store—that was the *correct* place for us to buy our boots.

This took care of everybody but me. As befits a stylish nation, the French have very slender feet— you generally can't even find wide sizes—but unfortunately, I don't; my feet are shaped more or less like a baby elephant's. I tried on roughly 20 pairs of shoes at the *Campeur*, tramping painfully up and down their special test ramp, before I finally gave up.

Luckily, Cybèle's French teacher, Isabelle, told her about a store near her home in the Sixteenth Arrondissement that catered to elephant men and other orthopedic curiosities. I visited Babar & Fils the following Saturday and walked out with a very expensive but extremely comfortable pair of squat shoes made by the BÄR (that is, "Bear") company in Germany that swaddled my feet so well I didn't care how they looked.

They were so comfortable, in fact, that Cybèle inspected them with deep suspicion when I got home. Between what she had learned from orthopedists when she was recovering from her stress fracture and more recently from the salespeople at the *Vieux Campeur* about the *correct* choice for our hike, she had become such a believer in firm, unsupple soles that she thought the soft BÄR boots might kill me.

But I loved my new boots, and I wasn't going to give them up without a fight. I showed her their entry in BÄR's online catalog, which described the square-toed, black, semi-military boots as a retro design (retro to what period I was afraid to ask), and pointed out to her that they were classified as hiking boots.

When that didn't convince her, I emailed the company, told them our plan, and asked if they thought these boots would be up to the job. A week or so later, the president wrote back. Herr Bär saying that he had hiked the Camino himself nine years before in his own boots and they had worked just fine. I should have no problem. Buen Camino!

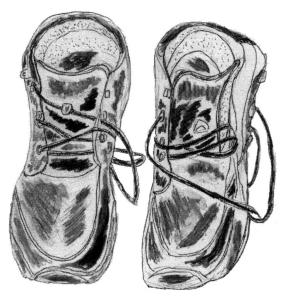

Die Bären

April 2012
Wherein yet another complication ensues.

Complicating everything that spring was an even bigger problem: preparing Masha for a new school.

For six years, Masha and her sisters had been at a school I will call the *École Jeunesse Dorée*, an English-French bilingual school with a French heart. It had gone very well at first—Masha and her sisters had all learned to speak beautiful French and plenty of other things besides—but after that glorious first year, things had gone steadily downhill for Masha, academically and socially, gradually at first, and now at an accelerated pace. By May, we had begun to feel that if we were going to rescue her last two years of high school, she needed to start fresh somewhere else, and as soon as possible.

Masha, a big Harry Potter fan, suggested English boarding

school, and we reluctantly agreed to look into it. We didn't like the idea of her leaving home at 16 or our paying the ruinous tuition, but after she and Cybèle took the Eurostar to London and visited one of the few schools that still had spaces available for the fall, she started to seem happier, and a few weeks later, when her admission to a school in Surrey arrived and she bounced through the following week happy as a convict who learns a pardon is on the way, Cybèle and I knew we had to follow through.

This gave us still more logistics to worry about. Her new school started one day after we were supposed to get back from Spain, which meant that over the next two months, we had to get her visa, her uniform, and what amounted to a scholarly trousseau together, all before we left town.

Between getting Masha organized, getting the apartment ready for our soon-to-arrive visitors, trying to deal with the British authorities for Masha's visa, doing my own work, planning our trip—and, on top of everything, preparing for the one-week art camp Cybèle and her friend Cathy ran at the end of every school year—we were now almost out of our minds with worry about various details, large and small.

At this point, reasonable people would have canceled the walk or scaled it back, but as you will have gathered by now, "reasonable" isn't one of my strong suits. In fact, I became even more determined to do the walk, as Masha's life away from home would now begin two years ahead of schedule. Ready or not, our life together was not going to last much longer.

May 2012

In which we discover we don't like walking or bicycling all that much.

> If you are not already used to walking or used to carrying a rucksack day in, day out, get in plenty of practice before you go. Consider joining your local rambling club at least six months in advance and go out with them as often as you can . . . start increasing the amount of weight and luggage you take out with you until you can carry what you need.
>
> -*The Way of Saint James—Le Puy to the Pyrenees*, Alison Raju

All the guidebooks we read (or rather, Cybèle read, then read aloud to me, selectively: I have a deep aversion to guidebooks and tend to lose them en route or even pre-route) suggested a serious training regime. Some people even take a long pre-hike hike to build up their strength and break in their boots. In a brochure we ordered about biking the Camino, *The Cycling Pilgrim*, the author, the inauspiciously named John Curtain, said that in preparation for his trek he had bicycled to and from work four miles a day, swam three times a week, gardened, walked his dog 40 minutes, and cycled "20 miles on bridleways and hilly ground on Saturdays with the bike fully laden for about two months before departure."

Cybèle wanted to start training immediately, but I kept putting it off. Back in New York, I once spent a few months training to run the marathon, only to tear up my knee the week before the race. There is a little glory in collapsing on your 22nd mile, but none if you collapse the week before the big day. You just end up with physical therapy bills and a T-shirt you can never, ever wear. Instead of drawing the correct conclusion that I should have trained more, and more carefully, I had deduced that it sometimes paid to prepare less.

In the end, we compromised.

One Saturday afternoon in May, we rented bikes from the Vélib' (vélo + liberté = bicycle + freedom) stand, the city's amazing municipal bike rental system. Vélib' had been around for four or five years, but we had tried it only once. At that time, the bike lane doubled as the bus lane on the bigger streets, and the idea of swimming with steel killer whales alarmed me. First, I am not very brave, and second, although Cybèle is much braver than I am, I thought it could be much more dangerous for her as she is deaf; she can't hear an engine or a even a car honk if she is not listening for it.[8]

That first outing, Thea and Masha were staying over with friends,

---

8   In fact, it turns out that bicycling in Paris really isn't all that dangerous—the year before, in 2011, not a single cyclist died in Paris, according to French police statistics.

so we only had Charlotte with us. She normally wouldn't have been too happy about this, but we bribed her by making our destination W.H. Smith, the English bookstore on rue de Rivoli. Cybèle and I had trouble unlocking the heavy gray bikes from their stands but fortunately Charlotte figured the system out right away. (I don't know if she is all that mechanically inclined, but compared to us she is a little Leonarda.)

Then we were off, and on our way down busy rue Cambronne. As we went, between the traffic and car doors opening and closing and Cybèle not hearing the honks, the *mot de Cambronne* kept crossing my lips.[9] From Place Cambronne we bore left on rue du Laos and down past Avenue Suffren[10] to the Champ de Mars— the long field that stretches from the École Militaire, France's West Point, to the Eiffel Tower—and then a right along the quay and across the bridge farther down to the Place de la Concorde to Smith's, where we bought Charlotte's reward (*Nineteen Eighty-Four*) and headed home.

Masha's turn came later. This was a more delicate mission because riding bikes on streets terrified Masha. She had seen Thea almost run over by a taxi once back in New York, and this memory had morphed into a general fear of her sisters being run over and then a specific phobia about bicycling. Cybèle had decided that to get Masha used to cycling again without being distracted by worries about her sisters' survival prospects, she needed to take her out alone one day after school.

They went with Cybèle's friend Sadie, an experienced city bik-

---

9   That is, *merde*. The euphemism comes from a popular account of the response of Brigadier General Pierre Cambronne, one of Napoleon's generals at Waterloo, to a message the British sent him, pointing out that he and the last of his army were surrounded and ought to surrender. While he supposedly used *merde* to mean, "Go to Hell," it has shifted usage over time. Now you can describe something as being "a load of old Cambronne" or use the *mot* as a verb, *cambronniser*. It was a perfect address for a business writer.

10   Sometimes I think half the streets in Paris are named for glorious losers. The namesake of this street, for instance, the gouty and disagreeable Vice-Admiral Pierre Suffren (1729-1788)—Admiral Satan to those who knew him best—was considered brilliant strategically but not a great leader of men. Military historians say he lost more battles than he should have because his captains resented his bullying and contempt. Charlotte's favorite place name in this genre was the *Square des Écrivains Combattants Morts pour la France*— the Square of Fighting Writers Who Died for France.

er with nerves of steel who whipped across the first intersection just as the light changed. Masha started after her, but right in the middle of the avenue, saw the oncoming cars and froze. Fortunately, Cybèle saw this and quickly pedaled up alongside her, grabbed her handlebars, and pulled her the rest of the way across moments before the traffic passed the intersection.

Masha froze once more on that outing—not a good sign—but when Cybèle told me about it in the evening, I rationalized that the Camino would be nothing like Paris. There wouldn't be nearly as many cars out in the country. And anyway, it would be good if Masha got over her old fears and learned to feel comfortable on a bike. Wasn't that one of the things you were supposed to learn as a kid, right up there with swimming? How could we let her go off to school without mastering such a basic skill?

The following Sunday afternoon, all five of us rode Vélibs to the Bois de Boulogne, five whole kilometers from our apartment.

This did not go especially well either. Charlotte and Thea dueled over who would go in front and who would go behind; Charlotte complained that the bike hurt her knees; and Masha was annoying just to make sure she wasn't overlooked. We didn't last more than three hours, in the end, and that was on more or less flat ground, and including a sullen coffee break.

We also hiked once. This went somewhat better. After dinner one golden night in June, we walked all the way to the Luxembourg Gardens in our hiking boots. I carried my pack too, to make for a more accurate simulation. It was a strenuous 37 minutes, after which we stopped for an ice cream at Amorino, the girls' favorite ice cream parlor, sauntered through the soft dusty paths of the old park, walked out the gates on the other side, and started back home. The girls turned crimson every time we passed a sidewalk café on our way through Montparnasse, but I observed no physical injuries.

I was red too by the time we got back—not out of wounded *amour propre* but because although it was not a hot evening, I was sweating like a pig.

I began to have second thoughts. What were we doing, leading an expedition like this when we had never even walked more than a day? And not only with the girls, but our friends? What had I been thinking? Could I even do this?

Then, to add another worry to all the others, just a few days before Leen, Carson, and Lola were supposed to arrive from New York, Cybèle came home wincing. She had been on her feet at her art camp that day and now felt some twinges.

"What kind of twinges?"

"Stress fracture twinges."

Oh no. We had been through this before. At best, a stress fracture meant six weeks of sitting. At best.

We whispered alternatives to each other that night, after the girls had gone to bed. She would stay in Paris and rest up a little. No, she would take a taxi from stage to stage, and we would meet her at the end of the day. Maybe she could ride a bike? Le Puy had a Decathlon; she could buy a bike in Le Puy. We considered every possible option before concluding that the best thing would be to try to walk the first few days, and if it was getting worse, she could take a bus back to Le Puy and pick up a bike.

But for now, we agreed that we wouldn't breathe a word of this to anyone. Leen, Carson, and Lola were arriving in the morning, and in fact were probably in the air now— and between the girls' continuous search for a way out and Leen and Carson being prudent adults, one word about Cybèle's foot could be a disaster.

The arrival of the New York delegation didn't reassure me. On the bright side, the girls, especially Masha, were glad to see them, especially Lola, who was excited about the walk, so we would probably have less to worry about on the kid management front. Leen and Carson, on the other hand, made me a little nervous, even though I had known them for at least 20 years, before they'd gone gray and I'd gone bald, almost as long as I had known Cybèle. My concern was that they were very observant people. There was something quick and birdlike about them both, not so much physically, though Carson was on the delicate side, as in the earnest way they paid attention to things. They lived in a world where everything was foreground, every detail important because every detail could kill you. Carson had become more that way over the last 20 years, as she had developed various allergies, from gluten to sunshine. As for Leen, I think was just born that way. Their capacity for detail didn't usually bother me much, but now, given what I knew about Cybèle's foot, made me giddy with anxiety that with once ungarded wince, we would be found out.

The night before we left, Cybèle laid everything out on on the living room floor to make sure we had absolutely everything we needed but nothing more. Leen, Carson and I stood and supervised. It was an impressive sight, and calmed me a little, as it seemed to me that Cybèle had worked out every detail. I felt as proud as Mamie Eisenhower the night before D-Day.

For the girls, she had picked the smallest backpacks she could find—18 liters, not much bigger than a daypack—and 22 liters for the two of us.

Cybèle had each of us pack just two T-shirts, two changes of underwear, three pairs of socks, a tiny rubber towel, a pair of flip-flops, a sun hat, a swimming suit, a one-liter aluminum water bottle, a polar fleece cardigan, and a rain poncho. She had had to push the girls hard to pack only those items, particularly the big floppy sunhats, but having seen her friend Caroline suffer the previous fall from a too-heavy pack, she was determined that each girl's pack would weigh less than four kilos (about nine pounds), and ours no more than seven (around 16 pounds).

We also made sure the girls' Kindles and iPods were in working order. Lola would keep them entertained for the first two weeks,[11] but after that, they would need other distractions. Some

---

11 Lola really was entertaining—a born storyteller with intense, deep-set gray eyes, who talked in a conspiratorial mumble. She was a font of information who had entertained the girls with facts about pyramids and mummies when she was younger and had now moved on to indie bands and no doubt shocking goings-on at the New York Performing Arts High School I never managed to overhear.

past holidays, we had had to pack a whole suitcase just for their books. Charlotte reads very quickly. Masha, the most literary of the three, tends to want to pack books too, but in a different way—usually new ones along with some old favorites, which she likes to keep with her like a cellulose security blanket. And Thea, not quite at the same stage as the other two, had tended to read their books but also had her own separate stack.

Besides her clothes, Cybèle carried a camera, a pack of cards, bandages, blister medicines, a box of hearing aid batteries, enough Pepto-Bismol for an army, and three guidebooks.[12]

Cybèle, Charlotte, and Thea also each carried a journal. My father had told me once that Jefferson had encouraged every literate member of the Lewis and Clark expedition to keep his own journal, because he believed that each point of view could be valuable, and I thought it would be interesting to have those other perspectives when we got back. I wanted this badly enough that I had succeeded in bribing Charlotte and Thea to do it. Only Masha refused. She'd done enough writing to know that I was

---

12   A French guide called *Miam Miam Dodo* (baby-French that translates roughly to "yummy-yum, nighty-night"), that ran from Le Puy to Saint-Jean-Pied-de-Port, on the Spanish border, and *The Way of St. James*, an English guide with pictures by Alison Raju. *Miam Miam* was better on food and lodging, but the English guide had more detail about the history of the chapels and villages that we would pass on the trail. As for the Pepto-Bismol, I had asked Lola to bring some along with her. They have stuff like Pepto-Bismol in Europe, of course, but I had found it was just not the same, at least not to this American stomach.

talking about real work.[13]

I had a headset for telephone calls, a tiny school-bus-yellow foot pedal I had ordered from Germany (because I sometimes interviewed people over Skype, then work up a transcript from the recording), and a tiny green notebook. I had my iPhone too, on which I had downloaded an audio book of *Don Quixote* and a lecture series on Cervantes delivered by an old professor of mine. And, of course, my laptop.

Leen and Carson looked skeptically at our backpacks. They thought we needed a larger size, with a heavier-duty belt to keep the weight off our shoulders, the kind they and Lola had. Leen also worried that Cybèle was carrying too much and thought the girls should carry more, but Cybèle refused to make any adjustments.

Their skepticism worried us. Leen and Carson are the kind of people who know things that are actually useful to know—Consumer Reports subscribers who stay at the cutting edge of sensible-shoe technology. It was Carson who had originally diagnosed Cybèle's first stress fracture, not the doctors Cybèle had seen

---

13 I'm glad I did that, because it did give me a good sense afterward of what Cybèle and the girls had been thinking. For example, Thea's journal begins with a title page, My Compostello Summer, written inside a neatly drawn scallop shell, and the following lists:

Why I don't want to go! Not necessarily in this order
    1. I have to be wearing ugly clothes all summer.
    2. I have to walk not shop.
    3. I have to WALK!! all summer!
    4. I have to wash my own dirty Underwear!
    5. I have to wear Biking shorts for the last 2 weeks.
    6. I can't go on the computer all summer.
    7. I have to carry all my stuff on my back.
    8. I only get back 3 days before school starts.
    9. I CAN'T GO SHOPPING!!
    10. I HAVE TO WEAR HIKING BOOTS!
Why I might want to go
    1. I might get tan.
    2. I will get Blonder!!
    3. I will get very strong (fit)!
    4. I will get very skinny!!

about it—and she even did it over the phone.[14]

In any case, it was too late to go back to the Old Camper to exchange our packs; we were supposed to be on the train to Le Puy in seven hours.

"How's your foot?" I whispered to Cybèle, as we got ready for bed.

She grimaced. "We'll see," she said.

---

14 Cybèle and I, on the other hand, tend to be overinvested in what Nabokov calls "unreal estate" and underinvested in the practical, a preference that had left odd gaps in the girls' education. I remember one summer, for instance, on a morning after we had moved into a furnished apartment out in the country, when the girls came to us with a strange object they had found in the closet—a long, folding table covered with padded fabric that was too tall to sit behind and too narrow to be a bed—and asked us if we had any idea what it was. Nor was this aversion to practical things like ironing boards an isolated incident. Charlotte claims, for example, that she once changed a burned-out lightbulb that her parents had forgotten to replace for three years, but this is a gross exaggeration.

First Sally

Le Puy-en-Velay to Saint-Jean-Pied-de-Port

If we had a keen vision and feeling of all ordinary human life, it would be like hearing the grass grow and the squirrel's heart beat, and we should die of the roar that lies on the other side of silence. As it is, the quickest of us walk about well-waddled with stupidity.

George Eliot
Middlemarch

July 7. Paris to Le-Puy-en-Velay, 541 km
Wherein our journey begins.

Over the years, I had gotten into the habit of pulling myself out of bed at 4:30 every morning to get a chance to draw and write without feeling I was stealing time from the family business.

At this point, I had become a bit vain about this perverse ability, the way some people are about drinking black coffee or downing vodka shots. The truth is, it wasn't so hard anymore. I slept lightly most of the time, and our two cats often started campaigning for breakfast around four, giving me a treatment that began typically by sprinting up and down the steep, glorified stepladder that led to the girls' rooms upstairs, a scamper that sounded like someone playing scales on the marimbas, and then, once Max, the fat marmalade, had built up some momentum, concluded by dive-bombing our bed.

But this morning, for the first time in months—maybe because Max and Ruby were already with our cat sitter, Agnès—on the one morning I had a real justification for my masochism, the unthinkable happened.

It gets light early in France in the summer, and I could tell I had overslept because it was now almost full daylight. I looked up from our futon in the living room (we had lent our bedroom to Leen and Carson so I could stick to my routine) and saw that Carson was in the kitchen, making coffee. I looked at my phone: 5:25—and our taxis to the train were supposed to arrive at 5:45! I nudged Cybèle awake, threw on my old bathrobe and the worn-out Birkenstocks I use as slippers, hurried up the stepladder, and woke the girls.

"Time to walk to Spain," I told Thea.

She growled.

A few minutes later, the girls came down the stairs in one Lionel Hampton cadenza, still pulling themselves together. Thea was having a minor fit about her hiking outfit.

"It's on the edge of retardedness!" she shrieked.

For the record, I thought the girls all looked good and told them so, but as usual, nobody believed me.

"The edge of retardedness!" Thea shrieked again, this time more because she liked the sound of the phrase than genuine fashion trauma. Meanwhile, our other two girls and Lola said nothing.

I kicked off my faithful Birkenstocks and laced up *die Bären*.

I felt excited but also unsettled—there are people under house arrest who get out more than I do. All the apartment's familiar things: the ancient toilet that you had to flush carefully, squeezing the handle like a clutch, or risk having the water geyser Old Faithful-style all over the bathroom; our closet-sized kitchen and the jazz station I liked to listen to while I cooked, whose purring DJs seemed to organize their playlists by stream of consciousness; the red-framed watercolor of the little red teapot Cybèle had painted for me when we first got together, which had stayed above all my desks ever since; the pigeons on the chimney pots across the street; beneath them, under the gray mansard roof, the old couple who spent their days watering their red geraniums, endlessly moving things on and off their terrace; and six floors below and two blocks down, the white-smocked, red-handed girls of the Boulangerie Pichard and the *pain tra-dition*, the third-best baguette in Paris – that whole world of rue Cambronne would have to get on without me for two months.

Boots on, packs zipped, we stumbled down the six flights of stairs to meet our taxis. We had a few minutes before our scheduled pickup but we knew the cabs

The view from 125 rue Cambronne.

would already be there[15] Cybèle had wanted to walk—Cybèle *always* wants to walk—but as we were taking a 6:30 train out of the Gare de Lyon, about six kilometers from rue Cambronne, Carson and I had persuaded her that just this once we ought to do it the easy way.

The one good part about having to take a cab was that we were in Paris, and if you happen to be going to the Gare de Lyon quite early one morning in July and find yourself gliding along the smooth green Seine, past the Assemblée Nationale, past the Musée d'Orsay, past Notre Dame, you're likely to feel more optimistic than usual about the human race. Even Thea's groans didn't bother me.

Meanwhile in the other cab, Masha confessed to Leen and Carson that she was afraid the walk would make her ugly. "Oh no," Leen said, "you'll be all toned and tan by the time you get to Santiago—*sinewy*," she said. (Leen is a lawyer; Carson is a writer—they both choose their words very carefully.)

"*Sinewy!*" Masha said. "But I don't want to be sinewy!"

We met Della and Enya in front of the old station, under the caryatids.

"Howdy, Pilgrim," I said, a joke I thought was pretty good for 6:15, but fell flat just then—maybe because it was too early or maybe because nobody else had watched as many John Wayne movies as I had.

Cybèle introduced Della and Enya to Carson and Leen. Della was as affable as ever—she should have been in the Canadian diplomatic corps. She had three daughters, like us, but the other two were older and in college. Enya was 15 and had grown a head or so taller since I had seen her last. She had switched out of our girls' school the year before, and I had missed this spurt. We had known her ever since we moved to Paris six years before,

---

15   As a rule, Parisian cabbies like to come early and start the meter running before the passenger arrives. But there wasn't really an alternative at the time: in New York, even toddlers learn how to hail a taxi, but in Paris you almost always needed to order cars by phone.

when she was a little dimpled thing, and it startled me now to see her so tall.

The grownups were all trying to be jolly—Carson and Leen were such old friends that having good-humored outsiders present made us all more sociable for this early in the morning—but Lola and our girls were quiet and sullen, especially Thea, who looked at me with a deep, abiding disdain.

Thea had always had an expression of flat-out contempt in her repertoire that I found unnerving, a nonplussed look that reminded me of the girl in *Paper Moon*, who keeps reminding her conman father throughout the movie that he owes her, say, forty-two dollars and thirty-seven cents, or whatever his current debt to her happens to be, and she had that "death to fools" glare on at full strength that morning.

On my way through the station door, I reached into a side pocket of my backpack for some water and suddenly felt something cool jet all over my hand. I turned my hand around, and it sprayed again. Now I pulled my hand back and stood contemplating the cool white stuff for a few seconds before I realized I had just sprayed a perfect pyramid of shaving cream all over my palm.

Thea roared, which under the circumstances was an unexpected bonus, like hearing Garbo laugh.

After I cleaned myself up in the restroom and bought the paper, we picked up croissants and coffee and walked to our platform. Cybèle, who remembered that Lola could be as absent-minded as Masha, warned her not to put her hat on the luggage rack, where she might forget it.

We didn't have much time to wait, which was too bad because the Gare de Lyon is a beautiful old station. It has the high spidery glass ceiling familiar from spy movies, and in the hall where they sell the tickets, a long mural of various landmarks in southern France, with real palm trees to put you in the mood. Like all the French train stations, it plays a jolly three-note riff before every train announcement—*ba Ba ba, the train to Lyon is departing in two minutes*—that sounds like a clip from a happy scene in an old New Wave movie, the interlude of cavorting in the park before the couple gets down to the real business of pouting and throwing things at each other.

Despite the foreboding I read into those three jolly notes, the train ride itself was a treat, as usual. I love the TGVs, the *Trains à Grande Vitesse*, which slice straight through the countryside at 300 kilometers per hour (186 miles per hour). Generally, by the time you finish your paper, you're halfway there, wherever you're going. The TGV is modern France's idea of what modern France should be—smooth, quiet, elegant—part of a 1975 future that somehow actually exists, except that on your return trip to Paris you can no longer transfer to the Concorde.

A few hours later, at the TGV station outside Lyon, we switched to a smaller, slower train, and the girls moved into the next car where Lola (still in her blue straw hat, which she had left on her head the whole trip, to make sure she didn't forget it) could continue her entertaining and no doubt highly educational seminar without any risk of being overheard by the Grups. By 11:30, we were winding the last 30 kilometers or so up a sparkling river gorge speckled with boulders, swimmers, and a few fly fishermen. Ten minutes before we reached Le Puy-en-Velay, I texted Thea: "Enjoy your last motorized transport for the next 1000 miles."

Out in front of the station, Cybèle took a picture of us with our packs under the LE PUY EN VELAY station sign: Leen squatting in front of all of us in the center, then behind her, Carson in her long-sleeved shirt to keep the sun off; Lola in her blue straw hat, her deep-set eyes watching Masha; Masha talking to me; Charlotte, looking straight at the camera with a *j'accuse* glower; Enya smiling; Thea smiling, but her arms crossed, to make sure no one took her for a *chouchou*[16]; Della smiling and relaxed, and behind us, a poster of Marilyn Monroe with frightened doe-eyes, an advertisement for an exhibition.

After our class portrait, the nine of us left Marilyn and made

16   "A teacher's pet." The French have better words for everything.

our way through the old southern town, with its cobblestones and orange tile roofs. We were in luck: we walked straight into the Saturday farmer's market just as it reached its late-morning crescendo, right when we had begun to think about lunch. The stands were bursting with fruit and vegetables, slippers and apple-peelers. All around us, the vendors were shouting *"Tomate tomate tomate!"* or whatever they were selling.

The girls stood talking while we shopped, joking with each other and enjoying the sun. After a while, Leen came up to me as I looked over some olives. She seemed anxious; it was about 1:30 and none of us had had anything to eat since 6:30.

"We've got to get moving," Leen said, with an edge in her voice. "The girls are getting hungry."

One was for sure, anyway, I thought.

As we left the market square to go find our *gîte,*[17] Carson and I noticed that Lola was walking along the cobblestones in an odd way, pigeon-toed and on tiptoes. Blisters already? This was not good. Cybèle was feeling her foot too, but she mouthed to me that it didn't seem to have gotten any worse.

Our gîte was in an old pink building that looked like it might have been a school at one time, but the front desk was done in IKEA noir, all flashy chrome and black lacquer, which made me think of ABBA and the seventies. The rooms lacked charm too, but in a more institutional way. Charlotte said theirs looked like the ward in *One Flew Over the Cuckoo's Nest.*

We borrowed some plates and silverware from the communal kitchen, joined two long tables in the gravel courtyard outside the building, and set out our picnic: two cooked chickens, a few pounds of cheese and tomatoes, two enormous loaves of bread, and a bowl of peaches.

---

17 A French bed and breakfast/youth hostel hybrid we saw a lot of that summer. Most gîtes we stayed in serve breakfast and sometimes dinner, and most rooms had four or six bunk beds. (Often, but not always – unlike hotels, gîtes didn't seem to follow any real pattern, except that the beds were generally hard and had no bedding and the bathroom was down the hall.)

After lunch, the first item on our agenda was to pick up our pilgrim passports—little booklets that you get stamped every place you stay and in some of the churches you visit to prove that you have made the pilgrimage. The guidebook said you could buy them in the cathedral gift shop.

To get to the church, Our Lady of the Annunciation, we walked first down into the heart of the old town, where the street names all had a medieval flavor: there was a Street of the Rope, a Street of the Ladle, a Street of Tables (as in merchants' tables), a Street of Jews, and finally, a Street of Pilgrims that led up to the cathedral.

The cathedral stands at the top of a steep volcanic hill. It's tall and domed, an enormous pile of marble zigged in black and brown candy stripes like some of the grander Italian churches. You take a long flight of 60 steps up to the dark porch of the church, which a local priest has described with slightly worrisome gusto as the Stairs of the Womb, because "you feel you are being welcomed by a mother... and feel you are entering her womb and she holds out her arms to take us in."

Although it's dark inside, and cozy as far as vast Romanesque cathedrals go, I'm not sure I would go so far as to say it is womblike. On the other hand, you could argue that if France has a birthplace, there is enough history piled onto this one hill that Our Lady of the Annunciation would be a good candidate.

Before the French, before the Franks, before the Visigoths, before the Romans, before the Gauls, five or six thousand years ago, someone looked up at this little volcanic mountain jutting up from the floor of the Le Puy valley and said, "You know, Trog, that would be an awesome place for a megalith."

We don't know much about those megalith-makers, but when the Gauls took over the region, they kept climbing this hill, and performing their own rites next to the megalith, and when the Romans moved in during the first century, they built a temple around the stone, and around 400, after they converted to Christianity, replaced that temple with a church, still without touching the megalith.

Eventually, the bishop renamed the megalith the Throne of Mary, and a Christian pilgrimage to Le Puy began. A few centuries on, someone got the idea that worshipping a rock was somewhat pagan and had it broken up. Some bits, however, were supposedly left in the floor, near the entrance we were stepping over now—I guess to be on the safe side.

Around the year 800, the object of the pilgrimage shifted to a statue the monks called Saint Mary of the Rock. Charlemagne visited twice, and most of the French kings followed his example, even after Saint Mary was replaced in the 11th century by a black statue that came to be known as Our Lady of France. Whether they were going off to fight in Spain, heading off on a crusade, or getting back from a crusade, French kings almost always paid a visit to Our Lady of France.[18] But the kings weren't the only devotees: Joan of Arc's mother made a pilgrimage here (women often prayed to Our Lady for an easy labor), and Joan herself supposedly had a special devotion to this particular Black Madonna.

Why they made Mary black is unclear. There are around 400 Black Virgins all over Europe, but for a long time, no one had a good explanation as to why. Shortly after World War II, a young American religious scholar, Leonard Ross, seeing a Black Virgin on an altar in southern Italy, asked the priest why the virgin was black, and the priest answered, "my son, she is black because she is black," an answer that didn't satisfy Ross, who went on to find a number of other equally unsatisfying answers. Some said it was the result of centuries of candle soot, but this is wrong, as most are painted black. Others have tried to explain the black virgins as images brought back from the Crusades, which doesn't work very well either, as even in Ethiopia, Mary is traditionally pictured as fairly light-skinned. Also, the features on most of the Black Virgins aren't African or Middle Eastern, and the idea that medieval sculptors didn't know what people looked like outside

---

18 The crusader connection is presumably why the church ended up with a lot of Arabic inscriptions, mostly fake except for one praise to Allah on a chapel door.

Europe doesn't hold up very well, as there has been more or less constant trade between Western Europe, the Middle East, and North Africa since Roman times. Nor were the Madonnas made of a black stone; most of the sculptures are in fact carved from locally available wood.

What seems most likely to scholars now is that the figure of the Black Madonna is an ancient earth-goddess pressed into Christian service. Many of those goddesses, including Artemis of Ephesus, Ceres, and Demeter (whose name is derived from Ge-meter or Earth mother), were traditionally portrayed as black, but their blackness represented not pigment but agricultural fertility. After the Christians suppressed all the pagan goddesses, "Mary, Queen of Martyrs, became the sole inheritor of all the names and forms, sorrows, joys, and consolations of the goddess mother in the Western World: Seat of Wisdom... Vessel of Honor...

Mystical Rose, House of Gold, Gate of Heaven, Morning Star, Refuge of Sinners...Queen of Angels... Queen of Peace," as Joseph Campbell put it in the third volume of his book *The Masks of God*.[19]

Le Puy's current Black Virgin looks gaunt and gothic. She wears an elaborate gold crown and a quizzical expression, like a hostess who is trying to look pleased to see you but can't quite place your face. Below her chin, the head of a little black Jesus with a matching crown peeps out of her bright embroidered robe, which was a cheerful yellow the day we visited.

The Black Virgin of Le Puy

I say "current virgin" because this particular figure is a 19th-century,

19 The black goddess retained her powers for Campbell, at least: his reflections on the Black Madonna at Chartres inspired him to pursue his famous studies in comparative mythology.

lead copy of the 11th-century sculpture, which was destroyed in the French Revolution. In August 1793, Jacobins tossed the original Black Virgin and Child in a manure cart and burned them in the main square. Afterward, the cathedral spent several years as a Temple of Reason, a house of worship of the state-sponsored Cult of Reason, before becoming a Temple of the Supreme Being under Robespierre, and then, under Napoleon, a Catholic church once more.[20]

All this destruction left a permanent mark on many French churches. Even today, they tend to be more sparsely decorated than the Spanish, Italian, or even the English churches, despite Henry VIII and Cromwell. If they have been restored, as this one was in the late 1840s, they tend to have been done up very flamboyantly, in ways that have more to do with *Hunchback of Notre Dame* ideas of the medieval than the real Dark Age thing.

Carson and Thea stopped to light candles—Carson, for her father, who had died a few years before; Thea, for Paola, a very Catholic family friend who had died a number of years before that, and also just for the fun of lighting a candle in the big dark church – while the rest of us walked on past the sanctuary to the gift shop.

In France, the pilgrim passport is mostly a souvenir—every church and many hostels along the Way have their own distinctive stamp and they are fun to collect—but in Spain, the passport is a serious business and something you do not want to lose. You often need your *credencial* to register in the pilgrim-only hostels. Many *refugios* won't give you a bunk unless you have it, and

---

20   In their atheistic phase, the revolutionaries decreed that all statues and crosses in cemeteries had to be replaced by a single inscription, "Death is an eternal sleep," and all church bells melted down. A new set of services were to be held that included sermons in praise of atheism, a flame supposed to symbolize truth, and girls in scanty togas and tricolor sashes who circled around a costumed Goddess of Reason, often played by the wife of an official or a former prostitute. (In Le Puy, one historian assures us, the goddess was a nice, respectable girl.) All this lasted about two years, until Robespierre sent the founders of the religion-less religion to the guillotine and brought in a religion of the Supreme Being. This in turn lasted until Napoleon brought Catholicism back. The Emperor had no special liking for Catholicism, but appreciated the political advantages of organized religion. "In Egypt, I was a Musselman; here I shall be a Catholic, for the good of the people," he once said.

perhaps more seriously, at Santiago they won't give you your *Compostela*, the diploma that says you made this pilgrimage—not a big deal for infidels like us but important to devout Catholics who want to make sure they get full spiritual credit for their trouble.[21]

While Cybèle waited in line to buy the passports, Della and I browsed through the books. Holding back a smile, she nodded over toward the entrance, where a plump young nun and a skinny monk leaned on an unoccupied counter and texted on their smartphones. It must be tough to be in holy orders today—everything you do that couldn't have been done in the 13th century makes you look like a character in a Mel Brooks skit.

After leaving the church, we walked up an even taller volcanic butte behind the cathedral to visit another unfortunate aesthetic consequence of the *citoyens'* vandalism, a 17-meter (52-foot) statue of Mary holding baby Jesus perched like a giant terracotta lawn sculpture that looks down on the cathedral and the whole valley.[22]

From the top, we could see the bell towers of the cathedral, as well as all of Le Puy and the surrounding green hills. Cybèle pointed out our pink gîte on the edge of town, but I had my eye on an ancient stone chapel to our right, which was set on top of an even more dramatic peak than the one we stood on. I suggested to Cybèle that we go there next but she thought that would

---

21   In addition to its role as the keeper of the Black Virgin of Le Puy, since around 1000, the church has also been a prime stop on the Camino de Santiago, one of the most important of many bonus stops pilgrims would make as they were passing through, like swinging by Mount Rushmore if you were driving out to Yellowstone.

22   Mary was partly under scaffolding for renovation while we were there, but I don't think we missed much, aesthetically speaking. The second tallest sculpture in the world from 1861 until 1886, when the Statue of Liberty lifted her torch, Our Lady of France was a joint project of some nationalistic clergy and Napoleon III. The clergy were looking for ways to reintegrate the Church into French life, and Napoleon III (whose ideas about religion were similar to his uncle's), presumably saw an opportunity to insinuate himself into the royal tradition. This new, unburnable Lady of France was a gift from the nation, including 300,000 school students whose centimes paid for the base, and the Emperor himself, who contributed 10,000 francs and the iron of 213 cannons seized from the Russians at the end of the 10-month-long siege of Sebastopol in the Crimean War. Whether that was all the cannons there were in Sebastopol or the recipe just called for 213 cannons, I haven't been able to determine.

be pushing the girls too much before our first day of hiking. I glumly agreed but made a secret resolution to go take a look at the mysterious chapel later that afternoon if I had the chance.[23]

Saint Michael of the Needle

23   Set on an extraordinary, 25-story-high lava butte that rises abruptly from the valley floor, the 1,000-year-old Saint-Michel d'Aiguilhe ("Saint Michael of the Needle") is only reachable by a flight of 268 steps that for some reason has yet to inspire any reproductive similes.

"We have to go up there tomorrow," Cybèle explained, pointing to a less dramatic but ultimately higher hill behind our gîte.

"Where?" Leen asked.

"There. That's where the *chemin* starts," Cybèle said. "That road, the long one there."

"The one that goes straight up the hill?"

"Yes."

No one but Leen liked the look of that.

As we walked back down toward the cathedral, we heard singing waft upward toward us and decided to crash the Saturday evening Mass.

This was an unusual event for all of us. Cybèle was a pagan from day one, and though a gentile, she, like many longtime New Yorkers, somehow considers the Jews to be her home team, for reasons I have never entirely understood. I was raised Catholic, but, as some Americans do, tend to describe myself as a recovering Catholic[24]; Leen is Jewish; Carson was religious, but not in any specific way; and the rest weren't anything in particular, as far as I knew. Our girls, at least, were not.

I enjoyed hearing the Mass again, even though it was a folk mass—guitars instead of organs—a very 70s phenomenon that I had disapproved of as a kid. I'd been right about that—aesthetically speaking, felt banners and turtlenecks couldn't hold a taper to cassocks, bells and incense—but as usual, maybe I had missed the larger point.

It seemed like a warm community, perhaps because we had arrived right before the Sign of Peace, my favorite part of the Mass, the moment you shake hands with the people around you. I thought of my own candle-lighting, bell-ringing altar boyhood *(Remember the time you were swinging the incense and started seeing*

---

24   I have since run into a phrase I like much better: the writer Edmund White likes to describe himself as a "mystical atheist," which sort of sums up my own attitude fairly well.

swirls and almost passed out? And the way Mom always had to keep Dad and Molly separated because they would give each other the giggles whenever they sang a hymn? And the time Father Cohan's sermon was interrupted by a loud thunk and we looked around and realized that an old man had fallen asleep and tumbled out of his pew?), and felt warmly nostalgic for five or ten minutes until the girls began to get restless and we ducked back out.

Outside the church, at the bottom of the Steps of the Womb, the *Chemin de Compostelle* began. We followed a line of shiny bronze scallop shells screwed into the cobblestones all the way down the steep hill. At the moment, we were just heading back to our gîte, but technically speaking, our pilgrimage had begun. After 12 years of talking about it, we were finally on our way to Santiago.

July 8. Le Puy-en-Velay to Saint-Privat-d'Alliers, 24 km

In which we meet Saint Roch.

Outside the breakfast room windows, the heads of an enormous group of pilgrims bobbed past.[25] This particular crew was a funny-looking bunch. Some of the men had big mustaches and with their walking sticks, looked like Asterix and Obelix, the comic book Gauls, off to fight the Romans.

Traditionally, pilgrims dressed in a long cloak and a broad-brimmed hat and carried a staff with a little gourd on the end of it for water or wine, a costume people wore all the way up to the late 19th century. A hundred years later, pilgrims still wear a uniform, but these days the French pilgrims at least are mostly bedecked in neon microfibers, shorts, and fleece from Decathlon's Quechua budget line. The only exceptions in our troupe were the New York contingent. Carson wore a somewhat clerical-looking hat with an enormous brim that I liked and a long-sleeved shirt, because she is allergic to the sun. Leen wore a higher class of microfiber. And Lola had on her pretty blue straw hat with a brown band and an old yellow T-shirt.

Soon we finished our coffee and croissants and joined the Quechua tribal parade ourselves.

The first hill out of town was steep, but not as bad as it looked from Mary's peak the day before. It was a bright, sunny morning, still cool but beginning to warm up. The girls began singing "It's A Hard-Knock Life," from the musical *Annie,* and charged ahead—even Lola, though she was a little wobbly because of her preexisting blistered condition.

Red and white splotches painted on lampposts marked our way, so the navigation was not difficult, which was a good thing because the adults were tired; we had all had hard-knock nights for

---

25 I'm not sure what the collective term for pilgrim should be: coven? phalanx? puzzle?

one reason or another.

Cybèle had gone to bed early with a migraine—she often has them right after a period of high-stress, like the prior week, when she had to deal with the trifecta of her art camp, our visitors, and packing for the walk.

My night had started out promisingly enough: We had turned in early, right after we got back from dinner. Stuffed and tired, I brushed my teeth, unrolled my new sleep sack, and tucked myself into my light silk cocoon. It was smooth and comfy, and as I pulled it up around me, I congratulated myself again on our splurge. It had definitely been worth it. I set the alarm on my phone, put the phone and my glasses under the bed, and turned over, ready to sleep.

But after 10 minutes, I began to notice that I was extremely hot, and in an unpleasantly sticky way, as if I had just crawled inside a giant sandwich bag. What did people use these liners for? Where could you possibly use them, outside of Antarctica? I looked up at the bunk above me, which bowed under a wire hammock. Cybèle was already asleep in that sack. How had she managed that? I wondered. A few minutes later, I fidgeted my way out of the sack and rearranged myself. As a blanket, the liner wasn't quite so bad.

Around 3, Leen woke up and pulled out her iPad to pass the time. She has the energy of a little kid, but as she's deaf, didn't realize how much noise she made shifting in her bunk. More shifting, more blue light from the iPad. More shifting. I woke up and after awhile, Carson stirred as well. Eventually, she reached up and tapped Leen. "You need to be quiet, Pounce," she sighed.

Then at 4:30, in Della's room, around the time I got up to work, she and Enya had been woken up by their roommates, a German couple who had decided they needed to repack before they left. They seemed to be going through everything—folding and unfolding, zipping this and tying that, and just when it seemed they were all done, starting all over again. By morning, our tolerant Canadian friend was ready to strangle them—particularly after she watched them chuck their packs in the back of their tour's support van.

The countryside was beautiful that first day, but we didn't see the same things. Cybèle noticed *"the old stone houses, horses, cows, roosters, and small villages high up on the hills. There were lots of wild-flowers – purple, blue, pink violet, yellow, and white… along certain paths there were tons of butterflies – white ones with black spots. The wheat fields were a gorgeous white gold."* Masha paid attention to the flowers too, particularly the *"papery red poppies, light pinkish-white daisies, and bright purple fields of lavender."*[26] For Charlotte, it was all discomfort and bad outfits, which, to be fair, are also prominent features of the Way. *"My feet really hurt because the insoles of my shoes are too thin. My backpack chafes my shoulders and neck. Dad's outfit is 100% beige: hat, shirt, shorts. Mom's t-shirt has dark patches sewn under the arms so it looks like she sweats loads. Masha keeps saying I look like a person recovering from cancer with my headscarf."*

I wish now that I had been tougher on myself and kept a journal too as we went along, but Cybèle reminds me that between walking and working, I didn't have much energy to spare at the end of the day. On the bright side, memory is a good editor. From that first day, I remember

---

26   I found out much later that although she had not signed up as a journal-writer, Masha did keep a journal for the first few weeks.

A pair of earnest young French women ahead of us who wore matching blue-striped shirts, had matching red tin mugs tied to their backpacks, and never smiled

A French mother with her eight-year-old son, who wanted to move every direction but forward

Our picnic—camembert, sausage, bread, and chocolate— in front of a very small and old stone chapel

—And inside the musty chapel, a peculiar statue of a pilgrim lifting his robe to a height that might get you arrested in Penn Station, and pointing to a wound on his thigh.

The exhibitionist pilgrim turned out to be Saint Roch or Roche, or Rocco to his Italian friends, the patron saint of plague victims, cattle, doctors, prisoners, bachelors, dogs, and dog lovers. We ran into him a lot over the next few weeks, usually in that same pose — showing off his boo-boo, often with a dog at his side.

On this stretch of the Camino, Roch turns up even more often than Saint Jacques (that is, Saint James or Santiago), probably because of his reputation as a healer of the bubonic plague, a periodic scourge in France from the

Saint Roch

mid-14th century, when it wiped out as much as 40 percent of the population of Europe, to the early 18th century. Wherever you see Saint Roch, you can bet they have seen a lot of plague at some time or other.

Saint Roch was born into a family of minor-league nobles near Montpellier in what is now southeast France, either in 1295, or 30 or 40 years later. *The Golden Legend*, a medieval compendium of saints' lives, notes that Roch had two unusual features from birth: a birthmark in the shape of a red cross on his chest, and an unusual capacity for holiness—even as a nursing infant, when his mother fasted, so did he.

At 20, after his parents died, Roch left the family village in the care of an uncle and set off on a pilgrimage to Rome. As he walked, he kept wandering through plague-stricken towns, where he would stop to care for the sick.

By the time he reached Rome, Roch had become such a famous healer that a sick cardinal had him summoned to his palace. At his bedside, Roch made a sign of the cross on the cardinal's forehead. The cardinal soon felt better, but Roch's medicine had an embarrassing side effect: it left behind a mark in the shape of a cross, which I gather was seen as a sort of allergic reaction to goodness.

Roch managed to outrun the embarrassed cardinal's men out of Rome but not the Black Death. Now that he was sick himself, however, no one remembered his kindnesses. Shunned by every town he passed, he found a place in the woods where he could stay, built a hut, and prepared for the worst.

But then his luck changed. First, a spring sprang out of nowhere. Then a clever dog found him, and began bringing him bread he had stolen from his master's table.

Not only did the dog feed Roch, he looked after him: in some versions of the Roch story, the dog licks the open wound on his leg that had been caused by the plague. That's why most statues of Saint Roch show him lifting his robe, pointing at the scar on his thigh healed by the dog, sometimes with the dog by his side.[27]

---

27   The dog belonged to a young nobleman named Gotard. In the version of the story "Englished" by William Caxton in 1483 says, "Which thing when Gotard had advertised oft that he bare so away the bread, but he wist not to whom ne whither, whereof he marvelled, and so did all his household." One day, after letting the dog make off with an especially nice loaf, Gotard followed him into the woods, and was amazed to meet Roch, who told him to stay away because he had the plague. Later, after Roch had recovered, Gotard came back and announced he wanted to become his follower. The holy man accepted, and then instructed Gotard to give away everything, beg for his food, and make his way to Rome. Gotard had a hard time doing so at first—the townsfolk were understandably annoyed to find the son of one of the town's richest families begging at their door—but after he left his hometown, the job got easier.

Once he recovered, Roch headed back to France. Every so often, he would be stopped by sick or injured animals that wanted him to heal them, and "when they were healed they would incline their heads reverently and go their way." Unfortunately for Roch and his woodland pals, when he finally reached his village, his uncle, who had run the town in his absence, didn't recognize him in his pilgrim outfit and had him thrown in prison. Too humble to tell anyone about the mistake, the saint languished in prison for five years, and then died. The end.[28]

And the beginning of Roch's fame.

At the time, the community of saints was organized much like health care today: for everyday concerns, you would pray to your local general practitioner, the patron saint who kept watch over your village or city, but if you had a specific problem, you might consult a specialist. When terror of the plague grew in the mid-1300s, Roch's career as a healer and a plague victim himself made him the obvious go-to saint for delivery from the Black Death.

The plague first came out of Asia in the late 1340s, by rodents carrying plague-bacteria-infected fleas into cities, driven there (according to the latest theory) by climate change: as Asia became warmer and wetter in the 1300s, rodent populations crashed. Fleas desperate to jump a sinking rat found ideal new vessels in the human inhabitants of the cities of China and later to points west.

It was a terrifying, brutal disease. Boccaccio wrote

> In men and women alike it first betrayed itself by the emergence
> of certain tumours in the groin or armpits, some of which grew as

---

28   There is a lot of uncertainty about Roch's biography, as there often is about saint's lives, including minor details such as the dates of his birth and death, and the place where he died. Some historians now argue that Roch lived from 1348 to 1376 or 1379, and died not in Montpellier but Vorghera, Italy. This kind of thing is why I have generally ended up more or less ignoring the documentary side of these stories, which are often hopelessly vague or confused. Sorting them out seems to me about as useful as deciding what year Spiderman graduated from high school—and beside the point, which is all about the feeling people had about the character. As Henry Adams said of the century before, in *Mont Saint Michel* and Chartres, "To understand the twelfth century, one has to be prematurely young."

large as a common apple, others as an egg...

After that came black spots, then fever, and then you might start vomiting blood. Once you saw the blood, you had a few days left at most, and then you were dead.

The 1347–51 outbreaks were the worst epidemics but not the last, and the plague continued to break out often enough that Roch stayed in people's prayers in France and in Italy, over the next century and a half. During a particularly bad outbreak in 1484, a group of Venetians even stole his body—or at least a body—from his hometown, Montpellier, and took it to Venice in the hope that his relics could protect the city from the next wave.

Despite his fame, it took 200 years before Roch received an official promotion to saint and even then, his popularity seems to have forced the pope's hand. I can understand the hesitation. Traditionally, a person needs several miracles for canonization. I would give Roch miracle-credit for the mysterious mark of the cross on the cardinal's forehead and maybe some of his healings, but I'm not sure about the dog episode, as it seems to me the dog did most of the work.[29] [30]

The hiking stayed easy after our picnic – a largely level lane that cut straight through farm after farm. Every so often, Leen would look out at the fields, the wildflowers along the path, and the old stone villages we walked through, and say, "This is unbelievable! Un-believable!"

Afterward, Thea admitted it had been a good day. *"It was really beautiful and it wasn't too hard, I mean it was kind of annoying and I don't want to do the whole thing but for a trip with my parents it's not*

---

29   Nor is the licking, strictly speaking, a miracle. A number of studies have found that if your dog is healthy, dog licks really are good for you.

30   Despite my reservations about Roch, you might want to get on good terms with him now, while the lines are short: Madagascar has suffered three outbreaks of an antibiotic-resistant strain of the bubonic plague over the last 23 years. The last, in October 2017, killed 170 people. Of course, Madagascar is an island and the doctors blame cultural practices that involve physical contact with the dead, but Saint Antibiotic doesn't seem to be coming through as well now as she once did.

that terrible," she wrote.

Around 3:30, we reached our destination, Saint-Privat-d'Allier, a narrow hill town whose main street seemed more a paved extension of the trail than a road. The hamlet had a tucked-in, almost Japanese quality, and clung to a ridge that looked across a deep gorge toward a ruin that must have been part of an old fort or monastery.

At our gîte, a well-scrubbed place with nautical red trim, the proprietors were just starting to check people in when we arrived. While we waited, we sat down at several picnic tables, took our boots off, and changed into our flip-flops. Thea, Charlotte, and Enya started playing cards. Masha—and Lola, always a loyal friend—began interrogating Cybèle about whether Masha would have enough time to pack and prepare for boarding school. Della began writing in her journal, as Leen reviewed the map for tomorrow, and Carson lay on a patch of grass in the shade and rested.

I took another long look at the ruins across the gully, thought about walking over to investigate them more thoroughly, then lay down on the bench, and fell asleep.

July 9. Saint-Privat-d'Allier to Saugues, 17.9 km

In which we meet various beasts of Gévaudan.

Early next morning, I tiptoed downstairs and found a spot to sit in the foyer. It was cold and would be dark for at least another hour, but the laptop kept my knees warm.

Twenty minutes later, two solid German women with short hair, matching thick-framed glasses, and chunky wooden crosses around their necks thudded down the stairs. They were startled, then annoyed, to find me on the landing and gave me a curt goodbye as they huffed out the door. If you ever want to bug an ascetic, just get up earlier than she does.

As the light rose, I noticed that the gorge on the other side of the street was filled with fog, making the old fort look like an island.

The Beast of Gévaudan

(from an 18th century illustration)

The gothic scene was appropriate: We were heading now into a part of the country that had been terrorized in the 18th century by an animal that came to be known as the Beast of Gévaudan, a creature Robert Louis Stevenson in his *Travels with a Donkey in the Cévennes* described as "the Napoleon Bonaparte of wolves," a monster that killed more than a hundred people between 1764 and 1767, and was never captured.

A German naturalist who pored over the eyewitness accounts of survivors recently published a theory that the reason they had such a hard time with the beast was because he was not actually a wolf, but a young male lion imported from Africa to satisfy the aristocratic appetite for exotica that had somehow escaped to the Cévennes.[31]

Whatever the truth, the beast's memory continues to terrorize even now, primarily through horrendous movies. We were scarred by one of those films ourselves when we got back to Paris that fall—a French picture that involves a young scientist, a handsome Native American, a beautiful prostitute with a PhD in martial arts, a pack of secret revolutionaries, and two aristocratic vampires with incestuous tendencies. In his review of the *Brotherhood of the Wolf*, Roger Ebert said it plays like "an explosion at the genre factory."

By the time we finished our bread and coffee, the fog had burned off and a lot of the romance of the scenery had evaporated along with it. Our path led first to an old chapel and tower that stood on the same ridge as Saint Privat and looked far out over the valley, and then turned and fell more or less straight down the hill to a river, a village, and a boxy hydroelectric station that straddled one channel of the river. High-voltage power lines stretched off in either direction. The landscape reminded me of the American West—gorgeous except for the manmade stuff, which tends to look as if it had been thrown out of airplanes by angry robots.[32]

The girls jumped, almost flew, down the steep hill, along with Cybèle, who had decided that her footache was actually nothing to worry about, and had gone back to being 49 going on 14. The rest of us, being middle aged and mortal, took slow and careful steps down the slippery granite slabs and loose gravel.

Cybèle and Thea waited for Della and me near the village at the bottom of the hill. Carson and Leen had walked ahead of them, and the four older kids had all disappeared. None of them had

---

31   His reasoning: the descriptions made by the peasants who had tangled with the beast and survived matched those of a young mane-less male lion, an animal they would not have recognized.

32   To be fair, Gustav Eiffel of Eiffel Tower fame built the village bridge, so I may not be the best judge.

cellphones, but this didn't concern me much. I assumed they had just zoomed through town and were now on the trail again. Sooner or later, I told Cybèle, they would get hungry and wait for us.

Della, Thea, Cybèle, and I went into the village store and bought bread and cheese and cold cuts for lunch. When we got out, we ran into Leen, who was waiting for Carson. As we waited with her in the tiny parking lot, I noticed an overwhelming silence. No kids went by, or cars, or much of anything, not even a dog. Even the stream and the power station didn't make much noise.

After waiting another 10 minutes, we decided that Carson must have somehow missed us and gone ahead with the girls. We started on the gravel path that wound up the steep hill behind the village, climbed a series of switchbacks and past a grotto for Mary, and then made another left, where the path stopped hugging the hillside, turned inward, and drove straight up to the crest. About halfway to the top, Cybèle and I began to worry that maybe Carson and the girls had all taken the wrong path when we left the village, but as we started climbing up through a steep abandoned orchard, we spotted Carson, who had been trying to find us and looked frantic. She had seen the girls, but they had raced right past her and she wasn't sure if they had seen her.

Near the top of the hill, we ran into the girls. As I had predicted, they had started to think about lunch and slowed down to give their food-bearing sherpas a chance to catch up. It turned out they had decided they would have more fun if they left the grownups in the dust. I'm sure this was true for as long as it lasted, but I suspect that what the French call a "bad quarter hour" (basically an earful)_ they got from us now outweighed the fun. We made a rule that they could walk ahead but had to make sure we could see them or arrange a place to meet, as none of them had a map. Scolding over, the grownups took off their authority masks, the girls took a break from their rebellion, and we became a friendly group once more. {Mostly, at least: Masha felt her telling-off *"honestly wasn't very fair, so I was in a big huff with the grupps for most of the afternoon."*)

We stopped for an early lunch at the first flat open place. As we ate, a wild, or at least stray, dog walked up to us. She was hungry but wary, a mangy fur-covered skeleton that couldn't even manage a proper bark. Before anyone could try to feed the poor thing, Della said we shouldn't touch her because she might have rabies and instructed the girls not to pay any attention to her. After a while, she wandered off. Things had evidently gone downhill for beasts of Gévaudan in the past 240 years.

But not for every beast, it turned out: A little while after lunch, a blur of striped wild boar piglets zipped across the path ahead of us.[33] The boar-lets were obviously well-fed, and much cuter than the starving cur.

Still, we started walking faster—where there are babies, there are mothers. I had never seen a boar in the wild myself before these three but I had seen plenty of fields that adult boars had dug for grubs as thoroughly as any rototiller and knew enough about them to understand that you didn't want to run into.

A crashing boar (after Cranach the Elder)

Hunting writers agree that the boar is one of the most fierce, intelligent, and dangerous animals in the forest. At least two French kings were killed in boar-hunting accidents. The beast even provoked Hemingway into an adverb. In one essay, he calls the boar "a really dangerous game animal":

---

33 This is apparently unusual: when boars are on the move, the herd (communists should note that the collective in French is compagnie) usually runs in formation, sows in front. Unlike our own enterprises, female leadership in compagnies des sangliers is the rule rather than the exception.

A wild boar's tusk is like a razor and about three to six inches
long. It makes a ghastly wound and once a boar gets a man down
it keeps driving into him in an insane rage until the man is dead .
. . A wild boar will weigh up to 200 pounds and ounce for ounce
and pound for pound is about as fierce and vicious an animal as
there is.

Boars are big enough and ferocious enough that even today, they
are not usually hunted *mano-a-suino*, but from a distance, either
shot sniper-style from a raised pillbox in a field or encircled like
a movie fugitive by teams of dogs and men in camouflage carrying big guns and walkie-talkies who don't stray too far from
their 4x4s.

In the unlikely event of a marauding pig, one authority advises
running away. But you're not out of the woods yet, so to speak:
they can run faster than you can. Whether you will presently
be boar-hash is entirely up to the boar. Don't bother trying to
play dead—boars are smart: there is one incident on record of a
person escaping alive by playing dead, but only one. Climbing a
tree might be a good idea, but keep in mind that a big pig can
"walk" his front legs up the trunk and reach as high as five feet
off the ground. Even swimming won't do you much good: boars
have been seen a kilometer and a half out in the open sea. Nor
are you necessarily safe in a car. There are more than 11,000
boar-related car accidents in France every year and boars are
strong enough and fast enough that even trains have occasionally suffered damage.

Fortunately, boars seldom look for a fight. Unless they are trying
to protect their young, their first instinct is to run away. Despite
being so fearsome, the big pigs are right to be wary; after all,
they were hunted to extinction in the British Isles before 1400.
They also suffered hard times in Renaissance France as forests
were cleared to make way for more farms.

Historians have speculated that the only reason boars managed
to hang on in France at all is because under the *Ancien Régime*,
the law limited boar hunting to the nobility. Ironically, this re-
striction turned out to be good for the pigs but bad for the aristocrats. In the years leading up to the Revolution, one of the

peasants' biggest complaints against the nobility was their monopoly on boar hunting. Boars could tear up the peasants' fields and they could do nothing to stop them. Even liberal aristocrats could not help: unlike fishing rights, boar-hunting rights could not be leased out.

When the Revolution finally came, the citizens' *fraternité* did not extend to boars. Often, even before they got around to chopping noble heads and burning chateaux, rural revolutionaries' first order of business was to go boarhunting.

Since 1789, however, humanity has done a lot to make things great for boars again. Crop yields rose, reducing the need for cleared land. There are more woods now in Europe than there were in the 18th century. In France, 25 percent of the land is covered in forest—14.8 million hectares, almost 50 percent more than in 1890, which in turn was 50 percent more than in 1790. In 1937, French hunters shot the country's last wolf—the boars' only natural predator, not counting human beings— and in the 20th century, we did our best to minimize that final menace too.

In a 1923 *Toronto Star* dispatch, Hemingway noted that during the Great War "when there was almost no shooting, game flourished unchecked all over Europe. One of the best flourishers of them all was the wild boar." In France, the local boar population grew because the animal refugees reportedly fled the fighting in the Ardennes forest in Belgium and headed south. French boars received a second boost in World War II, as firearms were prohibited in occupied France. All through the war, the boar's only threat was German soldiers who would sometimes combine boar hunts with hunts for partisans.

Today, climate change is helping the boars as well. Milder winters have not only made it easier for the piglets to stay warm, but more importantly, produced bumper crops of beechnuts and acorns, two of the boars' favorite foods.

All in all, these are the best of times for boars. Between 1974 and 2012, the boar population in France increased at least fourteenfold. Hunters kill over 700,000 of the wild pigs every year, yet some farmers complain that this is still not enough. "Some hunters are doing their bit but others prefer to hunt just on the weekends during the hunting season. They're not putting in the work," one Breton farmer grumbled to a reporter a few years ago.

Two kilometers on, the path opened out on a rolling field with a farmhouse in the distance. It was a warm clear day with only a few puffy clouds in the sky. Between a full stomach and the wide, level path, most of us were feeling fairly relaxed.

With one exception.

It was almost 2:20, and I had an interview at 2:30, but had just lost my cellphone signal. All morning, I had kept an eye on my phone connection, and even into the early afternoon, I had had five strong bars. Up and down and around boulders and trees, even with no trace of humanity in sight but a few long-distance power lines, I stayed on the grid. But now that the trail had turned into a long country lane with fields stretching out on either side and a barn and farmhouse ahead of us, my connection fell to three bars, then two, then vanished ... 2:26 ... I began walking faster, hoping the bars would come back ... 2:27... waving my phone around like one of those old coots who wander the beach back home with a metal detector, looking for lost jewelry ... 2:28.

Then as the lane turned left ahead of the farm compound, the signal bars began to come back. Leen found a nice footstool-sized rock under a tree where I could sit. Charlotte thought I looked funny sitting on a rock in the middle of a field *"with his weird hat and his computer on his knees."* ... 2:29.

But right after the others took a last picture and left me behind, I checked my phone again and realized my connection in this comfortable spot had fallen to half a bar. Not nearly enough. I gathered up my stuff, and hurried back up the lane to a place in the sun that was less comfortable but had a stronger signal and sat down in the warm dirt.

2:30 ... Oh no! I'd forgotten to write down the dial-in number in my little notebook. I scoured the laptop, found it, and called. Right on time. As the cheerful anthem swelled, I imagined thousands of consultants racing through airports, optimizing supply chains and creating tax efficiencies, leaned back a little and stretched my legs out across the path. Home, home on the grid.

At moments like these, I always feel a bit like a secret agent who's just defused a bomb at the last minute—first the buildup, then, red wire or blue wire? And finally, with luck and pluck, it's "Well done, Mr. Bond"—only now, just as I exhaled, a big tractor careened around the corner.

Two dogs lolloped ahead of the tractor, barking like canine sergeants-at-arms. With my phone in my left hand, thumb over my microphone, and laptop in my right, I wobbled to my feet and leaned backward just as the parade passed by and my call began.

Once the speeding farmer and his dogs turned the corner, I settled back down in the dirt, pinned my phone between my ear and shoulder, and started the interview. I was talking to two consultants about European telecom regulation, the subject of an article they wanted me to ghostwrite for them.[34]

When my call ended, I stuffed the computer back in my backpack, uncoiled my headphones from the shoulder strap, and turned on my recording of *Don Quixote*.

In the end, how you make a long walk like the Camino is likely to be a reflection of how you live the rest of your life. Some people are well prepared. They pay attention to their surroundings. They think things through. They have epiphanies but reach their destination with time to spare. My companions, for instance, had probably already finished our day's hike. I, on the other

---

34 I assumed they were sitting at a polished conference room table in London, but they may not have been. Increasingly, I find that work is becoming a virtual reality game for a lot of us, played while we're driving or in an airport lounge. I have gotten pretty good at shifting between physical reality and Workplace Radio Theater, but a lawyer friend of mine I'll call Zubin is the master. Not only has he learned to separate work from physical reality—he has negotiated deals on the Pont-Neuf—he's even crossed the multitasker's final frontier: the mind. A serious amateur pianist, Zubin says he has trained himself to negotiate and think about Schubert or whatever piece he happens to be working on at the same time—a four-handed variation, I guess you would call it.

hand, was still out wandering around the fields with *Don Quixote* and had just realized that it had been a while since I'd seen one of the red and white striped path markers—the one thing in the world I needed to pay attention to at that moment—and that in fact I was not on the path at all.

I looked around the field for a few minutes and tried to retrace my steps, with no luck until I saw a couple pass me a little to my left who seemed sure enough about where they were going that I decided to follow them, and once I'd locked in their coordinates, put my brain back on cruise control and hit "play."

An hour further on, at the end of those fields, I lost my couple, but the path came to a sandy patch with pine trees and the red and white stripes reappeared. I could also see far down the hill ahead of me more fields and then a town. This had to be Saugues, our destination. Thea called and tried to give me directions, but they didn't penetrate. They were very good directions I'm sure, but by the time she got through describing the third turn, I couldn't keep them straight. Anyway, I thought, she was probably over-engineering this—the town had about three streets, there had to be signs to our hostel, and besides, I wanted to finish my chapter. I thanked her, hung up, and hurried back to *Don Quixote*.

On a paved road now, the Don, Sancho, and I kept heading down the hill, past two new ranch houses set on terraced lots, one completed and another under construction. Two little kids took a shot at me with squirt guns from behind a hedge.

Once in town, I walked right through to the other side, realizing only after a kilometer or so that I had missed the turn for our hostel, then had to circle back. This took awhile; my feet had begun to ache, and I was moving very slowly, even for me. Eventually, after another call from Thea—I was late enough now that they had begun to wonder if something had happened to me—I found my way to our hostel.

It was a more institutional establishment than the night before, a large building that felt like a school without classrooms. The check-in clerk told me the number of the room Cybèle and the girls were in and I shuffled slowly down the hall to meet them, suddenly exhausted.

When Thea opened the door, the girls were in various stages of cleaning themselves up. I shucked off my pack, sat down on the unclaimed bunk, and had just started taking off my boots when Cybèle came in to the room with an armload of wet clothes.[35]

"Did the call go all right?" she asked, keeping one eye on my mouth as she started hanging the girls' damp T-shirts and underthings on our metal bunk bedstead.

"Fine," I said, peeling off my wet socks. Then, just as I began to lean back, she sat down next to me on the bed, landing with a bounce.

"We should go into town," she said, her brown eyes bright. "There are a couple of things we should see and I want to stop at a pharmacy to get some better insoles for Charlotte."

I nodded.

Despite two firm no votes to this proposal from my feet, I took a shower, changed my clothes, and 10 minutes later inched out the door behind the family, feeling ancient, while Cybèle, our girls, and Lola clicked ahead in their flip-flops, apparently no worse for wear.

First, Cybèle took us to a tiny museum dedicated to the life of Brother Benilde Romançon, a local hero of the town.

The museum featured dioramas in glassed-in artificial grottos that looked like the animated window scenes department stores used to put up at Christmas, except that these displays illustrated episodes from the life of Brother Benilde, patron saint of

---

35   One of the tougher parts of pilgrim life as a family adventure is that almost every day is laundry day.

teachers and accordion players.[36] The strangeness of the place charmed Cybèle but Lola and the rest of us took a quick glance and moved on. We could be a tough audience.

Saugues' English Tower

Outside again, we followed a painted white line of giant animal footprints down the street to our next destination, the Museum of the Beast of Gévaudan.

Unfortunately, the museum was closed, but just across the alley we saw a more somber memorial to an earlier set of monsters, Saugues's English tower. A number of the towns we walked through those first two weeks had similar fortifications—all tall, windowless stone bunkers, most of them thrown up in a hurry

---

36   Saint Bernilde, a 19th-century Christian Brother, was a gifted and inspiring teacher at the local school. Technically, his qualifying miracles have something to do with a cross some workmen had ended up with after his death, but I think the Vatican was more impressed with his day job. At his beatification in 1947, Pope Pius XII emphasized that Benilde had grown holy by "doing common things in an uncommon way" and enduring "the terrible daily grind." But Benilde took no credit for his talent: this font of goodness once confessed that teaching did not always come easily to him. "I imagine that the angels themselves, if they came down as schoolmasters, would find it hard to control their anger," he once said of his students. "Only with the help of the Blessed Virgin do I keep from murdering some of them."

during the Hundred Years' War in the 14th and 15th centuries. I had thought at first that they were called "English towers" because the English occupied those towns, but I read later that they were called English towers for the same reason we call bomb shelters "bomb shelters": they were meant to defend the townsfolk *from* the English.

To make matters still more confusing, most of the "English" were Basque mercenaries—*routiers*, armed bands that roved the countryside, sometimes on behalf of the English but more often on a freelance basis—Robin Hood and his scary men.

The history books describe the Hundred Years' War as a long struggle between France and England over who would rule France, but that's giving it too much dignity. As Henri Denifle, a 19th-century historian put it, the Hundred Years War was "an endless and grimly monotonous succession of massacres, fires, pillaging, ransoms, destruction, losses of harvests and cattle, rapes and...every sort of calamity."

The brutality stemmed partly from the fact that soldiers weren't paid, so there was always a "delicate boundary between loyal service and armed criminality..." as the historian Nicholas Wright observes. From the peasants' point of view, the armies consisted mostly of roving gangs who were largely focused on extracting money from peasants any way they could. "Pain was the mangle that squeezed out every available drop of wealth."[37]

The allegiance of the soldiers was often irrelevant to the peasants, who had, in essence, a choice between rival criminal gangs. As Wright says, "a peasant who saw his livestock being driven away by unidentifiable armed men towards a fortified place had neither the capacity nor, one would guess, much incentive to determine whether the plunder was for the benefit of an English or a French garrison."

You can see the desperation of the times in the architecture of

---

37   Nor were the higher-ups boy scouts. Henry V may or may not have said, "Once more unto the breach!" but he definitely observed that "[w]ar without fire is as worthless as sausages without mustard."

those towers. Unlike earlier and later French castles and fortifications, Saugues's tower and the other English towers we saw
were all ugly and sloppily built. I wouldn't do much better, I'm
sure, but given that when these people had time and money,
they were perfectly capable of building a cathedral, the towers
do look like an appropriate monument to a cruel and stupid ep-
och.

In the dining hall that night, we found ourselves surrounded by
a sea of noisy school kids. Expert lip readers, Leen and Cybèle
carried on their conversation without any problem, but the rest
of us had to shout at each other to be heard.[38]

Dinner was not as good as the dinner at Saint-Privat the night
before—a pasta salad and greenish chicken that sent memories
of lunch at Oceanlake Elementary School rushing back to me
like a stale Madeleine—but adults were issued unlabeled bottles
of awful but effective plonk, so I didn't mind much.

After dinner, I went off to try to do a little work.

Upstairs, I found a seminar room that had a wireless connection,
three or four big tables, and large picture windows with a view
of a playing field and the hills behind the town. A warm gold
light filled the room—it was around 9 now, on one of those long
summer evenings that seems somehow marinated in nostalgia,
as if you are already looking at yourself looking back.

At one point, Masha and Lola stopped by to ask if they could set
out on an expedition to a statue of Mary that was perched on
top of a hill behind the town. I didn't let it show but deep down
felt a little parental glee: after five hours of hiking, Masha had
decided that a climb up this steep hill would be a fun thing to do.
I couldn't wait to tell Cybèle. *Doctor, the experiment is working!*[39]

---

38   One of the great things about France is that summer camp isn't just a rich-kid
thing. Almost everyone can go. The camps (colonies) tend to be basic but wholesome
places. Many have a Catholic connection but the Catholicism is more something you
sense, like an institutional smell—one part macaroni to two parts floor wax— than
something you see.

39   In retrospect, of course, it's also entirely possible that I'd been had. Gullibility
was always one of my more winning qualities as a parent.

July 10. Saugues to Chapelle Saint-Roch, 21 km
In which we eat, and eat some more.

A soft white mist fell on the fields and the blacktopped road. We had pulled out our slickers and, as Decathlon doesn't make many colors, almost everyone matched someone else—red, red, green, green, blue, green. Moving in ones and twos up the long gentle slope, we looked like a roll of Life Savers. At the top of the hill, the Way missed the turn and shot straight out on a sandy path that wound through a grove of lean, wind-warped pines. And we were talking.

We talked a lot those first few days.

The grownups compared childhoods. Carson told me a story about a recent visit she made to her hometown in Alabama, where nothing had changed in 50 years—not even in the diner where she and her brother had sometimes spent their bottle-return money, except she couldn't order the grilled cheese sandwich now because of her gluten allergy. Della, who was from Vancouver, talked about her outdoorsy father and all the sailing, skiing, and hiking they had done together, while I talked about cozy times in front of the TV, out of that same northwest rain, watching old movies and *Perry Mason* reruns.[40]

I fell behind whenever she returned to the topic of her bicyclist. Normally, I'm as up for inspiration as anyone, but given our summer plan, I didn't want to hear about it.

Leen also gave us regular updates on how much distance we had covered. She had a sleek blue bracelet on her forearm that monitored her heart rate and calculated her average speed and time to destination, as if she were a slow-moving missile. Those first few days, the girls asked her every hour or so how far we had walked and how much further we had to go, but eventually they lost interest. Knowing didn't make the time go any faster.

---

40 "The nice thing about the weather here," Dad told me once, "is that it's weather that doesn't make demands on you."

At one point, a fellow Canadian Della and Enya had met at their hotel the night before caught up with us. After five minutes of reluctant chat, he hurried ahead, eager to get back to his regularly scheduled program of splendid isolation. I had imagined more pilgrims would travel together as they walked, Canterbury style, but there were many single pilgrims who prized their solitude. The younger women in particular tended to radiate a fiercely independent *la femme Nikita en vacance* energy that would make you think twice about tangling with them.

A number of authorities say the only real Camino is a solitary one and that may be true, but as far as I'm concerned, they are welcome to it. Unless you are a deep thinker or a saint, traveling solo would be hard going.[41] If I had tried this walk on my own, I am sure that sooner or later I would have started to tag along like a stray dog behind any group I could find. Particularly after my lonely afternoon the day before, I was glad to be with my herd again.

Around 10, the sun came out, and when we passed a farmhouse that had set itself up as a coffee shop for pilgrims, we decided to stop. We sat at long wooden tables outside the old stone house, and drank *café crème* and cocoa out of large blue, yellow, and orange cups, served with fresh cream from their own cows. If there were places like this at two-hour intervals all along the Camino, the cities would be empty.

Later that afternoon, the land turned swampy, and the good feeling of the morning wore off. We passed a marsh of white bleached stumps and a few cows who looked nearly marooned. The gang was starting to get impatient: We had walked two more kilometers than the 21 scheduled, according to Leen's watch, and still had not reached our destination. After one missed turn, on the 24th kilometer, even Della had begun to get a little tense— Cybèle thought she might be getting blisters.

After a little backtracking and a second look at the *Miam Miam*

---

41 Even some saints might find it tough. I suspect that's the real reason Francis of Assisi preached to the animals.

guide, we found our gîte, a gray stone lodge tucked deep in the woods about two kilometers off the trail. It had been built in the 1940s or 1950s, and the green shutters, Adirondack chairs, and general air of prim prosperity made me think of New England. Della and I had a beer in the garden and then I roused myself and got to work.

Like most gîtes, this place was run by just two people or maybe one and a half. Unlike an American hotel where there would have been four or five perky teenagers out front picking up plates and pouring coffee and two families of illegal immigrants behind the scenes doing the heavy lifting, the gîtes have to make do with very few employees. Hiring rules are still tight enough in France that the proprietors tend to do almost everything themselves. I'm not sure how they manage, especially as many places prepared dinner and breakfast for 20 to 30 people every day. That night, for example, the proprietor cum waiter cum maître d' hotel—a young man of around 30, good-looking in a clean-cut, gendarmey way—had 30 for a full dinner, with only a cook helping him in the kitchen. Despite that constraint, the food at the gîtes was often good. Tonight's dinner, for example, was very popular, particularly with Charlotte. (*Dinner was awesome + delicious: veg. soup w/ bread, then boeuf bourginion with pasta and vanilla/ meringue ice cream cake for dessert*)

Except for Della and Enya, we were all in one room that night, a high-ceilinged attic in an otherwise vacant house not far from the main building. The beds were laid out in two long ranks like the Seven Dwarfs times two, and it looked comfortable enough to me.

But there were two things wrong.

First, the room stank. Leen asked Cybèle to ask me if I would wash my shirt but I told her to tell Leen that it wasn't me. (Fortunately for my self-respect, one of our roommates was the guilty party.)[42]

Second, we were sharing a room with strangers—a German couple—and although they were very nice, the idea upset Thea. Up till now, Thea had only shared a room with people from our group, and she found the idea so frightening that she began to cry. These moments always surprised Cybèle and me—Thea was so articulate and tall, and good at holding her own with the older girls, that we found it easy to forget she was still just 11. When Cybèle tried to comfort her, she got angry.

A little later, though, Cybèle finally soothed her with an old remedy that seldom failed: she lay down beside her and read aloud a little Georgette Heyer, the witty English romance writer. *"No one could have called Mr. Standen quick-witted, but the possession of three sisters had considerably sharpened his instinct of self-preservation..."*

---

42   Many pilgrims found this kind of communal living hard—people are not used to it any more. We live in smaller households but bigger spaces (in the United States, for example, the average size of a new home is now 2,164 square feet (201 meters), up from about a 1,000 in the 1950s, even as families have shrunk)—and unless you live in one of a handful of very dense cities, chances are good you have not spent any time so close to strangers or even relatives. Personally, I didn't mind it, but then again I was usually so tired by the end of the day that a dry ditch would have been okay.

July 11. Chapelle Saint-Roch to Aumont-Aubrac, 23 km

Wherein we meet Dr. Tosquelles and his hospital for the criminally sane.

When life itself seems lunatic, who knows where madness lies?
- *Cervantes*

Quite early the next morning, I tiptoed downstairs from the sleeping loft and worked on an article in the kitchen, leaving the light off so I didn't wake anybody. Usually I like my early summer hours—I get to feel productive and larcenous at the same time, knowing I will be taking most of the normal workday off.[43] This kitchen, however, was a dank place where no one had cooked for years, and sitting there in the dark made me feel like a homesick squatter. More importantly, I had no Wi-Fi. When I saw the lights go on in the main lodge, I walked across the lawn and into the bar, ordered a *café crème* from the friendly gendarme, and got online.

This was better. While I worked, I could hear the proprietor getting breakfast together and the radio newscaster warbling the news of the countryside's non-events. I also had a good Wi-Fi connection, which given my dependence on the Internet, always feels as cozy to me as a hot wood stove.

All this reminded me of Grandma Voyles's little house in Baker, in eastern Oregon. She had a stove that was half electric and half wood, and in the morning from my bed on the davenport in the front room I would hear her clink the handle into the flat iron lid like a small manhole cover on the wood-burning side, then after she had lifted the lid and set it down next to the hole, crinkle some newspaper and toss it into the stove. Next would come the clatter of kindling against the paper, the rough *swick* of a match, and another clink as she set the lid back over the fire. The house would start to warm up with that dry fire heat that always feels

---

43 Ultimately, this makes about as much sense as thinking you're putting one over on the Man by taking a job on the night shift, but illusions have their value.

warmer than other kinds of heat, and it would soon be time for breakfast.

Eventually, my second breakfast came and went and we had to face the raw, wet day. On the road, we passed a group of French pilgrims, dressed in almost the same uniform as us—fellow members of the Quechuan tribe—who had stopped to attend to someone's blister. They told us to take a shortcut along the highway because the main path went up the hill and then almost straight back down to the highway, adding an extra kilometer for no good reason.[44]

This cut off a little mileage, but not enough to suit me. The trail stuck to the highway all morning, which was just busy enough we had to walk single file, and passed not even one pretty farmhouse serving coffee in large bright cups. *Miam Miam*, finding nothing to write about regarding this stretch, warned that we were entering a blank page zone, whose contemplation could draw the pilgrim into "a dangerous spiral where the infinite and the eternal mix in a glutinous spaghetti ... Quick, *vous êtes en danger, tournez la page!!!*"

Just before lunch, we reached Saint-Alban-sur-Limagnole.

Saint-Alban isn't much to look at—like many small French towns, it's a dreary beige mass, relieved only by the occasional bright discount store billboard. Even when examined on foot, you might not notice anything interesting about the place, except perhaps for an unusual pink castle—and even that structure

---

44 I have often found the French to be helpful in these sorts of circumstances. On a country road, for instance, if a cop is lurking around the corner, drivers will signal the fact to oncoming cars with their lights. My theory is that the arbitrary authority the French endure in their school days gives them a feeling of solidarity against authority that serves them well for the rest of their lives, like Marines who have a shared memory of bootcamp. (French schools are still tough by American standards—for example, a kid can easily come home not with just a few points on a quiz but *negative* points, as in, *What do you mean, Honoré, that you got a minus 17 on your French test?* And teachers can be mean in ways that don't happen anywhere in the United States but law school lectures and art school critiques.) The French also tend not to end up debilitated by that white middle-American notion I grew up with that most authority figures are more or less on your side and your boss is or should be your buddy. Nor do people have to struggle with the fiction that your company is a family, which can be emotionally inconvenient if, for instance, Dad decides to sell you and your siblings to a Chinese conglomerate or lay you off because you've just celebrated your 56th birthday.

seems unlikely to have had any significance. Yet during World War II, that pink castle was actually the heart of one of the most daring and ultimately perhaps most important revolutions of the 20th century.

The vanguard was an unlikely cadre—900 institutionalized insane people, a group of surrealist poets and artists hiding out from the Nazis, and a handful of psychiatrists and psychiatric nurses—led by a Catalan refugee who could barely speak intelligible French.

Their action began in 1940.

The Vichy government had requisitioned many of the mental hospitals still under its control, along with many members of their staff. This left the Saint-Alban hospital with only 26 people to run the entire facility, even as the inmate population swelled from 540 to nearly 900. At the same time, the Vichy bureaucrats had cut the hospital's budget and commandeered a lot of the produce from the castle's garden, leaving the hospital with no way to feed everybody.

Many other French mental institutions that faced the same situation that year let their inmates die. A few even accelerated the process: one hospital in Lyon turned a profit by selling food grown in the hospital's garden even as 2,000 patients starved.[45]

Fortunately, Saint-Alban had less dutiful leadership.

Life had taught François Tosquelles's how to improvise. As the chief psychiatrist of the Spanish Republican Army during the civil war, Tosquelles had already done plenty of things that would be unthinkable in peacetime, such as training prostitutes to work as psychiatric nurses. (They actually made very good nurses, he said in a 1989 documentary—their professional experience had taught them that everyone is crazy.) Later, when the

---

45 By the end of the war, between 40,000 and 50,000 people would die of hunger in the country's mental hospitals. Historians still debate whether they were deliberately killed, as in Germany and Austria (where as many as 300,000 of the insane, retarded, deaf, blind, and otherwise disabled were executed between 1939 and 1941 in what ended up being almost a trial run for the Holocaust), or were simply casualties of overly zealous Vichy bookkeepers.

Republicans lost and he fled to France, Tosquelles had set up a clinic in his internment camp at Sept-Fons to try to look after 16,000 depressed and often suicidal Spanish refugees.

Dr. François Tosquelles

Tosquelles arrived in 1940, evidently after some string-pulling by communists in the mental health system.[46]

After sizing up the situation in Saint-Alban, he moved quickly. First, he sent 124 healthier patients out to nearby farms, to trade labor for food. Others he had shown how to pick wild mushrooms. Still others he encouraged to make useful objects that

---

46   Tosquelles believed French communists were kind to him and other Spanish refugees because of the guilt they felt that they had not pressed France's government harder to intervene in the Civil War. As he said in a 1980s interview:

> They realized, after the fact, that if the French government or workers had supported the Republic, if they had converted the movement of the Popular Front into a revolutionary movement—and not a demand for paid holidays— the whole history of the world would have been different. But it's like Cleopatra's nose. Things are as they are.

they could trade to farmers for eggs, fruit, and whatever else their farms could spare. He also tried to take advantage of the bureaucracy when he could: after learning that patients with tuberculosis could get special ration cards, he made that diagnosis for some who were showing signs of malnutrition.[47]

That crisis averted, Tosquelles turned to a second, larger problem: World War II. He and a colleague, Dr. Lucien Bonnafé, a fellow communist and the hospital's official director, started a secret group of *résistants* among the staff, which Bonnafé christened the Society of Gévaudan.

In this too, they were successful. Throughout the war, the society managed to print clandestine books on paper parachuted in from London, smuggle arms to partisans, and hide Jewish doctors, surrealist artists, and poets Dr. Bonnafé had known in Paris.

Nor did the Society's impact end with the Liberation. One of the secret guests was one of France's best-known poets, Paul Éluard, who eventually wrote a book of poems about the months he and his wife hid on the third floor of the castle, Memories of the *House of the Mad*.[48] Even more importantly, it's also where Éluard met an artist named Auguste Forestier.

Forestier was not one of the political refugees—he had been a patient at the hospital since 1915—but he cut a figure bound to catch the eye of a surrealist poet: he had set up a workbench in a corridor on the ground floor that led from the castle's scullery to

---

47   The Saint-Alban hospital was also luckier than most in another way too: the Lozère is a Protestant region, and the mayor was on his side. Most of France went along with the Vichy regime in the south and the Occupation in the north, but a few isolated Protestant villages in these mountains played important roles in the Resistance, which some historians have traced to an adversarial tradition that went back to the bloody 17th-century wars between the Protestant Huguenots and the Catholic government.

48   That book's most famous poem is called "Cemetery of the Mad," but of the Éluard wartime poems I have read, my favorite is "Liberté," which was dropped by the Royal Air Force over France before the Liberation. It's awfully stirring. If you liked the Marseillaise scene in Casablanca, you'll love "Liberté." The first stanza begins:

On my notebooks
On my desk and the trees
On the sand, on the snow
I write your name.

an inner courtyard, where he would sit dressed in what doctors describe as a regal costume, furiously drawing, painting, carving animals (often ferocious Beasts of Gévaudan, whose jaws that bristled with real horses' or cows' teeth that he had found on the hospital grounds), or putting together elaborate model ships.[49]

Éluard took three of Forestier's pieces with him when he returned to Paris after Liberation. Picasso, a friend of his, agreed with him that the pieces were good, but they don't seem to have made a huge impression. However, for a younger artist Éluard knew, Jean Dubuffet, seeing Forestier's work was life-changing. Dubuffet began to collect not only Forestier's work but also to organize a museum for what he dubbed *art brut*, "raw art"— emotionally direct pieces by people without formal art training, including children and the insane. It changed Dubuffet's own work as well, leading him to be more direct, emotional, and at least on the surface, often a little crazy. "For me, insanity is super-sanity," he once explained. "The normal is psychotic. Normal means lack of imagination, lack of creativity."

But it was arguably in psychiatry that Tosquelles and Bonnafé had the greatest impact.

Often, while they waited at night for clandestine packages to be dropped or for fugitives from Paris to knock, the two would talk about what was turning out to be an interesting phenomenon: not only were the patients not starving, but now that they had work to do, many seemed to be mentally healthier.

---

49   The ships were a symptom of a lifelong obsession with traveling. As a young man, Forestier had been a compulsive traveler, but he had no money, and often got in trouble for trying to take long train rides without a ticket. His traveling days ended permanently at the age of 27 when he was sent to the hospital for a train-related offense—putting a line of pebbles on a railroad track that caused the train to derail. He insisted that he meant no harm by it and only wanted to see what would happen to the pebbles, but authorities committed him all the same. At first, he tried to escape, but after he started making art he stayed put happily enough until his death in 1958.

What they were seeing fit in with something Tosquelles had observed during the war in Spain: given real work, many of his
patients' symptoms would disappear overnight—*take two fascists
and call me in the morning*—and they began to think that maybe the
hospital itself made people sicker.

Tosquelles and Bonnafé began to question everything about the
institution. Why did we lock these people in? Why did we wall
them off from the town? Why did we wear uniforms, and make
them call us by our professional titles? "Nothing goes without
saying" became the hospital's new motto.

Even after the war ended, their self-examination continued, but
began to extend beyond the hospital walls, as they started to see
in their work not only a way to cure patients but society. Hitler
and Mussolini might be gone, but the attitudes that produced
them, that loved power and embraced oppression, had not.

In the late 1940s, the hospital's reputation spread among radical
psychiatrists, who came to Saint-Alban to see their new method,
which emphasized not only work (which some fascist psychiatrists had also liked) but democratic decision-making.

One of those affected by the method Tosquelles had begun to
call Institutional Psychotherapy was a young resident from Mar-
tinique, Frantz Fanon, who saw in Tosquelles's theory a way to
understand and resolve the psychological damage of colonial
racism. Later, through his books *Black Skin/White Masks*, and the
more radical *Wretched of the Earth*, Fanon made the case that the
sanity of both the subjugator and the subjugated could only be
achieved after colonialism had ended.

Fanon's books were very influential, not only in Algeria, where
he worked after his residency with Tosquelles, but among generations of radical leaders, including Che Guevara, Steven Biko,
Malcolm X, and the Black Panthers.

In the 70s, however, just as the idea peaked on the streets, Institutional Psychotherapy began to lose momentum within psychiatry. Psychiatrists who tried the Tosquelles's method seem
to have decided that, as Oscar Wilde supposedly quipped about

socialism, Institutional Psychotherapy was a nice idea but took too many evenings. At Nonette, an institution not too far from Saint-Alban that followed Tosquelles's methods, one critic complained that the hospital's constant meetings led to "nobody speaking about anything except the team and its tensions, crises, feelings, and reinforcement that the *jouissance* [intense pleasure] of this generates."

For a long time, it looked like fascist psychiatrists had won the postwar battle of ideas— 30 diagnoses developed by psychiatrists under the Third Reich are still used today.[50] In Saint-Alban, after Tosquelles' retirement, the hospital eventually went back to "normal." The walls were rebuilt, and before the hospital closed in 2015, it reportedly spent 10 percent of its budget on video surveillance. But Institutional Psychotherapy appears to be making a comeback. Recently, as more and more countries elect nasty populist governments, scholars have begun using their ideas to answer what Camille Robcis, a Cornell University historian who is writing a book about Tosquelles, calls the "What's the matter with Texas?" question.

Before we left Saint-Alban, everyone went into the store to shop for lunch, except Lola and me. She had promised her mother she would send her a card with a drawing on it every day but hadn't gotten around to it. The night before, she had borrowed Cybèle's watercolor set and dashed off several cards, and now she was desperate to send them off, so I volunteered to take her to the tiny post office to help her buy stamps and mail the postcards.

French post offices look like post offices anywhere but unlike an American post office, the people behind the counter aren't in uniform. In France, letter carriers drive yellow trucks and yellow bicycles and sometimes wear snappy blue jackets with the La Poste logo, but they aren't necessarily all decked out in blue.

---

50   One of the most famous, Asperger's Syndrome (discovered by Dr. Hans Asperger, an Austrian Nazi), was officially folded into autism in 2013, but in a recent book, *Asperger's Children*, Edith Sheffer argues that the autism diagnosis itself remains enmeshed in Nazi cultural values, because the Nazis believed everyone ought to be obedient and sociable.

Tosquelles would have approved.[51]

A few more kilometers down the road, we came to another town, and our next gîte. The last few kilometers had been along a small but fairly busy road, but once we passed through the high front gate of the Ferme du Barry, we felt far away from the highway, tucked in a snug courtyard enclosed by stone walls and a three-story brick and stone house, every surface punctuated with explosions of bright geraniums. The whole effect was picturesque yet compact enough to be a stage set. I felt like I ought to burst into song.

The prince of this little principality was a heavy-set man with salt and pepper hair who wore chunky black glasses that made him look like Buddy Holly's older brother. He showed me to our rooms, which were on the second and third floors, past old travel posters of distant destinations that partly covered the dingy wallpaper. The house was a little worse for wear but he had already opened all the long French windows before we arrived so it still felt welcoming and cheerful.

Dinner that night was aligot and lamb. Aligot is the region's signature dish—aligot is to the Aubrac what lobster is to Maine—and many restaurants and inns on the way into town had signs that said *Yes, we serve aligot!* It's a garlicky mashed potato concoction that is roughly one-third potatoes, one-third cream, and one-third cheese—a special local cheese called laguiole—and the result is something that looks like mashed potatoes but has the tensile strength of taffy, which in its last few minutes of preparation

Aligot!

51 This informality had surprised me when we first moved to France, and made me wonder why we like to have our packages and pizzas delivered by people in matching clothes.

must be stirred with a big wooden bat.[52]

For tonight's rendition, all the guests sat at long wooden tables in the dining room, and as the proprietor finished stirring the pot he beamed and made a show of pulling enormous ropes of the stuff into the air.

After dinner, Masha wrote, *"all of us kids went upstairs and started talking about Peter the Great and how he would use his slaves' stomachs for pillows. We ended up in a giant hexagon on the floor using each others' stomachs for pillows and doing funny accents."*

The adults, meanwhile, took a short walk to town. It was Della and Enya's last night with us, and to celebrate, Della took us out to the village cafe for an after-dinner drink. The place was empty except for the bartender, who was keeping an eye on a soccer match on TV as he cleaned up. Della and I had armagnacs. Cybèle, Leen, and Carson ordered mint tea. I was going to miss Della.

---

52 How and when aligot was invented is uncertain but there are origin stories of varying degrees of plausibility. One version sounds like Stone Soup: Three bishops met, one carrying potatoes, one carrying garlic, one carrying cheese, and not having anything else to eat, had an epiphany. The historical problem with that version is obvious: there were no potatoes in France before the 18th century. Another story is that once upon a time, a king traveled through Aubrac with a smaller retinue than usual. His wife was angry with him and wouldn't cook dinner, so he slopped a cheesy mush together for his entourage, *et voila!* However, given I had always understood not cooking the family dinner to be almost a job requirement for royalty of either sex, this seems unlikely too. I think the most credible is the story that famished pilgrims knocked on the door of the local monastery, begging for "aligot"—a bastardization of the Latin word "aliquod," an indefinite adjective meaning "anything"—and the monks at the nearby Domerie d'Aubrac, not having anything else, whipped up a bread and cheese porridge. A food called *anything* doesn't sound too promising, but maybe being potato-less, Aligot 1.0 wasn't very good.

The contemporary version, however, is delicious. Most health-minded people would try a bite and order green beans and a skinless chicken breast instead. As for me, I could eat aligot all day long.

July 12. Aumont-Aubrac to Nasbinals, 23 km

In which we meet the Demoiselles d'Aubrac.

We said goodbye to Della and Enya at a bus stop in the village the next morning.

They seemed sorry they had to leave and we were sorry to see them go. The girls were especially glum about it, and maybe tired now too, if they had stayed up late with Enya the night before. Cybèle had been right—the pair had added some jolliness to our company, partly because they are easy-going people and partly because we didn't know them quite as well as we knew everyone else, which had helped keep us all on our best behavior. Leen and Carson (and to a lesser extent, Lola) we had known forever, in every mood. Without Della and Enya, there would be less need to keep up what my dad used to call "party manners."

What made their departure even sadder was that it was a beautiful day and we were walking through the prettiest country we had seen yet—grassy hills that stretched on for miles. Periodically, Leen would stop short, look at the green rolling country, and say, "Un-Be-lievable! This is un-be-lievable!" And it was.

Cybèle took picture after picture of the endless grassy hills, the herds of reddish and cream-colored cows, and the bright blue sky. Carson was happy too, mostly because of the cows. In her bohemian days back in the 70s, she had spent a year and a half in Virginia, milking cows with a friend of hers, and just thinking about that time seemed to take her mind off her blisters.

These particular cows are famous. Some of the best cows in the world live in France, and some of the best cows in France live in the vasty fields of Aubrac. As one of the French tourist guides put it, *Who says Aubrac says cow!*

This is the literal truth: the most famous breed in the Aubrac is the Aubrac, a reddish longhorn that produces the Laguiole cheese used in aligot, bred for the high and often cold country by Benedictine monks hundreds of years ago.

The Aubrac is a hardy breed with some admirable, pilgrim-like qualities, including:

- Aptitude for walking
- Very strong legs
- Ability to take advantage of simple feed

An Aubrac cow can produce one calf per year. She is known for easy calving, good nursing aptitude, and longevity. Pure Aubrac cows weigh 550–800 kilograms and the bulls can grow to over a ton—900–1,200 kilograms—which is about average for larger European cattle breeds.

Every few years on a slow news day, the French news programs will run a feature about the region's dairymen, *les buronniers*, named after the *burons*, the half-buried slate-roofed barns in which the laguiole cheese is traditionally made. The buronniers, stocky, laconic, Depardieuian types, are always filmed on early

The Aubrac of Aubrac

foggy mornings milking the cows by hand into wooden buckets, squeezing 500 liters of milk in a wooden trough down to a paste in a dank, fire-heated stone barn, and then shaping the paste, also by hand, into 50-kilogram *tommes* roughly the size of a wheelbarrow tire, which they leave to dry in that cellar-barn for six months to a year.

It is true that the cheese is made only between May 25 and October 13, the traditional summer pasture period, from milk provided by those lucky cows that have been munching Aubrac's delicious grass and wildflowers, but I am sure most old-school *burroniers* are now off dancing gavottes with grape-stomping peasant girls in the green fields of the After-France. City folks always love the idea of country people hefting wooden buckets, preferably if they look impoverished in a virile, stubbly way. But when the camera crews aren't around, most of Aubrac's cows are milked by machine and the cheese is fabricated in a stainless steel, white-tiled factory owned by a cooperative, an organization with a happy name: the Coopérative Fromagère Jeune Montagne (the "Young Mountain Cheesemakers Cooperative").[53]

Part of the reason for the persistence of these almost-medieval images of France like the burroniers may also be that they are still part of living memory. Back in the 1970s, even as the Concorde rocketed from Paris to New York in four hours, parts of rural France were still more or less preindustrial. In a 2011 essay, Phillippe Planel, a half-English, half-French writer who grew up in rural areas of both countries in the 50s, says that while most English farmers had tractors by the 50s, he remembered seeing French farms plowing with mules as late as 1974. When Cybèle was a girl in the 70s, she remembers seeing women doing their wash in a channel near the Rive Oeuf, two hours outside of Paris. In 1984—two years after France launched Minitel, the first consumer Internet, and three years after the first high-speed TGV trains began running—18 percent of French farms still had no indoor toilet.

That night we stayed at a rundown dude ranch outside the town of Nasbinals.

---

53 Which is not to say that there aren't still plenty of agricultural traditions in France that are very much alive. Some of this is the product of the appellations d'origine (AOC) system, which serves to accentuate and preserve some regional specialties like laguiole, a kind of copyright regime that makes it illegal to market sparkling wine as champagne that is not from the Champagne region, brie from Brie, or Le Puy-en-Velay's special lentils from Le Puy—but some of it goes back to actual differences in the land. Not far from the Aubrac, for example, archaeologists have found evidence that several of today's cheeses were made in the region even before the Romans.

Thea, Cybèle, Carson, Leen, and Lola made a tour of the barn after we arrived, and spent some time patting the horses. Masha and Charlotte, on the other hand, just flopped on their bunks and read.

Their indifference had to do with a bad memory. One weekend in early September 2006, the year we moved to France, Cybèle had gotten the three girls a riding lesson at a small riding school out in the Sologne, where her father lived. Although she told the instructor that our girls had never ridden before, he took them out to a bridal path in the woods, at which point the horses all broke into a gallop and after a terrifying minute, threw their riders into the blackberries. When we came to pick them up, we found all three waiting in the tack room, bruised and bleeding. Masha got the worst of it: her lip had swelled to fishlike proportions—a trauma that may have been magnified in her memory because she had had her first day of her new school in Paris two days later.

By now, Thea had forgotten about the accident—she had only been five at the time, and after being bucked off the horse, had landed on her feet, like a trick rider at the circus—and taken some more lessons since then. But the other two had held their grudge.

The proprietors stabled us that night in a low-ceilinged, prefabricated bunkhouse. The place had floors that bounced a little when you walked and they had decorated it in an American cowboy theme.

The cowboy aspect I enjoyed—I love seeing Americana like this in Europe. Just as you find plenty of Americans who have tried to replicate bits of Versailles in Austin or Sienna in Scarsdale, there is also a subculture in Europe generally (but in France particularly, for some reason) that tries to lead a Western-theme life: bolo ties, ten gallon hats, and even the occasional rodeo. Sometimes you hear Franco-American country music on the radio. There was a song in Franglish that I remembered hearing on a bus in the Alps once that had the wonderful line:

but that was so far ago,
in San Francisco —

Judging from the décor and the gruffness of the proprietors, I didn't expect much from dinner. Burgers, best case. But the owners surprised us: they had not been able to un-Frenchify themselves when it came to the food. Dinner was fantastic, our best yet—aligot again, but even better than at Buddy Holly's brother's the night before, with more garlic and herbs, and a rhubarb tart as thoughtful as a poem.

July 13. Nasbinals to Saint-Chely, 17 km
In which we celebrate Charlotte's birthday and don't let the bedbugs bite.

A French woman who had arranged her lavender scarf into a turban fell into step with us for a while the next morning, as we made our way along a rutted lane. She had lived in San Francisco for a number of years, spoke good English, and walked with a careful saunter. She was now the principal of an elementary school north of Paris but missed California.

We met a lot of teachers on the walk. Teachers are on their feet all day long, so maybe it's not as hard for them physically as for a lot of other people. There is also something field trip-like about the atmosphere, particularly in France, which might appeal to some, I guess, though I don't think it would have appealed to my folks, who were both teachers.[54]

Then again, the French teachers, like the French generally, also usually don't hike for long. Lavender Turban, for instance, told me she walked a week of the Chemin every summer with her sister. Her father and mother used to come as well, but her mother died and now he was too old and couldn't manage it anymore.

This habit of a week's walk is the rule rather than the exception for French pilgrims, who often take 5 or even 10 years to complete the entire route.

It's not a matter of time; most people in France get five or six weeks off a year, sometimes more. Nor is it money; if you stay in the gîtes, the Camino is a lot cheaper than a lot of ways you might spend a month. Instead, I think it's an instinct for moderation the French seem almost born with—like table manners. It's a quality I admire and yet I think will remain forever foreign to me, like their ability to take just one chocolate out of the box,

---

54   And for whom *Gemütlichkeit uber alles* could have been the family motto. For instance: they always travel with their own pillows and lightbulbs, to make certain that they can read in bed. Something had gone very wrong with me, which for the record was not their fault.

or pour one glass of wine out of the bottle, and say, *Ca suffit!*[55] For the most part, the French pilgrims thought we were crazy to try to walk to Pamplona in one go. (We didn't dare tell them we were actually aiming for Santiago—they might have called the child welfare authorities.)

Lavender Turban asked me if we were making the walk for spiritual reasons and I could see I disappointed her when I said no, we were just walking.[56]

Meanwhile, the girls, bored with the Aubrac cows and the grownups going on and on about the cows and the spectacular scenery, were immersed in one of their imaginary games. *"For fun we played a game where we each had a character and we made up a story using our characters. Masha was a gypsy/spy, Charlotte was a vain fairy, Lola was the pirate queen and I was a ninja/mage,"* Thea wrote. *"In the story I wore a raven feather, super tight minidress bustier, blue leather leggings and knee high horseback riding boots with spikes on the soles."*[57]

---

55 Not that I think that as an American, I am uniquely weak-willed. In London, you'll see stores open at midnight with long lines of people waiting to buy beer and ice cream. In Munich, they serve beer in tankards the size of small aquariums and old ladies dig into cakes as big as their heads. Nor does self-discipline seem to be a southern European thing. Madrilenos' days are full of snacks and enormous lunches. Things in France may be changing—you see "maxi croissants" in Parisian boulangeries for instance, and hamburger-sized macaroons—and store hours are longer now than when we first arrived in Paris, extending temptation later into the evening, but in relative terms, the French remain models of restraint.

56 I was a little taken aback by the question; I think it was a measure of how many years she'd been in California that she felt free to ask me. Religion is still a personal business in France. In political discussions, for instance, the French consider it bad form to even speculate on a candidate's denomination—Cybèle earned a frosty silence from her French teacher one morning when she asked whether she thought Sarkozy's being Jewish would matter to French voters. At the same time, it's also considered wrong for politicians to mention God in speeches. This separation between church and state is so deep that if you want to be married officially, you have to marry first in the mairie (town hall), whether or not you have a church wedding. Yet even though the French pilgrims did not talk about it much, many of them seemed less irredeemably secular than we were. For the most part, I got the sense that the religious aspect of the hike was still part of the exercise for many *pelerins*, but a relatively minor one, like meditation in a yoga class.

57 Thea had picked up this interest in fashion from Masha, who had a frightening capacity for detailed fantasy. I remember a number of walks where she would pepper me with questions that drove me to distraction, e.g., If you had a fairy, what color would her wings be? And how about the walls of her winter house? But Masha was having less fun with this now than she used to: "...I got bored. It makes you feel retarded playing gypsy/ninja pirates if you are 16 years old."

The fields rolled on until we came to a crest and saw a gray church big as a battleship in a grove below us a kilometer or two away. I was thrilled: For most Europeans, old buildings are about as interesting as someone else's stamp collection, but to an American who grew up seeing nothing over 50 years old, an old tower or a distant steeple always feels like a victory over the ordinary.

This turned out to be the Domerie d'Aubrac, the reputed birthplace of aligot, a monastery and way station for pilgrims. It was founded in 1120 by a Flemish knight, Adelard of Flanders, to fulfill a vow he made on his own pilgrimage to Santiago, when, after being struck by thieves and a snowstorm, he made a deal with God that if he was spared, he would build a monastery to shelter pilgrims along the Way.[58]

Most of the 120-monk complex was burnt down in the Revolution. All that remains is a field of foundations, the church—an enormous stone barn with long narrow window slots and nearly bare walls—and another English tower.

Next door was a square, 18th-century stone building that looked like an old barracks. On the ground floor, we found the restaurant recommended

The interior of the Domerie chapel. by Lavender Turban. After Carson checked the menu to make sure there were gluten-free dishes that she could eat, we went inside.

Chez Germaine is supposed to be famous. I can't vouch for that, but it does deserve to be, in part because it has the most appealing address in the world: *Place de la fontaine et des fêtes, Aubrac,*

---

58 These monks were another important ingredient of the Aubrac landscape. Besides breeding the Aubrac, some authorities give them credit for inventing Laguiole and even for clearing what had been a dense forest into the treeless plateau we had been walking over the past two days.

La France.[59] It's an old inn, founded in 1742 by the Gros family, who still run it. Their specialties are aligot and tarts of unusual size, "a delicacy of 56 cm in diameter that nobody can resist," according to the menu.

We passed on Mme. Germaine's prize-winning aligot—after two dinners in a row, everybody but me had had enough and I buckled under the peer pressure. Instead, we had a relatively light cheese soup—relatively light, that is, compared to aligot. For dessert, the waitress put a sparkler on Charlotte's slice of tart and the eight of us sang "Happy Birthday."

Now we gave our 14-year-old a birthday card and a list of various presents we would give her once we got back home: a trip to IKEA to fix up the room now being vacated by Masha; a gift certificate to Starbucks, which had become her regular haunt with her friends that year (traditional Parisian cafes aren't friendly to teenagers); and a few other things besides. She liked all the presents but one: the shorter-than-usual walking day Cybèle had organized, which made her scowl.[60]

Before we left, I read a little about the history of Chez Germaine and the Gros family on the wall and looked at an old photograph of the late, not-at-all *gros* founder, a thin, serious woman who didn't look like she had had a weakness for tarts or aligot.[61]

From here, we had a short and easy walk to the next town. It was sunny and hot, but a pleasant, dry heat, and mostly downhill.

---

59   That is, "Place of the Fountain and the Festivals, Aubrac, France."

60   I couldn't figure out why at the time, but I'm beginning to understand the psychology; after all, you don't thank your captor for letting you out of your cell early.

61   To be fair, Germaine had earned her dourness, having faced down not just the ordinary wear and tear of running a restaurant and hotel, but several real disasters: during the war, the hotel had burned down. After the war, she rebuilt it, only to see it burn down again. Finally, she rebuilt it a third time, and this iteration has lasted. She had also had to endure some skepticism from people who didn't approve of her unconventional approach to aligot. In a 2010 newspaper story, her daughter Adrienne (who took over in 2000) recalled that people decried her mother's idea of whipping the aligot—it wasn't necessary, everyone said—but her mother was proven right in the end: in 1959, Mme. Gros' aligot had won a prize at a national agricultural fair in Paris. "She knew how to do everything. She was a ray of sunshine to everyone," recalled the daughter, who carried on the family tradition of not smiling for the camera.

On our way, we passed a patch of delicious, tiny wild straw-
berries, and then an old couple sprawled on the grass, taking
an afternoon nap. I recognized them—they were the blue-eyed,
trail-cured Austrians we had chatted with that morning. This, I
thought, is how to do it. For a minute, I imagined an unretiring

retirement out with Cybèle, the two of us as brown and spare as these two, ambling along for hundreds of miles as if it were the easiest thing in the world, stopping whenever we felt tired.

But for now we kept walking.

When we reached our gîte at Saint-Chely, the proprietor of the gîte asked us to leave our packs on the floor to guard against *les punaises de lit*—bedbugs.

From here on out, many of the gîtes were on their guard against *les punaises*, but somewhat worryingly, they all followed different preventive protocols. Some hosts would make you leave your pack at the door or in cubbyholes, or as at Saint-Chely, tell you to leave your pack on the floor of your room. Others would give you a garbage sack that was supposed to help you keep your *punaises* to yourself. Or they would spray your pack. Or they would go over your pack slowly and carefully, like customs officers checking out backpackers on the nonstop from Cali. Once we even had our packs inspected on the back porch by a guy wearing jewelers' glasses.

I didn't blame them for their paranoia. When I was growing up, "Don't let the bedbugs bite" was just something parents said to their kids when they tucked them in. But over the last 20 years or so, bedbugs have made a huge comeback. The reason is that like lice—which had almost vanished during my childhood but were a regular scourge that had visited our girls every three months some years—bedbugs have become resistant to the pesticides that kept them at bay in the 50s, 60s, and 70s.

Bedbugs bite like crazy but are almost impossible to see—you only know you've got them because of the itchy welts and the blood on your sheets. They are not even nice to each other: they mate by a method known as traumatic insemination, which is even worse than it sounds. All in all, *les punaise* are a good point to bring up if you ever find yourself on the con side of a debate about the existence of a beneficent God, or pro on the materiality of evil.

We heard horror stories of hostels shut down by *les punaises*, and ran into many pilgrims who were terrified of them. Solitary women tended to be especially vigilant, and would spray their bags and their bunks, and sometimes our bags and our bunks too for good measure. One young woman we met, who had walked all the way from Switzerland and looked unafraid of anything, told Cybèle she was thinking of going home because of the bugs. Curiously, we never met anyone who caught them or visited a place that admitted they had had a problem. Then again, who would advertise?

All along the French Camino, the French innkeepers tended to blame the infestation on the Spanish, who were supposed to have large, filthy gîtes. Some of this undoubtedly goes back to old stereotypes—"like a Spanish hotel" (*une auberge espagnole*) is old French slang for a sloppy place where you have to fend for yourself. If we had thought about it a bit, we would have known that this didn't make much sense: first, 99 percent of the Camino traffic is heading toward Spain, not away from it (not many pilgrims make a round trip anymore), and second, in a cleaning Olympics, the French and the Spanish would probably tie for the gold. I guess, as with *Spanish* influenza or the *French* disease, it's natural to want to blame someone else.

July 14. Saint-Chely-d'Aubrac to Espalion, 21.9 km

In which various things roll along.

Cervantes gets a number of things right about the experience of wandering through unfamiliar country. One is that what you see depends on who is doing the wandering. Cybèle, for instance, has a tremendous capacity to be where she actually is, particularly when her feet are fine (as was now the case), and noticed the flowers and the animals. For Carson, as was perhaps inevitable in a Southerner who wrote, everything triggered memories. Leen noticed the dogs, the scenery, and the distance, which she still tracked on her odometer.

Another thing Cervantes gets right is the surreal quality of the journey—the odd things you run into, made odder still because from the traveller's point of view, they turn up out of nowhere. I suppose there are surreal things at home too that we don't see because they are in front of us every day, but you notice them when you are away from home, and even more if you are walking. The pace gives you more time to digest the oddness—unlike, say, driving on the interstate, where you may also see odd things but don't have time to point them out to your companions, and in the end, if it was deeply strange, may not be absolutely certain you even saw it in the first place.

That day especially, the country seemed to abound in oddities.

In Saint-Côme-d'Olt, the main church's steeple was twisted like a giant puff pastry gone wrong. And not just a little wrong, but so off kilter it wasn't entirely clear to me how it stayed up. The winding streets of the ancient town kept doubling back on themselves, making the town feel even stranger, as if we were seeing several different crooked steeples, and in my memory the town looks like the *Cabinet of Dr. Caligari*, the silent German horror movie where all the buildings seem to be melting.

This twisting phenomenon turns out to be not all that rare. Supposedly there are 109 twisted steeples in Europe, 65 of them in France. Most of the time, they were caused either by building with insufficiently seasoned timber or by the sun melting the lead in the steeple. Saint-Côme-d'Olt's steeple had the latter defect until 1929, when it was struck by lightning. For some reason, the locals were attached to the twist, and when they re-built, the carpenters supposedly put it in again on purpose. But I have my doubts. The angles are so odd I don't see how you could build them deliberately.

As we turned a corner, we saw the two gloomy French girls we had set out with from Le Puy, the dour young women with the matching red tin cups tied to their packs and matching blue-striped sailor shirts. They looked slightly happier now, and I was surprised to find they recognized us too and could speak. They were finishing their hike today, they said, smiling in tandem.

In front of the church with the crooked steeple, Carson—who always kept an eye out for ice cream parlors, ice cream being one of the few goodies she could consume without worrying about gluten—spotted a sidewalk café with an ice cream freezer in front. After we sat down, a German pilgrim at the next table started talking to us. He was big guy in his late 50s, tall and hale, with big teeth and a booming voice. Not many pilgrims were curious about other people but he was an exception. He kept referring to us as Canadians—he might have assumed this after hearing the girls order their *boules des glace* in proper French. In any case, he volunteered that he had spent a few years in Cana-da, and liked it.

After our ice cream break, we walked on. The route to the next town, Espalion, followed the green and dreamy Lot River, through shady, mossy woods that felt almost like a jungle after all those sunny miles across the Aubrac moors.

The walk along the riverbank was flat and cool, which was lucky, because I don't think we could have taken much adversity that day. Masha was getting even more anxious about whether we would have time to get everything she needed for boarding school. (Her experience at *Jeunnesse Doree* had taught her that girls could be vicious if you had the wrong clothes.) Charlotte was more than tired of all the cows. Thea was annoyed about a number of things, some of which really were annoying. For instance: Masha and I kept forgetting whose toothbrush was whose, and we both kept using hers. Carson was suffering from tendonitis and communal life. Lola in particular was getting on her nerves. She and Leen sometimes had to share a room with her and with Masha, which would have been fine except Lola didn't take many showers because she had read somewhere that too many showers were bad for your hair. Leen and Carson tried to enlist Cybèle and me in a campaign to force Lola to change her beauty regime but I stuck to my usual—and I'm sure in its own way, equally annoying—strategy: sympathize with everyone but stay 700 miles away on the plains of La Mancha.

When we reached the outskirts of Espalion, I saw the second oddity of the day: a headless statue holding its head in its hands as if it were a rugby player getting ready to pass the ball. This turned out to be Saint Hilarian, who was said to have been decapitated by Saracen invaders in 730, on a hill behind the town.

Hilarian is a local saint, meaning the town recognizes him but he didn't make the All-Star list in Rome because no one could prove his existence. One of Hilarian's miracles is that he crossed the river riding on his cape. His other, showier, miracle is that after his Muslim captors had chopped off his head, he carried it back to town, washed it off in the fountain, and told his mother what had happened, as he had promised he would if he were decapitated.[62]

Odder still, I learned later, Hilarian is not alone—there are enough decapitat-

Saint Hilarian with fetching accessory

---

62 How or why he came to make this promise, the authorities don't specify. It's a mystery, as the nuns used to say to me whenever the catechism reached a point that didn't make much sense.

ed saints in France—134 at last count—that they could form not just a rugby team but a whole league if you brought them all together. Most of the time, the severed saints' stories are similar to Hilarian's: the saint crosses a river miraculously, gets himself decapitated, and after his decapitation, rinses poor Yorick off in a fountain and gives it to a woman. One of the most famous, St Denis, the patron saint of French kings and headache sufferers, supposedly walked six miles from the site of his beheading to the site of his burial, "carrying his own head and preaching a sermon on the way."

One theory as to why the French like this headless martyr genre is that it's tied to a pre-Christian tradition, like the megalith in the cathedral at Le Puy—buried and broken but so deeply embedded in the culture it keeps popping out every once in awhile.

As I thought about this, I began to wonder if this obsession was why the guillotine caught on in France. A few other countries experimented with the guillotine, but only in France did it really take off: the guillotine remained the country's primary method of capital punishment from 1793 until 1977 without a break, through seven or eight different governments. The French might have disagreed on occasion about whose head should end up in the basket, but never on how to get it there.[63]

In the beginning, however, the French did not like Dr. Guillotin's machine. It might have been a less painful way to be executed than hanging or low-tech head chopping, but it also had a lot less entertainment value. After its premiere in 1792, the spectators shouted that they wanted the gallows back. "No one minded seeing the condemned man's head being cut off, they were used to that kind of thing; on the contrary, they were disappointed that they could *not* see the condemned man's head being cut off,"

---

63   The only other country that has ever used the guillotine in a big way was Germany under the Nazis. The Nazis executed about 16,000 people by guillotine (most notably Sophie Scholl, a college student caught spreading anti-Nazi literature)—just a thousand less than the number of people executed during the Terror—but given the millions the Nazis killed, decapitation was clearly just a novelty. In comparing violence in the French Revolution with the Third Reich, one academic has noted that the Jacobins liked having a certain theatricality in their executions while the Nazis generally preferred industrial-scale killing in the forest or behind the gates of a camp.

writes Frances Larson in her history of decapitation, *Severed*. But whatever drawbacks it had as a live performance, by the end of the Terror, guillotining loomed large in the French imagination.[64] In the 19th century, almost every major writer wrote at least one guillotine scene and Balzac wrote five—an obsession that I think may have to do with his habit, which eventually killed him, of drinking 40 or 50 cups of coffee a day— and a family guillotine trauma involving an uncle convicted of murder.[65]

On the other hand, maybe they just like watching things roll.

When we reached the outskirts of Espalion, an international boules competition was in full swing in a park that stretched along the river. Some of the matches had spectators, who stood watching the little silver balls roll back and forth.

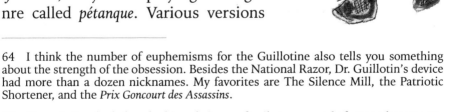

Charlotte was in a foul mood and unimpressed: *I have a blister on my toe – it hurts…I am so sick of bread and cheese…There was an international boules tournament. Who has an international tournament for a sport that is basically old men throwing metal balls at a target?*

In certain respects, her description wasn't precisely accurate. First, they weren't playing classic boules, *boules lyonnaise,* they were playing a subgenre called *pétanque*. Various versions

---

64   I think the number of euphemisms for the Guillotine also tells you something about the strength of the obsession. Besides the National Razor, Dr. Guillotin's device had more than a dozen nicknames. My favorites are The Silence Mill, the Patriotic Shortener, and the *Prix Goncourt des Assassins*.

65   Decapitation had played a big role in our family too, even before we became expats: Charlotte's first big word was decapitate. Aged 2 1/2, she ran to us one morning shouting that Masha had decapitated her Barbie. Where she learned this word we don't know for sure but I suppose the goldilocked Robespierre must have taught her.

of boules have been played more or less continuously in dusty squares around the Mediterranean since at least the Romans, probably since the Greeks, possibly even the Egyptians, but pétanque only goes back to the early 1900s.

Boules lyonnaise involves running three steps, a little like bowling, while *pétanque* doesn't require any steps, and uses slightly smaller balls. In both versions, the aim is to roll your balls closer than your opponents' to a smaller target ball, called the *cochonette*—"the little pig."

Pétanque was invented in La Ciotat, a town outside Marseilles. A cafe owner named Ernest Pitiot had a regular customer who had loved boules but then developed rheumatism and couldn't play anymore. To help him, Pitiot invented a new version that had a shorter pitch and didn't require as much movement—hence the name pétanque, from *pès tancats*—"feet planted" in *Provençal*—which made it possible for his crippled customer to play again.

The metal balls came later. Except for rocks in ancient Greece and an unfortunate experiment with cannon balls in revolutionary France,[66] most boules balls were made of wood until 1925.

Ball-making was a slow, tedious process—each ball was made on a lathe and then studded with nails—and even an experienced boule-maker could complete only four or five two-ball sets per day. The most serious limiting factor, however, was finding the right wood: the balls needed to be made of boxwood root, the hardest part of one of the hardest hardwood trees, but over the course of the 19th century, boxwood had started to become scarce because it was the only wood hard enough to be used as wheel hubs for stagecoaches. Then, during World War I, boxwood became even scarcer. Munitions factories used it for artillery shell casings and the main import sources in Turkey and the

---

66 In Marseille in 1792, 38 people died after some soldiers decided to play boules with cannon balls near a powder magazine.

Near East were cut off to the Allies.[67] Nor did the Armistice in 1918 end the shortage: to make a good boule, the wood had to be dried for at least three years.

Two young engineers who worked in the enormous Berliet car and truck factory outside Lyon decided to come to their country's aid by forging metal balls with the same machine that the munitions factories had used during the war to turn out cannon balls. In 1920, Paul Courtieu and Vincent Mille (who also happened to be the champion boulist of Lyon) tried molding solid metal balls but found they were too heavy, and hit on the idea of making a hollow ball. At night, after the pair got off their day jobs at the factory, they would test various kinds of metals, experimenting first with steel and then with other, lighter alloys, until, finally, in 1923, they presented the world with the bronze and aluminum *Boule Intégrale*, the Ultimate Ball.[68]

Charlotte was also not entirely correct either about pétanque being a sport only for old men: they were playing mixed doubles that day at the Espalion tournament, and the male half of the winning team was Dylan Rocher, the Tiger Woods of pétanque.

A 21-year-old native of Draguignan, Cote d'Azur, whom sports writers refer to as "la Machine," Rocher had been playing pétanque since he was four.

I'm a fan of any art pursued for art's sake, and professional boules-playing certainly qualifies. Considered as a moneymaking opportunity, boules compares unfavorably to poetry; even the best players can't make more than EUR 16,000 a year on the circuit. However, like many successful artists, Rocher is fortunate in having a patron (in 2012, he worked for the mayor of

---

67 Other civilian uses for wood blocks such as print engraving also got short shrift. "[W]hen either side fired a field gun at the other, bang went another wood-engraving," one English artist later lamented.

68 After some resistance from the national boules association, the Ultimate Ball was sanctioned for competitive play by France's boules federation in 1925, and Courtieu and his wife kept their factory rolling all the way up to his death in 1972. The glory of having invented the all-metal boule would undoubtedly have ruined many lesser men, but when Courtieu died in 1972, a local paper, *Le Progres*, noted that "Despite his success, he remained unusually modest, fleeing honors, wishing only to be a worker in the best sense of the word."

Draguignan, who didn't mind his frequent absences) and a supportive family; his father was also once a pétanque champion.

As for boules' reputation as a sport for codgers, "La Machine" Rocher has told sportswriters that he had never seen it that way. "No, because my family bathed in it. From when I was little, only pétanque mattered. All my friends played, so I never considered it a sport for the old." He said he could understand why people might think that—you don't move very much when you play pétanque—but he hoped he could get people to consider it as more than a pastime for old guys. "At a high level," he told an interviewer in 2012, "I want to erase the image of bob and pastis. I want to be taken seriously."[69]

That might seem like a lonely battle, but who knows? After all, one of the few clear morals that can be drawn from a close study of French history is that playing boules is fun—people have enjoyed boule in France for about 2,000 years straight, with just three recorded breaks,[70] and with some minor modifications, men and women can play it together.[71] There is international interest too: people play variations in Italy and Spain, France's former Indochinese possessions, and some US cities. It has also always been recognized as good exercise—Rabelais in the early 1500s declared boule a game "suitable for all ages." And at the very least, hanging around outside for an hour won't do you any harm—assuming you wear your *bob*. Our gîte tonight was a city-

---

69   The "Bob" is a kind of floppy, narrow-brimmed sun hat that became popular in the 1960s. The name supposedly refers to the Americans who wore them, who to the French all seemed to be named Bob. In American pop culture, it's probably most closely associated with the character of Gilligan on the TV show Gilligan's Island— which was, eerily enough, played by an actor named Bob Denver.

70   Two brief periods – first, under Charles IV and Charles V in the fourteenth century, when they hoped to focus people on more profitable pursuits, and then again in the early seventeenth century, when partisans of racquet (a precursor of tennis) got boules banned briefly. Even then, however, monks in the privacy of their cloisters kept the balls rolling.

71   The vocabulary of pétanque has some charm to it but if Rocher is serious about taking the sport out of the clutches of the geezers, he may want to squelch one tradition: if a player is skunked, 13-0, he is said to have "fait Fanny" – made Fanny, and must kiss a girl named Fanny on the fanny (that is, posterior). If a Fanny is not available, more traditional clubs and cafes keep a nude statue or a picture on hand for the purpose. To get to the bottom of this issue, see Mérou et Fouskoudis, *Le Fanny et l'imagerie populaire* (Grenoble 1982).

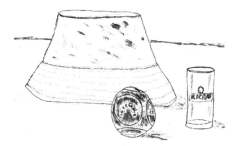

owned hostel in the center of Espalion, a 500-year-old town-house faced with butter-colored stone.

The house-minder opened the door with a scowl that looked a little like the gargoyle over her head.

"You're late," she snarled.

"I'm sorry, Madame," I said.

"You should have called."

"I didn't know we were supposed to call. The reservation just said between 5 and 7."

"Still, you should have called."

We didn't like the place any more than we liked her. There were several rooms with bunk beds, scuffed linoleum, and overhead lights that were either too bright or too dim. All the furniture, even the beds, was covered in white melamine and looked as if it could be washed down with a hose. But what really annoyed me was that we were forbidden to use the kitchen either to make dinner, as we had planned, nor, *monsieur*, to make breakfast.

Dinner turned out to be another low point. In a country where the basic formula of civilization is two parts gluten to one part animal protein, finding a place that could accommodate both Carson, the celiac sufferer, and Thea, the vegetarian, took some time. Earlier, Carson had avoided this problem by telling the people in the gîtes about her allergy before they made the dinner and to make doubly sure that they understood her, handing the proprietor a laminated card that she carried with her that explained her problem in French. But tonight, all eight of us had to agree on a destination, which exasperated the girls no end:

"Carson was being all martyry so we couldn't have pizza. Instead I had to have pasta with thousand island dressing! GROSS!" Thea wrote. Charlotte was also furious: *"We all really wanted to get pizza and Carson could have gotten risotto but she said it wouldn't be filling enough! We went to this other restaurant. It was really bad – my steak was burned and Thea had to eat the worst pasta in the world. Carson kept whining about how her omelet was too runny."*[72]

In our experience, it's usually the petty stuff that unravels groups of travelers. One couple wants to sleep in, the other wants to leave early. One faction wants to spend wildly more than the other. Or less. Someone is sick, and wants to make sure you don't forget it. Even agreeableness can become a source of tension: I remember taking a road trip around New England once with my brother Scott when I was working in Connecticut, and finally having to agree to take turns deciding what to do or where to stop, because neither of us wanted to take responsibility for a bad choice.

Von Clausewitz, the military thinker, classifies these kinds of stupid problems as friction, and notes that they have a cumulative effect, the way accidents do for the ordinary traveler, who, making a journey by post horses,

> arrives now at the last station but one, finds no horses, or very bad ones; then a hilly country, bad roads; it is a dark night, and he is glad when, after a great deal of trouble, he reaches the next station, and finds there some miserable accommodation. So in war, through the influence of an infinity of petty circumstances ... things disappoint us, and we fall short of the mark. A powerful iron will overcomes this friction, it crushes the obstacles, but certainly the machine along with them.

All in all, the evening was grim enough that I began to wonder how many more nights like this our hiking machine could take.

---

72   I should note here that the girls weren't nearly as grouchy as they sound in their diaries. Most of the time, they were exceptionally good sports —as the fact that their parents survived the walk suggests.

Leen was happy. Cybèle was happy. In my own way, I was happy too, but staggering. On the other side, we had Carson, who had bummed around Europe adventurously in her teens and early 20s, but would now certainly have preferred lounging by the pool in a five-star, teenager-free resort; Lola, who after some discussion with Masha had concluded that Cybèle and I were more or less unprosecuted criminals for not reserving Masha at least two weeks to prepare for boarding school; Masha herself, who was still anxious about making sure that she had every detail of her wardrobe right before she started her new life, and annoyed that I couldn't understand her anxiety, given that she was a beautiful girl and all the Sixth Form girls wore identical black skirts and black jackets; Charlotte, who had hated every step since Le Puy and would rather be doing almost anything else; and Thea, who liked the walk deep down—in almost every picture we have of her from that trip, she's beaming—but officially, to avoid being disowned by her sisters, did not.

Suddenly, the family's odds did not seem good, and in a few days, after the New York volunteers went home, could get worse. Cybèle had been right—having outsiders along had kept our family on good behavior. Without witnesses, I started to worry the rest of the trip would be like the last reel in most action movies, when the fight turns personal. *Yippikayay, Mom and Dad.*

July 15. Espalion to Golinhac, 23.4 km

In which we meet some great pretenders.

We were in green and hilly country now and on our way to Estaing, the hometown of Valéry Giscard d'Estaing, France's president from 1974 to 1981. I was curious to see the place. Cybèle remembered him because people often said he and her father looked alike. But I don't think this was too much of a trial for my beau *beau-pere*,[73] unlike say being a Nixon doppelgangster: Giscard d'Estaing was tall, slim, and distinguished looking. He had been popular too, particularly coming as he did after Georges Pompidou, Charles De Gaulles's former right hand man—a plump guy with bushy eyebrows who had the "appearance of being secretive, wily, a little cunning—which he was, to a degree."[74]

Carson found the perfect place for lunch just outside Estaing—a picnic table near a playground next to a gorge that overlooked the fast, green river; an old bridge over the river; and on the far bank, Estaing and the romantic pile of towers and turrets that takes up about two-third of the village, the ancestral home of the former president's ancient, noble family. Plains, Georgia, it's not.[75]

It's easy to imagine the boyhood of little Valéry, born in 1926, and his brother, Olivier, playing *cache-cache* among the busts of generation after generation of long-nosed Estaings in the chateau, fly-fishing in the Lot, hunting rabbits and wild boar in the high green hills that surround the town, never dreaming but still not entirely surprised that one of them would grow up to be president of France.

---

73 French for father-in-law. Belle-mere is mother-in-law. Is it any wonder French is the language of diplomacy?

74 At least according to one of his aides and successors, the secretive, wily, and slightly cunning Jacques Chirac.

75 For pre-codgers, this was the humble hometown of Jimmy Carter, the peanut-farming US president.

But it didn't actually happen that way.

The original Famille d'Estaing were a distinguished clan, founded by a comrade in arms of Richard the Lionhearted, who managed to stay on the front lines of French history from the Crusades until the French Revolution.[76]

The current crop of d'Estaings bought the castle in 2005 for about EUR 520,000, long after their hide-and-seek days were over. The *Freres* Giscard d'Estaing might have been to the manner born but when it comes to real estate, they are more to the manor aspired: In 1922, their father, Edmond Giscard, a prominent civil servant who served as minister of finance for the French-occupied Rhineland, and Uncle Rene, asked and received the Council of State's permission to add d'Estaing to their name. They traced their claim to a great-grandmother, Lucie-Madeleine d'Estaing de Réquistat (1769-1844), Countess de La Tour Fondue, goddaughter of the admiral and his half-sister Lucie, and possible descendant from an illegitimate line of Estaings in Puy-le-Dome.

Why Valéry's father, Giscard d'Estaing *ne* Giscard, went to all this trouble is unclear. A claim based on a great-grandmother who was just the goddaughter of the last d'Estaing and at least four or five generations removed from an actual d'Estaing (and down an illegitimate line) might seem like a stretch. But Giscard d'Estaing Sr. saw it differently. In an essay he wrote in 1940, after he had been a d'Estaing for 17 years, he argued essentially that sometimes a rose by any other name does not smell as sweet. For example, the name Michel de Montaigne "has the savor of a ripe fruit." If Montaigne had kept his father's name, Eyquem, he

---

76   The last d'Estaing, Admiral comte Jean Baptist Charles Henri Hector d'Estaing, had a colorful but largely unsuccessful career that ranged from India, where he was twice captured by the English; to Indonesia, where things went somewhat better; to the governorship of the Leeward Islands (which included Haiti), where things got worse (his efforts to import exiled French Canadians as colonists failed because they kept dying of tropical diseases); and finally to the American Colonies, where he tried to get even with the English by becoming a sort of naval Lafayette, with less success. Nor did Charles-Henri's bad luck end there. After coming home a non-hero, his wife died, then his only child, and finally, although he was a supporter of the Revolution, a gallant but ill-timed defense of Marie Antoinette and the discovery of some friendly correspondence with the hated queen earned him an appointment with "the Patriotic Shortener."

could not have represented the same kind of French wisdom to his contemporaries or to us as he did being Montaigne, a name that seemed to grow out of the earth. He would not, Giscard d'Estaing Sr. concludes, have been truly himself.

How much of your identity should be what you are issued versus what you cook yourself is an interesting question. Most of us mix and match to an extent, but in France I think there may be a stronger tension between the two impulses. On the one hand, the French have this connection to the land and to the family that people still take seriously. On the other, self-appointment—think of Napoleon's self-crowning and even the careers of Jeanne d'Arc and Charles de Gaulle— is also very French.

If Giscard d'Estaing Sr. changed his name partly to give his sons an advantage, he may have miscalculated. One of his son Valery's biographers notes that Edmond and his sons were teased for being aristocrats.[77] Unlike the English, the French aren't that keen on nobility. In recent years, almost none of the most prominent politicians have been aristocrats, though some have played them on TV. The closest, the dashing Dominique de Villepin, is mere haute-bourgeoisie. In fact, it's that upstart Sarkozy, the immigrants' son, who has the bluest blood of recent residents of the Élysée palace—his father, Pál István Ernő Sárközy de Nagy-Bócsa, belonged to a noble Hungarian line.

I have not been able to find out how the younger Giscard d'Estaings feel about that second name—what do you do if the family tradition is more or less phony? Valéry, at least, seems to have been of two minds about pretensions generally. On the one hand, as finance minister in the 1960s, he was known as a fairly no-nonsense *fonctionnaire*. Then, when he ascended to the top job in 1974, he dusted off a lot of the government's old gilt furniture and ran a very imperial presidency. Afterward, when he retired and became the equivalent of a county commissioner in his regional council in Auvergne, reporters noted that in his semiretirement, he changed his look again and became a rum-

---

77 Which was doubly ironic as their mother did have some actual backdoor aristocratic family connections to Louis XV by way of one of his mistresses.

pled country squire.[78] It was a dramatic enough difference that a reporter asked him why he had stopped dressing up. People expected the president to lead a formal life, he replied. In other words, it was just part of representing *la France*.

Deep down, however, I don't think Giscard D'Estaing ever had his heart set on being a regular guy: Why else would you spend EUR 520,000 on a castle a six-hour drive from Paris that you weren't even planning to live in, unless you wanted to make your father's name a little more real?[79]

But glamor always glimmers slightly out of reach: In the end, not even a fancy name, a castle, and a place in the history books seem to have been quite enough for Giscard D'Estaing, who in addition to his memoirs (*The Power and the Life*) and a few books on France and European politics, has written several romance novels. His second, *The Princess and the President*, published in 2009, got him briefly in the British gossip columns as it concerns an affair between a young Diana-like British princess and a tall, snappily dressed French president:

> "Do you think two people like you and me can fall in love?"
>
> "What do you mean by 'like you and me'?"

---

78 At least by haute bourgeois French standards, which is more or less a banker's Casual Friday everywhere else.

79 Adding some panache to your humdrum life as a commoner doesn't have to be that expensive. There are many people online who will happily sell you a title in France, Spain, Ireland, Switzerland or Italy for much less than EUR 520,000. Bargain hunters should note in particular a thrifty Scottish clan who will transform you into landed gentry for just £89. For the price of a middling seat at the opera, you get a whole new role in life, a square meter of the Highlands, and a certificate of lairdship with your name on it.

Title vendors say it's the only way to travel. As Nobility.co.uk puts it, "Once you have experienced what it is like to be a Lord or Lady, you will never look back, as the difference is a feeling of privilege and being honored. A Title is the ultimate status symbol, it says you are a V.I.P., it says CLASS."

To be fair, people do look at the titled differently. I know Thea told us that there had been a rumor flying around school all year that her science teacher was a Rumanian princess. I saw her once: she actually did have a regal air. Finally, one boy couldn't stand the suspense any more and asked, "So, Ms Sterza, is it true that you're a princess?"

"Yes," she said, then continued immediately with their lesson.

True or not, it's a great answer. It says CLASS, as Nobility.co.uk would say.

"Don't be a fool," responded Patricia. "I mean two people, one the President of the French Republic, and the other, a Princess in Britain. Can they really love each other, or is it just ridiculous? Answer me!"

I slowly stroked her leg, and her hand comes to mine. I dread to see a shadow in the half-open door of the unfortunate Fleuret, back for the tea tray, or worse, the indiscreet Major McCollum, lurking somewhere in the maze of the building.

"Yes, Patricia, I think it is possible," I said.[80]

Later that afternoon, even as a novelist who yet retained a certain animal something in his ninth decade looked out his study window and wondered whether his hero should arch an eyebrow as the countess entered the west salon or just ignore her and think of France, we were having a tough and not very glamorous time trudging on a gravel road up a very long hill.

First it was hot and sunny, and Thea remembered she had no sunblock on *"so I asked Dad to get Mom so I could have the sunblock but she was too far away. I decided to take a shortcut through the woods but I just ended up getting scratched by the berries. Anyway, I took the road but so as not to burn I had to wear my polar fleece!"* Then about an hour away from our hostel, burning was no longer a threat: the sky suddenly clouded over and the rain began to fall, lightly at first, then heavily. As we put our ponchos on, Thea and Masha started fighting. Thea claimed Masha was wearing her poncho. Masha denied the charge. How either of them knew whose was whose, Charlotte couldn't understand, as their jackets were both the same disturbing shade of watermelon and both the same size.

Charlotte and I decided to step off the road for a few minutes and wait under the trees until the rain let up. As we waited, a heavy but happy woman trotted by on a big horse, rain streaming off her cowboy hat and shiny olive slicker.

---

80 I suspect some of Giscard d'Estaing's longevity was the result of these books. A description in which an adoring young aide describes your alter ego as "larger than one would think by looking at his pictures, but he has no fat around the waist or stomach, and he dresses with care; in a fashion a little too classic, English-Italian, but very pleasing to me...I find him attractive," probably equals an hour of yoga and a bale of kale.

July 16. Golinhac to Conques, 20.7 km

In which we meet Saint Foy and learn all about monky business.

The girls lagged behind us the next morning, engrossed in a scheme to make their fortune running a summer camp in Lola's basement on the Upper West Side. Lola would teach art and tae kwon do (she had a black belt), Masha would teach creative writing, all three sisters would teach French, and together the four of them would clean up. The vision of all that money pouring in distracted them completely from the task at hand, and we kept having to nag them to pick up their pace.

At around three, the path left the fields for a forest and began to tumble almost straight downhill. Far below, we could see an old stone church and a few slate roofs poking over the treetops. At some point in the distant past, someone looked down from this crest or another of the green hills that surround the town and noticed that the whole valley had an oval shape, like a mussel shell (concha)—a curious association, considering we were more than 160 kilometers from the sea—but the name stuck: Conques.

We passed a marker about the village's patron saint, Saint Foy, *"a really cheerful sign about a 12-year-old who got beheaded,"* Charlotte recalled. A third-century Gallo-Roman girl, Foy ("Faith") had supposedly refused to make sacrifices to the public gods, even when the local governor had her tortured with a red-hot brazier. When some of the spectators objected, he ordered Foy's head chopped off, along with that of an equally stubborn neighbor, Saint Alberta.

Then the path became very steep, and we began rushing and almost falling down the hill toward our DAY OF REST. After 10 days of steady walking, we all thought of the next day the way Cybèle had written it on our itinerary—in big, red, capital letters. Weighed down by their 25-pound (11 kilo) packs and tortured by blisters, Leen and Carson were both looking forward to the break. The girls were even more ecstatic about the 40 hours or so of actual summer vacation ahead. Cybèle had mixed feelings. She knew the troops needed a little time off, but she was half afraid that once stopped we would stay stopped.

I wasn't so keen on stopping either. On the plus side, I would not have to hear my pack's annoying and apparently incurable *squeak squeak squeak* for a day, and more importantly, I would have a chance to catch up on my work. Squeezing your workday into the morning and the evening is possible, but just barely, and I was getting a little brittle.[81] At the same time, knowing that I would have to work the next day made me feel like I'd been bad and had to stay after school. But maybe there would be a nice café with Wi-Fi? A place where I could get a beer?

Several ankle-twisting switchbacks further down, the path dumped us in the town without warning, like the end of a steep playground slide, and we were surrounded suddenly by tidy, well-scrubbed stone and half-timbered houses, every window box brimming with red geraniums.

Conques is the Colonial Williamsburg of the chemin de Compostelle. No other town we passed through in France that summer or in Spain for that matter was was better preserved, no town more beautiful. It's a great place to wander and take pictures or to sit and ogle gargoyles. The downside is that Conques is not exactly a secret: because of the masses of tourists it attracts, the tiny village has the surreal, over-polished quality that restored places sometimes get—as if someone

Conques from our window in the abbey

---

81 This had not gone unnoticed. Leen, for one, kept telling me that there would be no shame in taking a bus to the next town so I could catch up on my sleep and my work, a thoughtful idea that I always responded to with a polite grimace. Cybèle, on the other hand, knew me well enough not to bother to make such a sensible suggestion. There was a reason she sometimes signed my birthday card "Your Co-Maniac Pal."

had Photoshopped each stone.

To the left of the church stood an enormous old five- or six-story stone building — the abbey, where we would be staying—and when we walked through the gate we could see that the cloister was buzzing with pilgrims all waiting to check in.

We waited there a long time, looking at the pedestals and stone heads that lay scattered around the courtyard like giant white chestnuts, and a throng of fellow pilgrims, mostly other gray-haired yet iridescent Quechanois. The only monk we saw in the abbey that day was the abbot himself, a tall thin man in a white cassock and rimless glasses who presided in a vague and genial way over the flock of volunteers who ran the place.

Several friendly but inefficient Englishwomen had been entrusted with the front desk. For some reason, the process of writing down names and figuring out how much each pilgrim owed took them awhile. The ladies seemed surprised each time a new group entered the office, as if they were in their kitchen back in Milton Keynes doing the crossword and a radio DJ had rung up out of the blue and asked them to name the top hit of June 1962.

The abbey was not always so short-handed. Ever since the monks acquired the relics of Saint Foy in the ninth century, Conques has been a prime stop for pilgrims—first for the cult of Saint Foy, and later as a stage to Santiago. Then as now, the pilgrim trade was the primary industry, but then it was a better employer: today around 250 people live here all year, but in the 1300s, the number topped 3000.

And they were probably all needed. Based on the volume of souvenirs and other bric-a-brac archaeologists have found along the way, some scholars estimate that as many as 500,000 pilgrims made the journey to and from Santiago every year. The Camino was so busy in certain periods that one 13th-century Arab traveler even complained about the traffic. From France, the trip is supposed to have cost the equivalent of about $3,000 in today's money, including food, lodging, and donations, though then as now, it could be done for a lot less or a lot more, depending on your stamina and your wallet.

Conques can be crowded in the summer.

But economically speaking, most of Conques's workers would just have been carnies at the carnival, selling food, wine, and souveniers—the monastery was raking in the big money. In the Middle Ages, Conques was a company town, and in Conques, as in many of the more substantial towns in France, that company was the monastery. The Benedictine monks of Conques managed a diversified portfolio that included Saint Foy's relics, beds for pilgrims, and extensive farms cobbled together from donations made to Saint Foy.

If the monks' farm at Conques was typical, it was probably a very good farm. Monastic farming tended to be more lucrative than the ordinary variety—one scholar estimates that French monastic farms were 81 percent more productive than the average peasant plot. The monks had a number of advantages over ordinary farmers: they did not have to worry about inheritances dividing and subdividing the estate, and then wasting space on boundary ridges or hedgerows. They also had more control over what they planted. For the ordinary farmer, if your lord specified the rent be paid in wheat, you had to grow wheat, but the monks could plant whatever grew best or paid most. And they usually did not have to pay rent, tithes, taxes, or tolls.

As many of the monasteries belonged to national and international networks, the monks could also think on a much bigger scale: the Domerie at Aubrac, for instance, had the considerable amount of salt it needed to make its cheeses and cure its meat brought by mule all the way from the Mediterranean, about 200 kilometers away. This wider view made the monks more ecumenical about their businesses too, and focused them on higher-value products that were easier to pack and transport, sometimes over great distances. Charlemagne reportedly had monks send him some especially tasty blue cheese from the Roquefort caves in southern France every year to his court in Aachen, 1,100 kilometers away. As well as cheese and beer, monks sold wine and, eventually, liqueurs.[82]

Other orders developed specialties that went beyond food and alcohol. The Knights Templar were military monks who over time diversified out of crusading and into a business that was something like a cross between Blackwater and Goldman Sachs. In addition to providing what we might call security services to pilgrims, the Knights Templar managed money for nobles, made large loans, and arranged letters of credit (basically, travelers' checks). A pilgrim could make a deposit in the Paris chapter of the Templars and withdraw it at any Templar chapter in Christendom. Some monks ran even higher-margin enterprises. The monks at Cluny, for example, elevated praying for the souls of the dead into an almost perfect business. The wealthy would make donations for the monks to pray and keep on praying for their loved one's souls, to get them out of the tortures of Purgatory. Donors' families could rest more easily, and the monks enjoyed a steady stream of premiums that came in generation after generation, without risk of any terrestrial payouts, like an insurance company that could outsource all the claims to God.

It's possible to make too much of the resemblances, but as I read up on the monks, I began to think that medieval monasteries actually had a lot in common with the modern multinational.

---

82 Including Chartreuse, the greenish cordial first distilled by Chartreuse (Carthusian) monks in France, which inspired the name of the color, but not Bénédictine, a liqueur that Alexander le Grand, a French wine merchant and industrialist, concocted in 1863. The brand-poacher claimed he based it on an ancient recipe that he had found in a grimoire ("a book of spells") in the library of an abbey sacked during the Revolution.

For one thing, the relationship with the state isn't entirely dissimilar, given the important role monks often played in running the king's government, and their exemption from the taxes the "little people" paid. For another, many monastic networks extended across multiple countries. The monks at Cluny oversaw more than 1,000 monasteries in Spain, France, England, and Ireland, for instance, and at one point, became so rich that they were independent not just of political oversight but also episcopal and even papal control.

But the biggest similarity I find between the monastery and the company is their self-consciousness. From the beginning, the monks were inclined to think of their institutions in an abstract way. This capacity to look at people and see not your brother-in-law and your cousin but cogs in a machine is an important skill in business, and one that in Europe at least seems to have started with the monks.[83]

There are subtler cultural resemblances as well. Like today's corporate cultures, the monks also made a point (or at least a show) of working hard. Saint Columba said a monk should always work "until the tears come," and one Benedictine motto held that "to labor is to pray."

The monks were also very businesslike in their time manage-

83　I doubt it's a coincidence that a monk, Luca Pacioli, published the first accounting textbook (1494).

Although Fra Pacioli doesn't claim to have invented the system of accounting (he says he just wrote down the method used by the merchants of Venice), it is striking that when he published the book, he had been a Franciscan monk—one of the least acquisitive orders—for nearly 20 years, and doesn't seem to have worried much about any higher purpose. Like Milton Friedman, he says that the goal of a business is "to make a reasonable profit."

A brilliant mathematician (he taught Leonardo da Vinci all he knew about math) and like Leonardo, an all-around genius (somewhat disturbingly, the father of accounting also wrote the first book of magic tricks), Fra Pacioli explains his method in a way that doesn't look all that different from the accounting textbook I had in business school, if you substitute cinnamon and skins for widgets, and it's better written. Pacioli sums up the essentials of all business in just five elegant lines:

Three things are needed by anyone who wishes to carry on business carefully:
    1) Cash and/or credit
    2) A good accountant
    3) Proper internal control
... The most important of these three is capital...

ment. In a world where most lives ran more like Toad's in the *Frog and Toad* books ("Wake me up at half past May."), the monks clocked everything by the hour. The French philosopher and intellectual historian Michel Foucault, in *Discipline and Punish*, describes them as "the specialists of time, the great technicians of rhythm and regular activities." Benedictines like the monks at Conques, for example, generally followed a schedule that went more or less like this:

- 12 a.m. First prayer service
- 3 a.m. Second prayer service
- Sleep, wash
- 6 a.m. Third prayer service, followed by instructions from the abbot
- Spiritual reading, work
- 9 a.m. Fourth prayer service
- High Mass
- Noon Fifth prayer service
- Midday meal
- Recreating, rest, private reading
- 3 p.m. Sixth service
- Farming and chores until twilight

Substitute meetings and conference calls for prayer, and the monks' lives start to look like that of the modern road warrior—in the gym by 5, meditation at 5:45, half a bowl of oatmeal, on the road by 6:12, in the office by 7, conference call to Sydney, on the plane to Düsseldorf, three meetings and a sales call, then a lonely hotel room that looks exactly like a thousand others; chicken breast, no sauce, steamed green beans, and an early night, and then up again far too early the next morning, to repeat the routine somewhere else. Welcome to Monastery by Marriott.[84]

But there is one important difference: the monks' machine was

---

84 Nor is it just the daily schedules that businesspeople and monks have in common. Rules against dating in the office (not dissimilar to the Benedictine stricture against having "particular friends"), an arcane vocabulary the rest of society neither understands nor cares much about unless something alarming happens (substitute subprime crisis for crop failure), special training or Botox to gain more emotional control (Benedictines frowned on laughter), and even the insistence on uniforms (and not just the gray flannel suits—what is the Zuckerberg hoody, anyway, but a very short cassock?) all seem very familiar. I could go on.

built to last. Only 62 companies listed on the Fortune 500 in 1955 are still on the list today, but Europe's monasteries stayed powerful for centuries. Monastic power began to ebb in northern Europe only with the Reformation, but even then, endured in some Catholic regions for a few hundred more years.

Where the monks went wrong might be a good subject for a seminar at Davos.

Some monasteries lost their reputation for restraint, which probably cost them a degree of goodwill. In the later Middle Ages, for instance, in the wealthy Saint Gallen's monastery in Switzerland, the monks ate seven meals a day and were allowed the equivalent of a keg of beer every week.[85] Peasants are also said to have resented the smell of roast chicken, a once- or twice-a-year treat for ordinary people that wafted out of the refectory windows a little too often for their liking.

Others spent too much on their headquarters. The Cluniacs built an enormous abbey—Cluny was home to the biggest church in Europe for 400 years, until Michelangelo built Saint Peter's in Rome—and the cost of building and maintaining the complex weakened them permanently.

This error was also brought on by another common mistake: over-relying on a single source of revenue. In the 1090s, during a flush period when he had conquered and looted some Muslim lands in Spain, Alfonso VI, King of Galicia, León, and Castile, doubled his traditional donation of 1,000 pieces of gold a year that his father, Fernando I, had made. A few years later, however, the easy looting dried up, and Alfonso stopped sending his donation, leaving Cluny in an awkward spot, the market for gigantic, half-built churches being fairly limited.

Then again, hanging onto the cash could also be a problem: too much wealth could make monastic orders what we would now call an inviting takeover target.

---

85 Most monks, however, faced the same pressure to be abstemious as the modern executive. Saint Benedict said "one hemina a day" of wine was probably enough—an ancient Roman measure equivalent to about nine ounces, or around two modern wine glasses—not so far off contemporary recommendations.

In 1307, for example, Philip the Fair, heavily indebted to the Knights Templar, had many of the order's members arrested, tortured into making a wide range of imaginative confessions. Confessions in hand, he had many of them burnt at the stake, then shut down the order, and appropriated their assets. Later, during the Reformation, some of the northern European kings were also quick to see the practical advantages of taking over the monasteries. In England, monasteries and convents owned about a quarter of the nation's landed wealth. It was said that if the Abbot of Glastonbury could marry the Abbess of Shaftesbury, their heir would have more land than the king—but Henry VIII relieved the pair of that temptation.

In the end, however, monastic power faded mostly after people started to believe monks weren't doing much more than hogging all the chicken. In the 1500s, Martin Luther, an ex-Augustinian monk, called for the abolition of all the monastic orders. "This kind of life finds no testimony or support in Scripture but has been made to look imposing solely by the works of monks and priests," he wrote in his essay, "The Pagan Servitude of the Church." "However numerous, sacred, and arduous they may be, these works, in God's sight, are in no way whatever superior to the works of a farmer laboring in the field, or of a woman looking after her home..." In fact, he wrote, they were often worse: "Vows only tend to the increase of pride and presumption."

When we were finally checked in at the abbey, the ladies pointed us toward our dorm, which was deeper into the building. We left our boots and bags in some ground floor cubbyholes, then Thea led us up a few cold flights of what she called *"a really cool/awesome spiral staircase made of stone,"* to a landing. There we found a large bare room with around 20 bunk beds, whitewashed walls, and big open windows that looked out on the slate-roofed church and its steeples and a forested hillside beyond.

A few hours later, we came back downstairs for dinner, and waited again in the cloister until they opened for business. It was cooler now that it was evening, and I didn't mind waiting in the twilit court with the white stone heads, even though I was very,

very hungry. After a few minutes, the abbot asked Masha to ring the dinner bell.

When he opened the door of the refectory, the hungry herd of freshly washed pilgrims rushed in and filled every inch of bench in the high-ceilinged, white-washed room. Baskets of bread and vases of roses were set at intervals on the long communal tables. It felt good to be in this happy crowd, which gave me a sense for the first time that not only were we doing something that many others had done over the centuries, but that the pilgrimage, in spite of everything, was somehow still alive. The abbot said grace and talked about various programs on offer that evening, and I felt slightly nostalgic for the Catholic life.

Not all of us were equally charmed. *"We listened to this priest go on for ages about all the stupid services we could go to,"* Charlotte wrote. *"Finally dinner arrived. We had:*

-salmon/pasta salad - GROSS

-Moussaka - GOOD

—Cheese - OK

Personally, I didn't think dinner was bad, but I could have done with a hemina of Bénédictine for dessert.

July 17. Conques—Day of Rest, 200 meters

In which we get to know Saint Foy better.

The abbey permitted only one-night stands, so in the morning we had to move to a dingy two-star hotel a block away. Along with our keys, the clerk gave us black garbage sacks for our backpacks, which made the place feel even grimmer. After everyone else went out, I opened the tall windows in our room and settled down to work, feeling thoroughly sorry for myself. The heavy wooden furniture and dark maroon bedspread gave the place a certain Simenon-ish quality that I wasn't in the mood for on such a sparkling day. On the bright side, for a period piece, the room had surprisingly good Wi-Fi.

At Cybèle's insistence, I took a break in the afternoon to go see Saint Foy's relics, which were just across the square.

I wasn't looking forward to it. I have seen a lot of relics over the years—cowls, bones, teeth, and hair; a few bodies laid out in glass cases, Snow White-style; mummies under mitres with jewel-buttoned eye sockets and tiny crimson slippers; and even the occasional pickled head. Being an overly sensitive soul, I tend to find this stuff a little macabre.[86]

But a visit to Saint Foy is not your typical visit to Saint Tussaud's. Cybèle was right—Saint Foy was amazing. As one blogger puts it, the statue is "so opulent and medievally bling-ed out, it's fabulous."

Foy's (Faith's) bones are tucked inside a seated gold statuette, parts of which go back to the seventh century or even before. The figure's head is made with a different gold than the body and seems to belong to a different gender, leading art histori-

---

86   I shouldn't hate these things so much, however, given that I owe my happy heathen life to them. More than anything else, those foul rags and bones tipped me away from Catholicism in the end. I had gone to Mass regularly all the way through college, at Saint Thomas More, Yale's spare blue chapel, which is so restrained it looks almost Quaker, but after graduation, on my first trip to Europe, the shock of all those grinning skulls convinced me not about everlasting life, as they were meant to, but its opposite.

ans to speculate that it may have belonged originally to a statue of Charlemagne or even a Roman emperor. Whatever the truth, she sits now in androgynous glory about a foot and a half high on a tiny bejeweled throne, beautiful but strange and utterly foreign, like a Mayan idol, her blue-black eyes staring at you from across 12 or 13 centuries.[87]

They say God moves in mysterious ways, and the saga of how the bones of a third-century, 12-year-old, Gallo-Roman girl from Agen in the Aquitaine ended up in Conques, a monastery 220 kilometers to the east, might be considered a case in point.

Saint Foy

In the 850s, the monks at Conques had a problem: Pepin, the Holy Roman Emperor, had founded a monastery at Figeac, about 43 kilometers west of Conques, and he wanted to shut Conques's doors and consolidate the two abbeys. The emperor didn't consider the narrow road to Conques very practical, and the rolling farm country around Figeac meant Conques's rival was not just more easily accessible but more easily supplied.

Today, towns solve similar problems with factory outlet stores and water parks, but in 855, you needed a saint's relics—preferably the bones of a famous or at least powerful saint.

The Conques gang, after a failed attempt to retrieve the bones of Saint Vincent from Valencia in Muslim Spain—the Muslims were no trouble but the Bishop of Saragossa shook down the monk who was bringing the bones back before he reached Conques—decided to go after a different set of relics. These belonged to another Saint Vincent, but this time closer by, in Pompejac near Agen. When they stole his bones, however, they took the opportunity to take Saint Foy's as well, like art thieves who after grab-

---

87 This kind of dazzle was always an important part of the show. As Bernard of Clairvaux noted in the 12th century, "by I know not what law, wherever the more riches are seen, there the more willingly are offerings made. Eyes are fixed on relics covered with gold and purses are opened."

bing the Mona Lisa decide to lift a Botticelli on their way out.

Then the monastery at Figeac upped the ante: Abbot Haigmar, who "was always eager to acquire the bodies of saints by trickery or theft," sent scouts to the town of Saintes to see if the remains of Saint Bibnus, a Merovingian bishop, could be spirited away. Fortunately, just at the moment the Figeac monks arrived, the Normans (that is, the Vikings) happened to attack the city. When the Sainteites went marching out, they left the relics to fend for themselves, and the monks from Figeac walked off with the loot.

Possibly to compete with this theft and its more exciting (and scholars say, probably fictional) origin story, a Conques monk wrote a livelier account of Saint Foy's theft. This revised version has a nice *Le Carré* -ish twist: a monk from Conques posing as a priest showed up at the abbey in Agen and spent 10 long years working there until he was finally entrusted with guarding Saint Foy's relics alone, at which point he grabbed Saint Foy and came in from the cold.

All this chicanery might give you the idea that the monks of southern France were a particularly bad bunch, which wasn't the case. Patrick Geary, a professor at Princeton, has found more than 100 accounts of what was called *furta sacra* (holy theft), by monks and private entrepreneurs, most of which occurred in the middle of the Middle Ages, between Charlemagne and the Crusades. A daring relic-theft became part of the saint's story, and often one of the favorite parts, in the same way we admire successful art forgeries or daring jewel heists. In fact, a good theft ("translatio" in Latin, as in the translation of something from one place to another) tended to increase a relic's popularity.[88]

"Far from condemning [thefts]...as sins against the fellow Christians from whom the saints were stolen, most people apparently praised them as true works of Christian virtue, and communities ... boasted of their successful thefts," Geary writes in *Furta Sacra:*

---

88   After all, who wouldn't want to check out the bits of Mary Magdalene's bones in Lincoln Cathedral, once you knew that Hugh, Bishop of Lincoln, later Saint Hugh, bit them off her arm in Fécamp Abbey *in* Normandy?

Thefts of Relics in the Central Middle Ages. They reasoned that the saints were so powerful that they wouldn't let something happen to them that they didn't want to have happen. Monks also waved away any lingering doubts by quoting passages in the Old Testament in which the Divine Will is executed through lying, stealing, and trickery.

But a dramatic theft-story was just the beginning of Foy's literary luck. Early in the 11th century, a monk named Bernard, who had been studying in Chartres, took an interest in the cult of Saint Foy. Stories that Foy was performing hundreds of miracles had reached him that were so remarkable he decided he had to go see for himself.

Once in Conques, Bernard conducted a thorough investigation. He collected dozens of miracles, so many that in his book he groups them by category (eye miracles, ear miracles, resurrected animal miracles etc.) to keep them straight. The first volume of the *Book of Saint Foy* has 34 chapters, and the second, 15. The titles of the first six are fairly representative:

1. How Guibert's Eyes Were Restored by Sainte Foy After They Had Been Torn Out by the Roots
2. A Similar Miracle About Gerbert
3. How a Mule Was Revived from Death
4. Another Miracle like the Preceding One
5. How a Man Was Killed in a Headlong Fall While he Was Attacking One of Sainte Foy's Monks
6. How Divine Vengeance Acted Against Those Who Wanted to Steal the Monk's Wine

As those headings suggest, Foy seems to have stayed a willful 12-year-old even after her martyrdom. Bernard deduces from her miracles that she likes jewelry but doesn't care about gold, is annoyed by mingy presents, and absolutely detests people who promise her something but don't deliver. She's also disgusted by sex—men complained to Bernard that if they had recently slept with a woman, even their wife, they suffered a burning sensation if they walked past her church without washing first. She could also be capricious, taking back miracles from backsliders, and freeing prisoners who ask for her help, regardless of their guilt.[89]

Her strange and sadistic "jokes" also suggest a child who doesn't always play well with others. For example, she advised a man who had prayed to her for relief from his hernia to go to the blacksmith, borrow a hammer, and pound his scrotum as hard as he could. Others are a bit funnier: my favorite is the feast day when the monks had no chance to feast. Custom dictated that whenever a miracle occurred, they were supposed to stop everything, chant a psalm, sound trumpets, and strike cymbals. Unfortunately, on that day, whenever they began to sit down at the table, Foy would perform a new miracle "so that they passed the day unfed, all the way to nightfall."

Weirdness abounds in medieval writing, but Bernard's accounts are exceptional. From the very first chapter of the Book of Saint Foy, "How Guibert's Eyes Were Restored," you can see you are reading a very original writer.

The story begins with Guibert, the godson of a priest named Gerald, meeting his godfather on the highway after returning from a pilgrimage to Saint Foy in Conques. Gerald, jealous of Guibert (who if I'm reading the story correctly, Gerald believes to be having a fling with his girlfriend), decides to attack him. Guibert pleads for mercy in the name of Saint Foy, but the angry priest jumps off his horse and plucks out his rival's eyes. Just at that moment, however, a bird swoops down and flies off with both eyeballs.[90]

Guibert recovers from the attack and starts a successful new life as a blind jongleur, a street musician. This goes very well—he told Bernard later that he made so much money as a jongleur that after a year he didn't mind being blind anymore.

---

89 The miracle of her freeing prisoners happened so often, Bernard reports, that the monks eventually stopped writing them all down and in fact had come to loathe them.

90 One of the winning things about Bernard is his candor in acknowledging the rough spots in the narrative. For instance, at this point in the story, he discusses a discrepancy in the eyewitnesses' description of the bird that flew off with Guibert's eyes. Wicked Gerald saw a magpie, while the more innocent bystanders reported seeing a dove. Maybe, Bernard speculates, the bird just looked black to the attacker but white to the innocent observers.

At this point, however, Guibert is visited in a dream by "a girl of indescribable grace" who tells him to go buy two wax candles in the church near where he lost his sight.

To get the money he needs for the candles, she says, he must first go to the church where a man will give him six deniers. Guibert, for unexplained reasons, goes to the church as directed but tries begging for 12 deniers. Everyone turns him down except for a man named Hugh who gives him six sols and one obol—just a bit more than Foy predicted.

Now Guibert buys the candles and makes his way inside the church. At around midnight, as he prays, two objects came flying toward him—"two light-filled globes like berries, scarcely larger than the fruit of the laurel tree, which were sent from above and driven deeply into the sockets of his excised eyes."

"The force of the impact disturbed his brain and in a state of bewilderment, he fell asleep," Bernard continues. Guibert doesn't get better right away, but as the matins begin, he is awakened by the choir and the chanting, and

> it seemed to him that he could make out the shadowy forms of shining lamps and people moving about. But because of the pain in his head he had almost forgotten who he was. Since he could hardly believe the truth, he thought he was dreaming. Finally the dullness that had taken over his brain gradually disappeared, and he began to make out the shapes of things more clearly.

In a conventional miracle-story, this would be the end, but in Bernard's telling, it's only the beginning: the monks give Guibert a place to live and set him up in the wax business, which must have been a good franchise in a monastic town.[91]

He makes a lot of money doing this, becomes arrogant ("for it is the nature of human kind"), and settles down with a like-minded, unchaste girlfriend, according to Bernard.

---

91 Wax was a convertible currency in many pilgrim stops. In addition to gold or jewelry, most important pilgrim churches accepted offerings in wax, at a set rate per pound. (Most but not all: the cathedral at Santiago de Compostela accepted only gold or jewelry.) Bell and Dale speculate that this was not really charity, as Bernard implies, but a kind of celebrity endorsement of the power of Saint Foy.

Saint Foy is so annoyed with Guibert's backsliding that she blinds him in one eye again, to encourage him to repent, and then heals him once he does. But eventually he slips once more, and she punishes him for his recidivism, in the usual way—and then they repeat the whole cycle several times. Finally, Guibert's lapses become too much for Foy, who resolves to blind him permanently. But before she does, he becomes a monk, and she relents.

I liked Bernard's description of Guibert as an old sinner, who sounds like a lot of former wild things—not so much repentant as worn out: "Now he is an old man, impoverished and held in contempt because of his shameless activity. He lives on the common dole provided by the brothers and is content with very little, very often just with an evening meal. He rejoices merely in easing his hunger, safe from the trouble of all his folly." The writer swears it is true and in fact, "I tracked down so much evidence that it is too boring to go over all of it."

Historians sometimes claim that people in the Middle Ages thought of themselves not as individuals but as worker bees who lived only for the family or to put another buttress on the cathedral wall, but reading Bernard makes me wonder. The preface of his first book, in which he whines about the three years he spent teaching in Angers before quitting his job to go to Conques and investigate Foy's miracles, and the preface to the sequel, in which he talks about how proud he is of the book's success (various bishops and abbots had ordered copies! – a big deal back before paper and printing presses), and the offerings to Saint Foy that the book inspired, sound somehow familiar, not much different from a lot of Facebook posts I see.

July 18. Conques to Livinhac-le-Haut, 24 km
Wherein we swim in the Lot and make the best omelet ever.

The girls had enjoyed their day off so much—an endless loll of long baths, fluffy white towels, and a delicious lack of adult supervision—that I felt badly when I had to knock on their door around 11:30 that night to tell them they had to go to sleep. I found them sprawled on their beds, watching a dubbed American film on TV, a war movie in which an injured American airman, for reasons they wouldn't stop to explain to me, was about to be parachuted on his gurney out of a B-24 into Nazi Germany. After waiting until his comrades said their tearful goodbyes and threw the bomb bay doors open, I turned off the TV.

All too soon, like the injured airman hurtling toward the earth, the girls were flung out of their comfy beds with real sheets and into the heart of enemy territory—the road to Santiago.

After a quick grumpy breakfast in the dark hotel bar, everyone pulled the black garbage sacks off their packs, cinched on their burdens, and left me behind in the dark hotel—I had to wait for an 8 a.m. call.

An hour later, I followed, out onto the sunny cobblestoned street. The pack was heavier than I remembered; every morning when I put it back on, the pack was always heavier than I remembered. I crossed an old stone bridge, passed a few half-timbered houses, and then I was out of town and back on the Camino. It was cool and damp on the steep path up through the trees and I turned on my *Don Quixote* lecture. About halfway up, just around the corner from a small chapel dedicated to Saint Foy, I misjudged a muddy switchback, slipped, and fell. Whether this was a joke of Foy's or just an accident, I took the hint, turned off Professor Echeverria, and began to concentrate on the business at hand.

A few minutes later, just after I had climbed out of the valley and into the rolling farm country once more, I passed the big German we had met at the café in Saint-Côme-d'Olt. He was walking today with a woman who seemed a lot less happy about the circumstance than he did. They had stopped to look at a map.

"Good morning!" he boomed, like a captain in an operetta.

"Good morning," I answered, an anxious corporal in the same show.

"I was thinking about you," he said, "I have been thinking, you should write a book about this: *How I walked the Chemin de Compostelle with seven women and became a real man! Ha ha ha.*" His big teeth shone.

His girlfriend grimaced and looked down at her map again.

"Take lots of notes!" he called after me, as I walked on.

Good advice, which as I sit now, trying to sort out my memories, I wish I had followed.

A few miles on, I saw a thin young man not too far ahead of me—dark hair, round *Where's Waldo?* glasses, blue-striped sailor shirt that made me think of *Jules et Jim*, and a stylish, broad-brimmed straw hat that hung over his pack. He walked easily and quickly, and after I had spotted the receding straw hat now and again on the rolling fields, lost sight of him.

I ran into him again an hour later, in one of those tiny hamlets along the trail that seem to exist mostly to sell coffee to pilgrims.

He was from Austria, he said, as we sat down with our coffees in the little café-cum-general store, and had walked the whole Camino three times. He loved it; he always told people, whatever your problem, the Camino is the cure.

As we talked, another pilgrim walked into the café, unslung her pack, set her poles against the counter, and ordered a coffee. She was stocky, carried a larger pack than either Waldo or me, and had gotten much more of a workout this morning than Waldo. We had been speaking English but switched to French when she sat down with us. His French was even worse than mine, so I had the unusual experience of smoothing over the linguistic edges of a conversation, which as I recall was not about much of anything, and could not be, given the limitations of the not-so-simultaneous translator.

After five minutes, she had had enough. "Au revoir, les hommes," she said, rising abruptly.

The three of us agreed we would meet at the next bar but of course we didn't.

After she left, the Austrian asked me what I did, and I told him I was a freelance writer. He said he was a kind of freelancer too. He lived in a small university town and sometimes led groups on the Austrian Camino. He also gave classes teaching people how to make their own muesli, and how to fast.

I decided to buy a sandwich for the road partly as an excuse to split up, and let the professional pilgrim go ahead. I don't know why, but I felt relieved to be alone again. This was unusual for me—although I spend most of my workdays by myself and have always lived with a fair amount of solitude, I have seldom sought it out in any conscious way.

As the morning wore on, though, the quiet began to feel excessive, and I regretted my decision to split up. I thought about the solitude that had grown up around me over the past few years, and it occurred to me that it was going to get a lot deeper from here on out. Masha's going away to school was only the beginning. More and more, I would be left to my own devices, and for better or worse, that was probably how it was going to be. Get used to it, buddy.

The trail led along a crest that looked out on the gingerbread rooftops of several Victorian farmhouses in the wide valley below.[92] The day had turned hot now, and I was very thirsty. I had forgotten to refill my water bottle at my last stop—I often rely on Cybèle to remind me about even the most basic of basics— and kept expecting to find a fountain or a faucet somewhere, but I didn't.

---

92   In the 19th century, the region had been home to an enormous coal mine and iron works, and you could see traces of the boom in all those old turrets and gingerbread.

A little later, I passed a cemetery, which made me feel gloomier still.[93] After the cemetery, I walked on down into Decazeville and crossed the main street, a row of boarded-up shops, and a few bars that had a "Stranger, keep out!" aura to them. I had hoped to see my coffee buddies, but they were long gone, and now I would probably never have a chance to ask Waldo a question that had occurred to me after we went our separate ways: what did you learn in a fasting workshop? Whatever its difficulties in practice, I had always understood the mechanics to be fairly straightforward. Soon I was out of the center of town and walking up a residential street of newish white stucco houses with terra cotta roofs that gave the neighborhood a certain je ne sais *Orange County* quality.

The rest of the crew had been having a hard day too. *"We walked and walked until we had lunch,"* Charlotte wrote. *"We had tuna and cheese sandwiches. It wasn't very good. I got really hot and Carson was having a meltdown. We went to a café and had Cokes."*

Afterwards, as they walked, Thea wrote, *"[w]e described what we wished we could have at that moment. The most popular things were: ice cold drinks, pool, fan and massages."* Carson wished she were sitting by the beach with a Moleskine notebook and a bowl of blueberries.

Near the top of the hill, I saw a church, and a few people standing out in front of the vestibule, including two very familiar faces—Thea and Charlotte! inspecting their latest pilgrim passport stamp.

A few kilometers on, the trail began to follow a quiet highway and then eventually the sidewalk across a standard-issue, four-lane highway bridge. Down below, we could see our old friend, the Lot, which was greener and wider here, and on the other side of the bridge and another kilometer up a gentle hill, our destination, the town of Livinhac-le-Haut.

---

93 I hadn't learned yet that cemeteries are actually an earthly paradise for the thirsty hiker. You can usually find a faucet near the entrance—people need them to fill flower vases.

Cybèle proposed that we stop for a swim. Carson wanted to press on to our gîte—her feet were hurting her, and she didn't think the water looked all that clean—but Cybèle was determined to make good on her campaign promise to the girls that there would be afternoon swims, and there had been none so far. In the end, Carson and Leen went on to the gîte, and the rest of us found our way down to a park that ran along the river. Officially, there were no hard feelings.

The park was about a half-kilometer from the road, upstream from the foundation of what looked like a monument but turned out to be the arch and base of an old suspension bridge.

I had assumed the bridge was blown up in the war but have since learned this wasn't the case. The bridge actually survived two world wars and four or five governments before it succumbed to decades of neglect in the early 2000s. I couldn't find much more online about it, except for a few stories about a small preservation group that had tried to stop its demolition. I would like to think it's because the local authorities are ashamed, as they should be: the bridge was built in 1833, which made it one of the oldest suspension bridges in Europe. Watching the slow collapse of that bridge over 25 years was a bit like having the Eiffel Tower in your backyard and letting it fall apart. It amounts to an architectural crime. Not murder maybe, but some grade of manslaughter.

This may seem excessive, but I've always had a strong feeling for bridges, I guess because they were the only structures on the Oregon coast that had any architectural distinction. The best there were built in the 1920s and 1930s, an eclectic mix of art deco details and gothic arches. Their designer, Conde McCullough,

Oregon's chief bridge engineer in that era, described them, accurately if not modestly, as "jewel-like clasps in perfect settings, linking units of a beautiful highway," and I remember always feeling a little exalted when we drove over one of them.

It's hard to imagine now, but when France first started building the new iron bridges, people had serious debates over whether a structure not modeled on classical architectural principles or built from local materials could be beautiful. The designer of a proposed suspension bridge across the Seine in Paris at Invalides, an engineer named Claude-Louis-Marie-Henry Navier, was even forced to waste a little of his considerable brain power defending the proposition that "an iron structure, if its appearance is that of grandeur and simplicity, can as much merit the appellation monument as a stone structure."[94] He lost that particular battle but won the war.[95] Between 1830 and 1850, 400 suspension bridges were built all over France. After that, however, suspension bridges fell out of favor for a time, not because of the design, but the materials: it took awhile for the metallurgists to figure out how to handle rust.

In the park next to the bridge tower, a few families sat at picnic tables, eating and talking, watching the dark green water roll by. We fished our swimming suits out of our packs, changed as discreetly as we could, and went into the river. Lola and Cybèle dived right in, then Charlotte and Thea. I followed, slowly and painfully, as I usually do.

But Cybèle had been right to insist on the swim. Once I got in, the water was lovely and the trees along the river shimmered in the breeze. I'm not much of a fan of swimming pools, maybe because I don't swim very well, but I do like flailing in real water, particularly after a long, hot hike. Even Masha, who had been in

94   A genius, Navier not only designed bridges but corrected some of Galileo's equations, and co-invented an important set of equations that are still used to calculate the movement of weather, ocean currents, water through a pipe, and air flow around a wing.

95   But not for aesthetic reasons. Construction went ahead, but in 1826, soon afer the bridge's completion, it started to crack, and had to be taken down. Navier had trusted his math too much and skipped building models with real materials to test his design.

a funk earlier that day, cheered up once Charlotte had pushed her off the dock and into the water.

The Lot at Livenhac

We arrived late at our gîte, an old ivy-covered house with a turret and a big stone kitchen on the ground floor that looked out on a lush back garden. Carson and Leen ran downstairs from their room in the turret just as we walked through the gate, anxious because we had to make our own dinner that night and our landlady had told them that the village shops would close in 20 minutes. Cybèle and I rushed out with the two of them, leaving the four girls behind.

At the store, Carson grabbed the last two packs of eggs, I picked up a pot of *crème fraiche* and a beer, and Leen and Cybèle found some some tomatoes, lettuce, and berries. On our way back, Carson and Cybèle slipped into the bakery and bought a half-dozen meringues, which were one of the only pastry treats Carson could enjoy because they have no gluten in them.

A little later, back at the gîte, we commandeered a thick wooden dining table in the kitchen that ran parallel to the stove and sink and got to work.

At the stove, Carson navigated around a big blond Irishman in a green shirt who was boiling potatoes. As I chopped tomatoes, I overheard an old French guy talking to the landlady. He had thick-lensed, black-frame glasses and the legs of a professional soccer player and as he stood shoveling the contents of a can of cold spaghetti into his mouth, explained between bites that he had bicycled to Santiago and was now on his way home. Usually he rode about 100 kilometers a day, he mumbled, sometimes more. Two minutes later, he threw away the can, washed his fork, set it on the drying rack, and went upstairs to bed.

For dinner, Carson made a salad and scrambled eggs with a fistful of herbs the landlady had given us from her garden and a dollop of *crème fraîche*, a trick I'd picked up from Julia Child's memoir. In her book, Child says that on her first day at the Cordon Bleu in Paris, her professor-chef made delicious scrambled eggs with *crème fraîche* and told the class that any dish, even something simple as scrambled eggs, could be delicious if you prepared it with care and love. The speech sounds more like Julia Child than a crusty old French cooking instructor, but that was how she remembered it. In any case, she was right about the recipe—Carson and I have talked about that meal now for years.

July 19. Livinhac-le-Haut to Figeac, 25 km
In which we go to the doctor.

We made our own breakfast in the gîte's old low-ceilinged kitchen, weaving awkwardly between the stove and our table, the big Irishman, the old French bicycle-machine, and four hungover hipsters. Carson was in a good mood—she and Leen had slept well in their tower, and she was still talking about our dinner the night before. It also didn't hurt that this was their last day on the hike.

Our girls seemed depressed—Thea was tired, Masha was sad that Lola would be leaving tomorrow, and worried, she remembers now, that without the New York contingent, "things were about to get worse quality-of-life wise." On top of that, Charlotte's right eye was bothering her.

Out on the trail, Cybèle and Leen charged ahead, absorbed in their soundless conversation. All of us were used to watching them talk without sound, and the girls, particularly Thea, often spoke without voice with Cybèle too, but it can seem funny to outsiders. A friend of mine remembers seeing them sometimes in the Yale Law Library when we were in school, silently chatting and laughing away. They must have driven the librarians crazy.

Lola and Masha followed in their silent slipstream, while Carson, Charlotte, Thea, and I trudged behind, resigned to not see the four of them again until they decided to stop for lunch.

The farms and orchards we walked through that morning were pretty but lacked any villages or rivers for punctuation. Carson and I were talking more than we had the past few days, the way people often do toward the end of any joint project, and after a while, the landscape began to pass by unnoticed, like the recurring background of a cheap cartoon – chimney, hedgerow, cow cow cow, chimney, hedgerow, cow cow cow. The hours passed pleasantly enough, until I noticed that we had seen the same brick farmhouse at least twice.

For the next hour, we tried to retrace our steps through this maze of old overgrown farms and began to feel progressively more exasperated. Why wasn't the trail better marked? Why had Cybèle and Leen just charged ahead? Why didn't they stop now that they hadn't seen us for an hour?

Even when we found Cybèle, Leen, Masha, and Lola getting our lunch ready, the petty annoyances didn't end. Without Carson's picnic-spot-scouting skills, Leen and Cybèle had chosen a place near a muddy lake that turned out to be midtown of a megalopolis of entrepreneurial flies. And Charlotte's right eyelid had ballooned even more.

At around three, we reached Figeac. It's not a big place—only 9,500 people live there—but from where we stood, looking down from the ridge at the river and the town, it seemed immense. Thea *"felt the way prehistoric people felt when they discovered fire: the Troyan-Voyles discover civilisation."*

A bridge in Figeac by Thea

On our way down toward the bridge, we passed a junkyard where someone had built a giant robot out of old metal buckets and pipes, one hand raised in a Greetings, earthling pose. I appreciated the gesture. We saw a surprising amount of sculpture and mysterious messages along the French Camino, I guess to take advantage of the captive audience. Occasionally too, people would leave out a box of fruit and a sign to serve yourself, pilgrim.

Across the river, we walked up several narrow alleys before we found our gîte—a dark, semi-converted storefront named *Le Soleilho* (the Sunshine)—and I volunteered to take Charlotte to the doctor.

This was hardly selfless on my part: I like going to the doctor in France. In the United States, doctors' offices tend to be serious places filled with nurses and paper-wranglers—there's a lot of money flowing through, after all, and money always adds a reverential hush—but not in France, where doctoring tends not to be a lucrative business. When specialists found out we were Americans, they would always ask how much their services would cost in the States and when we gave them an estimate, react either with outraged shock or a wistful, faraway look, picturing what might have been.[96]

That afternoon, the doctor who could see us had evidently just moved into his office, which was in a brand-new but cheaply built building up a hill behind the town, not far from an old cemetery and across the street from a row of car body garages and second-hand stores. Unusually for a country doctor, he had a receptionist or at least a share of a receptionist, and she buzzed him and told us to go in. He opened the door, reached up from his wheelchair to shake our hands—his right leg was in a cast and stuck straight out—then wheeled around back behind his desk, but sideways to us, which in combination with his being plump and mustached, made him seem shy.

It was a bare office with a picture window that overlooked several garage roofs and three parking spaces. A skeleton hung from a hook behind our chairs, admiring the view.

We sat down, told him the problem, and he asked Charlotte to come sit on a stool next to him on the far side of his desk. He picked up a light with the little funnel on its end and had just started to look at her swollen eye when his cellphone rang.

He had The Entertainer as his ringtone and it played another three bars by the time he rolled over to his desk to pick it up. After he spoke to the caller and made a note in his diary, he set the phone down, wheeled back to Charlotte, picked up the little funnel-shaped light once more, and continued examining her eye.

---

96   You really never know what you're going to find in a French doctor's office. A dermatologist we knew in Paris for instance had an office chockfull of bad ceramic sculptures and travel posters that went well with her fake tan. In the country, the office will be on the ground floor of the doctor's house. Often, the place will look like the workshop of a not-very-successful appliance repairman or the disciple of an alternative nutritional regime.

But before he quite finished, his phone rang a second time – *bum bum, de bummy-bum* — and as he rolled back across the room, Charlotte and I tried to hold back giggles.

He answered, made another note, and resumed.

We were all set for a third rendition of the jolly ragtime tune, but fortunately it didn't happen, or we would have started laughing in the poor man's face. As it was, we were barely able to contain ourselves until after he wrote Charlotte a prescription, gave me the brown form French doctors always give you to send to your insurance company, and sent us back out into the hot, white, afternoon, roaring.[97]

Our gîte did not serve meals and did not have a kitchen, so we decided to go out for dinner. We found nothing that looked good, and every option weirdly empty for a tourist town in the middle of July. Then we wandered into the main square and understood: food stalls had been set up, and hundreds of people were either sitting at long tables covered in white butcher paper, tucking into their sausages or aligot, duck, or snails, or lining up to buy one of these treats. My mood improved immediately, greasy street food being high on my list of favorite things, and greasy French street food being at the very top.

Carson, Leen, and Charlotte went to the steak-frite line. Cybèle and Thea went to the calamari and shrimp stand. Masha, Lola and I lined up for escargot—I had never gotten around to trying them before, but it felt like an unfinished task for my Franco-

---

97 Somehow, they manage to run most of the health system with that one brown form. It's a big reason French doctors are able to spend most of their time looking after their patients instead of a third on paperwork, as American doctors do, and France as a whole spends 11.5 percent of its GDP on health care and covers everybody while the United States spends 17 percent and misses millions.

phile merit badge and I was feeling brave.[98]

The liveliness of the crowd and the lack of a need to agree on anything made everybody feel better.   After dinner, we ordered ice cream cones and strolled lazily around the old town. Carson and Leen seemed far away already, although they would spend a few days in our apartment in Paris with Lola before they flew home. Leen kept thanking us and telling us they had had a fabulous time.

Not steak-frites.

---

98   To a former Oregonian, snails had always seemed too near the slug family for comfort. I thought they were pretty good, but all through dinner, kept casting a wistful eye on Charlotte's steak-frite.

July 20. Figeac to Cajarc, 31.5 km

Wherein we say goodbye to our friends and now have only ourselves to blame.

In the morning, we hugged Leen, Carson, and Lola goodbye. Lola promised Masha she would write to her at boarding school. We had walked a long way with them—two weeks and 250 kilometers—and although we were relieved that they had made it through without any serious problems, Cybèle and I were also anxious that their going home might set our girls to thinking that there wasn't any particular reason we had to continue what my sister's boys call "forced family fun."

The blow-up happened sooner than we expected—two minutes after our friends had left.

Masha and Thea get angry fairly often, but it blows over. Charlotte's anger is different. Most of the time, she keeps any annoyance to herself. Occasionally, however, the displeasure keeps building until it achieves a certain critical mass, which is why we shouldn't have been surprised when at exactly 8:17 at 8 rue Prat, Figeac, the family and the entire block were consumed by a blinding flash of rage.
She was sick of cows, sick of the countryside, sick of walking. Why did we have to do this? Why couldn't we be a normal family and have a normal summer? Why did we always have to do things that were hard and not fun? Etc.

Cybèle stayed calm. Even with the pillars shaking and plaster falling all around us, she continued to gather up the packs, methodically checking that we had packed the toiletries and filled all the water bottles.[99] Once Charlotte's sobs had died down, I

---

99 We had developed a few good habits, by this time. We always packed the night before, to save time in the morning; we always left our packs' rain covers on if the weather looked doubtful, so we never had to worry about pulling the cover on or off if it started raining; and we always tied things to the shoulder straps— damp, freshly washed socks; our ponchos, which made good picnic blankets; and my headphones. Yet everybody still managed to find their own way of doing things. "Charlotte always folded her clothes neatly and stacked them in her backpack," Cybèle remembered later. "Thea rolled her clothes—she heard somewhere that was the best way to pack. Masha stuffed her things in her bag, whichever came first."

offered her the option of staying with me—I had to stay behind to finish a column—but warned her that I would be starting the walk at the hottest time of the day and would not have time to take any breaks.

Charlotte pulled herself together in the end, but clearly under protest, with a look that said, *I am complying with this request, but you understand you will be hearing from Amnesty International very soon.* A few minutes later she and her sisters shuffled off after Cybèle—to the extent that you can shuffle down a cobblestone street without hurting yourself.

I didn't envy Cybèle that walk.

After they left, I settled down to what seemed now like a luxurious morning of silence, working for my favorite client. Most of my clients demand fairly straight-laced English that could be read by a machine and someday will undoubtedly be written by one, but *The Economic Times*, the Indian newspaper I wrote for, let me expound on almost anything, any way I liked, the loopier the better. This morning, I had promised to submit a 2,000-word essay about self-help books. It began as follows:

Seven habits of highly effective self-help book authors

If life had imitated art, Stephen R. Covey would have made a comeback. After a bicycle accident on a steep road outside Provo, Utah, in April, the 79-year-old self-help author was knocked unconscious and never regained his health. Instead, after nearly three months in the hospital, he died this week of the head injuries, cracked ribs, and collapsed lung he had sustained when he flew off his bike.

This was not quite the end that might have been expected of the author of *The 7 Habits of Highly Effective People*, one of the best-selling and most revered self-help books of all time. Flying down a steep hill too fast was not proactive (Habit 1), presumably did not begin with the end in mind (Habit 2), or put first things first (Habit 3). Nor did bicycling turn out to be part of a sustainable life style (Habit 7).

But looked at in another way, the distance between the preacher and what he preached should be encouraging to all of us: you don't have to be perfect to write a perfect self-help book, you just have to know how to write one....

I write slowly by journalistic standards, so churning out a long piece in a short amount of time, even something as silly as this, tends to take a lot out of me. I finished around 12:30 the way I always finished my pieces for *The Economic Times*—in more or less the same mental state as someone who just finished a marathon, or Rocky at the end of the first movie when he's bloody and shouting for his girlfriend—glad that it's over, regretful about the various things I could have done better, more or less reeling.

I mention this as a partial explanation of why, over the next eight hours, I broke seven habits of highly effective hikers.

1. Eat before you walk.

Normally, I would have picked up some lunch before I left town, but today I decided I had better start right away. I had a long walk ahead, and I thought that I would probably pass a *boulangerie* at some point. Instead of taking the long route back through town, I took a shortcut straight up rue Prat toward the river, took a right, then crossed the bridge, and followed the *chemin de Compostelle* up the hill behind the town.

At the top of the bluff, the trail turned left. I passed a stone cross and a viewpoint, and then a cellphone tower. Behind and below the tower, Figeac today was blanketed under a hot gray haze.

Soon I came to an octagonal obelisk 14 meters tall with no markings. I assumed it was a World War I memorial—in rural France, that's usually a good bet—but I later learned this was the Needle of Cingle, a mysterious monument that has a twin not too far away.[100]

It was about 1:30 now and I was starting to get hungry. I found myself walking through an industrial park and hoped I would run across some fast food. In America, some enterprising per-

---

100 Archaeologists think that these two medieval obelisks may mark the border of an ancient parish, but no one knows for sure, and there are no others like them in France. As one French pilgrim-blogger sums up the mystery, "L'énigme reste entière."

son would have opened a Dairy Queen or two to feed all those workers, but I didn't see anything like that—not even a candy machine at a gas station.

After a half-mile or so, I realized I also hadn't seen any red and white-striped trail markers since back near the Needle.

2. Keep track of your trail markers.

Getting lost is a familiar experience for me, so the thought that I might have to retrace my steps didn't bother me all that much. I wasn't angry, just disappointed, as good parents say. What did bother me was the uncertainty of the next quarter-mile. Should I keep going and risk the chance of slipping even further away from my destination or turn around and risk having to walk the same stretch of road all over again if I discovered I wasn't lost after all, just impatient? It felt like a strange game of chance, and I don't like games of chance; I've always been so lucky I have a superstition I'm owed a reversal to the mean.[101]

On my return trip, I spotted the red and white trail marker marking a turn. I had missed it because someone had stuck the decal on the backside of a traffic sign I had passed. Silly me.[102]

Back on the true way again, I resumed thinking about food. I thought about picking up something from a self-service foie gras factory outlet I walked past, a place with a cartoon goose as its symbol, but I decided to walk on past Goosey-goose. I like pate but I had no can opener, no knife to spread the pate with, and no baguette to spread it on.

Finally, I was out in the country once more, on a long straight road that dipped down and then up, with wide fields on either side. I was still a little hungry but began to feel better. This

---

101 Cybèle asked me later, sensibly enough, why I didn't check the map on my phone. The answer is, I forgot. I sometimes think I ought to be living in a halfway house somewhere.

102 In own my defense, this happened fairly often to all of us. It's not always easy to follow the *Chemin de Compostelle*, which some days weaves in and out of so many roads, lanes, and right-of-ways you would think it was designed by a cartographer with attention deficit disorder.

stretch had very few cars, and the wide fields gave me a sense of an orderly world, nicer than the dense scrub and broken-down farms we had walked through the day before. I was also up to a hilarious chapter in *Don Quixote*, in which the Don, who has sworn to free the oppressed, frees a gang of convicts on their way to the galleys and is beaten up for his trouble.

3. Never order an imaginary beer.

My mood stayed bright as I climbed a hill to Faycelles, a beautiful village of stone houses and flowers, and on three sides, a spectacular view of endless fields. When I got to the top, I would order a sandwich and a beer and sit out at a little iron table under a chestnut tree, happy as an Aubrac cow.

Unfortunately, Faycelles has everything you could ask for in a French village, except food. Like many villages in France and in Europe generally, the villagers evidently drive to a supermarket somewhere else to do their shopping.[103] At the crest of the hill, the village ended on the edge of a bluff, and the trail turned right. I debated whether to make a more thorough search, decided against it, and followed the trail out of town.

Near the edge of the village, a black cat watched me lazily from the top of a stone wall, but didn't bother to cross my path. My mood sank. Around this time, my companions—the Knight of the Woeful Countenance and the Professor (I had been alternating between the two every 45 minutes or so)—both began to annoy me, so I turned them off.

As the countryside closed in again, I could feel the solitude start to eat away at my confidence.

4. Don't try to find yourself. You may not like the company.

This should have been a prime moment for an epiphany—not

---

103 Much of rural France now shops at Walmart-like hypermarkets, particularly Carrefour, leaving the towns with less and less local commercial activity. The numbers of boulangeries, for instance, keep falling by 1,200 every year, according to government statistics. I may have also just missed the lunch hour; things often still close in the afternoon down south.

quite the road to Damascus, maybe, but the on-ramp to the road to Damascus. If I had taken a fasting lesson from my friend the Austrian hunger artist, I might have been in better shape. Instead, I just kept feeling grimmer. All I learned about myself was that I was tired, I missed my family, and I wanted to eat. Mostly, I wanted to eat.

5. Walk your own walk.

Some people like to walk quickly. Cybèle, for instance, is a speed demon. I used to joke that I didn't know when I was going to die, but I did know how and where: right in the middle of the intersection after the light had changed, with Cybèle on the curb ahead of me, looking back. I, on the other hand, am a natural-born ambler, which is why the decision I made now to start walking quickly was a mistake. In the end, the next three or four hours at a double-time pace probably didn't save much time, put me in an even fouler mood, and began to cramp my ankles.

6. Stop while you can still move.

I kept up the pace even when I went through another village, where for the first time in six hours, I saw live human beings.

Two pilgrims sat drinking beer on plastic lawn chairs at a little table in front of their gîte. Neither acknowledged me, and I felt annoyed, *bon* or *buen camino* being a standard and universal greeting.[104] Even an hour before, I would have stopped anyway and asked them where they'd gotten their beer, but by this time I had worked myself into a hypnotic fury, the kind I fall into occasionally if I have been driving for 10 hours or trying to finish some monstrously long report overnight, a fugue state where everything fades but the horizon and the horizon may be either where the pavement meets the sky or the beige of the desk meets the beige of the wall.

---

104 It is a lucky thing I don't live in the times when people felt obliged to duel at every imagined slight; I would have been long gone by now. But to be fair to my fellow pilgrims, I may not have been in the right kind of shape to acknowledge. I remember noticing in my 20s, on my first trip to Europe, that if you are by yourself too long you start to become invisible. The only people who can see you are dogs and children—and today, even they might have shied away, sensing that there was something off about the Pilgrim of the Woeful Countenance.

Not stopping was another mistake. One of the few smart things we did on the Camino was to take our shoes off for a few minutes every two hours. This tended to help keep the blisters away.[105]

Instead, I walked through the rest of the village until I reached a fountain in the nearly empty town green. As I filled my water bottle, I looked around. There was a lot of space between the buildings, which made the green feel more like a New England hamlet than a French village. One family was carrying boxes from their car into a church, either for a reception or a rummage sale. Everything else was still. A golden light had started to fall that I would have appreciated ordinarily but reminded me now that if I wasn't careful I might end up walking in the dark.

At the end of the square, the Way forked. The path nearer to me, the *chemin* proper, went off into the woods. The sign at the trailhead said 10 km to Cajarc. while 40 meters further down the road, the highway sign said 6 km to Cajarc. Earlier in the day, I might have stuck to the trail, but worried about ending up lost in the woods in the dark, I took the road more traveled by.

My thoughts grew grimmer still as I headed up a steep and winding highway into a fir valley. To stay off the narrow highway, I walked on top of a high gravel berm that separated the road from the valley below. The berm was flat on top and the angle below not steep enough to be frightening. I worried more about falling in front of a truck. I had worn trifocals for a few years now and the aquarium view from the lower, reading-third of the lenses sometimes added a little drama to uneven surfaces, particularly in fading light.

Another two kilometers up the long twisting highway, I saw a sign for the Cajarc dump, and began to breathe more easily, especially after an older man out for an evening bicycle ride whizzed past me. I thought about asking him how far we were from Cajarc, but just by being there, he had answered my question: people out exercising, walking dogs, or pushing strollers

---

105   On a hot day, I would even change my socks at the same time, as a special treat. I recommend it.

were usually a sign that the next town wasn't too far away. Seeing them always made me as happy as a sailor who sees a shorebird land on his rigging.

7. Always stick together.

Just after the sun had set, and after the two wrong turns I almost always make when I arrive in a town alone, I arrived at our gîte.

The gîte had a hedge and a picket fence around it and I remember that it looked unusually welcoming.[106] Home! I had finished my column, I had finished my walk, and through the window, I could see the kitchen, where Cybèle and the girls had *not* finished eating! And in fact, had just set five places on one of two red-checked oilcloth tables. Thea was cooking scrambled eggs. My lovely wife had set out a bottle of wine.

I don't think I had ever been quite as glad to see them.

After dinner, when I had begun to feel more or less human again, we talked to the big blond Irish guy we had met the other day, who was eating yet another plate of boiled potatoes. Patrick was an English teacher in a little school not far from Cork. He had walked the Spanish Camino from Saint-Jean-Pied-de-Port to Santiago the summer before and was back to do the French leg this year. The two were very different, he said. The scenery on the French part he liked better, but the Spanish Camino he found livelier and friendlier. He wore silver duct tape in patches on his feet, which paired with his buzz cut gave him the look of a sunburned android. He said the tape worked better than the expensive blister bandages everyone else used.

---

106   At least in my memory, it does. On the other hand, the light looks suspiciously like the light in my grandparents' backyard and the gîte like a house on a movie backlot. Not only is hunger a good sauce but for me at least it also has certain hallucinogenic properties.

July 21. Cajarc to Limogne en Quercy, 18 km

"And yes, it was very dangerous."

The next morning, Charlotte's stomach was upset, so she drank cocoa instead of her usual coffee. On the bright side, the antibiotics had kicked in and her eye looked a lot better.

I was not feeling tip-top myself. My stomach was fine, but the back of my right ankle couldn't hold much weight—I felt like I had been interrogated all night but never squealed.

Before we left town, we passed a wooden chainsaw sculpture of a funny-looking guy in a yellow shirt and blue overalls. This turned out to be Coluche, a comedian who wrote his most famous sketch, Le Schmilblic, at a café here.

Coluche's Schmilblic is a 70s parody of a 60s game show of the same name. You can find both programs on Youtube. Neither seems too funny to me, but present mirth hath present laughter, as Shakespeare says. In the original program, a host live from Paris asks people in rural France to define a mysterious object, the Schmilblic. The takeoff features Coluche pretending to be nine different people trying to answer the same question. In both the original and the parody, the contestants fumble through an answer and eventually the very superior host tells them they're wrong. Ha ha ha.

In each version, the humor is all about class—plain-speaking outsiders who don't want to admit they don't understand a word versus a snobby insider who makes fun of them for falling for the trick. Of course, as an extreme outsider, it is possible I missed the point. Or maybe I don't like it because, as Groucho Marx used to say, I resemble that remark.

The 60s program in turn was based on an even earlier comedy routine from the 50s, also called the Schmilblick, but spelled with a K, for some reason. This original sketch I liked more—it's an impenetrable, deadpan lecture by a comedian named Pierre Dac recounting the invention of an imaginary device in equally imaginary technical terms, the punchline being the occasionally comprehensible sentence "And yes, yes, it was very dangerous."

Despite our collective shakiness, we had left town early enough that the air was still brisk. Cajarc is a village of about a thousand people nestled in a valley of reddish cliffs that the Lot has cut over time. We were getting into a drier part of France now, and you could see it in those cliffs and the lighter green vegetation. The girls said the country reminded them of central Oregon, an association that led to a few collective sighs as they thought of grandma's pancakes, long lazy days at grandpa and grandma's house in Sunriver, and thrift store-shopping in Bend with Aunt Molly.

Françoise Sagan, the writer who put Cajarc on the French cultural map two decades before Coluche, wrote that the countryside near Cajarc offered the "fantastic and reassuring impression that France is empty." But although she could rhapsodize about the land—the hot dry Causses range, ruined villages, and shepherds and shepherdesses whose faces have turned "the color of the stone, because of solitude," she didn't write much about it. "It is very dangerous to speak of one's native country because it corresponds to one's childhood," she explained, "and writers are generally moved to tears by remembering themselves as children."

Instead, Sagan wrote books that one critic scorned as "luxury hotel existentialism," but she had no regrets. "It would be bad form for me to describe people I don't know and don't understand," she once told an interviewer. "Think about it. Whisky, Ferraris and gambling; aren't they rather more amusing than knitting, housekeeping and one's savings?...Anyway, I would have been the last person to have written convincingly about that."[107]

That the Cajarcois still claim credit for Sagan might seem extreme because the *enfant terrible* and her family moved away in 1940, when she was five, but you can't blame them for trying. After all, before Sagan, the last time a celebrity had taken any

---

107 Inadvertantly, however, her stories of bad behavior may have convinced a lot of girls to stick to their knitting, as it were. Masha says "she never makes those things sound like all that much fun. She's good at being glamorously bored."

notice of Cajarc was in 1623, when Cardinal Richelieu had the city walls torn down during the religious wars to make it harder for the Protestant town to defend itself.

Françoise Sagan

Plus, Sagan (the nom de plume of Françoise Quoirez[108]) really did do her best for Cajarc. Unlike the standard American biography where a small hometown is traditionally just the launch pad to glory (how often does Bill Clinton get back to "a town called Hope"?), many French families never leave their village entirely behind. In Paris, at least, people often maintain a dual allegiance between city and country—an intense love-hate relationship with their arrondissement and the small circle of friends they have known since kindergarten, and a more sentimental connection with a little town or even a particular house their family has visited every summer all their lives, maybe even for generations, and love in a way that is surprisingly whole-hearted and unironic. Even a tough-minded New Waver like Sagan, who might turn

108   True to her milieu, she named herself after a Proust character, the Princesse de Sagan.

on God, the Church, and her class, always stayed true to her old summer place. In Paris, Sagan might be "a charming little monster," as François Mauriac called her— the pop star novelist who published *Bonjour, Tristesse* at 18 and by her 20s was as famous and controversial as her friend Brigitte Bardot.[109] But in Cajarc, she remained skinny, little "Kiki" Quoirez. As she later wrote, "I come back from time to time and I am always the granddaughter of Mme Laubard—`you know, the one who writes books.'"

Sagan and her siblings didn't just favor Cajarc with an occasional visit—they were almost a one-family chamber of commerce. Her older sister, Suzanne Quoirez, who married one of the cofounders of the Carrefour hypermarket chain, was a close friend of Claude Pompidou, the wife of the rising politician Georges Pompidou, and took Mme Pompidou on a trip to Cajarc in 1960. Mme Pompidou loved it so much that she persuaded her husband to buy a house there, and he often visited the place during his premiership under de Gaulle and his own presidency afterward.[110] More impressive still perhaps, given that politicians always love to have a house in the country, was their brother Jacques's coup in convincing another Claude—this one, Paris's most notorious madame—to buy a converted sheepfold in Cajarc as a sort of

Hallo, Cajarc?

109 The title of her novel is from a Paul Éluard poem, the poet we met in the Saint-Albans hospital. The yarn on my crazy board is going to turn into a blanket soon.

110 Sagan took her friend Francois Mitterrand on a similar visit at one point in the 70s but didn't make a sale. This wasn't his last rendezvous with an occasional Cajarcois, however: in 1980, Coluche, the comedian with the Schmilbec sketch, made a run for president. This started out as a joke until a poll showed that he was supported by 16% of potential voters, after which Mitterand and others in the political establishment saw him as a rival and eventually pressured him to withdraw.

country retreat for her "Gazelles."[111] [112]

It's probably unfortunate Sagan didn't spend more time in Cajarc. Being young, rich, and famous as a rock star didn't really agree with her. Robert Hughes, the art critic, says in his memoirs that when he met her in 1972, she was 37 but already looked like someone in her 50s. Although her books sold 30 million copies altogether, she ran through all her royalties, and had to depend on the generosity of her friends the last few years of her life.

Considering the level of self-abuse she put herself through, however, she was quite durable. As Sagan's son once told a reporter, for someone who'd received last rites three times, she had incredible health. Despite the drinking, drugs (she spent some time in jail in the early 90s for cocaine possession), and a few high-speed car accidents, she made it to 69. In 2004, she died of a stroke in her home in Honfleur, Normandy. In accordance with her wishes, she was buried in Cajarc, near her parents and grandparents; her brother Jacques; her second husband, the gay

---

111 Jacques Quoirez was "[a charming, Falstaffian ne'er do well, a PR man, a fancier of cars – at one point he owned a spectacularly fast and handsome custom Lamborghini – and episodically, a pimp," at least according to Robert Hughes.

112 Quoirez was also a writer. Among other things, he ghostwrote Madame Claude's memoirs. Their book, *Allo, Oui*, starts out fairly well:

> *The telephone rings. I pick it up and I say, "hello, yes." I say "Hello, yes" because my name is Madame Claude and I have the habit – and now almost the obligation– to say yes to the men in agonies who telephone me.*
>
> *...It is not so disagreeable, nor easy, to be "Madame Claude."*

Madame Claude's rise to fame began right after the war. Maisons Close had been legal since Napoleon and flourished during the Occupation, but in 1945 in Paris and then in 1946 in France generally, legislators shut them all down. Maybe this was simply revenge for the good times prostitutes had enjoyed during the Occupation, but a writer for the satirical paper Le Canard Enchaîné saw it as a dodge by politicians to avoid dealing with more urgent matters: "There is no electricity. There is no coal. There is no wine. There are no potatoes and the disaster victims are without shelter ... Fleeing these depressing times, the Parisian municipal councilors devoted two long meetings to the removal of brothels."

But Fernande Grudent, "Madame Claude," was a pragmatic woman ("There are only two things people will always pay for," she later recalled, "and I couldn't cook."), who saw an opportunity. Necessity being the procurer of invention, she invented the call service. Instead of real estate, she invested more in her personnel—her "Gazelles"—mostly actresses who were beautiful but hadn't quite made it in the movies. From the 1950s to the early 1970s, her agency served several generations of high-flying playboys, from Jack Kennedy to Muammar Gaddafi.

Except for a few extended run-ins with the law, Madame Claude had a long and successful career, and died in Nice in 2015, aged 92.

American sculptor Robert Westhoff; and Peggy Roche, her partner of 20 years and a stylist for *Elle*.

An hour or so out of town, we passed a self-service coffee stand on the trail that included a bulletin board with photocopied pictures and descriptions of the town's most notable bridges, minerals, and people, including a scotch-taped picture of the young Françoise Sagan in full bloom.

We reached Limogne early, at around 12, but our free afternoon was less fun than we had hoped—one of those times when we felt less like a family out on an adventure than a band of unhappy hobos thrown together by unfortunate circumstances. Charlotte wrote:

> *We went to our gîte and bought food for dinner – Thea and I are going to make Mexican food. We got this cool soap that comes in sheets. We washed all the laundry downstairs. Mom and Masha had a fight because Masha refused to hang up the laundry.*

After the girls finished hanging up the laundry behind the gîte, where Cybèle hoped it would snap dry in the cold wind, they decided to go for a swim in the town pool. On the way, they looked for a new camera charger at the hardware store to replace one Cybèle had lost, but didn't find the right one, *"and I had to spend 20 minutes explaining to Mom why the adapter [they found] wouldn't work for her camera charger,"* Charlotte wrote. [113]

The swim didn't work out either. *"We went to the pool and that was nice but the wind was cold so we showered and left,"* Charlotte wrote.

---

113   Keeping track of everything when you have to pack and unpack every day isn't easy, and we often lost things. Most of the time, these were easily replaced incidentals—toiletries, for instance, which we lost so often that Cybèle now refused to pay more than two euros for a bottle of shampoo—but this latest material casualty had turned out to be a bit more trouble.

I had a better afternoon than they did, but not much better. Our gîte had once been either a town hall or a school, and although the rooms had high ceilings and big windows, the place felt sad and neglected.

Dinner was unpleasant too. An elderly Australian couple huffed abruptly out of the kitchen as soon as we walked in, which put me in a foul mood and made me want to reach for my cutlass. *You thumb your nose at me, sirrah?* The meal wasn't too successful either: Thea and Charlotte's dinner project hadn't gone very well. Limogne may be the truffle capital of France, but it's not a great place to shop if you want to cook Tex-Mex, particularly if you have to cook your not-quite-right ingredients on a half-broken stove. *"Thea insisted on making the guacamole and the rice wouldn't cook so we had bland guacamole, goopy rice, undrained beans from a can and lemon pork,"* wrote Charlotte. *"For dessert we all had peaches."* Thea didn't mind so much but Charlotte was furious. She likes her food plus she's a bit of a perfectionist, so a failed dinner in which she was implicated constituted a double slap.

After dinner it began to rain hard, and the harsh fluorescent tubes that lit the room coated the place with a horrible bluish light, like liquid homesickness.

The only good part of the evening was a chat Cybèle and I had with a woman from Toulouse during our after-dinner tea. She was in her 40s and had left her children and husband for the weekend. She wore her hair in a sensible corporate bob, had the posture of a star yoga student, and an unusually sunny temper. All in all, she didn't belong in this movie. What in the world would she be doing in this sad village, in a ratty, unhappy gîte, with a grumpy American family and a pair of even grumpier Australian retirees?

Spelunking, it turned out. Every few months, she liked to go off with a group of fellow enthusiasts and explore caves. Tomorrow, very early, she would meet her group and down they'd go.

Later, tucked in my bunk and listening to the rain, I wondered a bit about why you would pick spelunking as a hobby. Why would you volunteer to spend your free time crawling around in pitch dark, damp, and cold? And do it more than once? But then again, you could argue that spending your summer marching halfway across Europe, camping out in dank old school rooms, wasn't a terribly rational use of leisure time either. Pascal says somewhere that most of our troubles can be traced to Man being unable to sit quietly in his room. I think he may have a point.

July 22. Limogne-en-Quercy to Mas-de-Vers, 19.7 km

In which the dreary country makes some of us happy to have headphones.

In the morning, we had a quick breakfast and left around 8:30, glad to put Limogne behind us.

Now that we were on our own, I started listening to *Don Quixote* more often, and the girls plugged themselves in more too. Charlotte was listening to Asimov's I, Robot, while Masha had finished *Treasure Island* and now moved on to Dickens's *Dombey and Son*.

Few people were as wired as we were. The pilgrims we met were an electronically ascetic bunch, particularly in France. Some people listened to music, but often with peculiar proscriptions. Our Irish friend, for instance, said he never listened until after 11 in the morning. No one we met listened to books. We earned a few dirty looks because of our gadgetry—*quelle américain!*—but I have since learned that people always used to sing in groups as they walked the Camino, and that there is even a body of music that came out of the pilgrimage, facts that have made me feel somewhat vindicated.[114]

Other members of the family were better than I was at coming up with nonelectronic strategies to distract themselves from the walk. On hot days, Thea would look for sprinklers and wait until the water came sweeping by and soaked her. Masha would stop and pick blackberries, something she liked to do so much that she would slow the rest of us down, and Cybèle would tell her to quit.

But outside of Dickens and berries, at that moment, Masha was

---

114   There are even pre-modern precedents for my bad habit: I seem to remember Montaigne liked to read in the saddle. I also remember reading about a Renaissance Italian who had committed 400 books to memory —I suppose using the memory palace technique— who passed the time on his pilgrimage to Santiago working his way through his library, but my memory palace being more like a memory mobile home with a leaky roof, I haven't been able to find the references about these supposed facts anywhere.

not having a very good time, at least not that day:

> *I can't seem to get used to hiking. I absolutely hate everything about it. My back hurts because of the heavy pack. I have to scrape my straggles of hair back in a stupid bun. I have to wear awful ugly clothes all the time, and I'm always sweaty and sunburnt and my legs are covered with heat rash. I feel as if my legs are always on the point of giving out, and most of the time I am crying or very close to it…I feel as though mom and dad are testing us; seeing what we can go through before we give out altogether. I'm praying that we will stop in Pamplona.[115]*

We arrived at our next destination at around three. Compared to the night before, it seemed like gîte heaven—an old brick farmhouse framed by trees and flowers, way out in the country. The proprietor, an older lady, invited us to sit down and help ourselves to a drink—she had set out a few snacks, a pitcher of cold water, lemonade, and various Kool-Aidy syrups to mix with the water (a French alternative to soda pop that's probably dying out now because it's too economical). The lemonade was sweet and artificial, but I was thirsty enough that I enjoyed it immensely. While we waited for our hostess to check us in, Charlotte sat at a picnic table and wrote about the two donkeys in a paddock next to the house. *"One he-haws really loudly every time someone goes by. The loud one is white, the other one is grey. There is also a white Lab-*

rador here. She is really sweet. I finished the dried fruit and pretzels, but I am still starving. I hope dinner is good and involves meat, cheese, and potatoes."

Once we brought our packs inside, our prospects looked even brighter. We passed through a narrow, cluttered old kitchen and dining room and into a new addition that stretched out behind the former back door of the house, a multilevel glass and wood extravagan-

---

115 Masha's diary breaks off a few lines after this entry, but she kept writing — schedules outlining how she was going to excel at boarding school, which extracurriculars she would join, a page of poetry terms, and notes about a thriller involving "a strawberry blonde 3 year old, who wears ruby slippers and a Tarzan Jane costume. She has a plastic tiara with a fake sapphire. She is a gutsy, sturdy little thing with a critical mouth and an attractive imagination."

za. The Starship IKEA had a huge high-ceilinged kitchen, dining room, and lounge, and then stairs that led up to new bunkrooms behind. So far, so great.

But it didn't last. First, the Wi-Fi didn't reach our rooms. Tick one. Not a big deal, but a bit of a hassle for me. Then at around five o'clock, a younger woman took over from the nice old lady and made an announcement. Usually, this gîte served dinner, but tonight, we aren't, she said, without further explanation. Instead, they were offering a big can of cassoulet (a rich baked bean and duck stew that I adore but the rest of the family doesn't), and a share of a head of lettuce for eight euros a person. Tick two.

I would have thought people would be upset to pay eight euros for a partial interest in a can of beans and a fistful of salad, but most of the other pilgrims took the news in stride. Some of them even seemed to enjoy putting their own dinners together. One distinguished-looking older guy, a ripe pear of a man who might have been Jacques Chirac's younger brother, even put on an apron and poured the big can into a pot with a certain panache, as if he were actually cooking.

The older Australian couple we had met the night before were with us again that evening and the man was annoyed again, this time not because of us but because he was a vegetarian and cassoulet contains both duck and sausage. However, he was partially placated when he learned that jugs of wine were part of the ration. Fortunately, Cybèle had thought dinner might be a problem tonight, and picked up some spaghetti and salad along the way that day, so she gave them some of our surplus.[116] It wasn't a bad meal in the end but after all our jolly feasting of the past week, felt very mingy. We went to bed early again.

---

116   They helped us too: his camera happened to use the same charger as Cybèle, so she was able to get enough power to make it to Cahors, the next big town, where we could find a real camera store.

July 23. Mas-de-Vers to Cahors, 18.9 km

An account of how voodoo made Cahors the cheap wine capital of France.

Before we turned out the lights, Cybèle, Charlotte, and Thea made a pact to leave by seven so they could reach Cahors by lunchtime.

Charlotte was keen now on early starts. Although she generally hated mornings, she hated hiking more. If she had to walk, she wanted to get the misery out of the way as quickly as possible.

The next morning all five of us set off together at 7:30, but by 9 o'clock, the three speedwalkers had taken the lead and left Masha and me in the dust. My shins were getting worse—not enough that I couldn't walk, but enough to get my attention, as my grandfather used to say.

"Fair Cordelia," I said, limping along.

Not that her sticking with me had much to do with filial piety— like me, Masha is seldom in a hurry. My pace also had the added benefit of giving her more time to graze for blackberries, which were ripe and perfect on that leg of the trail. And so we ambled along all morning. Between my staggered steps and her berry addiction we must have looked like trained bears who had lost our circus.

Although I wasn't moving very fast, I was looking forward to our next stop. Cahors would be our first real town since Figeac, and with 19,000 people, the biggest we had seen since Le Puy-en-Velay. I also had high hopes for intemperate reasons: when we first moved to Paris, Hervé, my wine man, once pointed the town out to me on his map. In the Middle Ages, Cahors had a great reputation—Eleanor of Aquitaine and Henry Plantagenet served "the Black Wine of the Lot" at their wedding— but these days, much of the output has a certain Chateau Robitussin quality: dark, purplish, and often bitter. It is, however, delightfully economical. In Paris, I generally found it on the bottom shelf at the supermarché between the boxes and plastic barrels. If you pay more than three euros for a bottle, you're being robbed.

A little before lunch, our path joined a narrow two-lane highway. We could see the Lot at the bottom of the hill as it made a great green curve around the town of Cahors, most of which was squeezed in a horseshoe on the far side of the river. A string of pennants lined the length of the short modern bridge, and made our entrance feel a little festive.

At first glance, Cahors didn't look like a cheap wine capital. The main street had the usual sparkling sidewalk cafes and stately municipal buildings that always inspire confidence in French civilization. A quirky art installation added a little esprit too: all along the boulevard, an artist had knitted long, multicolored muffs for the lampposts and plane trees.[117] Nor did my opinion change after we found Cybèle and the sisters, made our tour of the town's cathedral—a spectacular building with multiple, mosque-like domes, which some scholars say was built by a bishop who had admired the buildings he saw on a crusade in the Holy Land—and treated ourselves to lunch at one of those bright

A tree muff grows in Cahors.

---

117   Actually, no! While trying to track down the name of this artist, I learned her name is Legion. The besweatered trees and poles were a local manifestation of yarn-bombing, which Wikipedia defines as "a type of graffiti or street art that employs colourful displays of knitted or crocheted yarn or fibre rather than paint or chalk. It is also called yarnstorming, guerrilla knitting, kniffiti, urban knitting, or graffiti knitting." Some critics have seen it as a kind of feminist graffiti.

A shopowner in Houston named Magda Sayeg is sometimes credited with being the mother of the movement. In 2005, Sayeg knitted a lavender cosy for the door handle to her shop because she wanted "to see something warm and fuzzy and human-like on the cold gray steel façade that I looked at every day," she recalled in a 2015 TED talk. The reaction was so strong that as an experiment, she knit a warmer for a nearby stop sign pole. People loved that even more, and she kept at it. "At this point, I'm smitten, I'm hooked ..." she said. Her work inspired groups of yarn-bombers in many different places, and gave Sayeg—a former math major who says she doesn't really know much about knitting—a career as a textile artist.

Today, the accidental artist travels the world making large-scale knit installations. She takes commissions, by the way. If you need a double-decker bus cosy, for instance, you might give her a call.

cafes, where I ordered my favorite salad.[118]

But then we set out to find our hostel, and discovered right off the shiny main street a sadder town of empty storefronts, alleys fogged with dust, and an unusual concentration of red-faced bums.[119]

It wasn't always this way. From the 1100s to the 1300s, a lot of the wine drunk in England was made in Cahors, shipped down the Lot to Bordeaux, and then exported. Over time—as happened in other towns with successful industries, such as wool cloth (in Florence)—Cahors families invested their profits in moneylending, and between wine and finance, they became rich. A century before, Matthew Paris, a Benedictine monk who lived in Saint Albans Abbey in Hertfordshire, wrote, "there was hardly anyone in all England, especially among the bishops, who was not caught in [the Cahorins'] net. Even the king himself was held indebted to them in an incalculable sum of money."[120]

Cahors today is just one more dusty town in south-central France but in the later Middle Ages, this lending business made Cahors a central square on the European chessboard, a place infamous enough that Dante in the *Inferno* paired Cahors with Sodom; influential enough that in 1316, the son of one of the city's leading families was elected pope; and desirable enough that a few

---

118   A *chevre au chaud*, a green salad with goat cheese toasties on top that is almost always good.

119   I often find French rural poverty more shocking than the American variety, in part because French towns tend to try harder to look their best, with flowerpots hanging from every main street lamppost and a lot of public art. The gap between those pretty main streets and the dusty back alleys can feel unsettling, almost embarrassing—like in a city when a well-dressed woman stops you on the sidewalk, you think to ask for directions, but then you notice her slathered lipstick and realize she is homeless and wants to bum a cigarette. France may be a wealthy country but there are still plenty of people who earn next to nothing, particularly in the suburbs and the country. In 2015, around 14 percent of the French lived below the poverty line, less than EUR 954 a month. That's not as bad as it would be in the United States, particularly if you live in a town where you can get around without a car and don't live in fear of being bankrupted by an ill-timed illness. Still, it's not a lot of money.

120   The Church was officially against usury, reasoning that usurers were profiting on time, and only God could make time. But this proscription doesn't seem to have slowed down the Cahorsins much. Instead of charging interest, they would simply make a loan in which the principal to be paid back was much greater than the amount paid out, "pretending not to know that whatever is added to the principal is usury, under whatever name it may be called," according to Paris.

months later, the bishop of Cahors tried to cast a fatal spell on that pope rather than let him take away the bishop's diocese.

For someone who likes inspiring sagas with clear morals, the story of how Jacques Deuze became the most powerful pope of the 14th century may not be for you. On the other hand, if like me you have a weakness for stories about little guys who over-come their scruples to outfox their enemies, you can do worse than Deuze's transformation from a violence-averse canon law-yer to the feared and formidable John XXII.

In Deuze's time, the divisions between church, state, and busi-ness were not at all clear. Not only was the pope the direct ruler of about one-third of Italy, but Catholic clergy ran a number of cities and towns all over Europe. Salzburg was run by a bishop; Quedlinburg in Germany was always run by an abbess; Le Puy-en-Velay was bishop-ruled; and in Cahors, the bishop had also always been the prince of the city. And often not just in an hon-orific sense, like being Lord Mayor: in Cahors, for example, one of the bishop's privileges was that he could leave his armor and his sword on the altar when he officiated at Mass.

Getting and keeping a post in the church was likewise a more rough-and-tumble affair than it is now. From a parish to a car-dinalate, posts were often bought and sold or simply given to well-connected friends and relatives. And in the 13th and 14th centuries, the election of a pope tended to be a bit like the story of Michael Corleone being elected Godfather, but with brighter clothes and fewer Italians.

Kings and other nobles often had a voice in the selection—and sometimes de-selection. In the years leading up to Jacques Deuze's papacy, Philip the Fair, the king of France, had one and possibly two popes murdered, and after their deaths, their suc-cessors had considered it prudent to take the French court's wishes very seriously.[121]

---

121   Understandably enough: in addition to his antipapal streak, Philip the Fair (fair as in good-looking -le Bel - not as in just) had crushed the Knights Templar, as noted earlier. He also does not seem to have believed in what we would call now a propor-tionate response. In 1314, for example, he had two brothers who were allegedly lovers of his daughters-in-law skinned alive, castrated, and then beheaded.

Philip's push against papal power began in 1296. After Philip had tried to tax the French clergy and abolish some of their privileges, Pope Boniface VIII asserted that not only had the king no right to do that, but come to think of it, the king should recognize the pope as *his* superior.

Philip disagreed. In 1303, after years of wrangling over who was *capo a capo*, Philip's henchmen accosted the 72-year-old Boniface in Rome and beat him so severely that he died of his injuries a month later. Benedict XI, the next pope, tried to make peace with Philip but failed. Benedict had a reputation as a very good, holy man—he was eventually canonized—but running the Church apparently required other qualities. He died under mysterious circumstances less than a year after his election, possibly poisoned.

His successor, Clement V, was a Gascon, who took more care to stay on the good side of Philip. One of his first decisions was to move the papal court north, near Avignon, in what is now southern France but at that time was part of the Holy Roman Empire.

Although Clement had more savvy, or at least more luck—his papacy lasted until 1314, when he died after a long but apparently natural illness—papal politics remained a risky business. The cardinals' next conclave was interrupted by Raimond of Budos, a nephew of the late pope, who arrived at the gates of the pope's residence about 20 kilometers outside of Avignon, at the head of an armed band that shouted, "Death to the Italian cardinals! We want a pope"—by which they meant "we Gascons."[122]

To underscore his point, Raimond and his thugs massacred a number of Italian clerics and bankers and pillaged the Italian cardinals' apartments. The cardinals didn't fulfill his request but

---

122   As this attack suggests, borders were much more loosely drawn at that time, and tended to be more like gang boundaries or sales territories than what we would think of as hard frontiers. Most of southern France, including Cahors, was not really part of France as we think of France today, but a hodgepodge of ill-defined duchies and kingdoms, some straddling the Pyrenees. This doesn't mean there were no disputes. One historian describes the region as a place "where the sheep were led and not driven, as even the straying of a flock on to another's territory could be the signal for outright warfare."

fled and refused to deliberate for the next two years. They only changed their minds in 1316, when the new French king, Philip the Tall (Philip V), the son of Philip the Fair, lured the cardinals to a palace in Lyon with promises that he wouldn't hurt them, then promptly locked them up, and planned to keep them there until the Italian, Provencal, and Gascon factions elected a suitable candidate.

They found a good compromise in Jacques Dèuze. The bishop of Avignon and cardinal of Porto, Dèuze had a good record as a diplomat, which was useful because the pope had his earthly Italian kingdom to worry about and faced nearly constant threats to its sovereignty. He was from Cahors, one of the financial centers of the world, and related to an important banking family, which could also be useful, because the wars and ecclesiastical skimming meant the Church was nearly always broke. And he had a reputation as a man of peace in an era when popes regularly took up arms against their fellow monarchs, a trait that Philip the Tall would have seen as a plus.[123] Best of all, at least from the point of view of the younger cardinals, he didn't look like he would last very long: he was 72, 5 feet tall, and appeared to be quite frail. (But only appeared that way: after Dèuze became John XXII, people noted that he had much more spring in his step than during the conclave. Some historians have speculated that he may have lied about his age.)

Like Michael Corleone, John XXII's first move was to settle his family business. In short order, he made five nephews cardinals and a few more nephews bishops. He named his brother Pierre the Viscount of Caraman, a southern territory not far from Toulouse, and gave him 60,000 gold florins (a lot of money at the time—the entire papal court of Avignon cost 48,000 a year to maintain). One nephew too stupid to be trusted with anything important John reportedly made his mustard-maker, which the Larousse Encyclopedia claims inspired the French saying, *Il se*

---

123 For the times, Dèuze was very squeamish about violence. Earlier in his career, when he was chancellor to King Charles of Naples, he persuaded the king to ban the bloody gladiatorial fights that were popular with every class of Neapolitan. Nor did he change in office: when he became pope and heard that the Neapolitans had started the fights up again, he excommunicated both players and spectators.

John XXII (from a detail of a painting by Pietro Lorenzetti)

prend pour le moutardier du pape (he takes himself to be the pope's mustard-maker), a phrase used to describe someone who is both arrogant and dense.

Whether for reasons of self-defense or family loyalty, even by the liberal standards of the day, John was an over-achiever when it came to nepotism. One historian, John Wealand, has compiled a five-page table of all the relatives the new pope appointed to one or another job, which he says is only a partial list. "The extent of the patronage of John XXII was so vast that it would be impossible to include all of the known relatives in a table of this kind. If one attempts to trace also the patronage extended to friends, the task becomes insurmountable..."

Of course, bringing so many friends and family into the Church hierarchy entailed some changes of personnel. Typically, the pope would have his prosecutors accuse the cardinal or the bishop whose mitre he required with a potpourri of real or fictitious crimes. This generally inspired the accused to retire quickly to a monastery or some other inconspicuous corner. But not always: when his turn in the docket came up, Hugues Géraud, bishop of Cahors, decided to fight back.[124]

Removing Géraud began in the conventional way, with a corruption charge that stemmed from his not paying the 3,000 or so guilders he still owed the papacy for his bishopric. (I get the

---

124   An outsider from Périgueux brought in by Pope Clement to set the diocese in order, Géraud had been given (or rather, suckered into buying) the bishopric of Cahors. The role included the nearly impossible job of governing a group of powerful families who didn't want to be governed, and trying to collect rents from tenants who had gotten out of the habit of paying their rent. Making the situation still more difficult, a prior bishop had tried to improve the diocese's finances by selling a half-interest in the city to the king of France, and Philip the Tall wasn't a happy shareholder. One of John's first messages from the king after he became pope was a request that he find a way to wrap up a lawsuit between the city council and Bishop Géraud that Philip worried might interfere with the old power-sharing agreement.

impression selling offices was somehow not considered a sin if you didn't pocket the money.)[125]

Even after his conviction, Géraud would not take the hint. Instead, he had a truly terrible idea about what to do with the troublesome pope. He had concluded, as Edmond Albe put it in his 1904 book about the Géraud case, that "[i]f the pope died, everything was saved." And maybe better than saved: many of Géraud's friends, some from Clement V's entourage who had also been displaced by John's people, would owe him a favor.[126]

In March 1317, papal police arrested two men from Toulouse in a tavern in Avignon who were caught carrying a tube of white powder and three hollowed-out loaves of bread, each of which contained a wax figure. The wax figures represented two cardinals and the pope, complete with tiny mitres. The men confessed to their role in a plot to hex and poison the pope, and before long, the papal police rounded up a group of conspirators that included members of Clement V's family, the de Gots (whom John was fighting to get back treasures he claimed they had stolen from the Church), assorted clergy in Toulouse, and Géraud.[127]

If little wax figures in costume sound like voodoo dolls, they should. We think of the voodoo doll as Afro-Caribbean, but this isn't true. Historians say it's actually a weird white people thing.

---

125 The bishop may have been short of cash because the crops had failed for two years in a row. Failed harvests would have made it harder for the priests in his diocese and other tenants to pay him. Credit may have been hard to come by in 1316 too; wine in those pre-glass, pre-cork days had to be drunk within a year, and two failed vintages in succession would have cut deep into the merchant families' cash flows. These were seriously hard times, lean enough that some Cahorsins reportedly turned to cannibalism. And more was still to come: 1316 was just the second of seven years of miserable weather and failed crops known as the Great Famine. a continent-wide scourge that may have killed 10–15 percent of Europe's population.

126 The book has a great title. In English, it would be translated as *Hugues Géraud, Bishop of Cahors: The affair of the poisons and enchantments of 1317*.

127 The testimony was fairly imaginative. The conspirators said that they concocted the powder from toads, lizard, rats' tails, and spiders. They also added flesh from the leg of a recently executed man along with some of his hair and nails, the rope that had been used to hang him, and the tail of a dead dog. On Good Friday, they took each figure, baptized it, and sealed it in a single piece of parchment. The one for John bore the Latin inscription Papa Johnannes moriatur et non alius (John dies and no one else).

"[T]he type of magic that is most recognizable as what we would term the 'voodoo doll' has its origins in the magical practice of Europe, not that of syncretic religion," writes Nathalie Armitrage in *The Materiality of Magic*. What we think of as voodoo dolls, she writes—wax or cloth figures that people would stick pins in, curse, and torture—have been made in Europe since the Greeks.[128]

The white tube of powder was also bad news for Géraud. Poisoning was considered just about as evil an act as a person could commit—a "very horrible, execrable, damned, unjust, and detestable deed" is how a French parliamentary document of 1474 put it.[129]

The stories the co-conspirators told didn't agree in all particulars, but after a moderate dose of torture they were close enough that prosecutors could point to Géraud as the deeply guilty ringleader. Even this might not have been so bad for him—after all, his minions had been stopped before anybody died— but just as the trial neared its conclusion, someone did. The pope's favorite nephew, the young Cardinal Jacques de Via, whom John had appointed to his old post as bishop of Avignon, dropped dead unexpectedly on June 13.

In the first interrogation by the pope, Géraud repeated what he had already told the inquisitors, blabbering so recklessly that modern historians have concluded he must have been very old,

---

128   Charlemagne tried to ban them; in 968, King Duff of Scotland reportedly broke into a sweat while witches held his waxen image over a fire; and in 928, after Count William II of Angouleme fell mysteriously ill, they later found three clay puppets buried in the ground. Today, deep in the heart of the country, wicked things may still be lurking: in his memoir, Notes from the Cevannes, the novelist Adam Thorpe writes that above a bread oven in an old house in the Cevannes he bought in the 70s, he once found a "legless, naked torso of a svelte 1950s doll, its nipples, navel and temples pierced by tiny nails. I guessed immediately that it was a witchcraft 'poppet', its lids closing creepily over sparkly blue eyes."

129   People considered poisoning a branch of magic, and thought of it as a singularly unnatural, inhuman crime; after all, the Creator had made certain insects and reptiles venomous, but not human beings. Beyond its occult aspects, being generally an assault by the server against the served, poisoning mixed homicide with treachery. The element of surprise also meant the victim didn't have a sporting chance, and made it likelier that he might die without a confession, increasing his odds of being sent to Hell.

very stupid, or very guilty.

Strangely, although the now-ex-bishop had already confessed to all the charges, and the pope, a good canon lawyer himself, thought the inquisitors had done a credible job, John interrogated Géraud six more times personally in July and August, before ordering the defrocked bishop put to death.

Why John went to such lengths is unclear. He may have wanted to confirm something Hugues had blurted under torture. It was common knowledge that you could get people to say anything if you inflicted enough pain, so the Church required an unforced confession before a conviction. (However, this rule had a fairly significant loophole: if the confession were not given freely, the accused would have to submit to another round of torture to refresh his recollection.) Or John may have wanted to make sure they had gotten to the bottom of the conspiracy. Witchcraft was the cyberterror of its day—mysterious, frightening, and increasingly popular—and John may have wanted to take no chances with it.[130]

It occurs to me too that John, still new at his job and maybe still not entirely comfortable with violence, may have spent that wet summer trying to find a reason not to make a decision he felt he had to make.

John was not obliged to execute Géraud—even after being convicted of a fatal poisoning, high-ranking people were sometimes just assigned a serious penance—but getting the ex-bishop out of the way would solve a lot of problems. It would improve John's relationship with Philip the Tall; it would likely be popular with his friends and family back in Cahors, and open a new position, to which he could appoint if not a family member (at this point, there couldn't have been many unemployed Deuzes left), then at least a local.

---

130 Witchcraft evidently worried John. A few months later, he wrote the first papal bull that treated witchcraft not as a superstition, but as a heresy. Previously, the standard theological position had been that only God could create something; the devil could only fool people. His rethinking had some important long-term consequences, the most important being that it set in motion 500 years of witch trials.

Géraud's execution would also probably encourage the resignation of Galhard de Preyssac, the bishop of Toulouse and another Clement V appointee (he had also been implicated in the Géraud plot); keep Clement's family, the Gots, and the whole Gascon faction quiet; and discourage further violence against John and the Deuzes—particularly by such unsavory means as sorcery and poison. Finally, punishing the bishop would reinforce an image of a powerful papacy after years of ugly infighting, which would in turn encourage priests to pay what they owed the Church. Subtract one foolish, loud-mouthed bishop from the ledger and all those other accounts balanced.

At the end of the summer, John finally gave the order.[131]

Whether or not making a public example of the consequences of being a deadbeat priest had been part of the idea of executing Géraud, it seems to have worked. Not too long afterward, the church's financial situation improved.[132] Between a more intimidating collection service, and John's reforms—better bookkeeping, clever sliding-scale formulas for clerical jobs and absolution of sins— Church finances stabilized. [133]

Ironically, John's successes may have made Cahors more powerful in the short run, but inadvertently contributed to the city's decline: a less precarious Church had less need of loans, and now, when he did need one, John turned more often to Italian bankers, which made sense, because most of the Church's wars were in Italy.

---

131   At some point in the first week of September 1317, Géraud may have been first tortured with the traditional punishment of simoniacs (sellers of church offices) of having his hands scalded in boiling water (to burn off the holy oils with which he had been anointed when he became a priest). Next, some accounts say he was skinned alive. Finally, everyone agrees, he was burned at the stake.

132   Clement V had been a shrewd politician—a back-slapper who had a good word for everyone and yet still managed to placate Philip the Fair—but financial acumen wasn't one of his talents. He had started his papacy with 1 million gold florins in the treasury but after wars and money to his relatives, left behind only 70,000 florins when he died.

133   For example, John set clerical office prices so it cost less to become a monk if you had one eye or were missing a few fingers. Different sins demanded different payments too, depending on the circumstance. Absolution for murdering your wife, for example, cost half as much as murdering your wife and getting a dispensation to marry again. John cared about loyalty.

As for John, the fragile old man no one had expected to last more than a year or two ended up being the longest-serving pope of the 14th century. One of the secrets to his longevity may be that like a lot of long-lived people, John maintained a very strict diet. After the attempted poisoning, he is said to have eaten only white food—milk, egg whites, white fish, chicken, and cheese—because it was thought harder to hide poison in white dishes. In any case, it seems to have agreed with him: white food and wariness kept John in the pink through his 90th birthday.

After a bad dinner in our dark but friendly church hostel (salty canned ham, canned green beans, tabouli, and a pink mousse with an unidentifiable flavor for dessert), Thea, Cybèle, and I made a twilight visit to the Pont Valentré. I should have stayed with Masha and Charlotte and rested my feet, but I wanted to see this up close: it's Cahors's most famous piece of architecture, France's last fortified bridge.

The Cahors wine I usually bought had an etching of Pont Valentré on its label, and the bridge is featured on most postcards of the town. The six-span, three-tower structure is beautiful, but melancholy too. It was begun by the city council in 1307, when Cahors was a nearly free city and Cahors merchants, traders and bankers to the world, but completed in 1378, long after the city had been ceded to the English, northern Italy had taken most of Cahors's banking trade, and Bordeaux had poached most of the town's wine business.

Financially stronger kings could raise stronger armies, and their wars hurt Cahors's wine trade, which was the taproot of Cahors's prosperity. As Michael Sanders writes in *Families of the Vine*, "Men absent at war or casualties of the frequent conflicts large and small, rising brigandry along road and river, export markets cut off by rival armies, ports closed by blockade, the destruction and pillaging of villages and towns, famine, disease – all these sent Cahors wine into a steep decline from which it was never to recover."[134]

The Lot ran dark and smooth that evening, and it was quiet enough that I could hear Cybèle and Thea's footsteps and my shuffle on the bridge's sandstone roadbed. Thea spotted a little gargolye of the devil on one of the towers, a touch added by 19th-century restorers. The sculpture alludes to a story that the devil promised to finish the whole bridge in exchange for the

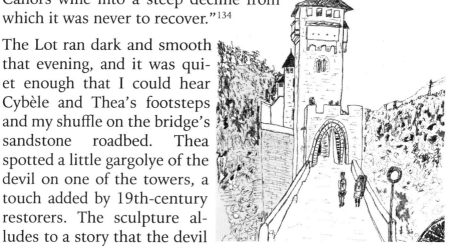

Pont Valentré

master builder's soul, but just before the devil finished the work, in order to prevent him from collecting, the builder designed the tower with a space for one stone that could not be set, leaving the bridge forever incomplete.

The story is apocryphal nonsense, of course, but I think the image does capture a certain truth about various unstable bargains with the devil that lay behind the prosperity of Cahors's great houses and maybe big institutions generally. As Archbishop Paul Marcinkus, the president of the Vatican Bank during its 1980s money-laundering scandal once observed, "You can't run the Church on Hail Marys."

---

134   Unlike wheat or barley fields, which can be burned one year and replanted the next, vineyards take 10 years to mature, and between 1350 and 1450, the Cahorsin vintners didn't have many stretches without mayhem. Bordeaux vintners, in the meantime, had a bit more peace and were able to plant more vines. Although the land was not as good for grapes as Cahors—it's rainier and cooler in Bordeaux—they eventually had more vines and their proximity to the coast made shipping to England much easier. Eventually, British drinkers got used to the lighter Bordeaux claret (a word that comes from clair, that is, clear), and after that, Cahors wines were used principally to give the Bordeaux a bit more punch.

July 24. Cahors to Montcuq, 24 km

In which we meet some heretical pescatarians.

It was a hot morning and we were marching up a long hill in the woods. Cybèle and the girls were on the march, that is; I was still on the shuffle. My ankles hurt even more today, partly because we were wading through an unusually thick blanket of gravel on a logging road. I wasn't in agony yet, but I could see the checkpoint for agony looming up ahead, and the guards were looking surly.

To distract myself from the heat and the pain, I turned on *Don Quixote*. Usually, this cheered me up, but even the Don failed me this morning. The Knight of the Woeful Countenance was talking about war, and how it had no glory in it anymore. In the old days, you needed courage, but now, with cannons, you could be as brave as you like, but if a cannonball lands on you, that's it.

Around 11, I caught up with my gang at a hamlet where everyone had stopped for a Coca-Cola break—the heat was intense enough now that coffee breaks were a thing of the past. Patrick the Irish android was there too, and the Australian couple. Everyone could see I was hurting. Patrick suggested cheerily that I might have to give up. After our Cokes, he sped ahead but the Australians stuck with us. The man, who had seemed boiled dry and angry the past two nights, expanded as we walked, teasing the girls about something or other and teasing me about chasing windmills. I noticed his red face less now and the bright blue eyes more, the way you do when you start to change your mind about someone.[135]

At some point, we stopped for our picnic and the Australian couple walked on, but we ran into each other again a few hours later, at a village fountain, along with a gangly and unusually friendly Frenchwoman in her 30s who had fallen in step with them. When I introduced myself, she laughed and said she knew me

---

135   Or maybe the Austrian hunger artist was right and the Camino really does cure whatever ails you.

already—we had shared a room two nights before.

I put my head under a tap to cool off—one of the joys of the ultra-short haircut—and the girls started a water fight with their canteens. For some reason, the Australian began to sing his national anthem, which was as unintentionally comic as national anthems usually are,[136] but he had a surprisingly deep voice, and sitting there under the inevitable First World War monument with its list of fallen Jeans and Michels, the anthem still felt poignant.

A little way out of town, we split up. The gangly Frenchwoman strode on ahead and the Australians left the path for a nice-looking gîte on the far side of a vineyard we were walking past now.

We reached Montcuq at around four. It's a picturesque hill town, complete with a pretty, round castle tower. To a French ear, Montcuq sounds like *mon cul*— my ass—which is the source of its only recent claim to fame: a TV comedian visited in the 70s and asked a number of old guys various questions about the town that were all designed to trigger the pun—"How's the air? How's the light?" etc. Har har har. Fortunately, the old guys were good sports, and between the Midi's two great traditions— tolerance and a tendency to beat the hell out of superior outsiders—they chose the former.

Unless provoked, people in the Midi (southern France), where we had been walking the past few days, have always tended to be exceptionally tolerant. In the 1200s, for instance, the southern

---

136   I don't think I'm being too harsh:

> *Australians all let us rejoice*
> *For we are young and free*
> *We've golden soil and wealth for toil,*
> *Our home is girt by sea...*

bourgeoisie paid lower taxes to the nobility and had more power in the towns, small-time aristocrats did not owe their betters much in the way of feudal duties, and everybody enjoyed some degree of religious freedom. Women had more rights here too than most places in western Europe, and even homosexuality was considered more or less okay: John Boswell, in *Christianity, Social Tolerance, and Homosexuality*, notes that the love poems from this region at that time tended to involve relationships between women and between men just as often as between women and men, and says that "statistically, the proportion of gay literature surviving from this period is astonishing."

The people of the Midi called this the spirit of *paratge*, which as near as I can tell amounted to a fierce determination to live and let live.

The political microclimate that fostered *paratge* owed itself to a number of happy accidents. Beyond the fertility already noted (particularly for grape-growing), the Midi is mountainous, and its many hills and mountains served as excellent places to perch fortified towns and castles. At the same time, the Midi also had more than its fair share of navigable rivers, which made it easy for goods to circulate.

This confluence of factors had helped make the Midi one of the richest parts of Europe. The region exported wine, dyed wool, olive oil, and grain to England and all over the Mediterranean, and imported spices, silks, and other luxury goods from as far as Egypt and Syria.

The region's openness attracted new ideas as well, and at least one new religion: Catharism, which turned up around 1100, imported by missionaries from Bulgaria.

Unlike the Waldensians, paleo-Protestants the Church felt the need to persecute only occasionally,[137] the Cathars quarreled not only with a few aspects of orthodox Christianity but with almost every proposition, beginning with Genesis: in the Cathars's opin-

---

137 Followers of Waldo, a preacher in Lyon who had some wild ideas about re-forming the Church so it was less corrupt and focusing the religion more on ordinary people.

ion, an omnipotent god, a God-God, would not have designed a world with so much suffering in it. A righteous God would not damn so many children to Hell, not to mention "an astonishing multitude of the dumb, the deaf, and the simple-minded, none of whom were ever able to do penance, none of whom had from God in any measure either the ability or knowledge to do good," as one Cathar wrote.

But if God didn't make this evil world, who did? The Devil, obviously. Beginning in Eden, when the serpent changed form and became a beautiful young man who kindled in Eve a desire "like a glowing oven" and seduced her with his tail, human beings never had a chance.

Like most religions, Catharism had its own set of pluses and minuses. One plus was that the Cathar creation myth made it much easier to explain bad things. There would also be no Day of Judgment: a good God wouldn't damn people forever, and a bad God (that is, the Devil) wouldn't have the power. On the down side, as long as we stuck to our wicked ways, the Cathars believed we would keep on being reborn ad nauseum, our sparks of divinity trapped in an unending succession of vile bodies.

The Cathars taught that only by leading a good life and abstaining from sex and any products of sex, such as meat, milk, and cheese, could people escape the unending cycle of rebirth.[138] Only if you died in this holy state, as a perfectus, could you shake off the mortal coil for good.

To become a *perfectus*, you had to be "consoled" (baptized or confirmed as a Cathar), which had its own special risk: the Cathars didn't believe in confession, so you could only be consoled once. Break a Cathar commandment after your initiation and you were

---

138   With the possible exception of gay sex: Boswell, in *Christianity, Social Tolerance, and Homosexuality*, argues that the Cathars may have seen the non-procreative aspect of gay sex as a plus. This could help explain why the inquisitors often referred to their adversaries as "traitors, heretics, and sodomites," and why even latter-day inquisitors like Senator McCarthy continued to associate radicalism with homosexuality. Traces of this tendency may have made it into the English language: Boswell says the vulgar English word "bugger" may be related to the French word for heretic—"bougre," that is, "Bulgarian"—the reputed nationality of those first Cathar missionaries.

doomed to suffer another incarnation. Rationally enough, this led many Cathars to put off *perfect*hood until they were lying in their deathbed.

For the hale, near-death conversion offered a number of practical advantages. You didn't need to jeopardize your temporal health through celibacy.[139] You could lean toward Catharism without fully committing yourself during the healthier part of your life. And if you weren't absolutely sure the Cathars were right, you could hedge your bets—keep going to Mass, for example, but get your house blessed by a *perfectus*—and put off your final decision until later.[140]

Although their Catholic neighbors and relatives sometimes found Cathar beliefs annoying (for instance, committed *bonhommes*[141] wouldn't eat your food or even cook their own if they had to do it in your old, meat-contaminated pot), the two groups seem to have gotten along most of the time, and by the early 1200s, Cathars could be found in every rank of Midi society. As one Catholic noted, "We [Catholics and Cathars] have been brought up side by side ... Our closest kinsmen are numbered among them. Every day we see them living worthy and honorable lives in our midst.

It is hard to say how long the *paratge* paradise might have lasted—there is usually a snake in the garden—but outsiders cut it short.

Looking back 800 years after the fact, it's hard to understand why the Church would feel threatened by a bunch of peaceful

---

139 At the time, celibacy was considered dangerous for men. Monks were bled to keep their chemistry in balance; some people blamed the death of Louis IX (Saint Louis) in Tunis in 1270 not on dysentery but on a rash vow to abstain until he got back to his queen.

140 Occasionally, people had difficulties if heaven's door turned out to be locked. If Cathar parents had a perfectus administer the consolation to their sick baby and the baby recovered, for example, the father might want to starve their daughter to make sure she moved on to a better world while the mother selfishly fed the baby and keep her mired in evil but alive.

141 "The good men," as they called themselves.

pescatarians[142] who had already been living in the mountains of southwest France for 50 or 100 years without hurting anybody. For some reason, however, beginning in the late 1100s (about a century before John XXII, in the last chapter), the pope, Celestine III, started to get very worried.

At first, Celestine just sent monks to debate perfecti and to preach against them, but this does not seem to have changed any minds, and the formal public debates they held with the heretics ended in name-calling. But in 1198, his much younger successor, Innocent III, lost patience, and sent in the inquisitors. The inquisitors made no progress either, however, and a few years later, Innocent threatened to excommunicate Raymond VI, the count of Toulouse and the most powerful noble in the region, if he didn't crack down on the Cathars.

The Cathars meet their new neighbors.

---

142   Like many modern semi-vegetarians, Cathars allowed themselves to eat fish. Church inquisitors were never able to figure out why.

Count Raymond wasn't a Cathar, but the pope considered him soft on Cathars, and when in 1208 a lone horseman rode up behind the pope's emissary and skewered him with a lance, Innocent blamed Raymond and used the murder as an excuse to launch a full-scale crusade against the Cathars.

For recruits to the cause, the pope's terms were good, as far as crusades went: for just 40 days of service a year and without the trouble of a long sea voyage, an anti-Cathar crusader received an indulgence for all his sins that would get him out of Purgatory sooner—the Church equivalent of a "get out of jail free" card. Sweeter still, the pope granted the crusaders the right to take heretics' property.

And that was enough to tear this entire civilization apart. As Simone Weill, the Jewish and Christian mystic put it, "[a] shady deal in salvation and the acquisitiveness of a rather mediocre man were all that was required to destroy a world."

But it took awhile. For the next seven years, a French noble named Simon de Montfort (Weill's "mediocre man"), and his thugs collected southern towns and castles one by one, either by siege or just trotting through the open front gate of a hastily abandoned village. Then Montfort died, during the third siege of Toulouse, and the war dragged on for 10 more years.[143]

---

143 Not everybody was upset about Montfort's death:

> *The epitaph says, for those who can read it,*
> *That he is a saint and martyr who shall breathe again*
> *And shall in wondrous joy inherit and flourish*
> *And wear a crown and sit on a heavenly throne.*
> *And I have heard it said that this must be so*
> *If by killing men and spilling their blood,*
> *Or by wasting their souls and preaching murder,*
> *And by following evil counsel, and setting fires,*
> *And by destroying barons, and dishonoring Paratge,*
> *And by stealing lands and exalting pride,*
> *And by praising evil and scanting good,*
> *And by massacring women and their children,*
> *A man can win Jesus Christ in this world,*
> *Then he surely wears a splendid crown in heaven.*

Some modern historians have quarreled with this view of Montfort as "an ecclesiastically licensed pirate" because he was also a very pious man. Personally, it strikes me as an accurate description, if perhaps a little unfair to pirates.

In all, between 200,000 and 1 million people had died to enforce religious homogeniety in the Midi —numbers that sound terrible enough today but were even more horrific at the time, given that the population within the borders of modern France totaled around 16 million.

And it wasn't over yet; it took another 75 years before the inquisitors and the French managed to eliminate the last of the Cathars. Even then, in some respects, the people of the Midi never quite surrendered their sense of independence. Only in the late 19th century, nearly 700 years later, did the majority of the population consider themselves French or speak standard French. Until the First World War, most people spoke *Provençal*. Even now, when you talk to southerners, there is often a surprisingly strong sense of northern France as another country.

Today, the Cathar name lives on mostly in various French products, including, ironically, the *Cathare*, a young, raw goat's milk cheese, dry and slightly sour, covered with charcoal powder except for a white Occitan cross. It's a delicious cheese—Charlotte's favorite—and if you were a *perfectus*, would be worth two or three extra incarnations. Cheese critic Max Shrem says the rendition he tried "transported him to cheese heaven."

We didn't like Montcuq at first. It's a pretty town, but we had arrived at around four, in 100 degree (40 degrees Centigrade) heat, and to get to our gîte, first had to climb to the town's highest point and then back down a country road that took us about two kilometers off our route.

Once we reached our gîte, however, we forgave everything. The place was built in and around an old mill, in a green and shady spot near the millstream, and our hosts had set a cold pitcher of lemonade for us out on a picnic table.

After our lemonade, the girls cooled off in the stream for a little while, where Thea admired the *"clouds of shiny turquoise and purple dragon flies."* Then they climbed into two big hammocks in the pleasantly overgrown backyard and read their Kindles. Our beds were in a converted stable behind the farmhouse, with curtains drawn between the stalls, a rough hemp drop cloth on the floor, and windows without any glass. A breeze blew through the window-openings, which made the stable feel almost luxurious.

The dining room was in another barn, set up on a raised floor with a missing fourth wall that looked out over the backyard. There was a single communal table and benches, and on the left, a grubby alcove kitchen where the proprietor began cooking furiously at about 6:30. He had a certain presence—for a short, chubby guy in a Hawaiian shirt, he radiated a surprising amount of charisma— and I would not be surprised if he had spent some time as an actor. I could have watched him work for hours. In any case, his intensity, the missing wall, and the raised floor gave the proceedings a theatrical feeling.

When dinner was ready, the guests all climbed three steps to the stage and sat down around the table. Our host and his wife then asked us to each give our name, our profession, and our age. Besides us, the diners included the host couple, our friend the gangly Frenchwoman, a Swiss tunnel engineer in his late 40s, his wife, and their 16-year-old daughter. The family had been walking the Camino for a week or so every summer for the past two years, and that was plenty, in their opinion. They thought we were mad to be walking to Pamplona (a story we had stuck to) and kept joking with Charlotte about adopting her and taking her back to Switzerland with them. The menu centered on a pasta dish that has not stuck in my memory, but Charlotte loved.

At the end of the meal, our hosts took out a little pilgrim puppet and bounced him across the table, explaining that the owner had once been a pilgrim, stayed at the place, and then after he finished his Camino, returned and bought the farm. He had been a thin, bearded guy then, judging by the puppet. I couldn't follow the whole story but I liked the idea of the puppet. Most of us have a set story to explain ourselves and I've wondered since then what my life might look like as a puppet show. You could probably design a whole psychoanalytic program around dolls like that.[144]

A family camping out behind the stable that had chosen to save their money and not have dinner with the stable-dwellers, were invited to come and join us for dessert, which consisted of a fruit tart and homemade liqueurs. This was nice of the hosts but felt a little awkward, as the young campers had to look up at us shyly from a few steps below the stage, like peasants visiting the manor.

After dinner, when everyone else had left to get ready for bed and the girls had gone back to their books and their hammocks, I stayed with the host a while longer. He asked me about Obama and plied me with more of his homemade hooch, all of which tasted to me like variations of anisette. We talked until it was nearly dark and I had worn out my French.

---

144   I found it interesting to see how our hosts had engineered so much more of a sense of community than many of our other gîtes simply by making us sit together, asking us to introduce ourselves, and then giving us their autobiographical puppet show. When you consider that nobody complained that we were paying top-dollar (as gîtes go—EUR 32 per adult, a near-gouge by Camino standards at the time) for pasta, a stall in a horse stable, and breakfast, being friendly was also smart business. Madame Cassoulet should take note.

July 25. Montcuq to Moissac, 38.5 km

In which we meet a troop of valiant Jewish scouts, Marcel Marceau, and the bravest town in France.

I worked well the next morning—it was cool and dark in the stable, and the moon was still out when I got up—so it was only when we walked over to the other barn for breakfast that I noticed something big was missing: pain. After three days of hobbling, my ankles felt fine.

My recovery was nicely timed, as today would be our longest stage yet—38.5 kilometers. It was also supposed to be a very hot day, so we left very early, while it was still dark, and walked back up the hill to Montcuq under the streetlights.

Most of the morning was hot but tolerable. By the afternoon, though, everything got worse. The temperature must have been nearly 100 again (40 degrees Centigrade), and Masha and I fell behind.

Not long after that, the two of us ran out of water, and after five or ten kilometers of endless sunflowers, lost track of the trail too and found ourselves walking along the shoulder of a busy two-lane highway. I promised Masha that we would stop for a drink the first chance we got, but we had no chance. Even when we reached Moissac, we weren't actually in Moissac. The town seemed to sprawl for miles, American-style—a dreary landscape of shuttered nightclubs, used car lots, and dealers in fake flowers and tombstones, brightened only by a few billboards of Technicolor burger eaters.

At this point, I was tired and thirsty enough to think the worst of anyone who had the misfortune of living in Moissac. But I was wrong about that. During the Second World War, some of the best people in France lived here. The Inquisition might have stamped out *paratge* in Montcuq and most of the Midi, but the inquisitors evidently missed a spot. *Yad Vashem*, the Israeli Holocaust memorial association, named Moissac a *Ville des justes*—a town of the righteous—one of the first three places in France's

36,000 municipalities to earn that distinction. Remarkably, in this community of 6,000 people, not a single person betrayed any of the refugees, including the 500 Jewish children they sheltered during the war.

The test the Moissagais passed that so many others failed began in December 1939, when the Éclaireurs israélites de France (EIF), a Jewish scouting organization, opened a home for Jewish refugee children in a townhouse facing the Tarn River at 12 quai de Port.

Although some of the kids felt encouraged when they saw the name of the town at the train station—Moissac shares the same root as Moise ("Moses" in French)—the town had no particular connection to Judaism.[145] The scouts had ended up there by accident. One of the EIF leaders, a 30-year-old Romanian immigrant named Shatta Simon (short for "Charlotte") had looked first in Normandy, where her husband had grown up, but not found anything. When she heard of a place available in Moissac, she took the train down from Paris, saw the house, admired its view of the river, the Pont du Napoleon, and the forest on the opposite bank—and with her usual decisiveness, decided on the spot to take it.

Initially, Shatta and the other EIF leaders had planned to build a kids' camp out in the country, to give their boy and girl scouts and other Jewish children a place to go if war broke out and the Nazis bombed Paris and other French cities. The EIF's founder, Robert Gamzon, had read about the devastation of Guernica and other civilian bombardments during the Spanish Civil War and wanted to keep kids out of harm's way.

However, by the time Shatta opened the colonie at 12 quai du Port in December, their fears had grown. In September, the Wehrmacht had marched into Poland, and Great Britain and France had declared war against Germany. In October, the Nazis began

---

145   There were so few Jews in Moissac that even basic elements of the religion were unknown to some Moissagais. One nun who volunteered to take the smallest EIF children to the city's municipal showers for their weekly bath came back saying that all the little boys were ill—not realizing that they had been circumcised.

deporting Jews from Austria and Czechoslovakia to camps in Poland. In November, the occupiers ordered Polish Jews to wear yellow Star of David armbands. Within France too, anti-Semitic feelings against the country's 330,000 Jews were running high, particularly for the 150,000 or so Jewish immigrants who unlike Shatta did not have French passports. Some French right-wingers argued that the Jews were trying to push the country into war against Germany.

After the Nazis marched into Paris, the pressure on Jews continued to grow—first against Jewish refugees from Nazi-controlled regions, and then against French Jews. Gamzon, the director of the EIF, wrote in 1941, "I still feel so French, so tied to the land and the people of France. But little by little, with all these decrees ... you get the impression that the country is pushing you away ..." One day, after a drink in a café with the directors of other scouting groups, one of Gamzon's colleagues clapped his shoulder when he pulled out his wallet to pay and said with a laugh, "'Save your money, old sport. You'll need it when you leave for America!'"

As the Gestapo and the French police began rounding up foreign Jews in the north and sending them off to the death camps, Shatta's choice of a southern home for the *colonie* turned out to be fortunate: Moissac was located in the southern, inland part of the country the Germans did not occupy in the first years of the war, and although the Vichy were nearly as anti-Semitic as the Nazis, they tended to act on it later.

Meanwhile, the scouts were able to live quite openly at the colonie. The younger kids went to the local school, and most of the older scouts studied a serious craft or trade, learning to be a seamstress or an electrician, for instance. (The directors of the EIF were a very practical bunch, intent on undermining old stereotypes of Jews as urban intellectuals.) When they weren't studying, the scouts were busy with a lot of ordinary scouting activities—hikes, games, sing-alongs (even Jewish songs), and sports. The boys had their own basketball team and would play against other teams around town.

But Shatta didn't let her guard down entirely. She would give children new names when they first arrived—- a new French first name if from outside France, and a silly nickname to use at home, to make betrayals more difficult. Many of the nicknames stuck: some of the scouts still used these names with each other 60 or 70 years later, when they met for reunions.

By and large, the EIF kids seem to have liked the place. There were fewer crying children than at other refugee shelters, and fewer meaningless rules. Nor did the directors care much about hierarchy—everybody spoke to each other in the *tu* form, like family—and the EIF was coeducational, at a time when that was still considered progressive. The boys liked roughhousing with Shatta's husband, Edouard "Bouli" Simon, and Shatta seems to have been good at making the children feel at home—one girl remembered that she never said "bonjour," but always "ma cherie."

Jouf (Cheek), Chameau (Camel), and the rest were organized into small groups who lived and ate together—patrols for the boys, clans for the girls—and kept together and too busy to spend much time with their memories. But even as they were encouraged to forget their personal history, they were pushed to embrace their collective identity as Jews. Shatta made proper meals for every Sabbath and elaborate feasts to celebrate the high holy days, particularly those that commemorated a persecution. At the end of every Sabbath meal, Bouli would lead the kids in a rousing chorus of an English hymn, "Raise your head, O people of Israel!"[146]

Of course, as is often the case even with peacetime childhoods, adults were privately scrambling to maintain that feeling of security. "URGENT, ARGENT!" Shatta would sometimes cable Paris. In the early years, some of the support came from a Rothschild fund and a little more from the EIF, but food was rationed, and

---

146   No one knew the hymn was by Handel, one boy remembered; they thought it was just something Bouli had made up. (I haven't actually been able to find a hymn with that title. There is a chorus in the Messiah that has the line "Lift up your heads," but the people of Israel don't make an appearance so I think Bouli may have made up the lyrics.)

she also needed to get 150 ration cards renewed every month by Vichy officials in the town hall. She traded trade wine coupons from the children's ration books for milk coupons on the black market, and grew vegetables in a field near the colonie.

Under pressure, Shatta's façade would occasionally slip: One girl remembered that if you crossed Shatta in some trifle, she would sometimes snap, "If you don't like it, ma cherie, tomorrow you can get on the train." "Get on the train to where? I was always a little afraid to ask," Ida Tieder later recalled.[147]

After Vichy tightened restrictions on Jews in the summer of 1942, Shatta sent the scouts out camping, which meant that when the roundups began in August, they were nowhere to be found. That fall, Shatta and Bouli shut down the colonie and turned the home into a clandestine adoption and travel agency. The children in greatest danger—German nationals, and foreign orthodox Jews who didn't speak much French—were smuggled over the border, either to Switzerland or Spain. Those who were either French or could speak good French were placed with a family in the countryside. To each kid, they issued one of three kinds of identification, also dispensed according to what they saw as the kid's perceived risk: the "false-false," papers that were entirely forged; the "real-false," genuine papers that had been somehow altered; and the "real-real," papers that used real forms and real stamps "borrowed" overnight from a local official.[148]

Not everything went according to plan for the scouts. In October 1943, Shatta learned that her brother Djigo, who had been running a similar operation for young adults in Auvillar, 20 kilometers away, had been arrested with his wife after being denounced

---

147 Shatta pushed herself so hard that at one point during the war, while she was pregnant with her second child, someone warned her that she ought to take it easier for the sake of her baby. She responded by saying, I need to worry about the children who are already here first. Fortunately, the baby was fine.

148 And not only did they do this for their kids; older scouts who had graduated to the Resistance delivered new identities to as many as 10,000 people.

by someone in the town.[149] But for the Moissac colonie, there were no bad surprises: by December 1943, the house was shut, and every last child in the Simons' files was hidden, smuggled out of the country, or matriculated into the Resistance. [150] Amazingly, none of the 500 children who passed through the Colonie starved or died in a death camp—and many had happy memories of their time in Moissac.

How did that happen?

Some of their good fortune had to do with the leadership of the EIF. Gamzon's foresight and Shatta's capacity for persuasion were both invaluable. Shatta, in particular, seems to have been very charismatic. She emitted a mysterious fluid, one person who knew her said.[151]

But they wouldn't have lasted a day without the help of the town.

---

149   Before his arrest, "Djigo," Dr. Sigismund Hirsch, was able to save 400 young Jews (16-25) by placing them with local farmers who were short of laborers because of the war. Like Shatta, he had a bold streak: he rented a house right next to the police station, figuring that would be the last place they would search, and even ate in a restaurant favored by soldiers and the police. But eventually, his luck ran out. After he and his wife were arrested, they were sent to Auschwitz. Djigo's wife, seven months' pregnant, was killed, but Djigo, as a German-speaking radiologist, was useful to Dr. Mengele, Auschwitz's sadistic camp scientist, and survived. His son and daughter also survived the war, safely hidden in Moissac by their aunt.

150   Although the EIF was never a huge organization – only 2000 at the time the war broke out – the older EIF scouts ended up being part of a crack unit of the Resistance known as "the Sixth, " not because there were five others but because the Vichy had renamed the EIF the sixth section of the French scouts. As the Sixth, they achieved a kind of mythical status with the Gestapo, who were never able to track them down. Only 100 of 2000 members died in the war, and they had some spectacular successes: in 1944, Gamzon and a band of 120 Jewish partisans, which included former scouts, captured an armored train and liberated two towns. In 1949, he and 50 of his former scouts emigrated to Israel.

The Simons stayed put. After the war ended, they moved down the street to an old mill, a much larger building, where they took in war orphans. They stayed there until 1951, when they relocated their orphanage to Saint-Maxim, north of Paris, to the wing of a chateau that had once belonged to a Rothschild. The couple ran that home together until Bouli died in 1993, at which point she retired, aged 84.

Shatta died in 2003, but the Maison d'enfants Shatta et Bouli Simon, is still open. These days, most of the residents are young immigrants, foreign children who have ended up with French passports for one reason or another, and asylum-seekers.

151   Once, Shatta not only talked a Vichy policeman out of deporting one of her boys but inspired him to help her: after their meeting, he began bringing food to the colonie every week.

And town residents gave them this help knowing full well that if caught they could be punished by the Nazis in ways as brutal as anything dreamt of by Simon de Montfort, the Cathar crusader.

Why the Moissagais behaved so well isn't obvious. The mayor of Saint-Michel, a nearby village, told Djigo at one point that he saw himself as part of a larger history of resistance in the region that went back to the Cathar crusade, the Catholic wars against the Protestants, and the Protestants' counter-persecution of the Catholics that his own ancestors had suffered.

But Moissac wasn't part of that Protestant tradition, and although the town had a significant monastic history, it had been a fairly secular place as far back as the Revolution.

One historian argues that those Jewish children actually owed their lives to the mild winter of 1930, when a sudden thaw in the mountains and heavy rains on March 3–4 flooded the Tarn River and sent a wall of water 3 meters over flood stage rushing through the valley, moving not at the normal 200 square meters of water per second but 8,000 square meters of water per second.

When the waters receded, more than half of Moissac was homeless. In all, 120 people and many farm animals were killed, and 1,200 homes destroyed. In a newsreel film taken after the flood, the town looks like the victim of a soggy carpet-bombing. Bit by bit, with almost no power equipment—one of the newsreels shows a line of men in gas masks tugging on a rope, trying to drag a cow carcass out of the rubble—they eventually cleared the debris and pulled their lives back together.

But they weren't alone. Inspired by that same dramatic newsreel footage, people all over France, Europe, and even Morocco sent donations.

Moissac never forgot their generosity. When the Jewish refugees began to arrive nine years later, the mayor, Roger Delthil, didn't see a lot of scruffy foreign Jews—he saw homeless people who needed a place to live. In a letter posted outside the town hall in September 1939, he wrote that the town had been asked to take in 1,500 people displaced by the war, and concluded simply, "We have a debt to pay." Fortunately, his constituents agreed.[152]

Cleaning up after the flood of 1930.

It goes without saying that the world is a richer place because of what the town did. Moissac alumni included one of the inventors of in vitro fertilization; an Israeli ambassador in Africa; Jean-Claude Grumberg, a playwright who has collaborated with Costa-Gravas and Truffaut; and Marcel Mangel—better known as Marcel Marceau, the famous mime.[153]

Despite staying only a short time in Moissac, Marceau made an impression on the colonie. The son of a kosher butcher, the 20-year-old from Strasbourg was an artist, a skill he used to alter the numbers and letters on identity cards, to make kids younger or give them a less Jewish name, depending on what they needed.

152 Such generosity was in short supply in those times, even far from Europe. In 1939, a bill in the US House of Representatives to raise the immigration ceiling in order to admit an extra 20,000 Jewish refugee children did not even make it out of committee. "Twenty thousand charming children," said Laura Delano Houghteling, Franklin Delano Roosevelt's cousin and wife of the U.S. immigration commissioner, "would all too soon grow into 20,000 ugly adults."

153 When they joined the Resistance, he and his brother took Marceau as their nom du guerre, after a gallant revolutionary general whose career Lord Byron summed up as "Brief, brave and glorious."

He could also speak German, and good-enough English that he later became a translator for the French army after D-Day. But most of all, people remembered how good he was at making faces, an interest he had had since his father took him to see a Charlie Chaplin movie when he was six.

This talent turned out to be a surprisingly valuable survival skill. Once, while pretending to be a scoutmaster leading a troop on an outing, he used mime to distract a group of children he was leading to safety in Switzerland. Later in the war, Marceau claimed he ran into a unit of 30 Germans alone one day, but quickly puffed out his chest, presented himself as an advance scout of a French regiment, and persuaded them to surrender their weapons to him.

Although a good storyteller and a compulsive talker who could charm women in five languages, Marceau always performed without words. He had various aesthetic theories for why he had chosen to create a wordless theater ("Do not the

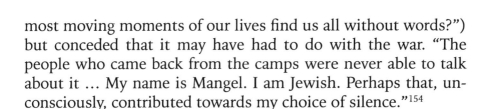

most moving moments of our lives find us all without words?") but conceded that it may have had to do with the war. "The people who came back from the camps were never able to talk about it … My name is Mangel. I am Jewish. Perhaps that, unconsciously, contributed towards my choice of silence."[154]

---

154 And I suspect may be why he called his character "Bip," the same word Shatta and Bouli used for the false-false passports.

As Masha and I wandered into the center of town late that hot afternoon, we saw Moissac's old gray monastery across the square. The entrance was through a stone porch big as a tunnel, crowded with nuns and monks in white who flickered in and out of the smoky darkness. Looking back on it now, I think they must have been a tour group, but at that moment, the porch looked like a portal to 1250.

"Should we take a look?" I asked. I was excited: Moissac had been a big deal in the Middle Ages, a major hub of the Cluny monastic network. All kinds of illuminated manuscripts came out of Moissac. Why, the abbey had been a center for the Cluniacs almost as important as Cluny itself!

"No," said Masha.

I didn't press the point; there was a certain edge in her voice. If I had insisted on exploring the cloister right then, after eight or nine hours of hiking—make that swimming— through 98-degree (40 degrees Centigrade) heat, half-dehydrated, half next to a highway, she would have used her last remaining strength to snap the head off the nearest gargoyle and bash my skull.

Instead, after a few of my signature wrong turns, we walked past the abbey and found the way to our hostel, at the top of a very steep street named, appropriately enough, rue Calvaire (Calvary Street). But that ended our trial: the hostel was a friendly place, run by older volunteers determined to keep pilgrims from going hungry.[155] At dinner, one grandmotherly lady took special care to find something vegetarian for Thea.

---

155   Friendly, that is, except for a German social worker who was horrified to hear we had walked all the way from Montcuq that day and told us she thought we were committing child abuse.

July 26. Moissac to Saint-Antoine, 25.4 km

Wherein we learn that Auvillar is the thing with feathers.

We got a late start the next day. Although we had another hot hike ahead, the abbey didn't open until 10, and I was determined to make a visit. Not stopping because we had too many miles to walk would be criminal, like visiting Paris and not going to see Notre Dame because you want to have plenty of time at the airport.

But although the Moissac abbey was definitely the place to be in the 12th century, it isn't anymore. Most of the manuscripts are in other libraries and in the 19th century, unsentimental railroad builders ran a line right through the middle of the complex. I wasn't entirely wrong about insisting we visit—the monastery still has a beautiful cloister—but making time for that stop meant we didn't get on the road until after 11, when the day was already as hot or hotter as the day before.

The Moissac Cloister

We were delayed even more because as usual the trail blazers had marked the route out of town sloppily and we got lost again, this time near the train station. Cybèle spotted another pilgrim who was having the same difficulty, so she decided to compare maps with him. He was dark enough that he looked like he might be South American but spoke no Spanish, English, or French, and turned out to be a very weather-beaten Austrian. In spite of having no common language, Cybèle was able to mime with him and together they figured out where we needed to go, at which point he folded his map and after a few more twists and turns, sped on ahead.[156]

For the next two hours, we walked down a dead-straight, tree-shaded access road on a high berm that separated the Tarn River from the Canal du Garonne. You could see the whole history of French transportation in that stretch: the river to our left, the canal, the railroad, and the highway to our right, all of it as tidy and cheerful as a Richard Scarry picture book. On the canal, white-*bobbed* boaters waved to us from the bridges of their big white boats. They cruised past almost at eye level, floating by like friendly aliens in Ray-Bans.

We made good time, but the path was so straight and flat that toward lunch I started to get a little bored. The French have a monstrous love of repetition and I began to pay attention not to the lovely green leaves of the endless line of trees at the edge of the berm but the snaky and somehow repulsive way their roots stuck out of the water.

I had a call at 12:30, so I found a nice spot and set up the office. Despite the weight, I liked having my working gear with me. It made me feel like an Inuit with his harpoon. Of course, moving from gîte to gîte where there would often be a nice dinner wait-

---

156 Cybèle has an exceptional talent for this kind of communication. She doesn't know much sign language, and in any case, sign language varies by country, but sometimes, if she meets a deaf person, even if they have no common language, she can somehow chat for ten minutes and then tell me that the man's wife died eight years ago, he is retired, and has one son, who is a real estate agent now but is going to night school to become a financial planner. The man doesn't like his daughter-in-law because she's a snob, but his grandson is a nice boy, so evidently she is doing something right.

ing for us at the end of the day wasn't exactly living like Nanook of the North, but it did make me feel pleasantly self-sufficient. A loaf of bread, a jug of wine, a four-bar Wi-Fi connection, and thou, and I'm pretty much set.

Thea and Charlotte made a mosaic out of shards of plane tree bark that lay scattered around me, but then left to catch up with Masha and Cybèle.

For the next 40 minutes, I sat leaning against that tree, interviewing a human resource director of an oil company about their new system for identifying high-performing talent. As I typed, I looked alternately at the canal and the wide, shining river, feeling very lucky not to be anybody's human resource, high-performing or otherwise.

A few kilometers ahead, Cybèle and the girls crossed a bridge and went over to a village that ran alongside the canal. *"We stopped for lunch at a big restaurant in a little tiny town,"* Charlotte said. Lunch met her standards, for a change. *"I had a salad, then steak with fries and one scoop of chocolate ice cream and one scoop of mango sorbet and Coca-Cola. It was really hard to walk again after lunch because we were so relaxed."*

I had hoped to catch up with them before they finished so I could get some lunch too, but even in a one-street town about three blocks long, I somehow managed to miss everybody for a good half hour. I walked up and down the main street, retracing my steps, and even after phoning Thea, still misunderstood the directions enough that I resorted to standing by a bridge I knew they had to cross to get back to the berm where they would find me.

I had expected we would stay on the dead-straight access road on the berm, but instead the path veered abruptly away from the canal, as if it couldn't stand the monotony any longer either. Suddenly we were on another bridge and then across the river, walking up a treeless road between endless cornfields, under a merciless blue sky.

We were in the hottest part of the day, around 100 degrees (40 degrees Centigrade) again, and the warm water in our canteens didn't last very long. Cybèle felt a scar from her skin transplant the prior year swell into a fat angry welt, something that hadn't happened before. At the same time, a heat rash erupted all over her legs. The rest of us weren't having a good time either. Masha started to get a heat rash on her ankles, and all three of the girls had now bowed to the indignity of hat-wearing. For what seemed like a long time, the next town, Auvillar, stayed on a hill in the far distance, where it hovered like the Emerald City.

Just before four, we finally climbed out of the fields and up the hill into the town. Most of Auvillar had shut at two and would reopen at five, but we found one snack bar that was still open, so we stopped for Cokes and I grabbed their last ham sandwich.

They say that civilization is only three meals away from barbarism, but in my case it's closer to two, and now, after three weeks of hiking, I was down to one. Before that sandwich, I was on the verge of turning into a raptor. I sat down, clawed the cellophane off the half-baguette, and devoured the whole thing in about 15 seconds.

Filled, I gained a few hundred millennia in intellectual maturity, and started to pay more attention to the town, which I now noticed was an unusually pretty place, and nicely situated. Auvillar is very old, and goes all the way back to the Romans. As usual, the legionnaires had picked a good spot: the town is perched on a cliff, high over the Garonne River, about halfway between Bordeaux and Toulouse (Auvillar's name is an eroded version of Alta Villa – high town).

Between the 17th and 19th centuries, thousands of boats passed by every year, stopping to pay a toll, and often to load up on Auvillar's two main products; faience pottery—a kind of painted imitation porcelain made with a tin glaze—and quill pens.

Faince had been around since the early Middle Ages, when it spread from the Arab world to Islamic Spain and then the rest of Europe, but the French market boomed in the late 17th century, after Louis XIV had forced the rich to melt down their gold and silver plate to pay for all his wars. Those missing plates created a huge demand for a presentable substitute, and faience fit the bill.

Auvillar had the right kind of clay and chalk to make good faience, but I'm not sure why it became a center for quills.

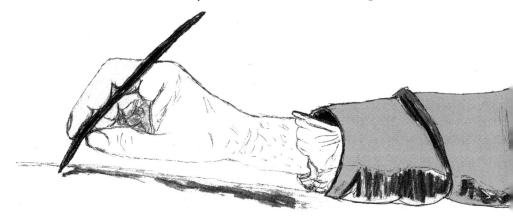

Then as now, the region seems to have been a good place to raise geese—and maybe that was enough; people liked goose feathers for quills because they were bigger than most other feathers and could hold more ink. [157] In any case, for most of the 17th, 18th, and at least half of the 19th century, quill-making was a good business: in 1832, Britain alone imported 33.6 million quills from the Continent. Technically, you could make your own, but

---

157 Goose quills were the Sharpies of their day—besides being able to hold more ink, they had a bigger tip. But they weren't right for every task. Crow quills, for instance, were smaller and considered better suited for drawing. Even on one bird, however, not all quills were created equal. Left wings were preferred because the feathers curved outward, creating an easier angle for the right-handed writers. Professionals preferred the first feather on the wing, but the second and third were okay for most people's purposes.

most people didn't, as quill making was a nasty job.[158]

But Auvillar's quill bonanza didn't last all that long, relatively speaking. Although quills had been the primary writing instrument in Europe since the sixth century, the town's quill business had only 200 good years before the invention of the fountain pen killed demand.[159]

There are usually tradeoffs as things become mechanized—I remember my grandmother saying that before the washing machine, clothes got dirtier but after they were washed, felt cleaner—but on the writing-instrument side, I don't think we lost a lot in the transition from quill to fountain pens. On the other hand, as much as I love keyboards, it seems to me that we may have lost something when we moved from the pen to the typewriter, particularly since the 70s in the United States, when someone decided that practicing penmanship stunted the imagination.

Not in France, however, where the good old days of legible script haven't ended. In l'Hexagon, handwriting still matters, and for

---

158   I remember Masha came home with a feather she had found in the playground one day when she was four or five, which she wanted us to make into a pen, and although at the time our concerns were hygiene-related, in retrospect, as I have learned more about the quill-making process, I'm even more glad we turned her down. Frederick Wong, in *The Complete Calligrapher*, says that a "quill in its natural state is covered with a greasy membrane on the outside and contains soft pith on the inside. Both of these conditions must be altered – in a process called `clarifying' or `ditching' – before the quill can be cut." If you want to try this at home, kids, the easiest way is to "heat the raw quill over an electric hot plate by holding it about ½ inches (4 cm) above the surface and rotating it evenly for 8 to 10 seconds. The heat softens the quill, shriveling both membrane and pith. Now hold the quill by the feather end and quickly place the barrel on the hot plate itself."

Next, according to one 16th-century authority, you cut away the feathery part of the feather (unlike in Hollywood, where Musketeers and Pimpernels are always writing with glorified feather dusters, people generally left the quill mostly bare), and then if the feather is "horish or skirtie [dirty or filthy], scrape off the same with the backe or heele of your penknife."

Nor were you done yet. At this point, you still had to shape the tip, and keep on trimming and re-sharpening that nib (that's what penknives were originally used for). At least you were supposed to: *MacCulloch's Commercial Dictionary* notes that as of 1832, the English hardly ever did. "Not one quill in ten is ever mended," the writer tut-tuts. Most people threw them out after about a week.

159   The French say the fountain pen was invented by a Romanian student in Paris, the English by an Englishman in London. Now quills are used only by calligraphers, who prize their sharp line, and by the US Supreme Court, where, by tradition, 20 goose-quill pens, neatly crossed, are placed each day at the counsels' tables. As most lawyers appear before the Court only once in their career, the quills serve as souvenirs.

a very practical reason: you can't get a good job without good handwriting. Many employers require job applicants to submit a handwritten letter, which HR will send out to a professional graphologist who analyzes your scrawl for clues to your personality. Does your writing tilt to the right? That's good—you're a "[w]ell-balanced, optimistic person who likes his work." Write in an embellished script? Be careful—you may be exposing your "[l]ack of cultural refinement; low intelligence; vanity; selfishness; immaturity; or dishonesty," according to *The ABCs of Handwriting Analysis,* by French handwriting analyst Claude Santoy, PhD.

Although the graphologists have added some Jungian vocabulary over the years, the technique reportedly hasn't changed much since the practice was invented in the 19th century by Jean-Hippolyte Michon, an ex-priest turned archaeologist and the pseudonymous author of anticlerical novels, and Adolphe Desbarrolles, who was also the founder of modern palm-reading.[160]

Personally, I don't think much of it, but that may be because I have the handwriting of a shifty underachiever, so I *would* say that. The one definitively true thing that can be said about Michon and Desbarrolles's science is that it has kept French penmanship up to an admirable standard. I don't think our girls will end up working in France, but if they do, they're set. Their years in French classrooms may have warped them in all kinds of ways, but they do have nice handwriting, which on the whole is probably a more valuable skill than knowing whether the answer on your Myers-Briggs personality test more likely to get you the job is by checking a) that you "easily see the general principle behind specific occurrences," b) like to "contemplate the complexity of life," or c) "prefer to isolate yourself from outside noises."

---

160 But Americans have no right to snicker. Robert Hogan, an American psychologist and personality assessment expert, has written that most personality psychologists regard our generally revered Myers-Briggs test "as little more than an elaborate Chinese fortune cookie."

Break over, we split up again. Thea and Cybèle charged ahead. Charlotte, Masha, and I made slower time. Now we were walking through more fields of sunflowers (*tournesols*—turn-in-the-suns, because they follow the sun during the day, giving a sunflower field the look of a stadium filled with vegetable spectators). The rolling yellow fields were spectacular, and the whole landscape looked to me just as French as French could be.[161]

At first, the stalks we passed were all beautiful and cheery, but after a few more kilometers, the sunflowers' heads began tilting down like ours, wilting under the heat. At some point, I remember, we passed a place where one of our fellow pilgrims had had enough, and scraped leering jack-o'-lantern faces out of the seeds. They weren't jolly sunflowers now, but more like Blake's:

> Ah Sun-flower! weary of time,
> Who countest the steps of the Sun:
> Seeking after that sweet golden clime

---

161   Thanks to Van Gogh, it's hard to think of the South of France without thinking of sunflowers, but these flower-filled fields are a relatively new addition to the landscape. Spanish explorers brought sunflowers back from the Americas as a decorative plant in the 1500s, but it wasn't until the early 1700s that an Englishman figured out how to make oil out of the seeds. Soon after that, Russian farmers started growing them as a crop. The Orthodox Church forbade the use of animal oil for cooking during Lent, but had not thought about vegetable oil, giving the farmers some built-in demand. In the 1820s, Canadian farmers began planting a Russian Mammoth hybrid, and eventually, particularly after European demand for sunflower oil surged in the 1980s, brought even bigger and better sunflowers back to Europe. This meant that what our American eyes took to be a quintessentially French scene was actually not only shaped by the vision of a Dutch artist influenced by Japanese print makers, but the flowers themselves were probably grown from seeds that came from flowers in Canada, whose seeds were originally engineered by Russian botanists who saw a way to profit from the demand created by Russian Orthodox dietary restrictions by using an English process to grind the seeds of a plant imported from Spain that Spanish conquistadors had brought back from Central America. It makes me think of Ezra Pound's poem "Portrait d'Une Femme"—"No, there is nothing! In the whole and all,/ Nothing that's quite your own./Yet this is you."

Where the traveller's journey is done.

Finally, at around 5:30, Masha had had enough. She went to the side of the road and started ripping sunflower stalks out of the ground. Those sunflowers were hideous, she shrieked. They looked like ugly showerheads and she was sick of them. She didn't want to do this any more. She *would not* do this anymore. I scolded her, but as this just seemed to make her even angrier, I decided to walk ahead with Charlotte.[162]

Five minutes later, I took a surreptitious glance behind us and saw that the vegetable carnage was over and Masha had started walking again, as I thought she might.

Charlotte was feeling better now—there's nothing like one sibling's tantrum to bring out the angel in another. To pass the time, we came up with ideas for inventions, an old game of ours. Our best that day: icy insoles to keep the feet cool, made out of that blue goo they use for ice packs. We also started making up songs about the Camino, sung to Broadway melodies. My favorite was a parody of "Maria" in *West Side Story*:

Camino,
I just walked a trail named Camino,
and suddenly I know,
my parents they are so,
insane—

But eventually we wore out that game too and staggered on in silence.

---

162 Masha had taught me the value of a tactical retreat a long time ago, particularly when I didn't have a strong counterargument. One case in point occurred when she was about four, while she was working on an elaborate block tower. She had been working on it for a while, and it had grown high and wobbly. As I walked by, she stacked one more block on top and the whole thing came crashing down. Blocks sailed in every direction.

"Goddam it," she said.

Oh dear, I thought, I had better start watching my language more carefully. I should say something. "Um, Masha, that's not really a little girl word," I said, as she surveyed the fallen city, "that's a daddy word."

She looked up at me, glaring. "It is too a little girl word, goddam it," she said.

We looked at each other for a few seconds before I nodded and left the room.

Our next gîte was outside a quiet village, behind a big iron gate wrought in an elaborate goose theme.

The house—a sagging, two-story ranch—was much less imposing than its gate, and judging by the vacant feeling of our upstairs apartment, the owners didn't seem to have had many visitors lately.[163] Our host apologized for the lack of Wi-Fi and the town's bad cellphone reception.

I did what I could without the Internet while Cybèle went out to forage for dinner. When she got back, she told us she hadn't found a store in the village, but she had seen an amazing little church, and found a restaurant with Wi-Fi.

After we cleaned ourselves up, we put our flip-flops on, I packed up my computer, and we click-clacked into town.

Saint-Antoine is an old village of around 400 people, most of whom live on either side of a narrow, pedestrian-only main street, if you can call a passage about as wide as a supermarket aisle a street. The church was interesting, as promised. Like the cathedral in Le Puy, it had been heavily restored in the 19th century. Some walls were stenciled flamboyantly like Victorian giftwrap, while others had older frescoed patterns that archaeologists had uncovered more recently. The statues, in addition to the usual suspects, included a three-foot high Joan of Arc, clad in fetching body armor, sword in hand.

We walked back down the street to the town's one restaurant, which for some reason specialized in food from Réunion Island, a French possession in the Indian Ocean 175 kilometers east of Madagascar.

In Paris, traffic and panhandlers often discouraged me from sit-

---

163 My guess is that people pressed for time skip this stretch of the Camino.

ting at sidewalk tables, but this street was so quiet, we decided to take our chances. After we ordered, Thea asked Cybèle if she could borrow her camera and walked back up the narrow street to the church to take some pictures. Cybèle was pleased—she had been encouraging Thea to do this, as a way to get her more interested in the hike.

The rest of us sat talking for a little while – it was pleasant outside, and felt more like sitting on someone's patio than on a street, especially as the shade from the rooftops crept over us. But after 20 minutes or so, Cybèle broke off suddenly and asked, "Where's Thea?"

I wasn't concerned but volunteered to go check on her and walked the block or so back up the street to the church.

I tried to pull open the massive old door, but now it wouldn't budge. I tried again. No, definitely locked.

"Dad?"

"Bug.[164] What are you doing in there?"

"What do you think I'm doing?"[165]

She sounded annoyed, but not traumatized. Our girls are thoroughgoing materialists and tend to be scared only by the tangible.[166]

"Is there another exit maybe?"

---

164 A pet name from way back, as in "cute as a …"

165 People talk a lot about parents giving their children complexes, but I think something could be said for the reverse. I know I have been disabused of many illusions about my own intelligence since we had our daughters.

166 Thea tells me that I was wrong about this. "I think you seriously underestimate how distraught I was. I was in fact very scared in part because the statues were terrifying and I was afraid of turning around on them, but also that the building might burn down. (I don't know why that occurred to me.) Also the vestibule between the sketchily lit church and the front door was pitch black so I really had to bet on there being nothing murderous around if I wanted to get out. Just saying." Still, it was a lucky thing it hadn't happened to me at her age, when I lived in dread of ghosts and aliens. I remember being alone in church once and believing that I had seen Mary move. After 15 minutes of being locked up in this church, I would have imagined Joan was ready to come after me with her broadsword.

"Would I be here if there were?"

"Take it easy. I'll go find somebody to open it back up."

I went back to the restaurant, and we told the waiter. A few minutes later, a heavy man turned into the main street, carrying an ancient key bigger than his hand, and unlocked the thick old door.

By the time we got back to the restaurant, it was still warm outside but getting too dark for Cybèle to lip-read so we decided to move inside. The restaurant had the woven strings of garlic, wooden beams, and white-washed stone walls you would expect in an old village cafe, but a few Christmas lights too, like an Indian restaurant, and old pictures clipped from magazines of palmy and volcanic Réunion Island.

Réunion food is spicy, which was a treat. As much as I like most things French, I missed spicy food. At the high end, the French have subtler pleasures—cognacs that unfold like novels, desserts with subtexts, and all those amazing cheeses—but by and large, in the heart of the heart of La France, you're eating various configurations of meat and potatoes. I wondered why the proprietors had decided to specialize in Réunion dishes and concluded, as they were a white family, that they probably had some colonial connection to the island.[167] But maybe there was no connection at all. There is often a theme park aspect to restaurants, and if for some reason the proprietors preferred Réunion recipes to Provençal and the trade could support it, why not Réunion?

The place made me think of road trips in the States and the little bits of Bavaria or Vietnam or Ethiopia you run into occasionally way out in the country, restaurants that usually give me a sense of triple homelessness – I'm in a town I don't know, eating in a restaurant whose owners have made a business out of foreignness but may not have been back home for 30 years, as I email somebody six time zones away—but I didn't feel that tonight.

---

167   Or they may have had a connection with one of the Children of Creuse, a group of 1,600 orphans that the French government plucked from overpopulated Réunion and resettled in underpopulated rural France between 1963 and 1982, often with less happy results than this restaurant.

This place was busy enough that it squeezed out that sense of foreignness, and too loud for me to make the call I was supposed to make at the end of dinner. The local cell phone tower still seemed to be out of order even here in the heart of the village, so going outside to make my call wasn't an option. Defeated, I emailed to reschedule my interview and relaxed. For the rest of the evening, I had no choice but to be entirely where I was. I kind of liked it.

July 27. Saint-Antoine to Lectoure, 23.5 km

In which we meet another Cybele.

Great goddess, goddess Cybele ... may all your insanity, lady, be far from my home. Drive others to frenzy, drive others mad.
Catulus

It was hot again the next day, but a steamier heat, like a greenhouse, and the fields seemed almost weighed down with sunflowers, melons, and artichokes.

"We walked all morning until we got to a town where we stopped for Cokes and watched Scooby Doo in French," Charlotte wrote. *"I accidentally hit Dad in the head with a baguette. He got a bruise."*

We reached Lectoure in the early afternoon. On our way up the main street, we passed the cathedral. Like a lot of the larger churches in the Midi built after the war against the Cathars, it looks less like a church than the castle of an occupying army. This one had few windows and a very tall Wicked Witch tower with parapets suitable for pouring boiling oil on mobs.

Our hostel was on the main street, and had a name like House of the Rising Sun. The front door was ajar so we walked in. Further inside, Thea noticed that *"The Common Room was painted the ugliest shade of pink, Blehk! [and had] all of these Indian scarves and random photos of Indian people [on the wall]...posters saying peace, creative attitude, love and happiness."*

No one seemed to be home at the moment, and the kitchen behind it was also empty. Someone had started making blackberry jam but evidently lost interest about halfway through the project, and the mess made the place look like a crime scene. Signs on the door of the small pink refrigerator warned in French and English not to touch the food inside.

Just then the landlady arrived, flouncing into the common room like Isadora Duncan. Her scarves and blond perm gave me the sense that she thought of herself as a free spirit, but she was actually too calculating for the role: the unflappable flapper managed to show us our stripped-down bunks, take our cash, and sashay back out into the southern light again, all inside of 10 minutes.[168]

After we checked in, I settled down to work at one of the common room tables while Cybèle took the girls to a spa built over natural hot springs, which they normally would not have thought much of, as the springs were neither very hot nor high-pressured. But they compared favorably to walking.

It's tempting to see people like our landlady and the spa proprietors as outsiders pushing aside the real France, but that's not really true. Hot baths and a New Age sensibility aren't anything new for Lectoure. Even in Roman times, when Lectoure had at least 5,000 inhabitants—a thousand more than today—baths and cults were already a feature. But back then, in addition to the hot springs, people visited because it was a center of the cult of Cybele, an ancient fertility goddess first worshiped in Anatolia (modern Turkey) and then adopted by Romans. Archaeologists have found 22 altars dedicated to her in Lectoure, more than anywhere else in the world.

No one knows why Lectoure became a capital of Cybeleism. Southern Gaul had had a few Greek colonies before the Romans arrived, and perhaps some of those colonists brought the religion with them. Lectoure was a hill town, and Cybele, besides being called the Great Mother and the Mother of the Gods, was also called the Mother of Mountains. Or the cult may have flourished here because Lectoure was an important military base and Cybele became a patron goddess of the Roman army around two centuries before Christ.

The Roman Army first drafted Cybele during the Second Pu-

---

168 Watching a performance like that, you begin to understand how it is that the French can be the 12th- most productive country in the world and never seem to break a sweat. We've seen that ourselves too: our dentist in Paris could examine and clean my teeth and have time left over for a chat and a handshake, all in seven minutes. And then there was Jeanette, our family friend in Saint-Cloud, who once, when she got home after a weekend in the country, had dinner on the table by the time her husband had unloaded the car.

nic War, in 204 BCE, according to several ancient historians. As Hannibal and the Carthaginians were closing in on Rome, the priests scoured the oracular Sibyllene books, looking for an edge, and found one: a prophecy that Rome would never be conquered if Cybele was on their side. The Romans asked the Oracle at Delphi for a second opinion, and when the oracle concurred with the Sibyllene diagnosis, sent a delegation to make a forceful request to the kings of Pergamon in Anatolia that they lend Rome their ancient idol, a black meteorite that Cybele's priests in Rome later incorporated into the head of a figure.

Cybele

(After a Getty Museum sculpture)

Like my Cybèle, Cybele[169] the goddess proved to be a powerful ally: soon after the Romans brought her to Rome, they managed to beat back Hannibal and the Carthaginians.

Now the Romans faced an awkward situation. Although they were delighted with their victories, they did not like the idea of keeping Cybele around.

The trouble was not so much the goddess as the company she kept— the Galli, her transvestite priests. If the Galli had just been gay it would not have been a problem— the Romans didn't have anything against homosexual activity[170] —but they didn't like transvestism, and the Galli "cross-dressed, wore makeup, frizzed their hair, drenched themselves in perfume, and acted like women." They may also have been eunuchs, but there is some debate about this, as the Galli were all Roman citizens and citizens were not allowed to castrate themselves.

---

169   The eagle-eyed will note that this Cybele is spelled *sans accent*.

170   In fact, they did not even have a word for it. On the contrary, being exclusively straight was considered a little eccentric. Historians have noted, for example, that the Emperor Claudius was the only one of the first 15 Roman emperors historians believe to have been exclusively heterosexual. Married or single, freeborn men were expected to desire male and female slaves and prostitutes and act on it. The rules were more or less the same as in an unenlightened executive suite, in that peers and social equals were out but adult underlings all fair game.

Most Romans were not too keen on the cult's practices, from orgiastic dancing and self-slashing with knives, to an initiation whose highpoints included a baptism in which the baptisee stood in a pit under a grate as the blood of a sacrificed bull rained down on him or her. The historian Stephen Benko speculates that their ceremonies must have been a bit like a punk rock concert.[171]

In the end, the Romans engineered a compromise. The cult could stay in Rome, but the priests were allowed to leave their temple only once a year to carry their idol through the streets and wash her in the Tiber. Also, oddly, given that Cybele was now part of the official pantheon, ordinary Roman citizens were not allowed to take part in her ceremonies, a rule the authorities managed to enforce for the next few hundred years, after which Cybeleism evolved into a popular religion.

How she broke out of her cloister is unclear. Historians know only that when she became a popular goddess, her worship was not an upper-class fad: judging from the inscriptions left on the bull altars in Lectour, Cybeleism as a popular religion seems to have bubbled up from the more downtrodden layers of the Roman social pyramid. In Lectoure, slaves, freedmen, and women donated most of the bull altars; at one year's festivities, women donated seven.

All that fervor meant that Cybele was one of the last gods to lose out to Christianity. The last pagan emperor, Julian the Apostate (330–363), who had been raised a Christian but turned against it as an adult, even tried to fashion Cybele-ism into a counter-Christian religion. As one scholar has speculated, the cult was well-suited to "appeal both to those who were attracted by the esoteric and 'mystical' while at the same time preserving a sense

---

171   Other historians argue that the more lurid details may have been cooked up by ever-inventive Christian imaginations. It should be noted, however, that the Cybele myth does have a fair amount of castration in it. In one version, Cybele falls in love with Attis, a youth of godlike beauty, but before they get together, his family sends him away to marry a princess. Just as the marriage song is sung, Cybele suddenly appears, her beauty so transcendent that Attis, in a fit of passion, goes crazy and castrates himself. At this point, his father-in-law—for reasons that I understand even less—follows suit. Three days later, Cybele brings 98 percent of Attis back from the dead.

of being Roman, something that would have been impossible for rival cults such as the cult of the Egyptian goddess Isis."[172]

Julian, like his half-brother, Constantine the Great (272-337), who presided over the conference in Nicea in 325 that gave us the Nicean Creed (the prayer that begins "We believe in one God"), thought a lot about Christianity. An accomplished philosopher, he sounds quite sincere, both when he writes against Christianity and when he writes in favor of Cybele. He was clearly not the dissipated *pass-the-wine-and-the-slave-boy* emperor you see in the movies.

In Julian's essay "Against the Galileans," a name he may have used to make Christianity sound like a small-time foreign cult, he asks a number of questions that this heathen would also like answers to, such as, why would God *not* want people to eat from the Tree of Knowledge and learn the difference between good and evil, as that's the most important thing of all to know?

Finally, he asks, what has your god done for you lately?

> Asclepius heals our bodies, and the Muses with the aid of Asclepius and Apollo and Hermes, the god of eloquence, train our souls; Ares fights for us in war and Enyo also; Hephaistus apportions and administers the crafts, and Athene the Motherless Maiden with the aid of Zeus presides over them all. Consider therefore whether we are not superior to you in every single one of these things, I mean in the arts and in wisdom and intelligence ... if we who have not given ourselves over to the spirit of apostasy, fare better than you in soul and body and external affairs, why do you abandon these teachings of ours and go over to those others?

But Julian died before he could really turn Cybeleism into the Pepsi to Christianity's Coke—and after his short two-year reign, he was succeeded by a solid string of Christian emperors who eventually suppressed Cybeleism and other competing religions.

Some scholars have argued that Cybele actually did survive but

---

172   Cybeleism was the oldest of a number of cults that migrated from the Near East to Europe in Roman times that historians often label "mystery religions." The cults of Cybele, Isis, Mithras, and sometimes Jesus are included in this category. Most are chock-full of virgin births, sacrificial deaths, and resurrections.

gradually morphed into Mary. One case in point: Constantine, who made Christianity a legal religion during his reign and converted himself on his death bed, had a temple to the Magna Mater (one of Cybele's titles) built in his new capital city of Constantinople. Zosimus, a pagan historian, notes that Constantine ordered an old statue of Cybele brought from Greece, and placed in the temple, but that he had directed that the statue be "mutilated." He had the lions removed from the sides, and her hands adjusted into a Mary-like pose. "[W]hereas before, she had seemed to hold back the lions, she had now been transformed into a kind of pious figure, her eyes looking toward the city and protecting it with her solicitude," writes the art historian Phillippe Borgeaud. In being moved to the new Christian capital, "the Mother of the gods, had lost her ancient attributes and assumed the loving, protective stance of the...Mother of God, her close neighbor. But she did not forget her origins."[173]

Even now, however, the Magna Mater herself still keeps popping up: my Cybèle (and a surprising number of other women about her age we have met over the years – also usually artists, for some reason) got her name from a New Wave movie her parents liked, known in the United States as *Sundays and Cybèle* and in French by the less catchy title *Cybèle ou les Dimanches de Ville-d'Avray.* [174]

---

173 Other aspects of paganism seem to have stayed with us as well. Blue, for instance, was the color of Rome's Vestal Virgins before it became Mary's color. As the historian Ramsay MacMullen puts it, "there was never any total eclipse of paganism: prayers, holy images, candles, bells, holy water, holy dust, the blood of holy persons, little bags worn around the neck with spells inside them written on papyrus all had their roots in the pre-Christian world." And of course, pilgrimages, which were also quite popular with the Romans.

174 *Sundays and Cybèle* was a big movie in 1962—it won the Oscar for Best Foreign Picture. It's a sad, beautifully shot black and white film about a veteran of the French installment of the Vietnam War who overcomes his guilt about accidentally killing a little Vietnamese girl through his doomed friendship with a French orphan girl, Catherine. The girl eventually tells the veteran that Catherine isn't her real name—that the nuns at the orphanage made her change it from a heathen name. The veteran begs her to tell him her real name but she demurs until finally at the end, as a Christmas present, she gives him a matchbox. Inside, he finds a tiny piece of paper on which she has written her true, pagan name, *Cybèle*, a poignant, bittersweet moment that occurs shortly before the film's tragic end (it's a New Wave film, remember). Unfortunately, time has not been kind to *Sundays and Cybèle*. It's hard for people to watch today, because as one blogger puts it, people are "creeped out" by the premise of a friendship between a man and a 12-year-old girl.

July 28. Lectoure to Castelnau-sur-Auvignon, 16.5 km

In which Don Quixote gets me lost again and I pine for the Warrior Princess.

Cybèle has two complaints about my listening to audiobooks when we hike: first, that they slow me down—which is true—and second, that I appreciate the landscape less when I listen to them—which is not.

The morning after Lectoure, for instance, I remember vividly, the way you occasionally remember a dream: I was alone on a wide white path, rounding a hill between two sets of leafy trees, a landscape so perfect it looked almost like an oil painting by one of the old masters. Sancho and Don Quixote had just met a wagon

> full of the strangest figures that can be imagined, and conducted by a frightful demon that drove the mules. The cart being altogether open ... the first figure that struck the eyes of Don Quixote, was death itself in human shape; next to which appeared an angel, with broad painted wings: on one side, stood an emperor with a crown (seemingly) of gold, upon his head ...

I can see them now, rounding the bend toward me, a strange bunch that turned out to be a traveling theater troupe. The players were all still costumed, preparing for a play called the Parliament of Death. The chief of the players, driving the cart, plays the devil, and tells Don Quixote,

> "If your worship is desirous of knowing anything else concerning our affairs, question me freely, and I will answer with the utmost punctuality, for, being a devil, I understand everything."

On the other hand, if part of the purpose of the walk is to get somewhere in particular, Cybèle has a point. That morning, for instance, after one of the actors had pounded a bell-covered pole on the ground, scaring Don Quixote's horse enough that Rosinante threw the knight from his saddle, I suddenly realized that

I had lost my way again.[175]

If I had been following the family, this wouldn't have been a problem, but I'd stayed behind to work that morning—I'd owed another labor of love to the *Economic Times,* so I was on my own once more. Had the trail followed a river or a valley or both, I would also have been okay, but I was walking now through rolling hills that ran on for miles in every direction, and the last trail marker was at least half a chapter behind me. A little later, when

175 Of course, my disorientation might have been a function not just of listening but also my choice of book. *Don Quixote* is one of those books that is so complete in itself the real world can start to feel like an extension of the page—especially if you too are trudging down a dusty road in a silly hat on a pointless quest.

my white lane met a paved two-lane highway without any trail marks, I decided I had better turn off *Quixote* and turn on my Google map. The blue pin bounced up and down, insisting, "You are here, You are here, You are here," but we were so far out in the country, "here" was hard to define. All I could tell from the map was that I was somewhere between Paris and the Pyrenees, and that I already knew.

Gers is one of the least populous and most remote provinces in France, which may be why Alexandre Dumas decided to make it the home country of D'Artagnan, the young bumpkin who makes good in *The Three Musketeers*.[176]

I can understand why D'Artagnan would have taken the first nag out of Gers. The countryside is pretty but after that one stretch with the white path, very little of the land had the kind of showy scenery I needed to stay on track. This irritated me, particularly because now that I had turned off my book, I was getting bored.

I'm not very good at tolerating boredom, and I've always had a horror of it.[177] In retrospect, I think I even infected the girls. When Masha was still in her stroller, I found a Walkman with a speaker, and used it like a car stereo. By kindergarten, when she was out of the stroller and we had put Tito Puente away, I started to tell her a story to pass the time as I walked her to school in the morning.

---

176   By coincidence, Dumas seems to locate Gers just north of La Mancha:

Imagine to yourself a Don Quixote of eighteen; a Don Quixote without his corselet, without his coat of mail, without his cuisses; a Don Quixote clothed in a woolen doublet, the blue color of which had faded into a nameless shade between lees of wine and a heavenly azure; face long and brown; high cheek bones, a sign of sagacity; the maxillary [jaw] muscles enormously developed, an infallible sign by which a Gascon may always be detected, even without his cap ... Too big for a youth, too small for a grown man, an experienced eye might have taken him for a farmer's son upon a journey had it not been for the long sword which, dangling from a leather baldric, hit against the calves of its owner as he walked, and against the rough side of his steed when he was on horseback.

177   One of my first literary productions was Ben's Things to Do Magazine, which I sent to my grandmother while she was in the hospital when I was seven or eight. It included a story, a puzzle, and a dot-to-dot picture. But the mania began to appear even earlier: my parents and grandparents often used to repeat a story that when I three, when we were moving out of one house, the parents and grandparents left me in front of the television while they moved boxes. All morning, they carried everything off to the U-Haul—my bed, my toys, the lamps, and the furniture, and I, the little stoic, didn't care. Then they came back for one last box. "Not the TV!" I shouted.

Over the next few hundred miles, that story became *The Warrior Princess and Masha*, a spaceship and boarding-school saga filled with plenty of what Cybèle sometimes calls hang-cliffters. Block by block, *The Warrior Princess and Masha* evolved into something like a radio serial, complete with theme music and commercials. Sound effects I delegated to the audience. Each episode lasted 20 minutes, just enough time to get from home to school.

The Warrior Princess was a strong and unflappable heroine a lot like Cybèle; Masha was her brave sidekick. In most of their adventures, the duo were assisted by Masha's best friends, fellow classmates from Queen Vidya's Academy (a Spartan boarding school for brave orphan girls where every day began with a run, an icy morning swim, and a tasteless but highly nutritious bowl of mush called wariola). I'm not sure how the cadets learned anything because their classes were often interrupted for intergalactic fieldtrips, mostly missions to thwart a large cast of villains: Miss Evil, Queen Vidya's wicked opposite; Miss Evil's old nanny, the wicked Babaganoush; Princess Trixiana aka Pretty Little Miss Evil; and Trixiana's father, Baron von Oushagob, the fattest man in the galaxy. But I digress.

Having Masha as a main character, however, had one drawback: when Charlotte and Thea started going to school, they wanted their own stories too, so we ended up having to alternate between programs every day. First I would tell Masha's story, then Charlotte's—the *Adventures of Alicia and Alana,* with Red the Sailor and his pal the Talking Bear and Captain Nell the Pirate Queen—and finally Thea's *Early Adventures of Tamara,* a Warrior Princess spinoff that enabled me to reuse some of Masha's back-lot.

Of the three, Masha was the happiest about her story. Charlotte liked her story well enough, I guess, or was at least polite about it. Thea, however, could be a tough audience. Like many talented actresses, she wanted to direct. "Stop. No, I don't want that to happen. I want the mermaids to find them. And can you put a baby in?"[178]

We kept up that storytelling routine for so many years that even now part of me is still on the Upper West Side, barreling down Columbus Avenue, past Mani Market, past the 99-cent store with the plaster Marys and angels in the window, down to the turrets of the Natural History Museum, and right to PS 87, the William T. Sherman School; and later, in Paris, zigzagging through the streets past our *boucherie* and *boulangerie*, our *fromagerie* and our *fruiterie*: left on Rue Mademoiselle, past the elementary school with the climbable wall; right on Rue Quinault, left on rue Meihac, across rue de la Croix Nivert to rue du Theatre, across rue Commerce and past the patisserie with the great *chocolat fondants* and Place Zola, the Warrior Princess flying and swooping and leaping beside us all the way.

I would get so caught up in these stories sometimes, particularly when we got to a denouement I had been saving for Friday morning, that when we rounded the last corner before the front door I would be all but teary-eyed and breathless *when suddenly,* the wicked Baba in her bat-winged suit descended on Masha; or Alana, forced by the wicked arch-thief Seven-Fingered Jack to steal the incomparable Blue Magoo, had the jewel snatched away from her at the last possible moment by Captain Nell the Pirate Queen; or Tamara jumped off the castle wall onto the fruit seller's awning far below, bounced across the street where she swung herself around a lamppost, knocked two of the baron's men out of his oversized hovercraft, and sped out of town.

So I took it hard when Masha decided in seventh grade that she

---

178   Thea would also make up some of her own stories occasionally—but she could be so convincing, I didn't always know it. In first grade, for example, the year we moved to Paris, she told me about a cooking class at school that the mother of a friend of hers who ran a bakery taught sometimes. She mentioned this off and on over the next few weeks, giving me occasional details about the menu—because, she said, they were getting good enough that they cooked lunch for the teachers once a week. This went on long enough that at one school event that fall I went up to the mother and thanked her. She looked at me absolutely mystified. It turned out that all that fall, not only had I been telling Thea a story, but she had been telling me one right back. Even now, I still remember the cooking class—all the little kids lined up in their starched white aprons, spoons in hand. I remember it more clearly than a lot of things that did happen.

was too old for me to walk her to school anymore—somebody had overheard me and teased her about it. How would Queen Vidya manage? What would become of the brave and perpetually hungry Daisy and Avalanche, Daisy's giant snuggly snow-cat? No more *Tune in tomorrow for another exciting episode of the Warrior Princess and Masha ... doot-dah dah dahh!?* Charlotte's and Thea's stories kept going a year or two longer but they too creaked to a halt eventually. I tried to be mature as this time ended, but deep down, I felt as if I had been fired from a favorite job.

"Banish plump Jack, and banish all the world."

I suppose every family has variations of routines like this. Even offices can be that way sometimes, if you've spent enough time together. Not in terms of telling long, strange stories semi-obsessively but in how the things we say—the inside jokes, the catch phrases—become a part of who we are and eventually, who we were. As usual in the Troyan-Voyles conspiracy, we just took things to extremes. As I think about it now, it occurs to me that the Warrior Princess may have had something to do with why we were on the Camino de Santiago, which when you get down to it is just another walk with a story attached.

After another hour or so of wandering, I stumbled onto the correct path again, and turned *Don Quixote* back on. As the path dipped into a gully at the bottom of a hill and a dark wood, a country squire dressed entirely in green rode up beside the Don, Sancho, and me. He was a man of "about fifty; he had some, tho' few grey hairs; his features were sharp, and in his looks appeared neither levity nor moroseness: in short, his appearance bespoke him a man of consequence." He looked over Quixote; Quixote, Sancho, and I looked him over, and before I knew it, I had climbed through the woods to the top of a hill, and the day's destination—a tiny town with a big name, Castelnau-sur-l'Auvignon—"New Castle on the Auvignon."

Most of the buildings on Castelnau's main street were relatively new and I didn't see a castle, either new or old. Near a little war memorial, a concrete semi-circle that looked like half of a budget

Stonehenge, an unusually detailed plaque explained why.[179]

The man who answered the door of our gîte was a tanned skinny guy about my age in shorts, glasses, and a goatee. You could imagine him running a beach-related business in California, where his name would be something like Kris with a K. He directed me through his newish ranch house to his backyard, where Cybèle and the girls were already lolling in and around a little pool he had just retiled. (I had the feeling that like the flapper at our last gîte, he had a knack for getting a lot of things done without moving very fast.) I smiled, not only because I was glad to see everyone, but because far in the distance—behind the pool, beyond the fields that stretched out far below us— I could see a hazy white line at the horizon that I knew had to be the Pyrenees.

That night, the girls took one room; an Austrian woman, Cybèle, and I shared another. The Austrian was not happy with this arrangement. She was terrified that we would give her bedbugs, even though Kris had already examined our packs very methodically through jeweler's glasses, but she warmed up after Cybèle let her spray our bags with insecticide.[180]

Dinner was jolly—an older Norwegian couple, schoolteachers; our Austrian roommate; and our hosts, Kris and his wife. Kris's

---

179 The plaque recounted the story a film producer should option of a Resistance cell that had operated very successfully in the town during the war, out of a hidden room in the elementary school that the mayor had found for them. There were three or four partisans in the group, including a female radio operator code-named Simone. Through most of the war, Simone and her band kept at it, sending messages and arranging parachute drops. As in Moissac, no one in the town betrayed them. The best part is that the ending was very cinematic, and unusual in being happy, at least for the partisans: when the Nazis finally moved in, our heroes defended the castle for awhile, and when they couldn't hold them back any longer, ran out the back way one by one, and blew up the castle just as the German reinforcements rolled up. Cue *La Marseillaise*.

180 I got the impression on this trip that Austrians don't get out much. This woman, for instance, spoke no English and only a little French. I tend to think of Austria as a sort of fraternal twin of Switzerland but it's not true. They might seem to have a lot in common—mountains, chocolate, and morally flexible bankers—but the cultural wealth of the country of Strauss and Freud is less evenly distributed than in other European countries: only 10 percent of the 8.5 million Austrians have a university degree, and nearly that many (600,000) are functionally illiterate, according to one government estimate.

wife was a quiet, pretty woman who also seemed very capable but a little too formal for her role as a gîte hostess, as if the gods had made a mistake along the way and right at that moment in a posh Paris suburb a bohemian lady was passing out canapés and cocktails to her elegant neighbors.

"We had dinner around seven. Salad to start then rice with chicken and vegees," Charlotte wrote. *"The dessert was a wonderful warm chocolate fondante with homemade raspberry ice cream that tasted like smashed berries and whipped cream. NEW BEST MEAL! I wish we could stay here forever!"*

Kris told us they had gotten into the gîte business by accident about 10 years before. One night a German pilgrim knocked at the door and asked if they had a room available. Kris said yes, and it went on from there. I wonder sometimes how much of life starts this way, with a case of mistaken identity that turns into a real identity—like the psychologist Konrad Lorenz's experiment, when he found that goose chicks would consider him their mother if they saw him 12–17 hours after they hatched.

Late in the dinner, after the wine went around the table once more, Kris told a story about a French couple he had heard about who had gone to China with their dog. They had stopped in a restaurant, and through hand signals, motioned that the dog needed some water. The waiter took the dog back into the kitchen and a few minutes later, brought the dog back out—on a platter.

The guests didn't know what to say and we all chuckled awkwardly. Kris's wife winced. Not long after, she quietly trundled him off to bed and we all called it a night.

July 29. Castelnau-sur-l'Auvignon to Montréal-du-Gers

In which we meet castaways and outcasts.

The next morning, we passed through the town with the funniest name since Montcuq—Condom—where we took a picture of the girls in front of larger-than-life statues of D'Artagnan and the Three Musketeers, and ran into the Norwegian teachers we had met at dinner the night before.[181]

For most of the day, we followed the Ténarèze, a ridge route used since neolithic times by animals, shepherds, and invading armies because it's the easiest way to get to the Pyrenees without crossing any rivers. Paleontologists have found the skeletons of 90 different species in the Ténarèze, including four never seen anywhere else. The latest discovery, in 1992, was the paleomeryx, a ruminant that looked something like a cross between a deer and a giraffe, but is thought to be an ancestor of the rhinoceros.

If I had known this at the time, I would have told Thea. She is the family expert on the prehistoric, because for some reason, French grade school teachers are obsessed with the subject. Just as American schoolkids are forever studying the American Revolution and the Civil Rights Movement, the young French get alternating doses of the *prehistoire* and Napoleon. The Napoleonic obsession I understand but I'm not sure why they feel this way about the prehistoire. Maybe it's because of the Lascaux cave paintings, which are in southern France. Or maybe it's their fascination with places they imagine lack rules, like Tahiti, the Sahara, or Las Vegas.

Post-prehistoire, the Ténarèze stayed busy as well. Caesar drove his legions this way and most other Iberian-bound invaders followed him. Even imaginary people took this path: in 1910, in a nice bit of detective work, one French scholar, Léopold Médan, argued that Robinson Crusoe must have returned to England by

---

181   The town's name actually has no relation to what the English used to call a French letter and the French referred to as a *redingote anglaise* (an English riding coat).

way of the Ténarèze.

In modern shipwreck movies, the credits start to roll when you see shiny boots on a beach, but in the 17th and 18th centuries, a castaway's troubles were far from over when he was found. It takes Daniel Defoe several chapters and many adventures to get his hero back by ship to Spain and then overland through France to England. Médan deduces that because Crusoe says he did not take Saint James's Way out of Pamplona, which he reports was impassable on account of snow, his only alternative would have been nearer the coast—that is, the Ténarèze.

Crusoe reaches France after a tough crossing of the Pyrenees that includes close calls with snow, a bear, and wolves. He does not have much good to say about the mountains, mostly because of the wolves:

> For my part, I was never so sensible of danger in my life; for, see-ing above three hundred devils come roaring and open-mouthed to devour us, and having nothing to shelter us or retreat to, I gave myself over for lost; and, as it was, I believe I shall never care to cross those mountains again: I think I would much rather go a thousand leagues by sea, though I was sure to meet with a storm once a-week.[182]

We talked a little that day but in general, it was a fairly solitary stretch. We were all comfortable enough walking by this time that the Camino had become a mobile living room in which the girls and I—only Cybèle still paid much attention to the land-scape now—tried to keep ourselves amused as best we could.

---

182   One chapter in the Pyrenees section does contain an attempt at comic relief—a strange anecdote in which Crusoe's man Friday, to make the company laugh, lures a bear to climb up a tree after him, crawls out on a limb, shakes the limb he and the bear are standing on to make the bear dance, and in the end, after a little more kidding around

> stepped up close to him, clapped the muzzle of his piece into his ear, and shot him dead. Then the rogue turned about to see if we did not laugh; and when he saw we were pleased by our looks, he began to laugh very loud. "So we kill bear in my country," says Friday. "So you kill them?" says I; "why, you have no guns."—"No," says he, "no gun, but shoot great much long arrow."

Ha ha ha.

I'm actually not sure what's supposed to be amusing about that, but on the other hand I have had similar feelings watching Quentin Tarantino films.

Masha was still listening to *Dombey and Son* but would stop the recording every so often to relay the better bits to me. Thea and

Charlotte were working out a plot for a science fiction story they planned to write, and talking again about redecorating their rooms, which they intended to rearrange the minute Masha left for boarding school.[183]

Our breaks had become somewhat less sociable the past few days. By this time, the girls were thoroughly bored with their parents, and had begun to pull their Kindles out of their backpacks every time we stopped, like unionized workers determined to take their full coffee break. Cybèle didn't like this but I let it

---

183   I have always found kids to be brutally unsentimental about these transitions. Charlotte and Thea's big sister might be leaving for boarding school in another country but at that moment the chief impression it made on them was that now they would each have their own room. It reminded me of a time in high school when I left the house in a huff for reasons I no longer remember, and took a walk so long that when I cooled down and returned four or five hours later, I learned that my youngest brother, Tye, had already asked if he could have my bed if I didn't come back.

go most of the time. I tend to be more sympathetic to some kinds of antisocial behavior than she is, and I also didn't want to push them any harder than we already were.

What bothered me more was realizing that this adventure would probably be one of the last we took together. First Masha would be gone, then the others. Soon, there would be jobs and partners and their own lives, without a lot of time left over for their parents. If Cybèle and I were lucky, the girls would look back on this summer as one of many adventures, like a half-forgotten episode of the Warrior Princess. And if it didn't, our Camino would be one of the exhibits recounted to a future therapist about their parents' crimes—another weird, exhausting thing Mom and Dad forced them to do. Either way, whether they remembered it as a great story or a terrible one, the adventure would be over, and in any case, what did it matter? As Cervantes says at the conclusion of *Don Quixote*, through his alter ego, "The sagacious Cid Hamet addressing himself to his pen, 'And now, my slender quill, said he, whether cunningly cut, or unskillfully formed, it boots not much...'"

The girls joke, not inaccurately, that they have been inside more churches than most people who actually go to church, but we somehow missed one just outside of Montreal du Gers that has an unusual feature I would like to have seen, which is shared by 60 churches in the region: a low side door that was once the special entrance for Cagot.

The Cagots' treatment was an unusual exception to the general rule of paratge in the Midi. They were shunned by their neighbors in southwest France for hundreds of years—forced to live outside their villages, stick to carpentry and a short list of other professions; not walk barefoot, touch or share food with other people; and advertise their pariah status by wearing a goose's foot pinned prominently to their clothes. Even the Church offered them no comfort: they could only enter the village church through a special entrance like the one we had just missed, and take communion from the end of a long wooden spoon.

What provoked this treatment is unclear. They didn't move

around, like the Roma or the Travellers in Ireland. They had the same religion. They spoke the same language as their neighbors, and probably even looked the same, although some people claimed you could tell Cagots by their lack of an earlobe, while others said they were shorter and swarthier than other people in their villages.

Some people have theorized that they were the descendants of Vikings. Others think they were part of the 8th-century Moorish invasion. In any case, whatever first set them apart is now utterly forgotten.

The Cagot category was officially abolished during the French Revolution, but the persecution lingered well into the 19th century. The Cagot have all but disappeared now—only one woman, Marie-Pierre Manet-Beauzac of Tarbes, has claimed her heritage. A believer in the theory that they were the descendents of Moorish soldiers, she has told reporters she still sees short swarthy people in towns near her that she believes to be Cagots. But even now, neither French nor French-Cagot want to talk about it.

Manet-Beauzac said she can still feel the prejudice sometimes. "In some places, the hatred lingers. Even now. The Cagots may be silent but I can still hear it."

Our hotel that night was just beyond the little stone town of Montreal du Gers, a roadhouse in a gully outside the city walls. The ground floor of the old house had been converted into a bar and the upper floor had four or five rooms, clean and bright in a scrubbed-raw way, like an old but well-run hospital.

 Kris the surfer dude had warned us at breakfast that the proprietor could be tough. Correct, he said, but tough. He was right about that: she seemed like someone from another time, a poorer, sterner France. She wore tortoise-shell glasses and had her hair pulled back in a severe bun that gave her an angry intellectual look, as if Simone du Beauvoir had decided one day to chuck philosophy and open a restaurant but was now having second thoughts.

When we arrived, I asked her if she had Wi-Fi. "Non," she said. Not "no, sorry about that," or "sorry, I'm getting it next month," but just plain old "non," as if I'd asked whether it would be all right if we stayed up all night rehearsing for a flamenco competition.

But for some reason, her severity didn't extend to the décor. The counter had *"a water fountain where a stork in glasses barphs water every ten seconds. The toilette seat is clear with starfish and shells floating around inside...On the wall in our room there is a painting of the town with trees and flying chickens,"* wrote Thea.

Dinner tasted good to me, but our hostess seemed so depressed and lost in her thoughts I wondered why she bothered, particularly as we were the only guests, and she wasn't making much money off us. All through the evening, she stayed gruff, coming and going with the dishes—vegetable soup, cucumber and tomato salad with ham and boiled egg, duck for the main course, apple pie for dessert. After clearing the dessert plates, she left us alone to watch the Olympics on the TV over the bar. France was swimming. On French Olympic coverage, it seems like the French are always swimming.

Everyone slept well that night, I think, including Madame de Beauvoir. In the morning, on her front porch, she or her kind-hearted twin wished us a good journey and then with a shy smile told us our daughters were beautiful.

July 30. Montréal-du-Gers to La Hargue, 23 km
In which we visit a haunted house.

The next night, we stayed in a crumbling chateau that was being renovated by a young English couple. They had fixed up parts of it in a way that would have done Jamie Oliver proud, but hadn't been able to finish the whole manse yet. Entire wings were blocked off and looked like they might fall down at any moment. Cybèle wrote:

> It was just us and two friendly cats – the place was beautiful – a gorgeous Japanese tree with pink puff ball blossoms. At one side through the gate was a patio with a greenhouse filled with flowers and then a long lap pool that the girls thought was a fountain. We swam there for a while. Then we took a bath! – a real luxury. The last time we took a bath was at Conques, which seems like a hundred years ago.

When dinner was ready, our hostess took us to a long table at the center of their gravel patio near the greenhouse. As we were their only guests, having that single table set added a spooky, gothic air to the meal, as if we were in a *Town & Country* remake of *Beauty and the Beast*. A small shy woman with a crooked smile, she would bring us courses at intervals, then disappear. The food was skimpy and not especially good, but it looked pretty.

After dinner, Charlotte and her sisters went back to play some more with the cats, Taffy and Nipper, then *"went back on the swing and Masha entertained us with her oh so hilarious 'super pooper' dance routine."*

The girls were all in good form that night. Charlotte in particular was beginning to feel better, now that we were getting close

Taffy

to Spain. *"My left boot has a hole in the side and both heels are worn down so Mom says I can throw them away in Pamplona when we start biking. Score!"*

Not long after dinner, I had an interview with someone out in California, but because I couldn't get any cell phone reception in our room and the chateau did not have Wi-Fi, I went signal-hunting up the hill behind the house.

Outside, the sun had just set but the sky was still pink. I walked up the gravel lane past a sty where seething masses of piglets converged on several enormous sows. At a wide spot in the lane a little further up, I opened my computer, and called my interview subject, a woman in California who had made her fortune in software and then reinvented herself as an organic beef rancher and organic farm banker.

I liked her—she had a confident, no-nonsense quality I hadn't expected. She said she got into the organic agricultural loan business after deciding that the old business model of making as much money as you could, raping and pillaging as you go, then spending what you had made on philanthropy, no longer made sense. Why not do some good now?

It was dark by the time I got off the phone and crunched back down the gravel road to the house. The pigs snorted as I passed.

July 31. La Hargue to Dubarry, 25 km
In which I say goodbye to Don Quixote.

In the morning before breakfast we talked to the landlord, a big guy who had bad teeth but by way of compensation, looked like a youngish Depardieu.

Cybèle told him about a dog she had shooed away from a rabbit outside our window the night before. He grimaced in a friendly way and said he wished she hadn't done that, as the rabbits kept getting into his vegetables. I guess when you get down to it, *MacGregor v. Cottontail* is a dispute usually seen from the vantage point of people who don't have a garden.

Our host told us they had ended up there not because they wanted to be in France particularly, but because he had always wanted to live in the country, heard you could buy farms for not much money in southern France, and when they drove down here to find out, discovered the rumor was true.

They had been there for 12 years now and didn't get back home much anymore. They kept pigs and chickens and geese, but I got the sense that the business side of the adventure hadn't worked out very well. Luckily, though, after his neighbors saw how nicely he had fixed up their place, they had started hiring him to renovate their houses too, and I gathered the couple got by on his carpentry.

Despite that limitation, he seemed to feel good about the life they had built, and he was right to feel that way. They were living the way they had wanted to live, one that a lot of people, even millionaires like the retired software magnate I had spoken to the night before, dream about for years before they ever try—if they ever take the plunge.[184] But even discount dreams can be expensive. I had the impression that, as is often the case with couples doing something out of the ordinary, the dream belonged mostly to him, but she had paid more for it.

After breakfast, I went back to *Don Quixote*. I was getting near the end now, and the story was turning sad on me, as the Knight was beginning to realize he had been deluded all along. I guess it was inevitable given the time and place Cervantes wrote the novel, but I think Twain found a more satisfying ending for that other great road story, *Huckleberry Finn*, when he has Huck light out for the territories. Then again, I would; even after so many years in Europe, I'm still an American at heart, and for better and worse we have a gift, even a genius, for not facing the facts.

---

184 But as far as the idea of moving to France is concerned, the couple wasn't unique. In 2012, British-born people represented 5 percent of the French immigrant polation. They tied with Spain as the fourth-largest immigrant group in France, after Portuguese (7 percent), Moroccans (7 percent), and Algerians (7 percent). In recent years, the Southwest has been a particularly popular destination. The 40,000 or so Brits who live in southwest France are a far cry from the 400,000 who lived in Spain in 2012 (or 240,000 who live there now, according to Spanish government statistics—the number has fallen dramatically in recent years) but it's still sizable enough that some southwestern villages are up to one-third British.

August 1. Dubarry to Aire-sur-l'Adour, ~~24~~ km

Wherein we attend the tale of Patrick the Irish Android and face some undeniable knobs of reality.

The unusual thing about August 1 was that there was less of it than we had expected.

We were tired, because our room the night before had been a stuffy, low-ceilinged attic, and resigned to another dreary day of hiking through miles and miles of more flat fields.

But just two hours into our seven-hour ordeal, at around 11:30, we passed an old communal washing basin on the outskirts of a town and realized we had already reached our destination.[185] Cybèle had miscalculated! She was disconcerted but the rest of us were ecstatic. It felt like a snow day.

But the festive feeling didn't last long. Aire-sur-l'Adour had a lively quality, like a port city, but there was not much to see, we

Aire-sur-l'Adour

---

185 Washing by hand is a recent enough phenomenon that a number of the towns we passed through still had municipal washing basins, which look just like a small swimming pool, but with sloped sides for easier scrubbing, and often a roof for shade.

were too early to check into our gîte, and it had begun to rain.

To pass the time, we sat down under an ancient stone portico that had been a cattle market for a few hundred years and ate a chilly picnic. While we were waiting, our old friend Patrick the Irish android walked up. He was staying at the same hostel we were and decided to wait with us.

Patrick was in a good mood—we were now only two days away from Saint-Jean-Pied-de-Port, the end of the French Camino, and he would be going home soon. As we waited on the cold, smooth stones and looked out at the light rain, he told us a bit more about himself. He had hoped to be a policeman, but couldn't qualify, for reasons he didn't go into. Instead, he got a job as a teacher in a poor town outside Dublin—where ironically, his crew cut made some of the kids think he was an undercover cop. Now he taught English at a high school in a small town outside Cork, and he liked that much better, though most of his students weren't much good. "We can't all be university-bound," he said.

Every summer, he tried to take a big trip. The past two years, it had been the Camino. Next year, he hoped to hike up Mount Kilimanjaro in Africa. He liked to do things like that, he said, where you could tick the box when you were done. Right now, however, he seemed to be thinking mostly about going home. He had it all planned, he said, looking out toward Ireland through the drizzle: he would get a taxi from the airport but then would have the cabbie drop him a few miles outside his town, so he could walk into his village with his backpack on and his big wooden walking stick and stop at his pub, to make it look as if he had hiked all the way. That would be a laugh.

Our gîte that night was much more Catholic than the last few places we had stayed, with devotional posters everywhere, along with instructions about what was and was not allowed. Outside every room, the proprietor had pinned up big pieces of brown paper on the plywood partitions and encouraged guests to leave messages, like a wallpaper guestbook. By and large, people obliged, writing a number of effusive testimonials about the host, his gîte, and the pilgrimage. Personally, I found the place dark and dank, but that may have just been the weather.

> "On the wall by the dining table was a row of rubber pieces that
> go on the ends of crutches – I asked what they were and the owner
> told me the story of a guy who walked from Germany on one leg
> up to l'Aire Sur l'Adour then got sick and was sent back home. He
> died and his wife sent the rubber pieces of his crutches to him,"
> Cybèle wrote.

I'm still not quite sure what to make of those brown rubber
stops. Did the wife consider them testimony to a miracle of
some kind, that her husband had made it all the way to this
town from Germany, despite his illness? Or as an accusation,
like the bed knobs on Don Quixote's deathbed—evidence that in
the end even the best stories can carry us only so far.

August 2. Aire-sur-L'Adour to Pimbo, 28 km
Of geese and their livers.

From the bottom of the hill, after a day of walking through bright cornfields, the farm on the ridge above us looked ominous, almost like a prison camp—a long low building with a corrugated aluminum roof. "There's our gîte," I said.

Nobody laughed.

When we reached the crest, we discovered that Stalag 17 really was part of our gîte—a duck and goose farm owned by our hosts. In the flowerbeds in front of the long barn, the farmer had put up plywood cutouts of cartoon geese. Inside, in the dark, the geese honked madly at us as we passed.

I don't like geese, but I discovered I do like geese farmers, at least the two we stayed with that night.

Our landlady seemed pleased to see us—they had never had Americans stay with them or a family, so we were a novelty on two counts. I think she also missed having kids around: her own were grown and lived in another town. The couple had two houses and the newer house was ours for the night but we would walk over to their house for dinner and breakfast. I was glad we had decided to have her cook for us; we were several kilometers from downtown Pimbo.

Dinner began with a nice tranche of their homemade pate de foie gras, some of the best I have ever had. It wasn't quite like this encounter with foie gras recorded by Brillat-Savarin, the great nineteenth-century food writer:

> All conversation ceased ... when the loaded plates had been handed round, I saw successfully imprinted on every face the glow of desire, the ecstasy of enjoyment, and the perfect calm of utter bliss.

...but it was close.

This might seem like an ur-French moment, but it's not. Like the sunflower, foie gras is also a relatively recent edition to France. We think of foie gras (fattened liver) as a French dish, but the French are actually fairly new to the game.

Archaeologists have found 5,000-year-old reliefs of Egyptian farmers force-feeding geese. Later, the Romans picked the trick up from the Egyptians, and later still, the Jews learned it from the Romans (through some loophole in the dietary laws, foie gras can be kosher). Much later, in Germany and Bohemia, when the Jews had migrated far away from places where they could get hold of olive or sesame oil, they had to rely on *schmaltz* (goose fat) for their cooking, and that led them to introduce foie gras to northern Europe.

In the Middle Ages, references to foie grass as a Jewish delicacy turn up here and there, but it was Bartolomeo Scappi who put foie gras permanently on the gastronomic map. Scappi, the personal chef of popes Pius IV and Pius V in the 16th century, loved the goose livers he bought from Jewish farmers outside Rome. One of the world's first celebrity chefs, Scappi published some of the first recorded foie gras recipes in his popular cookbook, *Opera dell'arte del cucinare* (1570).[186]

It wasn't until the 18th century that French foodies decided that foie gras was one of the best foods going, and made Gascony the center of the foie gras trade.

But if the Jews were mostly in northeast Europe and Italy at that point, why had French production settled in Gascony? My guess is that the answer involves the fodder used to plump all those livers. Traditionally, most recipes called for geese to be fed a mash of figs and soaked grain balls, or marinated bread crusts. But in the 18th century, they began to use corn (maize).

Corn was a miracle plant. It could produce three times as much cereal per acre as wheat and had a shorter growing season. The disadvantage for French gourmands was that corn requires a lot of sunshine, which meant you could only grow it in the South-

---

186   The book broke ground in a number of ways. It also contains the first illustration of the invention that made pasta plausible: the fork.

west. Plus, corn farming is labor-intensive. Like distending goose livers, which requires force-feeding the geese three times a day, raising corn takes a lot of work. I suspect this combination of factors helped make raising foie gras better suited to poorer peasants trying to scratch a living out of their smaller plots of land in the South.[187]

There is a lot of controversy around the process of inflating those livers. On the pro side, some scientists have found that the geese don't seem to excrete pain-related hormones in the 12–18 days when they are being fattened up before slaughter—and it is true that they don't have a gag reflex, so you can fill them up like sand in a bottle. However, other people have said the birds eye the feed room warily once the force-feeding begins.[188] In the 90s, a European Union court concluded, in a curious decision that must have pleased no one, that although the birds do feel pain, the pain the farmers would suffer from being treated like criminals and deprived of their livelihood would be worse.

Whatever the practice does to Gascon farmers' karma, it doesn't seem to hurt their health. For reasons scientists still struggle to explain, Gascons live longer on average than anyone else in France—who in turn live two years longer than Americans. One reason is that Gascons have fewer heart attacks, despite all that pate. Some authorities argue that goose fat is different from other kinds of fat. Others point to the wine: the local variety, made from the tannat grape, has five to ten times more procyanidins, a chemical also found in the wine of a region of Sardinia also noted for long-lived people.

---

187 These days, most foie gras is actually made from duck liver, because ducks require only two feedings a day, but our hosts had maintained the tradition, I think (though I recollect having duck for our main course).

188 There is actually a long tradition of opposition to the practice. In Moby Dick, Herman Melville rails against it:

> I tell you it will be more tolerable for the Fejee that salted down a lean missionary in his cellar against a coming famine; it will be more tolerable for that provident Fejee, I say, in the day of judgment, than for thee, civilized and enlightened gourmand, who nailest geese to the ground and feastest on their bloated livers in thy *pâté de fois gras.*

Our landlady's husband came home from work toward the end of dinner and joined us. A lifetime of the Gascon diet certainly hadn't hurt him. He had good posture, bright blue eyes, and a lot of opinions. He farmed and did some carpentry on the side. Like many people we met, he and his wife had traveled a fair amount—he knew our neighborhood in Paris and had visited Egypt and Miami. *"They were nice and funny even though they were kind of old fashioned, racist and never heard of Starbucks!!!"* Thea wrote. *"They told us how they had gone to a Moroccan restaurant and then read in the newspaper that the restaurant had used all the cats in the region for the tagines! Ewww!"*

A luckier dog

He also talked about their last visit to Paris, where they went to a Chinese restaurant but he couldn't figure out how to use chopsticks. That reminded him of another story—about a cousin of his who had traveled to China with her dog. She and her husband had gone to a restaurant, motioned that they wanted to give the dog some water, and—

Cybèle and I looked at each other. Evidently the slaughter of French tourists' pets is rampant in China. The ambassador should register a protest.

August 3. Pimbo to Pomps, 25 km
Parsley, sage, rosemary, and pimbo.

We slept fairly well that night, except for Thea *"because every time I started dozing off I would hear a buzzing in my ear so I would shake myself awake. IT was horrible."*

By morning, Thea had around 30 bites on one side of her face. Charlotte had even more bites, but they were more evenly distributed. Charlotte wrote: *"I feel like McDonalds for mosquitos ... I hope tomorrow there are less mosquitos because I think that I will need a blood transfusion if this goes on."*

Cybèle had worried at first that they might be bedbugs, but at breakfast, the farmer's wife apologized and said they were definitely not bedbugs.

For breakfast, she made eggs and crepes with maple syrup—a special un-French treat for *les filles americaines* —and then, with a grandmotherly air, watched the girls eat. Thea, happy to have something besides a roll and hot chocolate, dove in. *"It was actually kind of embarrassing because I had said that I usually don't eat very much in the morning and then the next day I went and ate about 2 kilos of food,"* she wrote later.

Then we were off.

The first village we reached was named Pimbo, which means "thyme" in Provençal. This was appropriate because we were now walking through field after field. There wasn't much to distinguish one field from the next; the guidebook Miam Miam noted on its page about Pimbo and its environs that this was the 10th or 11th blank descriptive-page in the book "and in truth, I tell you ... this book is a scam." Yet even here, in the middle of nowhere, Cybèle found a few memorable things:

Lately on the trail we've been seeing signs posted up on the trees saying

"Obstacles are placed for you to overcome"; "Happiness is not in things but in yourself." The girls find the signs very annoying. Many of them are posted on little blackboards with school-like cursive writing and signed L'Alchemist—very mysterious. There have also been rest stop areas—ghostly because we've never seen anyone using them—one place had a hammock and an easel with a Japanese painting of three stones sitting on top of each other and a couple of sitting areas made of chopped tree trunks and umbrellas—and some of the time we find wood boxes filled with various fruits and a note saying "Servez-vous, Pelerines."

Once in awhile, on this part of the trip, we would also pass some strange stone buildings: very small barns, raised on stone legs about four feet off the ground (I suppose to keep out the vermin) that looked like they might walk away. Sometimes too there were round stone huts, which were once shelters for shepherds, and loosely stacked stone boundary walls that must have had a purpose back when there were farms behind them but now served mostly to keep the pilgrims on track.

A shepherd's shelter   A strange barn

There weren't many hikers in this section, but there were a few recurring characters. The most memorable was a young woman I thought of as the Swiss Killer. Tall, painfully thin, with ice

Things were dead at the office.

blue eyes, she never smiled, and I could always hear her walking sticks creeping up on us steadily long before we saw her, like the theme from *Jaws* played with aluminum poles.

At our next gîte, a 50s cinderblock building that reminded me of my elementary school, the lady in charge was a bit curt with the grownups but friendly with the girls. When she saw how badly bitten Charlotte and Thea were, she gave them some lavender oil to keep the mosquitoes away.[189]

Before our hostess went off to cook dinner, she told us and the other guests who were sitting on picnic tables in the schoolyard outside the building that we were responsible for setting our places. In similar circumstances, most people would have just dealt out the knives and forks, but I sometimes think the French have a gift for making things more attractive than necessary: while we were waiting for dinner, one young woman picked blue wildflowers and set them in little water glasses on our picnic tables.

---

189   She was right -- the girls said the oil actually did do the trick.

I was glad we were going to eat outside in the twilight rather than under the fluorescent lights in the grim cinderblock dormitory, and to be with people after those endless empty fields. We talked to an older French couple, retired teachers whose children were grown and gone. The wife was a short plump woman, with short hair, bangs, and glasses. Her husband was a big guy with a gray walrus mustache. He had a large military crest tattooed on his forearm that made me think he had spent more than the usual number of years in the service. His feet were covered in bandages but he didn't complain and didn't even seem to notice. But although he looked tough, he was actually quite shy. When he spoke, he always faced his wife, so his comments would glance off her before they got to us, as if we were playing conversational billiards. They talked mostly about their children.

August 4. Pomps to Sauvelade, 26.5 km
Wherein Charlotte dazzles a troop of girl scouts.

Toward the end of the next day, we passed a field where Cybèle saw perched on ferns, masses of butterflies that looked like kites, "black and cream, diamond shaped, and when they opened their wings, orange and black," and then reached a massive gray building that looked vaguely mosque-like, the 12th century Benedictine Abbey of Sauvelade.

At the entrance, we noticed a group of girl scouts who stood outside the church in their red berets and then went in one by one. We followed a girl in, and noticed that the confession box was open for business. *"The priest sat on one side—the door covering him and on the other side a girl scout with a red beret sat facing the pews—her ear to the wall dividing her from the priest … ,"* Cybèle wrote.

Inside, you could see that the proportions of the church were not quite right. the high domed ceiling looked cut off, like a house divided into two, which in fact it had been. During one of the wars in the sixteenth century between the Catholics and the Protestants, the Huguenots knocked down half the abbey, and then converted the surviving wing to a Protestant church, which the Catholics took back in 1630. For such a peaceful place, the Midi has seen a lot of fighting.

After her confession, a scout mistress gave each girl a red and white scarf, which she would tie around her neck before going to join her friends outside the church. Cybèle noticed that *"[s]ome of the girls looked around 8 years old. They stared at Charlotte who walked right past them in her neon pink mini shorts, long brown legs in boots and tank top, listening to her iPod."*

August 5. Sauvelade to Navarrenx, 14 km
In which we meet a backward pilgrim and a philosopher.

When we left Sauvelade, the weather was gray and cool, and we found ourselves on a logging road heading through a pine forest. We had a short walk that day because Cybèle had wanted to give the girls an afternoon at the swimming pool in Navarrenx, but the sky looked so ominous, I didn't see a swim in our future. At least not a voluntary one.

We passed a dying toad in the middle of the road. Cybèle wrote that it had *"his tongue hanging out, bits of gravel stuck on it. He was still breathing—Masha asked if we could pick him off the road so he wouldn't get squished by a car. I picked him up using a plastic bag as a glove and put him on the grass – he did not move –his body was already getting cold. … I think he had another two hours left to live. We've seen a few dead animals along the way—a dead baby rabbit, a fox, flattened toads, mice, and a deer."*

Seeing dead animals upset the girls. They didn't see much death at home, outside of the occasional pigeon, and on our street, the sides of beef being wheeled into the butcher shop, or more occasionally, the sides of horse to the horse butcher. Urban children grow up fairly sheltered from certain aspects of reality: I remember the story of one of Charlotte's classmates who was asked to give an example of a homonym who raised her hand and answered, "Chicken! There's the kind you see on farms and the kind you eat."[190]

Midmorning, we met an old man walking toward us. We had met him the night before, in Le Sauvelade. He had a neatly trimmed white beard, and was dressed again today all in khaki. He looked like he could be an uncle of Tintin, and was, in fact, Belgian.[191]

---

190 On the other hand, European butcher shops and delicatessens do tend to be more direct about meat and will often keep it attached to their contributors' hides and hooves, as a sign of authenticity, I guess. It's a world far far away from the McNugget.

191 The boy-detective hero of the *Adventures of Tintin*, one of Europe's favorite comic book series, created by Belgian cartoonist Georges Remi, who wrote under the pen name Hergé.

So why was he walking back to our last stop? Had his camper broken down?

> "He told us that what he does is drive his Vespa for about 5 km, then walk back to his camper, then drive the camper to his Vespa and get on it and scoots for another 5 km and so on," wrote Cybèle. "He cooks and sleeps in his camper and doesn't have to worry about bed bugs. But what a way to do the Compostela! It makes the whole thing absurd! It is absurd!"

He chatted with us for a minute, then looked up. "The clouds are getting very dark," he said, "I should go."

Uncle Tintin was right to worry. The rain began to fall just as we left the woods, lightly in the fields and then more heavily as we neared the old walled town of Navarrenx, at which point it turned into a terrible run-for-your-life torrent that crashed down on us like rain on a movie lifeboat. We rushed through the narrow, eave-less main street looking for a cafe but every joint was crowded (there being nothing to do in Navarrenx when it's wet but drink bad coffee and wait for the rain to stop), and after we reached the town hall, had to backtrack to the first cafe we had passed, a crowded place with an oppressive Ye Olde Knights theme.

It figured.

Navarrenx looks like one more charming old village but don't let its picturesque stone walls and flowerpots fool you. The town is cursed. We had spent a disastrous July there three summers before, in which we were rained on half the month, lost one of our cats for a day, and shortly after her recovery, injured (I twisted my ankle chasing the cats down the stairs in the middle of the night).

The 400-year-old house we rented one miserable summer

It's a tiny town, just four by five blocks, squeezed in by five stone walls. The houses are all tall and narrow, packed together in a way that seems quaint at first but after you've been there a few days, starts to feel claustrophobic. Particularly on a wet day, the main street matched the description of another French street that native son Henri Lefebvre described as "an ordinary street, with its little shops, its rows of windows stretching drearily along like gravestones in a cemetery."

There is a brass memorial plaque on the wall of Lefebvre's house that includes the coat of arms of the village in the top right and left corners, a statement in French about his life, a photograph of his long face in the lower right-hand corner, and an English translation on the lower left. The translation is exactly the same as the original except for some reason omits his service in the Resistance:

> This huge house belonged to Henry LEFEBVRE (1901–1991), one of the last great Marxist philosophers and one of the founders of urban sociology. Professor of philosophy, dismissed by the Vichy government in 1941, he was director of research at C.N.R.S., then a professor at the University of Strasbourg and Nanterre until 1973. He left behind a work of philosophical and sociological importance.

I loved the ironic note that the huge house (*maison formidable*) had belonged to the great Marxist. You don't usually see snide village social commentary insinuated into the text of a monument.

It's also an appropriate parting shot, as Lefebvre had spent a fair amount of his career noting the many ironies of modern French life. Perhaps best known for a three-volume opus called *The Critique of Ordinary Life*, Lefebvre railed against any number of aspects of modern life, which he saw as an endless relay between dreary work and dreary fun, all *Métro, boulot, dodo* (commute, work, sleep), with only fleeting moments of being truly alive.

Lefebvre argued that modern people suffered not only from the alienation of labor but the alienation of leisure. Maybe the factories and the mines were better now than they had been, but as one of his disciples put it, "Who wants a world in which the guarantee that we shall not die of starvation entails the risk of dying of boredom?" What we needed to do now was to fight for more genuine moments in which we were not deadened by our routines and had a chance to live.[192]

Personally, Lefebvre seems to have done his best to fight capitalist boredom in all its guises, stocking up on lively moments in a wide-ranging career as an anthropologist, sociologist, Marxist critic, and ladies' man. One of the women in his life—and there were apparently a lot of them, including four wives—described the long-faced southerner as having "the head of Don Quixote and the body of Sancho Panza" – a nasty description that I think probably worked on several levels.

Although Lefebvre published 72 books and is still influential, you may not want to brush up on your French before you read him. His lectures were supposed to be fun, but some authorities say his writing is better in translation because the translators tend to dress up his literary style. Gossips have speculated that part of his informality stems from a habit of dictating his books to beautiful young typists he had either seduced or was trying to seduce, and I imagine that might have been a distraction.[193]

You might think a Marxist philosopher would be above such bourgeois pursuits as chasing secretaries, but I get the sense that Lefebvre's Moments doctrine kept him as involved in the ordinary as the rest of us. Consider, for instance, his critique of Sartre. Lefebvre derided existentialism, which he called "excrementalism," and even claimed in one review that he had had similar ideas as an adolescent but fortunately realized in time that they were no good. However, to his credit, Lefebvre did admit to one friend that he hated Sartre because of his "success

192   His philosophical children, the 68ers in France and the Yippies in the United States, didn't have a very sustainable ideology ("Never Work" is a great slogan but as an economic plan it obviously could, well, never work), but I am sympathetic to their concept that boredom is counterrevolutionary. There is something about watching a bad TV show, for instance, which does feel soul-destroying.

193   Lefebvre once said that he had only had three passions in his life—philosophy, the Communist Party, and women—and all of them had been a disappointment to an extent. Of the three, he seemed most bitter about women. They are just incapable of seeing the ordinary life for what it is, the old radical once complained. I remember being surprised when I learned that Frenchwomen only got the vote in 1944, but if that's the way the old left intelligentsia thought, maybe I shouldn't have been.

and glory, money and women"... while he was stuck with "a hard and mediocre life ... working on real problems."

I doubt existentialism was quite the gravy train Lefebvre imagined, but he is more perceptive, as are most of us, when his *amour propre* is not involved. For instance, I like his ideas about landscape, which I imagine he had occasion to reflect on a lot when he retired to his mother's old *maison formidable*. Highchurch communists might find him a little sentimental when he starts talking about the country—when it came to the land, Lefebvre seems to have been a Frenchman first, a Marxist second—but he does make an interesting point:

> How many times have we all 'strolled' through the French countryside without knowing how to decipher the human landscape before our eyes! We look with the eyes of unskilled aesthetes who confuse natural facts with human facts, who observe the product of human actions – the face that a hundred centuries of working the soil—have given to our land—as though it were the sea or the sky, where the wake of man's passage quickly fades away. We do not know how to see this reality, so near and so vast, these forms creative labor has produced. City dwellers getting away from it all, intellectuals at a loose end, we wander through the French countryside simply for something to do, we look but we are unable to see.

Instead of viewing human activity as separate from the landscape, he said, we should consider people as part of nature, and see a town, for instance, as an exo-skeleton that humanity has built gradually over the centuries, "shaping its shell, building and rebuilding it, modifying it again and again and again according to its needs."

This was certainly the case with Navarrenx's walls, which have been built and rebuilt over at least two-thirds of a millennium. But it may not have been quite the communal project that Lefebvre imagined. First, like most of the *bastide* towns, it had a military function, so the local barons probably funded the fortifications. Second, what public works Navarrenx's overlords, the viscounts of Béarn, didn't fund, the townsfolk would have paid for with taxes on salt, wine, and beer. As one historian puts it, "the mighty walls of late medieval towns stood as sober testimony to their inhabitants' unquenchable thirst for alcoholic beverages." It's strange to think that through all those centuries of rain, when people had looked out of their tavern door, sighed, and asked Jean to bring them another *picher*, they were also adding incrementally to their walls, like sozzled coral.

After lunch, we went back out in the rain and scurried down the narrow main street to our *pension*. A young man, who turned out to be the proprietor, opened the door and showed us to our rooms. He bounded up the stairs ahead of us, past landing after landing filled with dark furniture and ancient light fixtures, talking at high speed as we climbed, at the rate of about half a chapter per flight. As we neared our floor, Pre-Raphaelite locks bouncing behind him, he grumbled about his two Spanish guests. It was two o'clock and they were still sleeping! Why were they still sleeping? He wanted to clean their room before it was time to get dinner started but it didn't look like they would ever get up. We saw them later that afternoon—plump men with perfectly pressed clothes, sunglasses (which they weren't going to need), shiny slicked-back hair, and shinier loafers. They looked like extras in a Fellini film.

We were in our host's good graces, however—he was impressed when he discovered Cybèle could lip-read not just in one language but two. She thought he was probably religious—she had found religious people were often more observant about her deafness, something she had mixed feelings about, as they sometimes offered unwelcome advice about miraculous cures.

"All afternoon since it was raining really hard we stayed in Mom & Dad's room and read and caught up with our journals", wrote Thea. *"It was really cozy."* Later, we saw our friend the Austrian bedbug-exterminator, who was staying here as well. Cybèle wrote that *"...she was happy to see us and to have her own room. She said, "A room all for me! Just me!" We're happy to see her too—having a familiar face in these small villages is really nice; it makes it feel much less lonely."*

The coziness of our room with its heavy antique furniture was a big contrast to the stripped-down municipal gîtes we had been sleeping in lately. Cybèle wrote that it had *"the luxuries of sheets, bedside lamps, pictures on the walls and books on the tables and we can bring our backpacks in the room."* Above our bedstead was a kitschy painting of the Moulin Rouge.[194]

Most of the guests, apart from the *señores* and our Austrian friend, ate dinner together at a big round table in the old doi-ly-ed dining room.[195] *"It was awkward because none of the grownups were talking to each other,"* Charlotte wrote. *"Dinner was ok—we had green soup, fish with ratatouille, green salad with cheese and mini-muffin/ scones with melon."*

I felt sorry for our animateur,[196] who worked hard to try to an-imate, or rather reanimate, this pack of zombies. As he darted in and out of the kitchen with course after ambitious course, he told us that he had walked the Camino himself a few years before. He covered about 45 kilometers a day, which he said is what the original pilgrims did—they couldn't leave their farms for very long, and unlike us, they had to walk back.

---

194   Here is another mystery: why do hotel rooms always have pictures of faraway places?

195   I thought at first that our long-haired, be-sandaled host had just borrowed the place from his grandmother for the summer, but he told us later he had collected all the antiques himself.

196   Another of my favorite French words. Animateurs and animatrixes are what we in the United States would call camp counselors or kids' party organizers.

August 6. Navarrenx to Chateau de Joantho, 18 km

In which we hear the echo of a 480-year-old slap.

We had a fairly short hike that day, so before we left Navarrenx, we walked around the corner to see the tall old house we had rented three summers before and made one circuit of the ramparts above the town. After that, we walked out the old stone gate, took the bridge across the Gave River, passed a subdivision or two, and began walking through another long stretch of empty countryside.

As Lefebvre observed, people always leave their traces on the land. I think this happens not just in obvious ways—like the bridge or the ramparts of Navarrenx or a short stretch of train tracks in the woods a few kilometers outside of the little town[197] —but sometimes in what artists call "white space," the empty parts of the canvas. Béarn, the region we were walking through now, isn't exceptionally unpopulated by rural French standards, but for a region that used to be one of the richest parts of Europe, located at a strategic point between two of its most powerful countries, it's a surprisingly blank canvas.

Land can't tell a lie. In Europe, particularly, there is usually a reason "[t]here is no there there," as Gertrude Stein would say. In Béarn, I think you can make a case that the empty green land we were walking through now had to do with the life and death of Jeanne d'Albret, the viscountess of Béarn and last queen of Navarre.

Jeanne d'Albret, queen of Navarre

---

197 The ramparts date from when Navarrenx was a fortified city that defended the Kingdom of Navarre from France. The bridge had been built initially for pilgrims in the 13th century. The train track was a memorial to the Gurs concentration camp, where the parents of some of the Moissac children were held before being shipped off to even worse camps and where the philosopher Hannah Arendt first saw the banal face of bureaucratic evil before she escaped to Spain.

Decisive, capable, brilliant, and beautiful, Jeanne d'Albret was part of a bumper crop of charismatic queens the 16th century produced, including her friend Elizabeth I and her enemy Catherine de Medici. Jeanne was the only child of Henri II, the king of Navarre and later France, and Marguerite de Navarre (née d'Angoulême), sister of King Francis I of France. She was Navarre's queen from 1555 to 1572—and more importantly, the leader of what was briefly the United Provinces of the Midi, a Protestant league that tried for a time to make itself independent of Catholic France.

Jeanne inherited her titles by birth, but like Henry VIII, became a leader of the Reformation for more personal reasons. In her memoirs, she recalls a day her father caught her and her mother studying Doctrine—the Calvinist catechism—with two Protestant scholars. After the clergymen fled her mother's chambers, her father "slapped my mother in the right cheek, and gave me a caning, while severely forbidding involvement in Doctrine, which cost me bitter tears and kept me in fear and sadness until [his] passing."[198]

Henri's anxiety was understandable. All over Europe at that time, princes were lining up on one side or the other regarding the ideas of Martin Luther, John Calvin, and Reformation theologians in general. These divisions and the Pope's habit of excommunicating Protestant leaders and having them burned at the stake made her mother's support of the reformers potentially dangerous to the French and Navarese royal families to which she belonged. Marguerite's conversion could have had shattering political implications, on the order of Eleanor Roosevelt joining a communist cell or Michelle Obama showing up at a White House dinner in a hijab.

Jeanne's father's slap also shows that even an aristocratic woman needed courage to win a degree of independence at that time. Her mother might have been one of the richest and highest-ranking women in France, a savvy diplomat, and one of the country's

---

198   The actual word in the translation is "their," but from the context I think she means her father.

best-known writers, but as powerful as she was, she could go only so far against the ruling order. [199]

Jeanne's own struggles began early. In 1541, when she was 12, her parents and her uncle arranged her marriage to William the Rich, Duke of Jülich-Cleves-Berg (and brother of Henry VIII's wife, Anne of Cleves), a match intended to bring the Hapsburgs of Germany and Spain and the French Capets closer together. For her father, marrying her off to William would also advance his aim of reuniting the part of Navarre on the south side of the Pyrenees the Spanish had taken a hundred years before.

But there was one minor obstacle: Jeanne hated the idea. To get her to the altar, her uncle King Francois had to have her flogged and then carried up the aisle. Even then, she never consented and she had had the presence of mind earlier to sign several papers in front of witnesses before the wedding that said as much.

Jeanne did get her way in the end, accidentally. Her mother had included a proviso in the marriage contract that said she did not have to live with her husband until after she reached puberty, but before that event, Duke William had a dispute with Charles V, the Holy Roman emperor, and asked Francois to back him up. When Francois refused, William decided the French were

---

199 Marguerite de Navarre was a diplomat, writer, and intellectual who kept a number of theologians clear of the stake and received fan mail from Erasmus. Among her most notable works is a series of short stories called the *Heptameron*. The bits I've read have some nice repartee. Unlike most Protestant thinkers, including her daughter, she could be funny. Consider this conversation between a lady named Geburon and three women as she tells the story of a woman who manages to hold off the advances of a cordelier (a rope-maker):

> "It strikes me, Geburon," said Longarine, "that it does not need much virtue to refuse a Cordelier. On the contrary, I should rather think it impossible to love such people."
>
> "Those who are not accustomed to have such lovers as you have," replied Geburon, "do not think so contemptuously of Cordeliers. They are well-made, strapping fellows, can talk like angels, and are for the most part importunate as devils.
>
> Accordingly, the grisettes who escape out of their hands may fairly be called virtuous."
>
> "O by my faith!" exclaimed Nomerfide, raising her voice, "you may say what you will, but for my part I would rather be flung into the river than go to bed with a Cordelier."
>
> "You can swim, then," retorted Oisille, laughing.

useless allies, and quit their alliance. Francois, not wanting to waste a good princess—a valuable diplomatic commodity at the time—had the pope annul the marriage.

In 1548, after Uncle Francois died, another uncle, Henri II, became king. He proposed a French suitor for Jeanne, the charming and handsome Antoine de Bourbon. Uncle Henri favored the match as a way to further consolidate Navarre with France, but Jeanne's father didn't like the idea, for precisely the same reason. So now she opposed her father again—this time because she *liked* the new suitor, but with her uncle's support, she still got her way.

At first, her marriage with Antoine went well. In the early years, people close to her said that she had "no pleasure or occupation except in talking about or writing to [her husband]. She does it in company and in private ... the waters cannot quench the flame of her love."

Eventually, however, Antoine managed to douse that flame. For a variety of reasons, the couple weren't very well-suited to each other: he was a charmer, but not especially honest, and Jeanne seems to have been honest to a fault. As she wrote in her memoirs—expressing a sentiment critics say is almost unique in 16th century autobiography, "I have always deemed that if a person. is not satisfied with herself in herself, the satisfaction others may have of her is only a half feeling of contentment in her conscience."

There was also Antoine's philandering. In 1555, the same year they jointly inherited Béarn and Navarre, his mistress had a child.

But his least forgivable act, perhaps, was trying to wangle Jeanne out of her throne. Shortly after her father's death, he attempted to get the Navarese Estates General in Pau to ratify him as the next sole ruler before she could reach town. Not surprisingly, given that the locals viewed Antoine as a foreigner, the Estates General refused, and waited until they could install the couple as joint sovereigns.[200]

Their religious differences also grew more serious over time. Like her mother, Jeanne was a woman of strong convictions. Just two months after her father had died, and she and Antoine had taken the throne in Navarre, she declared herself a Protestant to her court. "Now that I am freed by the death of my said father two months ago ... a reform seems so right and so necessary that, for my part, I consider that it would be disloyalty and cowardice to God, to my conscience and to my people to remain any longer in a state of suspense and indecision."

Antoine flirted with Protestantism, but only when he thought he could gain some political advantage for Navarre by it. He hoped somehow that by threatening to skip Mass he could provoke Philip II of Spain to give Navarre back.

In another era, the two might have managed despite having so many differences, but with war breaking out between Catholics and Protestants, they had to take sides. In 1560, the couple announced their conversion to Protestantism publicly, but he soon went back to the fold, and pressured her to follow. He once had her taken to Mass by force and another time, briefly took their son Henri away from her.

In 1561, she left Antoine for good during the Colloquy of Poissy, a peace talk in which Catherine de Medici, the queen of France, tried to work out a compromise between the warring Catholic and Protestant factions. Jeanne broke with him when she learned that Catherine was pressuring him either to disavow his wife or to have her locked up in a nunnery. Before he could decide, however, she fled to La Rochelle, a Protestant stronghold, and then headed south to Gascony, where she managed to evade an army and make her way back to Béarn. There, with nothing left to lose, she soon instituted her own pint-sized Reformation.

Over the next few years, Jeanne became one of the first Christian

---

200 It's not surprising that they would find Antoine suspicious. France at the time was still more or less a foreign country to the Navarrese— people in Navarre had a hard time even getting their new king's name straight, writing it as "Anthoyn de Bozboo" or "Borboo."

leaders in Europe to give her subjects the freedom to choose their own religion, and had the Bible translated into Basque, her subjects' first language. Unusually for the period, she did not believe in enforcing her own convictions through violence. "I do nothing by compulsion: I condemn no one to death, or to imprisonment, which penalties are the nerves and sinews of a system of terror."

Meanwhile, Antoine stayed on with the Catholics. When the next round of the religious wars broke out, he fought on the Catholic side, and died after a battle in 1562.

After his death, Jeanne revoked her earlier pledge to permit freedom of religion in Béarn—on second thought, why give people the freedom to be wrong?—and assumed not only a role as ruler of Béarn and Navarre but also as leader of a region that was coming to be known as the United Provinces.

Then suddenly, Jeanne died. She was only 44, and some people thought she had been poisoned. More recently, scholars have begun to suspect tuberculosis.

Had she lived, Navarre and the other southern lands might have remained a United Provinces of Midi, southern bookend to the United Provinces of the Netherlands[201] that the Protestant Dutch were fighting to establish against the occupying power, Catholic Hapsburg Spain. Instead, on Jeanne's death, her kingdom went to her son, Henri IV. Navarre stayed Protestant at first, but a few years later, after he inherited the French throne too, Henri IV made one of history's great sharp turns and converted to Catholicism. "Paris is worth a Mass," he supposedly quipped.

To Henri's credit, however, instead of betraying the Protestants altogether, he issued the Edict of Nantes (1598), which guaranteed religious freedom to Protestants, and then issued a mirror image of the same edict in Protestant Navarre, giving Roman Catholic Navarrese a similar guarantee of tolerance. After six miserable wars, two declarations of the king settled everything: now no one in France needed to fear for their life or their afterlife.

---

201   Or Staaten —that's where we get the place names for Staten Island and the United States.

This might have ended happily enough—after as many as three million deaths, most people must have had enough of religious wars—and even after Henri's assassination (on the 12th attempt), his Edict stayed in force. But in the late 1620s, Cardinal Richelieu had Louis XIII revoke the political guarantees that had made the Protestant parts of France semi-sovereign provinces, which he thought threatened the kingdom's security. Later, in the 1650s, the Catholics started persecuting Protestants again, and in 1685, for reasons that nobody understands even now, Louis XIV revoked the guarantees of religious tolerance entirely, and plunged the kingdom into 25 more years of sectarian terror.[202]

Midmorning, we met Uncle Tintin again. We chatted a minute about the weather—it had turned out to be a nice day!—and then pushed on.

Like most ethnic and social cleansings, Louis's crushing of the Protestants seemed advantageous to the cleansers in the beginning. The government gained from the theft of Protestants' assets, the Church regained lands requisitioned by Jeanne, and Catholic businesses lost some of their most formidable competitors. In the longer run, however, Louis had weakened his country permanently. "He had banished, or destroyed, during his reign, about a million of his subjects...He loaded his kingdom with debt and overwhelmed his people with taxes. He destroyed the industry of France, which had been mainly supported by the Huguenots," a pro-Protestant historian named Samuel Smiles

---

202   Intent on making France entirely Catholic again, Louis XIV gave Protestant clergy 15 days to leave the country and rank-and-file Protestants just a few weeks to convert. People who didn't comply were subject to a variety of punishments, as extensive as Hitler's Nuremburg laws and affecting all levels of society. Protestants couldn't work for the state; couldn't be a midwife or a doctor; couldn't even be a servant; washerwomen were excluded from their places at the river. Louis' officials also invented even more imaginative ways to bedevil people. One of the most effective was billeting Catholic soldiers in Protestant homes. If you were suspected of being Protestant, soldiers had the right to move into your house and take whatever they want. This was so notorious that the US Constitution specifically prohibits the practice.

This created a terrible dilemma for French Protestants, particularly because Louis XIV had made emigration illegal. Some tried to worship in secret, often in forests or in ruined churches, and at night. A number took part in a bloody guerrilla war in the Cevannes mountains that dragged on from 1702 to 1710. Others managed to escape.

argued in the 19th century.[203]

No region was harder hit by the crushing of the Huguenots than the Midi, where about two-thirds of France's 800,000 Protestants lived. After the revocation of Nantes, the Midi lost at least 200,000 people to death or emigration. This amounted to a lot of people for the region—Toulouse, one of the biggest cities, numbered only around 40,000—and it seems to me, was probably a big reason we were walking through empty fields now.

Our next stop was the Chateau de Joantho. I know there is an estate somewhere near the village of Chateau de Joantho but somehow we missed it. I don't think we missed much, however—even the French guidebooks don't have anything to say about the chateau or its owners except to observe that the Joanthos must have been important people because they had a big house. Our gîte was similarly unmemorable, a converted firehouse at the edge of a one-stoplight village whose principal features were a church and a pizza parlor, all in the middle of endless wet fields. If Jeanne d'Albret's lungs had been as strong as her will, the village, Béarn—and Europe—might have been very different.

Charlotte, for one, wasn't too upset about the lack of sightseeing opportunities:

> "We went to the church but it was locked. Booya!" she wrote. "We brought our pizzas back to the hostel and ate them on a picnic table outside. Mine was kinda gross. I had ham, cheese and potatoes on it. We had bananas for dessert and Thea poured a glass

203   The departure of those highly skilled Protestants helped make France a relative latecomer to the Industrial Revolution, and gave all its neighbors an economicad-vantage. The countries where the Huguenots fled—England, the Netherlands, Prussia, and Switzerland—all profited from the infusion of some of France's most highly skilled and entrepreneurial people. Some historians argue that the entire Industrial Revolution happened first in England largely because of the Huguenots' business and mechanical expertise.

of water on daddy. I finished all the Percy Jacksons (twice) and Beka Cooper so Masha and I were stuck reading this dumb French magazine called Femme Actu. It was all about losing weight and making your kids crazy."

August 7. Chateau de Joantho to Ostabat-Asme, 23 km

In which we meet some swell people.

The next morning, not long after we set off, we ran into Uncle Tintin again, still in his perfectly pressed safari suit. By now, meeting him had started to feel like a familiar routine, but he told us he had calculated that because he was going more slowly than we were, this would be the last time we would cross paths. I felt sad about that, but at the same time, I found his example encouraging. The idea that you could travel backward, slowly, and still reach your destination felt hopeful to me, perhaps because I've spent so much time engaged in pursuits that, in the end, felt like a long backward hike.

This may be a genetic predisposition. An image of Masha as a baby keeps coming back to me now: when she first learned to crawl, she just had a reverse gear, and the harder she tried, the farther she would move away from her intended destination. Slip sliding away, as Paul Simon says. Frustrated, and not quite sure what she was doing wrong, she stopped crawling after that, and for a while would only walk, hanging on to our hands, like a tiny New York straphanger. I'm not sure she ever quite got over that. She's an independent girl, but even now, she's more of a hand holder than the other two.

Uncle Tintin's scooter

We passed Uncle Tintin's tan Vespa a few kilometers later, pulled over to the side of the road.

Around noon, the fields gave way to high, grassy hills, and we reached a bluff where the three main tributaries of the French *chemins de Compostelle* meet. From here, the chemin from Vezelay, the chemin from Arles, and the chemin from Le Puy flow into a single path that leads on to Saint-Jean-Pied-de-Port, and then over the Charlemagne Pass to Roncesvalles and Spain.

A chapel marks the spot, along with a picnic area below, where everyone stopped to admire the bare hills behind us and the blue Pyrenees ahead. It was a spectacular view, but the girls would have kept on going if they had had their way. The picnic tables were just downwind from a herd of cows, so the place stank, and our lunch that day was mostly leftovers—some undistinguished bread (a lot of the bread in the French countryside is not very good), knobs of cheese, stumps of salami, and a slimy store-bought tortilla.[204]

Then we reached the bottom of the hill, and the land changed again.

We were in the Basque country now. Technically, we had been for two days—"Navarrenx" in Basque means "Bedstead of Navarre"—Navarre being the outsider's name for the ancient Basque homeland. But here it looked like a different country: white chalets with red trim, white cows on green meadows, and enormous gray stone houses. The older stone houses were huge and barnlike, and some actually did have animals living on the ground floor.

Our gîte that night was in one of these old piles, but built most-ly of dark wood and plaster, with a low ceiling that made the house feel almost like an extension of the modern barn across the street. On the ground floor, in the kitchen, curly strips of yel-low flypaper hung in the corners, covered with flies. Our host, an old farmer in shorts and sandals, would shuffle by and check in on us periodically, making the rounds the way he probably did with his cows, looking us over with a proprietary air. I half expected him to pat my flank as he passed.

We were stabled in the town of Ostabat—*Provençal* for Hospital, because of its long career as a pilgrim stop. The nicer parts of

---

204   The Spanish scrambled egg and potato pie, not the Mexican taco wrapper.

the town are at the top of the hill, and the not-so-nice (where we were staying) next to the main road at the bottom. It's been that way since the 12th century, according to a sign on the swanker main street up above.

Cybèle and I were intrigued, but we were in the minority. Thea noticed *"a door hanging off its hinges right next to a sign that said, "Ostabat, a lively town." Yeah right! Maybe it was 600 years ago!"*

The ground floor walls of the oldest houses were made of stone and included stone mosaics in flower or star patterns that framed a few utterly incomprehensible words also written in round stones or ceramic bits. The words seemed to be half Xs and Ks, like a particularly unfortunate draw of Scrabble tiles.

This was the Basque language, which looks truly strange. Basque is not only not a romance language, it's not even Indo-European, so even the roots are all unfamiliar.

The *Euskaldunak*, as the Basques call themselves, are as unusual as their language. For starters, they are the only people in Europe who didn't begin their European career as a marauding tribe from somewhere else. DNA tests have shown that the people who live in the Basque country now are closely related to the people who lived here 7,000 years ago, before agriculture. The Basques are old enough that their folktales tell of a race of giants that did not know how to make iron, which some have suggested may be an ancestral memory of the Neanderthals.[205]

---

205   Seven thousand years is enough time to develop some interesting folk wisdom, and Jon Aske, a Basque scholar at Salem State University in Massachusetts, has translated some of the proverbs. My favorites, in Basque alphabetical order:

Bururik ez duenak, hankak ibili behar
If you don't have a good head, then you better have good legs.

Dagonean bonbon, ez dagonean egon
When there is, spend lavishly, and when there isn't, that's life.

Egarri dagoenarentzat, ur loirik ez
For one who is thirsty, there is no muddy water.

Ez egin oihanean, eder ez denik kalean
Don't do in the forest what you shouldn't do in the street.

Gilen, bihar hilen, etzi ehortziren, etzidamu ahantziren
Tomorrow will kill you, the next day will bury you, and the day after will forget you.

Haurrak hazi, nekeak hasi
One's troubles really begin when one begins to raise children.

Not much is known about the early Basques. As with many other ancient cultures, the Basque pagan religion focused on a goddess, Mari. The Basques worshipped her until their conversion to Christianity in the late Roman era, but even after their conversion, they retained a preference for matriarchal power.[206]

The Basques first begin to come into focus—at least a funhouse mirror focus—in the Middle Ages. Aymeric Picaud, the French monk who wrote the first pilgrim's guide (circa 1140), evidently didn't have a good time in the Basque country. He says the Navarese—whose name, he claims, comes from the Latin, *non verus*, that is, illegitimate (as in bastards)—wear black hooded capes, black kilts, and rawhide sandals. They also

> eat and drink repulsively. For in fact, all those who dwell in the household of a Navarrese, servant as well as master, maid as well as mistress, are accustomed to eat all their food mixed together from one pot, not with spoons but with their own hands, and they drink with one cup. If you saw them eat you would think them dogs or pigs. If you heard them speak, you would be reminded of the barking of dogs...

> This is a barbarous race unlike all other races in customs and in character, full of malice, swarthy in color, evil of face, depraved, perverse, perfidious, empty of faith and corrupt, libidinous, drunken, experienced in all violence, ferocious and wild, dishonest and reprobate, impious and harsh, cruel and contentious, unversed in anything good, well-trained in all vices and iniquities, like the Geats and Saracens in malice, in everything inimical to our French people. For a mere nummus [a small coin], a Navarese ... will kill, if he can, a Frenchman.

About the only vice he doesn't accuse Basques of is cowardice. After describing their alleged habit of flashing their private parts at each other when warming themselves and their obsession with bestiality (which he claims is so widespread that they have

---

206 For centuries, up to and including Jeanne d'Albret, Navarre had a reputation for producing clever queens that was well-enough known that London theater audiences supposedly knew Shakespeare was being ironic in *Love's Labor's Lost* when he made the misogynist Ferdinand the king of Navarre. Nor was this preference confined to the aristocracy: the Basques had a similar regard for women in general and maintained a tradition of passing inheritances through the female line all the way up to the modern era, a quirk that has irked many visitors and most Spanish civil authorities for the last 2,000 years.

to lock up their mules, in order to secure them for themselves), he concedes that "they are considered good on the battlefield ..."

Nor have the Basques lost their reputation as fighters since then. One of Don Quixote's closer calls is a duel with an angry Basque who can barely speak Spanish but insists, *"Me kill you or me no Biscayan."*

More recently, during the Spanish Civil War, Basques fought hard for their independence—Francisco Franco leveled Guernica, a Basque city, in retaliation for their resistance—and one Basque terrorist group, the *Euskadi Ta Askatasuna* (ETA), kept fighting through all four decades of his dictatorship. In 1973, they succeeded in assassinating his heir apparent, Admiral Carrero Blanco, and only in 2011 did the ETA finally renounce violence.

What's more unusual about the Basques than their fierce reputation—after all, a lot of people with mountains in their backyard (Corsicans, Sicilians, and Afghans) have a reputation for belligerence—is that they have also always been very open to the world. Despite the Pyrenees, the Basques have never been stay-at-home hillbillies. As Mark Kurlansky points out in *The Basque History of the World* (2000), Basque mercenaries helped the Romans defend Hadrian's Wall. Basque whalers and cod fishermen may have reached Newfoundland a hundred years before John Cabot. Columbus sailed on Basque-built ships and had a Basque first mate. Basques also built Magellan's ship, and some Basques signed on as his crew, making Basques among the first people to sail around the world.[207]

Two Basques, Saint Ignatius of Loyola and Saint Francis Xavier, founded the Jesuits, the most learned and arguably the most globally minded order of the Church. Basques also punched above their weight with Mammon as well: they were among the first successful multinational capitalists, experimenting with tariff-free international trade and competitive pricing to break monopolies, and during the Industrial Revolution, became lead-

---

207 They were adventurous in other respects as well: Basques were the first Europeans to develop a fondness for some of the world's favorite American exports—tobacco, hot peppers, chocolate, and corn.

ing shipbuilders, steelmakers, and manufacturers. As Hemingway writes in *The Sun Also Rises*, a novel in which Basques play an important role: "These Basques are swell people," Bill said.

But beyond the house mosaics, we didn't find a lot of the native genius on display at Ostabat. It was a quiet town. I liked it well enough, but there wasn't much to see. The rest of the afternoon, I stayed at a bar with Wi-Fi—well, to be precise, *the* bar, which fortunately had what may well have been *the* Wi-Fi—and worked.

When I got back to our gîte, I met our friends, the old French teachers—the short woman with the gray bangs and the big guy with the walrus moustache. He was sitting on the steps of our gîte, his bloody feet stretched out in front of him. She was dressing his dirty bandages without flinching or disgust and he sat watching her take care of them with a certain detachment and not even a wince. I admired them both. In situations like that, stoicism has something to be said for it.

We ate our dinner at a picnic table outside our door, next to the street. As we ate, a long parade of farm trucks and machines thundered by, *"monstrous machines – dinosaurs out of a Miyazaki movie,"* Cybèle wrote. *"Some have tanks at the back and huge spiral forks in the front. Some have huge vacuum-looking shovels in the front."*

Dinner was not great—the choices in the grocery store were limited—but we were all tired enough we shoveled it down without much outward complaint.

Privately, however, Charlotte was about to boil over again. *"I am so tired of this stupid walk!"* she wrote. *"I can't bear another three weeks of this! On the plus side I have a rest day pretty soon. Tomorrow we arrive at Saint-Jean-Pied-de-Port and Masha and Dad go back to Paris to try and get Masha's visa for England so she can go to boarding school."*

August 8. Ostabat to Saint-Jean-Pied-de-Port, 18.9 km
In which we reach the end of the beginning.

Hil arteraino bizi, han arte ez izi.
(Live until you die. Until then, don't panic.)

–Basque proverb

We started earlier than usual the next morning. Masha and I had to catch a two o'clock train from Saint-Jean-Pied-de-Port, and we were anxious to reach the town on time. Or rather, Cybèle was anxious and kept telling us we had to hurry and I followed in her emotional slipstream.

The hills were steeper and greener here, the houses even more chalet-like, and most of the farms, with the exception of our gîte of the night before, very tidy. It was a golden, almost alpine, morning and although we were supposed to be hurrying, it was not the kind of country you want to rush through. Charlotte and I were walking together, chatting with a talkative young Belgian. As we crossed a quiet two-lane highway, he was telling us that he and his father had spent a week on the trail but then his dad had to go back and now he was going on alone and—

Suddenly, a car came roaring over the crest of the hill 50 meters away. The driver hit his brakes and veered to our left with a terrible screech, all before we even had time to sprint the rest of the way across. It was a close call; afterward, I tried not to think of what would have happened if the driver had been going just a little faster or we had been walking a little slower.

The Belgian kid walked ahead now but we ran into him later at a farmhouse, where the owners had set up a few tables out front, two or three big insulated tanks of uninspired coffee—almost American car dealer coffee—and a basket where you could leave a euro or two to pay for what you took. He was smoking and for some reason seemed a little embarrassed for Cybèle to see him with a cigarette in his hand. After our quick coffee break,

we walked on up through the narrowing valley, alongside a fast and narrow creek, until we reached Saint-Jean-Pied-de-Port. The town had a lively frontier feeling to me, another port city, like Air Sur l'Adour, even though there is no water to speak of in Saint-Jean besides that stream. On the other hand, in the old days it actually had been a kind of port (a foot-port, as the name puts it)—in the sense that it was a place where goods were brought for trading, and even now it was a trading post of sorts—the last stop for many French pilgrims and the first stop for everybody else.

Normally, we would have celebrated, as Saint-Jean marked the end of the first half of our trek—732 kilometers down, 773 to go. But first, Masha and I had to get through an annoying 1,600-kilometer detour.

Second Sally

Saint-Jean-Pied-de-Port to Paris to Saint-Jean-Pied-de-Port

The Caterpillar and Alice looked at each other for some time in silence: at last the Caterpillar took the hookah out of its mouth, and addressed her in a languid, sleepy voice.

"Who are YOU?" said the Caterpillar.

Lewis Carroll

Alice's Adventures in Wonderland

August 8. Saint-Jean-Pied-de-Port to Paris, 818.5 km

In which Masha and I visit the future and aren't sure we like it.

In the waiting room of the little yellow station, Cybèle dumped all the clothes out of her, Thea's, and Charlotte's backpacks, separated them into two piles—the things we wouldn't need when we started biking, which Masha and I were going to bring back to Paris; and the things we would still need, which they would take with them. *"It was super embarrassing because we had a huge mountain of clothes in the middle of the station,"* Thea wrote. *"There wasn't enough space in mom's tote so Charlotte had to make a bag out of Dad's windbreaker to carry everything."*

The night before, in the back of the Alison Raju guide I was supposed to take back to Paris, Cybèle had written two pages of notes:

Things to take back to Paris

- *Backpacks*
- *earphones*
- *ipods and touchphone*
- *2 guide books for French part*
- *journals*
- *Uno cards*
- *foot pedal?*
- *sketch books*
- *(pens crayons?)*
- *Thea's bracelet*
- *Memory card*

Things to bring –

- *1 sheet sleeping bag (cupboard above your desk)*
- *Scrabble game (cupboward b/w drawers + scooter)*
- *Keys out of mail box*
- *Computer case*
- *Print out Spanish itinerary*
- *adapter for camera*
- *a shirt for Ben*

The little train to Bayonne.

Then Cybèle, Charlotte, and Thea wished Masha and me luck and suddenly the two of us were on the train, alone.

It felt strange to be in a machine again after all those weeks of walking. At first, I enjoyed it—our little train rocked gently along the right bank of a wide but rocky stream where people were all fishing, swimming, and soaking up the summer—and after all those miles of trudging at five kilometers an hour, watching the land whip by so quickly felt luxurious, like flying on a private jet.

Then I started to feel anxious. In addition to some of the girls' clothes, Cybèle had evidently stuffed about a half ton of worry into the shucked backpacks.

While she, Charlotte, and Thea enjoyed their Day of Rest, Masha and I would be back in Paris, pleading with bureaucrats. This was our last chance to fix an absurd but increasingly serious problem: the British wanted to see a French residency permit for Masha before they would issue her the visa she needed to attend boarding school, but inconveniently for us, the French don't actually issue such permits, at least not to foreign children.

Thanks to my life as an expat, I've had a fair amount of experience dealing with any number of government offices—I could almost teach a course in Comparative Bureaucracy—and in my opinion, for pure Alice in Wonderland insanity, nobody beats the Brits. The Americans can be extremely unclear. The French can be insane, but there's often a certain *frisson* of logic stirred in that adds a pleasant tartness. But the British—and to be specific, the privatized, post-Thatcher British—have raised paperwork almost to a performance art. In this particular situation, what had made Masha's visa such jolly good fun was that not only had the government privatized the consular service, but also that this service had subcontracted the help line to another company, to whom you had to pay £10 to talk to someone about your problem. And best of all, the help line was staffed by very patient, pleasant Spaniards whose only fault was *that they did not know any British immigration law.*

I had paid £40 now for four of these conversations, and they had all ended the same way: initially well, with a seemingly reasonable recommendation about how to handle this problem, and then badly, when I tested the solution against the clerks at the consular services office. My last call was in May, when the operator had agreed that my suggested alternative to the missing French residency permit—a certificate from Masha's old school that proved Masha had been a student in Paris for the past six years—might work.

I had the school prepare a transcript, and one afternoon in June, made one more sortie to the consular office, which is located in a bunker out near Saint-Denis, one of Paris's tougher suburbs.

We arrived early and sat in a waiting room along with people from a dozen countries who were also trying to get visas. The walls were covered in fading British travel posters and an enormous flat-screen television that played an endless travel commercial of that green and pleasant land. The lush loop of the United Kingdom in all its apple-cheeked, Union-jacketed glory felt out of place in the drab waiting room, like a Tory campaign commercial playing in one of Her Majesty's minimum-security prisons.

Eventually, our turn came, and I pushed our papers across the counter.

"But where's your proof of residence?" asked the clerk, a French North African.

I explained the problem and gave her the school certificate.

"Non."

"But the woman on your help line said—"

"*Non.* I need her *carte de sejour.*"

"But minors don't have *cartes sejour* —," I explained, my voice rising. "You must know—"

At that point, the maître d' of the operation, a smooth and friendly Indian guy, ushered me away from the clerk's window and explained to me sympathetically that there was no problem—all we needed to do was to go back to our home country and apply for the visa from there. He smiled.

"But that's in New York—"

His only response was a sympathetic tilt of the head—

"That's ridiculous—"

—and one last noncommittal smile, after which he showed us the door.

Since then, I had been on the phone with a counselor at her new school, a British lawyer, and a French lawyer to find an alternative. Only the French lawyer had an idea: he recommended we get a *carte de circulation,* a paper occasionally issued to foreign children who live in France but need to travel on their own across international borders. This was easy to get, he said. Same-day service was even possible. You'll just need to pick up that card from the Prefecture, go back to the consulate, and *voila!* the English will book your visa.

But after our earlier experiences, I had my doubts. A lot had to go right in Paris tomorrow: we had to get this special French document in the morning, arrive with said document at the visa services office in the afternoon, obtain Masha's visa, AND get back on the train by 3:30 in order to continue on to Roncesvalles the next day.

We changed trains in Bayonne. When we reached Paris, Masha and I stopped for dinner at the McDonald's near Gare Montparnasse. It's a busy commercial area, but nothing I had ever been overwhelmed by before. Now, though, after a month outdoors, it looked to me like Times Square, and the McDonald's itself felt like *Blade Runner*-on-the-Seine.

After dinner, we walked home up rue de Vaugirard and home to our stuffy apartment. Per Cybèle's instructions, we put all our backpacks in sealed garbage sacks in the bathtub in case we had brought home bedbugs, and then fell into our bugless beds.

August 9. 65 rue Cambronne to the Prefecture de Police, 1 rue de Lutece, Paris, 3.9 km; Paris to Bayonne, 764 km

In which we slay the Twiddle.

At 7:30 the next morning, Masha and I joined a long line of anxious foreigners in front of the *Préfecture de Police*, an old, gray, bullet-nicked building in the center of Paris, very near Notre Dame, where most foreigners' visas are processed in Paris. The building would only open at eight, but we wanted to make sure we wasted as little time as possible waiting in lines inside the building.

At precisely eight, the guards unlocked the massive front doors and took us into the building in groups of eight. When it was our turn, they opened a second curved glass door, ushered us into a kind of air lock, locked the automatic door behind us, and then opened a second door. Here, they checked our bags, ran them through X ray machines, and had us empty our pockets and walk through metal detectors, just like airport security, after which we were free again—at least in the sense that we now had a whole building of offices to choose from, each with its own set of lines and forms and numbers.

I had been there enough lately that, for once, I knew where I was going: straight through to the courtyard, and right, ground floor. So far, so good! At 8:08, I set our forms, cards, and passports on the counter with a certain degree of confidence, like a card player setting down a good hand. *Read 'em and weep, Doc.*

"But where is the mother?" the clerk asked, after she examined my suddenly not-so-royal flush. "You can't get a *carte de circulation* without the mother."

I called our French lawyer, who said we should get Cybèle to write a note explaining the situation, along with a scan of her passport. I phoned Thea, who mouthed the message to Cybèle, who then went out to find a photocopier and a fax machine somewhere in the tiny town while we took the Métro home and waited for her scanned letter and passport to arrive.

Two hours later, we were back in line again, a much longer line than before, but eventually we got to the front and re-*bonjoured* our friend the clerk—

"But this letter isn't original—"

"Her mother is not in Paris. There wasn't time to get a letter here."

"Then I can't help you," the clerk said. But as I gathered our papers together and we turned to leave, she asked, offhand, "Why do you need it, anyway?"

I explained.

"Oh, that wouldn't work," she said lightly. "If she is going to live in the United Kingdom, she will no longer be a French resident, *non*?"

I just stared at her. Sometimes French logic can be shattering. Why hadn't that occurred to me before? *Cogito ergo dumb.*

"So what should we do?"

"I don't know but the *carte de circulation* is definitely not what you need. Can you talk to the British?"

In the courtyard of the *Préfecture*, I smoothed out some of our papers on a car hood and tried to figure out what to do next. A female cop who stood leaning against the wall smoking shouted at me to respect others' property, so I gathered up our papers and walked over to the shady side of the yard.

It was now 11:20. In an hour, we were supposed to have our appointment at the consulate, where I needed to deliver a document that I didn't have, and now, it turned out, could not get. In four hours, we had to be back in Montparnasse to catch our train. If we didn't get this straightened out now, there was a good chance that the rest of our summer would all be wasted on a trip to New York to get Masha's visa.

But I had one last card to play: the name and phone number of an actual British civil servant the British lawyer had given me, someone at the Embassy.

"Oh," she said, after I explained the problem. "You seem to have been caught in a bureaucratic twiddle."

"Exactly," I said.

"Well, go ahead to your appointment at the visa center, and take the proofs of residency you do have. I will call them and take care of it. Cheers."

I thanked her, hung up, and called a cab.

When we arrived at the visa bunker in Saint-Denis 20 minutes later, the Indian maître d' came rushing to the door and brought us straight to a counter. Now they checked every box, took Masha's picture, and in a few minutes, resolved everything to their satisfaction. All the way through, everyone was smiling and wishing Masha well, and then we were on our way.

I felt immensely grateful to the entire British nation as we walked out of there, practically singing *God Save the Queen*—never mind that we had spent days and days in May and June trying to fix this same problem, blown a lot of money trying to resolve it, and the Brits had created the problem in the first place.

Back on our TGV, rocketing south, I started to think about what it must be like for all the immigrants who deal with these authorities without the benefit of lawyers, savvy friends, and a common language—all advantages we had. Living in the rich world, where you hardly ever have to show your papers to anyone, suddenly felt like an enormous privilege.[208]

---

208   And one I suspect we may not enjoy for much longer. Historically, states' appetite for control has tended to fluctuate. In the three decades before World War I, for example, passports were considered an artifact of backward regimes—something that the Russians and Ottomans still had but everyone else had outgrown. Now the authorities have fingerprints and sometimes even your retina prints on file—and that's only the data they tell you about. Theoretically, this should speed up frontier crossings, but I have a feeling they will find more imaginative ways to slow people down. *Any thoughts to declare, ma'am?*

Third Sally

Saint-Jean-Pied-de-Port, France, to Santiago de Compostela, Spain

He knew...that the plague bacilllus never dies or disappears for good; that it can lie dormant for years and years in furniture and linen-chests; that it bides its time in bedrooms, cellars, trunks and bookshelves; and that perhaps the day would come when, for the bane and the enlightening of men, it roused up its rats again and sent them forth to die in a happy city.

Albert Camus
The Plague

This section is for my daughters, with admiration.

August 10. Bayonne to Saint-Jean-Pied-de-Port, 54.5 km; Saint-Jean-Pied-de-Port to Burguete, 25 km

In which we meet Roland.

We were very tired in the morning, mostly because we had ended up having a late night.

My optimism was to blame. By the time we reached Bayonne, we were too late to make the connecting train to Saint-Jean. We went out for a celebratory dinner, then, far too late, began looking around for a room—the one detail I had forgotten. A few blocks away from the station, I discovered Bayonne is a much prettier town than I had given it credit for, but unfortunately for us, a lot of people knew that already—every hotel we passed was full.

After midnight, exhausted and almost staggering, I suggested we just camp out behind a high, schoolyard wall, but Masha vetoed that suggestion, so we kept walking.

At 1:30, we walked into a dingy hotel near the station where the night clerk sat reading. He was a young man with a sympathetic look. After a glance at his computer, he told us he might have something but needed to talk to someone first. Come back in 20 minutes.

Back near the station, the last of the tourists were heading home, leaving the square to the bums and other professional night people. When we came back, we followed him behind his desk, up a narrow creaky staircase that spiraled several flights up to our garret. It was decorated in a late *Midnight Cowboy* style, but compared to a concrete schoolyard, looked more or less five stars to us.

Ordinarily, we might have slept in, but we had a long way to go in the morning, and decided we would take the 7 o'clock train to Saint-Jean Pied-de-Port.

The hotel's breakfast room opened at 6:30. Given the dinginess of our room, I hadn't expected much, but like the night clerk, breakfast exceeded expectations. Emerging from the dark stairs down from our garret, we had to squint as we walked into the breakfast room. The light was almost blinding, flashing off the silver, white linen, and whiter china, bright as a dining room on a cruise ship run by archangels. Masha drank her hot chocolate, I had two coffees, and after we devoured a basket of hot fresh rolls, we set off to the train station again.

Our first few minutes on the two-car train, I tried to work, but then gave up and just watched the river, which stayed in full sparkle all the way to Saint-Jean. I felt tired but happy—in the end, the bureaucrats hadn't defeated us, we had made all our connections, we were only a few hours behind Cybèle and the girls, and it looked like we would get to Santiago after all. Plus, today's hike was supposed to be one of the most dramatic parts of the Camino—a 1,000-meter climb up and over the Pyrenees!

We bought our lunch at a *boulangerie* near the station, strapped our sandwiches to my backpack,[209] and walked on up to the old town. It was hot and very sunny. On the main street, we went into a pilgrim outfitters' shop, where I bought Masha a hat and a pair of shorts—she had forgotten hers in Paris and her black leggings would be far too hot for our climb today. I also bought a new *bob* for myself—after a frantic search, I realized that I had left my hat with Cybèle two days before.

Then we were off, up the pass that would lead us over the Pyrenees and into Spain. As we started up the first hill, I called Thea, to let them know we were on our way. She said they were fine and about two hours ahead of us. It was supposed to be a long hot day, and they had wanted to get an early start, so we had agreed to meet at our hotel in Burguete, on the other side of the pass.

Supposedly, Charlemagne and Napoleon both crossed the

---

209 Unlike Masha and the rest of the family, I still carried a backpack (although I had swapped the red pack in Paris for a smaller school daypack). I always keep the laptop so close to me when we travel that my father-in-law used to call it Little Brother.

mountains over this particular pass—even now it's often called the Charlemagne Route. Although the first few miles were steep, it still felt quite civilized. We stopped for a coffee break at about 10, at a café with a stone terrace that looked down toward Saint-Jean and the valley beyond the town, then climbed for another hour, and when we saw a second cafe, decided to stop again. This was a sad place with sticky tables and a lot of flies. The proprietor was nowhere to be found, but inside, an ancient man had been left sitting on an easy chair behind the counter, motionless. The poor near-mummy mumbled something about the proprietor being busy, so I helped myself to two cans of Coke from the refrigerator behind the counter, left two euros near the cash register, and wished him a good day.

Those two places lulled me into thinking this would be the pattern–a climb, a coffee break, and another climb. But we were in the mountains now, and we didn't see any more cafes. We didn't see anything really but one bare bluff after another, and vistas that kept getting longer and longer as we climbed.

Despite the endless views, we didn't see Cybèle, Thea, and Charlotte ahead of us—they were making good time. *"We walked fast—Thea and Charlotte were terrific,"* Cybèle wrote.

> *"The trail was on the road for a while and then veered into the side of the mountain. We ran into sheep with bells around their necks and a blue stain on their backs and horses. The mountains stood out clearly in the blue sky. The mountains just kept going."*

The hills were bare, as in Aubrac, but steeper, and the country more empty—wide-open spaces that made me think of Montana. The original pilgrim's guide says that you feel you can almost touch the sky here, and it's still true.

Masha and I met only sheep on the trail—all the sensible pilgrims had left much earlier in the day. The Pyrenees are formidable mountains—people die up there in the winter with some regularity—and all the guides consider this stage serious business.

The landscape was big enough and empty enough that I started thinking it must have been an easy matter to escape from Spain to France during the Spanish Civil War or from France to Spain during the Second World War, but this doesn't seem to have been the case.

During the Second World War, this German-occupied section of the French border was patrolled mainly by older Bavarian reservists who knew mountains and weren't strong enough for the Eastern Front. And if the Bavarians didn't get you, plenty of others might, because the Spanish authorities had agreed to send escapees they had caught back to France. Despite the obstacles, an underground railroad opened up, but fares were steep: Jews paid 4–5,000 francs per person to be led across—roughly EUR 1,000 now. Gentiles paid less.

Today there is hardly a border at all—it would take talent to get stopped for anything—and crossing the frontier is about as big a deal as crossing a US state line. For us, France ended not with a guardhouse or a marker but with a bleep on my phone and a change in signage.

The Spanish trail markers were very different from the casual red and white tape on the French camino—the authorities had set up proper, street-sized signs, navy blue with a stylized gold scallop. Here in the mountains, the signs were numbered consecutively and planted along the trail at absurdly short intervals—I imagine because numbering makes rescues easier.

Up ahead, Cybèle, Charlotte, and Thea were pushing on.

> "We finally got to the top after five hours," Cybèle wrote. "The views were stunning and so was the nature on the mountains— the purple heather and yellow bushes and purple thistles. It was

wonderful—I felt close with Charlotte and Thea that day."

As usual, Masha and I were talking. Or I did, anyway. Poor Masha – as we climbed, between the exertion of the walk, my weariness from the night before, and a little dehydration (we had forgotten to fill our water bottles in Saint-Jean), my end of the conversation became progressively more free-form. Whatever she didn't already know of our family history or my personal history came out as we trudged up those long hills. By the time we reached the top, the free associations were tumbling out at a fast and furious pace—I had even sung her some of the more memorable TV commercials of my childhood.

And the words kept pouring out, almost uncontrollably — not only that *Oscar Mayer has a way with B-O-L-O-G-N-A* but all kinds of things I had scarcely remembered that for some reason now seemed suddenly important to tell her. The feeling reminded me of some of the times when my parents said goodbye to me at the airport in Portland, on my way back to college, and Dad would start emptying his pockets, giving me money to make the trip back to school more fun, loading me up with newspapers, trying to share still more before I left.

By the time we reached the Spanish timberline, around four o'clock, we were very thirsty. As Cybèle noticed when they passed through here, the trees were different on the south side of the pass, *"white with moss, tall and slender and if on the side of the mountain shaped like an L."* Then we bounced down our first, tree-covered hill, in shade almost as pleasant as a drink of water, and we were in front of the massive stone abbey at Roncevaux, which is called Roncesvalles on this side of the pass.

We staggered into the first bar I spotted, a dark high-ceilinged room in a hotel not far from the abbey. Masha had a Coke and I ordered an extremely large beer that was still not big enough for the job.

Thirsts nearly quenched, we glanced at the large gray monastery and next to it, a statue that some kids were playing on, an abstract figure who has fallen off his horse. I saw Don Quixote everywhere now, and I assumed it was my poor knight, but as any

French student would have guessed, it's a statue of Roland, of *Song of Roland* fame, the strange medieval epic that's been bludgeoned into the heads of French schoolchildren for the past 150 years.

The Story of Roland (from a window at Chartres)

The oldest poetical version of the story is in Norman French and was written around 1100. It recounts the end of a military campaign into Spain by Charlemagne, fought by a number of Franks, including Charlemagne's nephew, the brave Roland, on the Roncevaux Pass about 300 years earlier.

The original runs 4,000 lines, but the plot can be summed up in around 20: their business in Spain finished, Charlemagne's forces return to France over the pass at Roncevaux. Roland is bringing up the rear, along with his friend and comrade, the trusty Oliver. Suddenly, they see Moors behind them.

Oliver: You better blow your horn, Roland. There are a lot of Saracens out there but we'll be okay if Charlemagne sends reinforcements.

Roland: I'm a brave Frank. It would be shameful to blow my horn for mere Saracens. I shall not shame my king or sweet France.

Oliver: But there are a LOT of these guys. Really, you should blow that horn.

Roland: Forget the horn. I won't let down sweet France!

Oliver: But think of us. You've got a thousand men here. If you don't blow your horn, we can all kiss our sweet France goodbye.

Roland: I will attack yon pagans with my faithful sword Durandel.

Oliver: Whatever you say, boss. But I don't think this is a good idea.

After a long and valiant fight, the Moors mow them all down.

A Latin prose version of this battle thought to have been written before the Song is part of the Codex Calextinus, the same collection as the first pilgrim guide. It's a chapter in a longer *History of the Life of Charlemagne and Roland*. The putative author is supposed to be a contemporary of Charlemagne—Turpin, archbishop of Rheims—but scholars now agree that the story was written several centuries later.

Charlemagne's vision

Pseudo-Turpin's history begins with Charlemagne suffering from an imperial midlife crisis, with "no desire to embark on new conquests or to engage in new wars but rather to allow himself to rest." But then he sees a path of stars in the sky, and for the next several nights, he starts to wonder what this sign might mean. Finally, one night

> [a] knight of splendid appearance, more handsome than words can describe, appeared to Charlemagne one evening in a vision as he sat in deep meditation.
>
> "What are you doing, my son?" the knight asked.
>
> To which the king responded, "Who are you, sir?"

Saint James, it turns out, and the stars are his sign that the emperor should free the saint's tomb in Galicia and liberate Spain from the Saracens. After three visits, in which James promises

Charlemagne that if he does this, Saint James will win a crown from the Lord "and your name will be praised until the end of time!" Inspired, Charlemagne embarks on a series of four wars to free Spain from the Moors, and wins.

The *History* was one of the 12th century's most popular books— dozens of copies were made[210] — and like many bestsellers, it's exciting but not particularly well written. Charlemagne, for example, is described as brown-haired, handsome, and around eight feet tall with eyes that glowed like hot coals. "Any man at whom he stared with those wide eyes in a fit of anger became instantly terrified," which was understandable, because Charlemagne was so strong that "with one swing of his sword, he could split an armed knight seated on a horse in half from head to saddle along with the horse as well ..."

The first city Charlemagne attacks on his quest to free Spain is Pamplona, where after laying siege, the walls tumble down Jericho-style. His crusade continues through a suspiciously large number of stops on the Camino, up to and including Santiago de Compostela.[211]

Roland's story is somewhat different in this version, featuring a three-day fight to the death with a formidable but evidently not too bright giant, Ferragus, a descendant of Goliath, who confesses to Roland during a short truce that his only vulnerable spot is his belly button.

This version also ends with Roland's martyrdom on the Ron-

---

210 Back then, given that copies were mostly made on what we would now call a print-on-demand basis, but on sheepskin and by hand.

211 The book also includes a shamelessly happy ending for the bishop of Santiago, who may have commissioned the story: at a council of Spanish bishops after the war is over, Charlemagne and the prelates agree that in the future, the bishops of Santiago de Compostela will be the most important bishops in Spain, entitled to the proceeds of an annual gift from all the landowners in Spain, and that all the Spanish prelates would have to obey them. Not long after this was written, one 12th-century historian, Rodrigo Jiménez de Rada, the archbishop of Toledo, noted that this history could not possibly be true. The places mentioned in the book had not been conquered by Christians until 200 years later, and Charlemagne could not have been responsible for opening up the pilgrimage from France to Santiago de Compostela, given Roland's defeat at Roncesvalles. Amazingly, however, plenty of modern guidebooks still serve up the same old story about Roland and the Moors.

cevaux Pass. In this version, he does blow his horn, sensibly enough, but it does not make any difference in the end.[212]

In fact, neither version gets the story right. There was a historical Roland, and he did go on a campaign with Charlemagne to Spain in 778, but their errand was to assist Charlemagne's ally, the sultan of Barcelona, not to defend a Christian king. When that campaign ended, and the horde headed back home to Germany. Roland and many of his men were ambushed near Roncesvalles, but by Basques, not Moors.

Fictional or not, between *The Life of Charlemagne and Roland* and the *Song of Roland*, stories about the knight have had a deep impact on France, first in the Middle Ages, and then again in the 19th and 20th centuries.

People had always known the story in a vague, but the original epic resurfaced only in the 1830s, when an Oxford University professor found an Anglo-Norman version of the poem. However, as anti-English feeling still ran high in France, French scholars became enthusiastic about Roland only after they found two versions in Old French.

For most of the 19th century, even as the fortunes of the French fluctuated, French medievalists used the *Song of Roland* as a way to puff up national pride. Even when there weren't many objective reasons to feel encouraged, the French still had the *Chanson*. Sure, Paris might be under siege by the Prussians, but what did that matter in the long run? Even if the Germans won a few battles, they still didn't have anything that could touch *Roland*.

One reason for the popularity may be that the moral is so ambiguous: the Song is an epic you can wear with anything. As Isabel N. DiVanna writes, "the nature of `Frenchness' was not constant for all groups throughout the nineteenth century, and, as a result, neither was Roland." Monarchists, Republicans, Communists—people of nearly every political stripe used this story about the defeat of an 8th-century Frankish knight—who,

212 I think that's a clue that the Chartres window illustration is from this version of the story.

as part of Charlemagne's entourage, probably spoke some kind of proto-German—to encourage people to fight for *la Patrie*.

After Roncesvalles, Masha and I had two more kilometers of easy walking through flat pine woods, past an eerie sign memorializing several witch trials and burnings that had been held there in the early 1500s, and then we were in Burguete, a long old town of white, half-timbered houses and shutters painted in bright primary colors.

We reached our hotel at eight o'clock, just in time for dinner. Cybèle, Thea, and Charlotte were sprawled all over the room, watching the Olympics.

I felt exhausted but ecstatic: we had made it to Paris and back right on time, with Masha's visa trouble finally sorted out. We had managed to get over that 1,000-meter pass, the last half without any water. We were nearly done with the first half of our adventure. And now we were all together again, at least for a little while.

August 11. Burguete to Larrasoaña, 27.4 km
Regarding the old shell game.

The next morning, we ate a dismal breakfast of cello-phane-wrapped *papier-maiche* croissants and bad coffee in the dark hotel dining room the night staff had been nice enough to leave out for us. The hotel might have been called El Peregrino (The Pilgrim), but it was a real hotel, not a gîte and evidently did not attract any pilgrim riffraff. Its other, more sensible, civilian guests were rising later. After breakfast, Cybèle and the girls went on ahead while I stayed behind to knock out a column.

The days were getting shorter now and it was still dark when they left. Out on the trail, Cybèle admired the dawn as it rose through the pines, but the girls were thoroughly unimpressed. Charlotte wrote *"we got mad at Mom for some reason and made up a lovely poem about the sunrise:*

> The sun is rising, Bloody Yay!
> It rises every single day!"

Cybèle tried to put a good face on the day's walk for the troops, but deep down, she wasn't crazy about this section of the hike either. *"I've seen a lot of toilet paper on the sides of the trail—a lot of it is paved with stone, cut stone steps—the path is wider, almost as wide as a country road—it feels more like a road than a trail through the countryside."* Midmorning, as they walked through a cement factory quarry, Charlotte slipped on some gravel and got a dramatic scratch on the back of her leg.

Charlotte was very glad that we were almost finished walking. Masha, on the other hand, didn't mind walking, and was still terrified by the idea of biking, so she had now started lobbying Cybèle to keep walking instead. Even if we had to hike 40 kilometers a day, she said, it would be better than biking. Thea, meanwhile, still seemed secretly content and ready for anything.

There were more people on the Camino now, and a different bunch. The trail on this side of the Pyrenees was clogged with

Spanish families with young children; older Americans and Australians; and, fresh-faced young people from many countries with shiny boots and backpacks.

More pilgrims also had scallop shells tied to their backpacks, many with a red crusader's cross stenciled across the back.

Although Catholicism was in the background of the *chemin de Compostelle* in France, it seemed more front and center here and I began to think more about how strange it was that James, a Galilean fisherman turned itinerant preacher, would have ended up buried in Galicia, in northwest Spain, thousands of kilometers from home.

Today, the Santiago pilgrim's office website says only that James's relics were found during the reign of King Alfonso II (792-842), but it glosses over the particulars. The Church's traditional version had it that after preaching in Spain, James went back home to the Holy Land, where he was beheaded. At this point, his disciples decided he should be buried back in Spain. Conveniently, a magical stone boat appeared just then and ferried them all back to Galicia, where a pagan queen named Loba (She-Wolf) invited them to bury the holy man on a mountain where a dragon dwelt, hoping the dragon would kill them. Instead, the dragon exploded. They buried the Apostle right there in the mountains, where the miracle of the dragon had occurred.

Santiago's stone boat
(detail from a Compostela altar)

Despite that auspicious start, the tomb was lost for many years, until a shepherd following a red star found the tomb, at the place that we now call Santiago de Compostela[213]

Stone boats and exploding dragons are a great origin story, but I suspect the "discovery" of Santiago's relics and the development of the pilgrimage had more to do with the usual quest for money and power.

In the early Middle Ages, the Christian kingdoms of northern Spain were in a strategically difficult situation: they were poor and weak—isolated from northern Europe, and far behind the advanced Muslim civilization that dominated most of Spain.

The gap between the two groups was vast.

Cordoba, the biggest city of *Al-Andalus* (Muslim Spain)[214] had a population of perhaps 200,000, making it the second-largest city Europeans had ever heard of, after Constantinople. Even a cloistered, 10th-century German poet, the nun Hrotswitha of Gandersheim, had heard about Cordoba's riches, and called it "the glittering ornament of the world."

Sister Hrotswitha was not exaggerating. Cordobans enjoyed the benefit of Arabic numbers, Greek medicine, compasses, wind-mills, weight-driven clocks, paper (which didn't get north of the

---

213   The authorities have always been equally vague about the precise location of Santiago's tomb within the cathedral. In 1056, one account of a group of pilgrims from Liège notes that the group had to hire a guide to show them where to find Saint James' relics, but don't mention anything about a tomb. One historian who has made a close reading of the 12th-century *Pilgrim's Guide* also notes that the writer talks about the cathedral in very precise terms but glosses over whether pilgrims could actually see Santiago's tomb. More recently, 19th and 20th century archaeologists have found plenty of bones in and around the church, but nothing apostolic. Some scholars began thinking that Compostela, instead of meaning "field of stars," as people had often romantically interpreted its etymology, may have actually meant Compos Tella —"burial ground." The most imposing tomb identified by archaeologists in the vicin-ity of the cathedral belongs to a fourth-century heretic named Priscillian, which had inspired its own pilgrimage for a time. Priscillian advocated a more ascetic version of Christianity than the Church preached, and for reasons I don't understand, the Ro-mans considered Priscillian enough of a threat that the emperor had him executed on the presumably trumped-up charges of studying obscene doctrines, holding nocturnal meetings with shameful women, and praying while naked. Currently, the pilgrim of-fice website says only that the cathedral was built over Santiago's tomb.

214   I refer to Muslim Spain throughout for clarity's sake, but specialists now usually prefer Al-Andalus to describe Islamic Iberia in the Middle Ages.

Pyrenees until the 13th century), and a better class of steel. Culturally too, they were years ahead: in 960, the caliph of Cordoba supposedly possessed a library of 400,000 volumes. By comparison, a hundred years later, the fact that Diego Gelmírez, the first archbishop of Santiago de Compostela (circa 1100), had amassed a library of 15 volumes by the time he reached middle age, which was considered enough of an achievement that a contemporary biographer found it worth noting.[215]

The northerners meanwhile had no cities to speak of and not much in the way of resources— the northern kingdoms did not even mint their own money. Northerners relied on barter, old Roman coins, and the occasional gold and silver coins that came in from France or Muslim Spain. In Galicia, 11th century records show, for example, that a parcel of land had been sold for "a mare and an excellent cloak and a cow" and a share in a church for "a splendid roan stallion and a good cloak."[216] Even the kings were broke: Ordoño II, king of Galicia and Leon, had himself crowned in the baths of Rome's Seventh Legion in 914, and afterward, used the legionaires' old bathhouse as his palace.

But some of them thought big: Ordoño's father, Alfonso the Great, the king of León, Asturias, and Galicia, had styled himself Emperor of All Spain, and to help back his claim, took Saint James as his patron saint.

At the time, a powerful patron saint was an important part of any Christian king's entourage. The Carolingians and the Merovingians, for instance, had three: Saint Martin of Tours, Saint Denys near Paris, and Saint Remigius at Rheims.

The patron saint served two functions. First, he (or she: I don't get the impression that gender mattered) looked out for the king and brought him good fortune (including enabling said leader to "live long, father children, defeat [his] enemies, win land and booty, attract followers and perhaps above all be remembered,"

---

215   And to be fair, building a library is a big deal if you have no paper. To make a copy of the Bible, for example, required about 200 sheepskins.

216   Churches in Spain at that time were often a kind of franchise business you could own, like an Arbys or a Jack in the Box. Disputes over shares and rights of title rose fairly often.

according to historian Richard Fletcher). Second, he played a public relations role, by making the king's power seem more enduring, even if his dynasty had not started very long ago.

This meant that choosing your patron saint was not a casual decision. As Fletcher puts it:

> In early medieval Europe saints' cults did not simply happen: they were made. Perhaps that statement is too sweeping. [It would be better to say that] small-scale, local and popular cults might be transformed if influential people were persuaded that it was in their interests to show devotion to one, or several, saints' shrines.

Why Alfonso chose Saint James (Santiago) nobody knows. Although the Apostle's tomb had been "discovered" in Compostela in the first half of the ninth century, and a small church built and dedicated to him, he was still relatively obscure before Alfonso decided to make him his patron saint around 900.[217] In Santiago's favor, however, was the fact that he was an apostle, which made him a five-star general in the army of saints. Alfonso may also have been genuinely grateful for his help in putting down a pretender at the beginning of his reign.

After dispatching the unlucky Count Froila of Galicia, Alfonso named Santiago his kingdom's patron saint and closed the deal with what I suspect was a fairly typical signing bonus: restoring land the count had seized from the church at Compostela and presenting the Apostle with a gold, bejeweled cross. Later, to stay on his good side, the king also rebuilt his church and extended its lands.

More surprisingly, Alfonso did not move Santiago's relics to Oviedo, his family's first city, or to León, where they would have been more easily accessible to the rest of his realm. At the time, as we saw with Saint Foy in Conques, relics were often "translated" to give a royal family an extra charge of holy power or a monastery or cathedral an added attraction, but Alfonso left the

---

217   He had other options, including his family's special relationship with two Roman-era saints, Facundus and Primativus, who were martyred at Sahagún around 300. Their martyrdoms had a miraculous side too, though more weird than impressive (when their heads were lobbed off, they gushed milk as well as blood).

relics in faraway Santiago de Compostela.

It could be Santiago was already too popular to move. Maybe, even at that time, the story of the stone boat was too much a part of Santiago's story for people to accept his relocation. Or maybe the relics could be more easily defended up in the mountains, because Alfonso had to worry about both Vikings and North African pirates on the Galician coast and attacks from Muslim Spanish armies on the Leónese plain. It could also be—and this is just a guess—that Alfonso believed that keeping Compostela the center of the Santiago cult would strengthen the kingdom's hold on Galicia, which then as now was hard to reach from the rest of his kingdom. In any case, Alfonso and his successors let the sleeping saint lie.

But that didn't mean Alfonso and eventually the other northern Christian kings didn't have big plans for the Apostle. As the historian Americo Castro wrote, "A relic of such magnitude meant as much in the tenth century – when the boundaries between the spiritual and the material were blurred – as the petroleum of Iraq does in the twentieth":

> For the Hispanic monarchs the pilgrimage was a source of holiness, prestige, power, and wealth, which the national monasticism was not in condition to take sufficient advantage of. It was necessary to bring in 'engineers' from outside to organize an adequate system of do ut des [I give that you may give back] between Spain and the rest of Christianity and thus elevate the importance of the Peninsular kingdoms both with respect to Islam and to Europe.

These days, if you find yourself with a windfall this valuable, you might call Shell Oil or McKinsey to help you handle it. Back then, the go-to guys for spiritual asset development were the Cluniac monks.

And the boys from Cluny delivered. As the art historian Arthur Kinglake Porter put it,

> Surely no capitalist of the XIX century ever promoted more shrewdly, nor any diplomat of the XVI played politics more cleverly, than the Cluniac monks, who to, if not for, their own advan-

tage, set all Europe a-journeying, quite literally, to the ends of the world. The rulers of the great abbey were quick to realize the success of the pilgrimage, and far-sighted in driving, at an early date, their fingernails firmly into the carrot of Saint James.

This did not happen all at once. In the early 1000s, Sancho the Great of Navarre gave Cluny monasteries at San Juan de La Pena and San Salvador de Leyre, near Pamplona. In the 1090s, Alfonso's grandson, Alfonso V, gave several monasteries to the Cluniacs in his realm and promised an enormous annual donation. By the mid-1100s, a whole string of Cluniac monasteries stretched at convenient, Days Inn-like intervals all the way from the Roncesvalles Pass to Santiago.

I had a good morning: I made my deadline and left the dark hotel about 9:30. Surprisingly, I could also still walk. Despite our epic hike the day before, my feet were giving me no twinges at all. In fact, I couldn't even feel them. They felt more like paws than feet now, all puffed up with a hide on the bottom. It also helped that the path was still mostly flat and sandy, and shaded by scrubby pinewoods, like our last hour the day before.

Toward noon, I ran into a young Greek couple, and walked with them for a little while. They were friendly and spoke some English. The two were both between jobs and had thought hiking would be a nicer way to spend the summer than staying home and being unemployed.

I enjoyed talking with the Greeks, but after a few minutes, they stopped to wade in a stream and I sensed I had begun to wear out my welcome. As I pushed on, the young man looked up at me from the water and asked, "Is it true that the Germans are planning on putting identity chips in everyone?"

Of course, the northern kings and the Cluniacs didn't build the pilgrimage alone. Imaginative churchmen played a big role too. Diego Gelmirez, the bishop and eventually archbishop of Santiago de Compostela, played a particularly important role.

Gelmirez, who became bishop in 1100, was a tough man in a tough time— contemporaries called him the "crozier and catapult of Saint James." In his earliest portrait, he is shown sitting on a throne next to Alfonso VII, dressed just like Alfonso and capped with a similar crown. Alfonso is looking at him somewhat anxiously, which is understandable, because while the monarch is pictured holding an orb in his left hand and a scepter in his right, the bishop is armed with an acanthus leaf (symbolizing immortality) in his left hand—and in his right, an upright, unsheathed broadsword.

Bishop Gelmirez and Alfonzo VII

Both the temporal and spiritual leader of his diocese, Gelmirez did a number of things to draw more pilgrims to Santiago de Compostela. First, he scared off the pirates. In 1115, he ordered two top-of-the-line, 100-man galleys from Genoa to encourage the Norman and Saracen pirates to go marauding somewhere other than the Galician coast. It took more than a decade of battles, but he won eventually, and safe sea passage made the trip much more popular with English pilgrims. He also put soldiers on the payroll who knew something about sieges, which was important because land-based bandits would periodically try building castles to shakedown pilgrims and challenge his authority.

He had a number of magistrates on hand as well, as a further measure to persuade townsfolk that there was more money to be made treating pilgrims well than in robbery. He also seems to have persuaded Queen Urraca the Reckless, Queen of the Kingdoms of Leon, Castile, and Galicia, to make Santiago de Compostela what we would now call a duty-free zone, which helped turn the town into one of northern Spain's most important trading hubs.

Gelmirez made the cathedral itself a bigger attraction too. He "translated" the remains of Saint Fructuosus from Braga, Portugal, to the cathedral, which, as Fletcher puts it, "topped up the charge" of the cathedral's holiness. To raise its profile, he cajoled Queen Urraca into making a pilgrimage to Santiago instead of Jerusalem.

The bishop rebuilt his cathedral on a grander scale too, with the help of Muslim prisoners and a French bell-maker. Modern conveniences added during the renovation included a cloister—he had been embarrassed when pilgrims from north of the Pyrenees said they were surprised the church didn't have one—and a fountain big enough for 15 pilgrims to bathe in at once. The fountain itself was supplied by an elaborate internal water system connected via a mile-long covered viaduct that provided not only enough water to operate the fountain but also enabled the cathedral to withstand a siege—an event that occurred at least once on his watch, laid not by pirates or Muslim invaders but powerful local families annoyed by his rules and his taxes.

Finally, Gelmirez persuaded Church leaders to agree that an apostle's tomb deserved to be not just a bishopric, but an archbishopric, and so important that the archbishop ought to report not to the local king or any Spanish prelate but directly to Rome.

This campaign worked on a more or less congressional basis—elaborate arguments followed up by what the contemporary biographer calls "many big presents." As noted in Gelmirez's *Historia Compestelana*—a gangster's memoir disguised as a history of Galicia—the fee and consideration to the church hierarchy included 100 ounces of gold, a gold reliquary, 100 marvedis, 211

Poitevin shillings, 650 Milanese coins, 20 Toulousin coins, "et cetera." The "et cetera" included a 40-mark silver dish formerly owned by al-Musta, the Muslim king of Zaragoza; a golden cross and crown; a chasuble worked in gold thread; and 40 marks from Gelmirez's own fortune. There was some embarrassment when one of the reliquaries turned out to be only gold-plated silver, but Gelmirez showered the prelates with a few additional "blessings" to put the unfortunate oversight behind them.

Gelmirez may have also hired a Cluniac monk from Poitou named Aymeric Picaud to write something about Saint James to promote the pilgrimage. Around 1140, during Gelmirez's tenure and possibly with his connivance, Picaud compiled and perhaps also wrote the popular anthology usually called either the Book of Saint James or the Codex Calixtinus.

This five-volume anthology included:
   1. The Book of the Liturgies: a book of sermons and homilies about Saint James.
   2. The Book of the Miracles: a book of 22 miracles attributed to Saint James (most of which happen to people far from Galicia, either at home or on route to Santiago).
   3. The Book of the Transfer of the Body of Saint James, explaining how he ended up in Galicia.
   4. The History of Charlemagne and Roland, supposedly written by Charlemagne's friend, Archbishop Turpin (noted earlier).
   5. A Guide for Pilgrims to Compostela (also noted earlier).[218]

The compilation is known as the Codex Calixtinus because each book has a preface supposedly written by Pope Callixtus II, a Frenchman with strong ties to Cluny who led the church from 1119 to 1124 and gave Gelmirez his archbishopric, but scholars are fairly sure that Calixtus's forewards are all forgeries.[219]

---

218 There are also appendices of sheet music, including the first polyphonic piece for three voices. Unfortunately, musicologists say, it reads better than it sounds.

219 Maybe even a double forgery: some historians have argued that there was no Aymeric Picaud and that it was actually written by a Spaniard pretending to be an intolerant Frenchman.

Copies of the collection were made and circulated all over Europe—a piece of propaganda that raised James's stature, enhanced the newly made archbishopric's status, and convinced many people that a pilgrimage to Santiago would be an interesting and important trip to make.[220]

Cybèle and the girls reached Larrasoaña about one o'clock, *"which was good because it turned out we had no reservation so we had to wait in line at the Albergo Municipal,"* Thea wrote. *"They made us show our passports and everything. We have to sleep in the same room as 50 million other people."*

Like most Spanish towns we walked through, Larrasoaña was laid out along a single strip rather than a grid, French-style, but it still took me awhile to track down Cybèle and the girls. The town was crowded with pilgrims, more than we had seen anywhere before, and as usual I marched off first in the wrong direction. When I did find the *albergo* (hostel), Cybèle told me I had to go to the office across the street right away, because the lady had not let her reserve me a bunk.

In the old, tin-ceilinged office, the clerk carefully inspected then stamped my pilgrim passport and allotted me the second-to-last free bed. After that, I claimed my bunk back at the hostel, and went out with Cybèle and the girls back to look for a snack. We found a cafe and sat down next to four Irish girls who were flirting with two prim young Spaniards. The girls had their feet up on the little tables and sat smoking and laughing and knocking back pint after pint. The guys laughed nervously, like missionaries who have wandered into cannibal country.

On our way back to the albergo, a goose suddenly charged at

220   And it worked. Even today, you will find many pilgrim websites that quote liberally from the Codex Calixtinus, without noting that it's filled with half-truths, outright lies, and outrageous slanders.

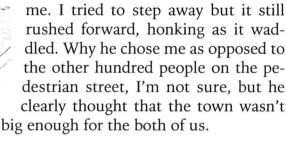

You ate my father.
Prepare to die.

me. I tried to step away but it still rushed forward, honking as it waddled. Why he chose me as opposed to the other hundred people on the pedestrian street, I'm not sure, but he clearly thought that the town wasn't big enough for the both of us.

His minder, a large goose-shaped man in a baseball cap, apologized and prodded him with a stick in another direction. The bird complained loudly but did as Father Goose directed.

Back in the albergo, we cleaned up, then lolled on our bunks for an hour or so. The hostel was a whitewashed barn jammed with metal bunk beds, every one of them claimed with a backpack on the bed. No one here seemed concerned about bedbugs. This worried us at the time, but not later on. Evidently, the French were wrong about the origin of the punaise. Wherever the pests came from, it apparently wasn't Spain.

Around 7:30, we went back out for dinner. I remembered that the Irish girls' cafe had a cheap pilgrim's special, so we ended up there, crammed on both sides of a long bench. An American woman sat down next to us. She was in her late 50s and from New York but had lived in Paris for 20 years or so. She had a C sharp Brooklyn accent but spoke beautiful French, and was doing the walk with a French friend, a woman about her age. She had married a Frenchman but they were divorced and she had stayed on.

It was a warm night and after dinner, outside the albergo, the five of us sat together around my computer and watched an old movie called *Romancing the Stone*, one of a limited stash of DVDs Cybele had picked up at a shop in St. Jean. It was a guilty pleasure to sit and watch a silly movie with the girls but still a pleasure, and I mostly ignored the superior looks of more earnest pilgrims who were already getting ready for bed.

August 12. Larrasoaña to Pamplona, 16.9 km
In which we end the walking half of our Camino.

As it was Sunday and we were in a one-room barn of a hostel with no place where I could work without waking at least a dozen people up, I had decided to sleep in.

But I woke up early anyway. The parents of the four or five families who shared the room with us were packing. Light from the fathers' tiny head-mounted flashlights bobbed all over the bunks and the high ceiling as they stuffed their backpacks shut. Then they were gone, and I tried to go back to sleep, but a few minutes later, a wave of slightly less organized and slightly louder people stirred, and the same thing happened all over again. And again.

The reason for all this early morning activity, it turned out, was that the municipal *refugios* in Spain were filled on a first-come, first-serve basis, so people often left long before sunrise to make sure they got a bunk at the next stop.

We got out at 6:30 and we were the last to leave—which Cybèle liked because it made the two of us look relatively easy going, even lazy, and not the martinets the girls imagined.

A few kilometers down the road, we stopped at an outdoor cafe right off the trail that was open for breakfast. It was an idyllic place—the tables were all set on a flagstoned patio next to an old stone millhouse with a stream rushing behind it and pine woods behind the stream. We ordered coffee and fresh tortillas (the Spanish potato and onion quiche, that is) that they had baked two minutes earlier in the outdoor brick oven, and it was so good that we shared a second slice and would have had still more if the earlier birds had not already eaten the rest.

I wish I could do more justice to that breakfast. Hemingway, who spent some time fishing in Burguete, could have done it. It would be hard to top his description of driving into Pamplona, for instance, in *The Sun Also Rises*:

> away off you could see the plateau of Pamplona rising out of the

plain, and the walls of the city, and the great brown cathedral, and the broken skyline of the other churches. In back of the plateau were the mountains, and every way you looked there were other mountains, and ahead the road stretched out white across the plain going into Pamplona.

That is all still true but there are also suburbs to get through now, some nice and some not so nice, another cement factory, and near occasions of freeways. Still, it was a short easy hike, only 13 kilometers, and we reached Pamplona before lunch.

To enter the old city, we walked through a park up a hill, the four- or five-story walls of the town on our left, and then through an old baroque gate, the Porto de Francia.

We checked into our hotel, a two-star place on the second floor. The hotel manager, a big bald man, seemed to find the sight of us more depressing than was warranted, all things considered. One of his staff—all strikingly handsome young Indian and North African men—led us to our grim and tiny room, which had one narrow window and white-painted cinderblock walls.

I had expected Pamplona to be a white stucco town because of all the stories you read about the annual running of the bulls, but it's not like that at all. Behind its tall gray walls, old Pamplona is actually a very dark city, filled with shadows and narrow alleys.

The one exception is the Plaza del Castillo, the central square, which looks like it should belong to a capital city, as indeed Pamplona was, in the distant past, when it was capital of the Kingdom of Navarre. There are a lot of cafes on the square but the grande dame is a cafe mentioned in *The Sun Also Rises*, the Iruña.[221] You can still walk in and have a nasty argument with your mean ex-pat friends if you like but the day we were there, the customers were mostly families ordering the set lunch, watching Sunday soccer on giant plasma TVs. It's as clean and well-lighted a place as you could ask for, in a high-ceilinged *fin de siècle* way, with iron columns, an ornamental tin ceiling, and a big window that faces the square. Whatever his other faults, Hemingway had good

---

221   The café is named after the Basque word for Pamplona, which also turns up a lot in graffiti scrawled on the city's walls and walks.

taste in cafes.[222]

The Iruña

Spanish critics have noticed many shortcomings in Hemingway's understanding of Spain, but given that he spent only 40 days in Spain between 1923 and 1925, and then a few months during the civil war, I'm not sure how anybody could have done any better. To my uneducated eye, about the only thing Hemingway leaves out of his descriptions of northern Spain is the Camino de Santiago. You would think that with all the dust and pain involved, the pilgrimage would appeal to him, but he never mentions it directly.

This seemed like a simple oversight until I read that he converted to Catholicism at 19, and practiced the religion for the rest of his life. He became a believer after being hit by a mortar on

---

222　The Iruña doesn't make too much of a fuss about the Hemingway association except for an unfortunate lifesize bronze statue of a grinning Papa leaning against the bar.

a battlefield in Italy during the First World War, when he felt his "soul or something coming right out of my body, like you'd pull a silk handkerchief out of a pocket by one corner. It flew around and then came back and went in again and I wasn't dead anymore." When they brought him to the hospital, a priest gave him extreme unction and he asked to be baptized.

Although Hemingway didn't write about the Camino in any overt way, H.R. Stoneback of Notre Dame has argued that you can find many traces of the trail in his work. In *The Old Man and the Sea*, the fisherman's name is Santiago, and there are stars all over the place—like Compostela, which as noted earlier is sometimes translated as "the field of stars." And Stoneback notes that Hemingway gave his Nobel Prize to a church outside Santiago de Cuba, which is the destination of the Cuban Camino.

Professor Stonebeck also makes the case that you can look at *The Sun Also Rises* as a pilgrim's story, as all the stops coincide with old pilgrim's stops, from the time Jake Barnes walks past "the rigid north and south of rue St. Jacques" in Paris, down through Bayonne, Roncesvalles, and Pamplona—and prays at the Cathedral at Pamplona. The more persuasive detail to me, however, given that almost every major town in France was a pilgrim stop, is that the narrator's name is Jake—Jacob being a variation of James; in Germany, the Camino is even called the Jakobsweg. As Lady Brett Ashley tells Jake at one point, "That's a hell of a Biblical name you've got there."

But if the idea of a pilgrimage really is fundamental to *The Sun Also Rises*, why doesn't Jake light out to Santiago in the end, instead of San Sebastian before going to Madrid? I think there are two possibilities worth considering. One, which has been suggested, is that Saint Sebastian, a handsome martyred soldier, is traditionally considered to be the patron saint of gay people, and that Jake Barnes's problem *vis-à-vis* Brett is that he's gay. A second alternative, which I find more plausible (because Jake insists more or less specifically several times that he isn't gay), is that he goes to the coastal town because Saint Sebastian is also the patron saint of soldiers. There, the emotionally and physically wounded pilgrim hopes to find, if not a miracle, then at least some solace. As Jake puts it,

> It was a splendid place to swim. You could lie on the beach and soak in the sun and get straightened around inside again. Maybe I would feel like writing.

We walked all over Pamplona that afternoon, visiting various churches, including Jake Barnes's cathedral. It all felt old and mysterious, and looking back on it now,

Statues of monks in the church of San Saturnino.

I could see why an American eye like Hemingway's would see something interesting in the contrast between his young, liberated traveling companions and the old city.[223]

Hemingway at a Pamplona bullfight in the fifties (from a photograph by Francesc Catalá Roca)

In the evening, after going out for more tortillas, we turned the TV on in our room and watched the closing ceremonies of the London Olympics. The spectacle made me feel very old and out of touch. After our weeks outside, I didn't know what to make of all those cars and trucks and 50,000 extras roaring around the stadium, like a ballet about traffic. Not even James Bond parachuting in with the Queen or the Churchill lookalike popping out

---

223 To his credit, Hemingway also saw Spain through less romantic eyes when he was older. During the civil war, he discovered that most of his matador friends were fascists, and later, when he visited Pamplona again in the 1950s, wrote to his wife that "he loathed the whole damn bull business now."

of the center like a chorus girl out of a birthday cake redeemed it for me. After 20 minutes, we turned it off and watched *The Matrix* instead, which felt similarly plastic, but at least had a plot. Then we went to bed, even though for once, we didn't have to get up early: we were going to pick up our bicycles in the morning, and Decathlon didn't open until 10.

Back in January, we had intended to rent bikes, but as I looked into it, I realized that it would actually be cheaper to buy budget bikes from Decathlon than to rent fancy mountain bikes from one of the Camino rental agencies. Ordering the bicycles had required a little doing, but with some help from our friend Jess in Madrid and a little emailing back and forth with Pilar at the bike shop, we had managed:

From: PILAR ESQUIVEL (PAMPO166) pilar.esquivel@decathlon.com>
To: Bennett Voyles <benvoyles@yahoo.com> Sent: Tuesday, July 31, 2012 12:58 PM
Subject: Re: DECATHLON PAMPLONA
Hi!!
I need know what day do you need the bikes and if you want put in there any portabagages!!
I think that your sizes are this:
FATHER: XL
MOTHER: XL
AND 3 SISTER: NEEDS SIZE L.
Pleasse answer me if you need portabagages in the bikes and I will have all ready.
Thenks for all.
Best regards
Pilar Esquivel.

Dear Pilar,

We will want to pick up the bikes on Monday morning, August 13. I think we will need portbaggages
on the two adult bikes and front baskets for everyone. How many liters of space do the portbaggages
have? I have not seen them and am not sure how many
we will need.

Also, do you have any rear-view mirrors for bicycles? My wife is deaf and it would be nice if she
had something to help her that way.

Thanks very much,

Ben

Dear Ben!
The portbaggages have 21 kg of weight wich one
also we have one trailer the 49.95 euros with more
capacity, if you want for any bike.
The front baskets only have one capacity for 8 kg,
there not serve for lead a lot of weight.
I think that it´s better that all bikes have portbaggages, but as you whichever you prefer.

And yes, we have a rear- view mirrors for the
bikes, if you want we will put one in your wife´s
bike.

Attentivey
Pilar Esquivel

August 13. Pamplona to Puente La Reina, 24.2 km

In which we saddle up for the next adventure.

In the morning, I put on my backpack, and then Cybèle and I picked up the shopping bags in which we had been carrying most of the clothes. We said goodbye to another comely youth in the hall of mirrors, and marched out the high front gate of the old walled city with the girls.

We walked for a long time through the snap-together strip malls and warehouses in the modern outskirts without seeing a place to stop for breakfast. Finally, I spotted a guy carrying a big plastic sack of breakfast rolls and without a word, we started following him like a pack of hungry strays down a side street and into a dark sports bar.

He turned out to be the son of a father-son team who ran a not-too-clean or well-lighted place illuminated mostly by a soccer highlights report on a big screen TV. They served only *café con leche* and those dry rolls, but I was hungry and it tasted good to me. The son also seemed kind, a factor that tends to raise my opinion of the food, whatever its objective qualities.

I felt anxious about this next stage of the trip.

We had a few reasons to be anxious. By now we had gotten very used to walking all day long. It wasn't comfortable exactly, but it had become a familiar routine.

As I mentioned earlier, we also hadn't biked much. Even that statement overstates. I could probably count the times I'd been on a bike, all the way back to grade school. Cybèle too hadn't ridden much since she was about 15, which was now nearly 35 years ago. And the girls had probably ridden three days their whole childhood, including back when they were small enough to ride in tagalong trailers. Masha's second-grade birthday bike went so unused that it took years before the shiny streamers fell off the handle grips.

There were other worries too: Masha's old bicycling phobia, and those mysterious knee pains Charlotte had complained about on our test flight in the Bois de Bologne in Paris. Cybèle's deafness—she can't even hear a horn unless she's listening for it, particularly not in traffic or the wind. And Thea's being so slight, that a strong wind might knock her over.

Personally, however, I was most worried about being locked up with my thoughts for six or seven hours a day. The past two days without a book had been hard enough—I was still almost in mourning for Don Quixote—and I wasn't so sure how I would manage for two weeks with only the median line to distract me.[224]

Out of the side street and back on the bright main avenue, we walked past a brand new office park that looked as if it had just been unwrapped. They weren't bad buildings—lots of glass and a fair amount of wood, set far back from the wide sidewalk and the wider empty boulevard—but seemed insubstantial after the old stone city and then the scrubby industrial blocks we had been walking through.

The Decathlon on the other hand felt oppressively genuine, a white cinderblock box with its name stenciled across a long low wall in enormous blue letters like identification numbers on a battleship. The store wasn't open yet when we arrived, so we found a tiny scratch of shade along one side of the building, squeezed ourselves into it, and waited. The girls pulled out their Kindles immediately, without a word.

Across the parking lot we could see an overpass and on the other side of the overpass a McDonald's. We might have been in Bakersfield.

When the door finally opened, we told a cashier that we had come to pick up our *bicis*, and asked to see Pilar, the Decathlon manager I had been emailing.

---

224   I am not alone in this aversion. One 2014 psychology experiment found that if left alone in a room for six to fifteen minutes with nothing to do but administer electric shocks, 67% of men and 25% of women preferred to shock themselves than be left alone with their thoughts.

The young woman came up, said hello, and led us to the store's bicycle section. The mechanics had already wheeled out the sturdy, black ten-speeds and were tightening this gear and making adjustments to that. One of the younger bike mechanics spoke some English—in compliance with that universal law that young people who do anything technical always know a bit of English—and advised us on what else we needed.

Three hours later, we stood near the front door next to our bikes, dressed in iridescent shirts and padded bicycle shorts that had the sheen and at least on me the general look of an endangered sea mammal. Cybèle and I had kept our hiking boots[225] but the girls wore new sneakers, as after 700 kilometers, their boots had fallen apart. At home, they would have had a fit about having to wear black and white, seven-euro store-brand specials, but just now this was the least of their worries. We also carried elongated helmets decorated with hot-rod stripes except for Charlotte, who had chosen a round helmet that looked like a white cannon ball; five reflective vests; two sets of what they called portbaggages (saddlebags that rested on the rear wheels); five bicycle locks; three spare tires; six spare inner tubes; a tube of goo for repairing said inner tubes; a pump; one rear view mirror for Cybèle; one front basket for Cybèle; and a Spanish guidebook on biking the Camino by a guy who called himself Kapitán Pedales (Captain Pedals), although none of us can read Spanish. I thought it might be nice to have a map.

On the other side of the checkout counter, near the entrance, Cybèle began packing all the stuff into the saddlebags that she had attached to her bike and my bike. The two of us planned to carry everything, as she thought it would make the bicycling easier for the girls. I would be carrying my backpack and two rear bags, while Cybèle had two rear bags, and a front basket in which she would carry all our water bottles.

As their mother packed, the girls and I stood watching her, slightly dazed. People stepped around us as if we were mannequins and examined the big black bikes. A few even squeezed

---

225   Die Bären, in particular, were still in surprisingly good shape.

and admired our special padded granny seats, which, to be fair, did have an invitingly voluptuous look to them.

It was 2:30 or so when we finally left the store and back out into the white heat. Remembering the hard time we had finding a place to eat this morning, we decided to go up and around the interchange to the McDonald's on the far side of the freeway. This wasn't too much of a sacrifice: I like McDonald's in Spain; they serve a nice gazpacho.

As we ate, Cybèle began to get anxious to start riding, but as usual, I was more relaxed. What was there to worry about? Sure, it was about 3:30 now, but we had only 25 kilometers to cover, and thanks to the advanced technology of our Rockrider 5.2s, getting to our destination wouldn't take long.[226]

The first hour, it certainly seemed that way. We were wobbly, but didn't find riding too hard. Even Masha didn't seem to mind. The road out of the city was on a slightly downward slope, subtle enough to feel like a gentle push, and we zipped right through more of the just-built edge of town. After our weeks of walking, the speed felt almost dreamlike, particularly once we found the smooth, freshly paved bike path that led through more new housing developments and a recently unpacked college campus. It was only when we were definitely out of Pamplona and in the country, when the bike path ended and a string of new blue and yellow shell signs led us down a freshly paved side road and out into the fields, that things began to go wrong.

On the other side of the field, we pedaled into a newish subdivision and our blue signs vanished. At around 5:30, Thea, who had been pedaling like lightning far ahead of us, as if she had been here before and knew where she was going, suddenly wheeled back to wait for us to catch up, just as a car came around the corner right behind her.

The next millisecond lasted a very long time, at least for Cybèle and me, watching Thea in the middle of her arabesque and the

---

226   Where did they get these names? Rockrider I understood, even Rockrider 5, but why 5.2? Did they think it sounded more substantial somehow? Or more cyber?

grill of a car directly behind her. Fortunately, the driver saw her, so everything was fine, but it easily might not have been.

Normally, we would have given her hell for this, but Cybèle was anxious not to panic Masha—she told me later she didn't want to remind Masha of her old traffic trauma (watching two-year old Thea running toward the sidewalk's edge in New York, in front of a blur of yellow cab), so she just asked Thea not to ride so far ahead.

We stopped now and fooled with the guidebook for a bit to see if we could figure out where we had gone wrong, but Kapitán Pedales was not especially clear. For the next 20 minutes, we wandered around the cul-de-sacs of the subdivision, until two women who were driving by stopped, asked us if we needed help, and and gave us a motorized escort back to the Way.

After more houses and more fields, we pedaled into a tiny town that seemed to consist only of a cafe, a traffic light, and a cemetery.

On our right, catty-corner to the cemetery, a two-lane highway ran straight down the hill and out onto an endless plain. I liked the look of that long straight road, which would eat up at least five of the ten kilometers we had to go in about five minutes. But then we looked at the map again, and Cybèle realized that in fact we needed to keep going straight. We pedaled alongside the cemetery, where the road turned into a lane, then past a marker for a young priest who had dropped dead there two days into his Camino, for reasons I couldn't make out, then veered left through a field that led directly toward a massive butte topped with long white windmills.

> "Now look, your grace," said Sancho, "what you see over there aren't giants, but windmills, and what seems to be arms are just their sails, that go around in the wind and turn the millstone."
>
> "Obviously," replied Don Quixote, "you don't know much about adventures."

When we reached the foot of the butte we just stood for a minute, looking up.

It was late in the day now, and the whole scrubby hill, almost a cliff, had started to turn orange. After some searching, we found a steep, rocky path that switchbacked up toward the windmills like a pilgrimage trail for penitent rabbits. Making turns was impossible because the gravel was too deep, so at the first turn we got off our bikes and started to push.

Three mountain bikers in Lycra pedaled past us, but two more turns and even those buff Power Rangers had to get off and walk. Then the path turned into bigger rocks and large, slippery boulders. I began to doubt whether we were still heading the right way, but just then we met an older couple walking down the hill —evidently returning from an evening constitutional that had not taken too much out of them—and they reassured us, by smiling and patting our arms as they strolled past, that we were heading in the right direction.

I would not have found that narrow path fun to climb under any circumstances, but it was hell to push a bike up. Between the roots, the gravel, the stones, and the sheer weight of the bikes, the girls began to get frustrated. Masha and Thea bore it stoically enough, but Charlotte threw her bike down on the brush once, then sat down and cried. Cybèle lay her own bike down, walked back to Charlotte, pushed her bike up for her, then went back to push her own, and repeated this procedure for the next few switchbacks.

I wasn't too worried about getting to the top; I was more concerned about what we might find once we got there. Would we have to take a similar pathless-path down the other side, and in the dark? And after that, would there be other hills like this?

Above us now, we began to hear a low hum, almost a moan, coming from the crest. The windmills! At a distance, they look delicate but Don Quixote was right—up close, they're definitely evil giants.

Thea stopped and turned to me:

"I hope you have a heart attack and die."

She said this coolly, without tears or regret, as if she had considered all the facts in the case and come to an unavoidable conclusion.

The moans from the crest grew louder.

At the next switchback she turned toward me again:

"Why are we doing this? We aren't religious. Nobody is enjoying this. Mom's not enjoying this. *Even you* are not enjoying this. We're just doing this because YOU ARE CRAZY."

I didn't say anything. It occurred to me that she might have a point.

Why *were* we here, anyway?

In the old days, people often had practical reasons for making the pilgrimage. You could get a reduction off your long and painful time in Purgatory. You might pay off your side of a bargain—give me a child and I'll walk to Santiago.[227] You might do it to atone for a serious sin (at some periods, for an extremely serious sin, people could even be sent on a perpetual pilgrimage, an open-air life sentence.) Sometimes, making the pilgrimage was a condition for receiving an inheritance.

You could also do it as a job—the rich and powerful would pay people to make the trip for them, and the not-so-rich might leave a bequest in their will for someone to make the trip on their behalf.

---

227   Such vows were taken very seriously. Foy wasn't the only saint who went in for miracle repossession: an Englishman with a broken arm made a vow to Saint James to make a pilgrimage to visit James' hand in Reading Abbey. The saint, believing they had a deal, heard his prayer, "but when the man failed to fulfill his vow intervened again to break the man's other arm."

Others came for the shopping. Pilgrims were exempt from most tolls while they were on pilgrimage, and as noted earlier, Santiago was a duty-free city.

A pilgrimage was also a legal lark—one of the few trips you could make away from home that wouldn't necessarily get you branded as a vagrant and whipped or worse. Women could even go, if they had permission from their priest.

"...but the road was there already."

Pilgrimages have also often served as a form of what anthropologists call "costly signaling." In the Orkneyinga Saga, an account of the pilgrimage of Earl Ronald of Orkney and his lads to various holy places in 1151, brawling and pillaging all the way from the Isle of Orkney to the River Jordan and back, the narrator concludes that after they got home, "They all passed for men of more importance after the journey they had made."

There is probably still a bit of this going on now, particularly among secular pilgrims, the people politicians call the yoga vote. I know that before we made our Camino, I looked at people who had made the journey with admiration and envy, the way I still look at marathon runners, polyglots, and PhDs.

On our own pilgrimage, we had met a few people who were doing it for more serious reasons, especially some of the single women. We didn't hear many stories, but there was something fragile enough about these women that despite their discipline that you could see they were trying to get through something grim and sad—a death in the family, a lost relationship—and hoped to find some peace.

In the end, however, most of the reasons people make the pilgrimage still beg the question—as they always have. As my favorite Camino writer, the ever-eloquent G.G. King, puts it:

> The kings of Spain had built a highway to assist pilgrims in the twelfth century: but the road was there already. The Romans had built a military road as sign and condition of their domination: but the road was there already. Palaeolithic man had moved along it, and the stations of a living devotion today, he had frequented; there he made his magic, and felt vague awe before the abyss of an antiquity unfathomed ...[228]

It was twilight when we reached the top of the hill.

We walked along the ridge of Alta de Persdon, the Peak of Forgiveness, under the windmills, past a sculpture that shows up a lot in the guidebooks, a black iron silhouette of a troupe of medieval pilgrims. Between their spindly cartoon legs, we could see the big valley stretched out behind them. On the other side

---

228 I have not found any evidence that the Paleolithic part is true, but when you are out there, it does sometimes feel that way.

of a rough, mostly unpaved parking lot, I saw a gap in the brush where our trail began again, and more hills beyond that. All this bad geological news had caught me offguard: for some reason, I had imagined that once we were out of Pamplona, we would be on the plain, in Spain, zipping easily from *taberna* to *taberna*. But as useful as optimism can be, it's no match for geography. I hadn't remembered my Hemingway well enough: "every way you looked there were other mountains."

Once we crossed the parking lot, I looked down and saw we had another steep path ahead, but this one was even worse, more like a staircase of big rocks than a proper trail. Cybèle and I looked at each other, trying to figure out what to do next.

Just then, a young mountain biker who looked a bit like a friendly hobbit walked up and asked where we were heading.

"Don't go that way," he said. "Take the road over here."

This was a whole lot better—we flew down the mountain on a smooth paved road and then joined a narrow and fairly level two-lane highway for the next 10 kilometers. The road was busy but not bad, and it looked like, with luck, we would reach our refugio before dark after all. Thank you, Frodo, wherever you are.

When we reached the outskirts of Puente La Reina, I realized I didn't know where our *refugio* was, and Kapitán Pedales had no suggestions. We passed a fancy hotel that looked a bit like a ski lodge, and as it was now almost dark, Cybèle thought we should stop and ask for directions. Normally, I would have resisted this suggestion. Although I have spent a good chunk of my adult life as a kind of information mendicant, I hate to ask anybody for anything, particularly directions. But at that moment, with night settling in, I didn't object. The two of us walked in to the hotel and left the girls outside to watch the bikes.

The hotel reminded me of the lodges in the US national parks, the grand old ones with flagstone fireplaces and massive wood beams, a bully place for Teddy Roosevelt but far too nice for irridescent *bicigrinos*. No one stopped us at the door, however, and we walked through the high-ceilinged lobby to the front desk, where the receptionist told us that our destination was fairly far away, up a hill on the other side of town, and as far as she knew, didn't take reservations. She would be happy to call and see if they had any places left. Unless we wanted to stay here—

"How much is a room here?" I asked, leaning on the oak counter, suddenly noticing that my legs were feeling wobbly.

"Well, we have a hotel upstairs and a refugio downstairs."

"How much is the refugio?"

"You're five people? Ummm—30 euros."

"Each?"

"All. Dinner is separate. The buffet is next door. You can lock your bikes up in the sheds outside."

We floated out of the lobby. DAD and MOM futures closed sharply upward.

August 14. Puente La Reina to Los Arcos, 43.7 km

¿Qué pasa, bicigrino?

In the morning we had breakfast in the cafe upstairs—fresh orange juice, coffee, and the inevitable tortilla. The lodge did not look quite as grand as the night before, but still posh by our standards, and a pleasant contrast to the pilgrims' quarters in the basement, which had low ceilings, bare overhead pipes and felt a little like steerage class on a cruise ship. Not that we were complaining.

On our way out of town, we stopped at a church tucked away on a narrow street of yellow stone buildings but the door was locked. Further down the street, the door to a second church was also locked.

Charlotte didn't say, "Booyah!" but she and her sisters weren't too upset by this trend.

Then we were on our way, at least for the next hundred meters, where I took a wrong turn and got us lost. This was impressive in its way, given that Puente La Reina's population is only 2,500, many of those people live on the far side of the wide Rio Arga, and the ancient, six-arch pedestrian bridge we were looking for is such a landmark that the town is actually *named* after the bridge.[229]

In the old days—and probably even now, if we had been out the door earlier—we could have followed the crowd. As the Arthur Kinglake Porter noted in *Romanesque Sculpture of the Pilgrimage Roads*, Puente La Reina had once been a prime stop on the Camino:

> The pilgrimage road may be compared to a great river, emptying into the sea at Santiago, and formed by many tributaries which have their sources in the far regions of Europe. All these streams,

229 Queen Muniadona of Pamplona, the Puente's Reina, had it built for the pilgrims about a thousand years ago.

gathering force as they descend, flowed together at Puente La Reyna, whence the river runs in its full strength to Compostela.

The surface of the bridge was rough and sandy and the sides so low that we walked our bikes single file over the Arga to the tall townhouses on the opposite bank.

Puente was quiet this morning, but in the Middle Ages, it must have been quite a town. G.G. King describes it as having been full of "thieves, robbers, pickpockets; also the professional cheat, or confidence man; and the relic-monger ... fiddlers, story tellers and jongleurs, and many of the same occupation as S. Mary of Egypt."[230]

Puente la Reina

The towns like Puente La Reina that grew up along what the Spanish still call the Camino francés (the French Way) to cater to the European pilgrim trade tended to be quite cosmopolitan. They attracted settlers from all over Europe, including Gascons, Bretons, Germans, Englishmen, Burgundians, Normans, Tolosans, Provencals, Lombards, as well as Jews and Muslims from Muslim Spain, "and many other tradesmen of divers nations and foreign tongues," according to a medieval chronicle quoted by Castro. One 13th-century miniature that illustrates daily life on

---

230   That is, a prostitute.

the Camino shows two musicians, a Christian and a turbaned Muslim, playing their viols together, a jar of wine between them.

The Camino brought other things to Spain as well, beyond money and new faces.

For the Spanish Church, the Camino served as a kind of pipeline for orthodox Catholicism. After the Muslim invasion in the 8th century, the Spanish Church had fallen out of sync with Rome and the rest of the Church, but in the 11th and 12th centuries, French monks helped align the churches in the northern Spanish kingdoms back in line with the rest of Europe. The monks also played a role in changing Spanish handwriting writing: prior to French contact, the northern Spanish still used the alphabet they had inherited from the Visigoths, but as the pilgrimage grew in popularity, the French converted the Spanish to the script used by most of Europe.[231]

The Camino also introduced French and Italian sculpture and architecture. As Porter puts it, "The history of Spanish Romanesque sculpture might be graphically represented by taking a pen, full of ink, and tracing with it upon wet blotting paper, the road of St. James."

But it would be a mistake to see the pilgrimage as just a French and Italian cultural funnel; the influence went the other way as well. In 1906, French art historian Emile Bertaux went so far as to say that as far as Romanesque sculpture (the period of 1000–1200) was concerned, "the Pyrenees did not exist."[232]

As Porter says, "One style stretched from Santiago along the pilgrimage road to Toulouse and Moissac and Conques. This art is neither French nor Spanish. It is the art of the pilgrimage,"

231　The Visigothic alphabet has some appealing qualities—it would clearly be a better world if we all wrote our Os in the shape of a heart—but as Charlemagne had understood when he ordered the ancestor of our modern alphabet be used across his empire, standardization has some practical advantages.

232　This seems logical enough, but in the early 20th century, people found it hard to accept. In the nationalistic atmosphere of the 1910–20s, Bertaux's conclusions were often resisted. It took Porter and King, two Americans, to demonstrate that there was actually no difference between the ecclesiastical art and architecture on either side of the Pyrenees.

Porter wrote, noting that the same itinerant craftsmen and artists carved the sculptures in all the churches the whole length of the Camino. Nor was the visual exchange limited to Christian iconography: G.G. King found that every church along the Camino, the monastery at Cluny, and even Notre Dame in Paris contain Arabic motifs that architects had borrowed from the Grand Mosque of Cordoba.

As we zipped along on our bikes, we caught up with the early-risers we had missed earlier, and now started to pass whole battalions of pilgrims.

Although the sculptures might be the same on this side of the Pyrenees, the pilgrims were different. They were younger, and there were a lot more of them. There were also fewer of our fellow Quechuans here (although Decathlon may be an even bigger deal in Spain than France, and Spain a little less well off, I got the impression that Spanish perigrinos anyway don't like to stint on their outdoor gear). We also kept meeting Asians and Americans with shinier packs and spiffier outfits than we had seen in Le Puy. Many more had scallop shells tied to their backpacks too. A few of the French pilgrims on the way to Saint Jean-Pied-de-Port had had the shells dangling from their packs, but not nearly as many as here.

As with a lot of things on the Camino, that shell has a story behind it.

The ancient Greeks liked the scallop, maybe because they associated it with the vulva, and used the shell as a symbol of Aphrodite. The Romans liked the scallop too, and continued to associate it specifically with Venus—the Latin name for the scallop is *veneria* (in Spanish, scallops are still called Vieira). Medieval Spanish Christian architecture also incorporated a lot of scallop shell patterns.

Pilgrims have been wearing scallop shells as souvenirs of the Santiago pilgrimage since at least the 12th century. Picaud, the 12th century guidebook writer, noted that in Santiago de Compostela, you could buy shells next to the cathedral entrance, along with wine flasks and sandals. The shells made for a good souvenir: they had a lot of scallop shells in Galicia, and they were durable. You also couldn't find them on just any beach, so they would be exotic once you got home.

In statues and paintings, Saint James is usually pictured with a scallop shell pinned to his hat—which Charlotte pointed out is fairly bizarre iconography, as it suggests he's on a pilgrimage to visit himself. The shells became so closely associated with this particular pilgrimage, in fact, that in French, scallops are still called Coquilles Saint-Jacques, and in German, Jakobsmuscheln.

About half of the pilgrims' shells had another symbol stenciled on top of the shell: a blood-red cross, shaped like a sword blade.

Charlotte hated those stenciled shells right away, and I could understand that — visually, Santiago's bloody dagger-cross doesn't scream peace on earth, goodwill toward men. If you didn't know anything about it, you might think it was a hateful, fascist symbol—not quite a swastika, but close.

Unfortunately, you'd be right.

The red dagger-cross began its career as an emblem of the Order of Santiago, also known as the Order of St James of the Sword, an order of military monks founded in the 12th century to protect pilgrims to Santiago from the Infidel.

In more recent times, the dagger-cross has also been popular with Spanish fascists and lives on even today as an

Santiago's dagger cross

emblem of the good old days—Spanish neo-fascists sometimes trot out banners emblazoned with the Cross of Saint James at their rallies.[233]

But not every traditional souvenir has survived: archaeologists have also found, particularly in the Low Countries (but not the British Isles, for some reason) not just metal pins decorated with a shell, a cross, or Santiago, but joke pins so vulgar that social historians have wondered how or whether people actually wore them—vulvas in pilgrim hats with penis staffs, penis pilgrims carrying vulva pilgrims—the variations go on and on.[234] Surprisingly—or maybe not so surprisingly—hoards of these mass-produced joke brooches have been found all mixed up with the more serious variety, and Jos Koldeweij of Radboud University in Nijmegen, The Netherlands, suggests that people may have even worn both kinds at the same time.

The biking was easy at first that morning. It was a cool gray day, and the path was mostly flat, with a few gentle hills. The good thing about following an old path is that there is usually no nonsense about scenery. Unless you're following a Roman road, paths will usually follow the easiest route, like water finding a channel. Aside from the clusters of pilgrims we passed, it was a fairly easy ride.

So far, we were doing well. Masha was not nearly as anxious as we had worried she might be. Charlotte complained about her

233 Latter-day crusaders also like the dagger-cross. The late Chris Kyle, a US Navy SEAL sniper in Iraq, "tattooed one of his arms with a red crusader's cross, wanting 'everyone to know I was a Christian.'" But western civilization may have made some slight progress in 800 years. In his memoir, American Sniper, Kyle wrote, "'I don't shoot people with Korans. I'd like to, but I don't."

234 Scads of these things have survived. Scholars have noted at least 10 different varieties of vulva-pilgrim brooches. (See Jos Koldewej's article, "'Shameless and Naked Images': Obscene Badges as Parodies of Popular Devotion." Some of them really are quite funny—I would draw a picture but this is a family book.)

knees but kept pedaling. Her round white helmet gave her the look of a disgruntled junior colonel in a banana republic ready to listen to any credible coup proposal, but for now she soldiered on. Thea, meanwhile, rode as if she had been born in the saddle. She usually sat almost sidesaddle and made the pedaling look like light work even on the hills. Cybèle and I were working hard under the weight of the saddlebags, but they did give us some extra ballast when we got to more slippery sections. *"At the beginning we were fine until it turned into a dirt, gravel road—then it was Crap!"* Thea wrote.

I was doing all right, all in all, but I still missed the Don and Sancho. I also found I missed talking to the family and other pilgrims. Sometimes, pushing a bike up a hill, I would have a few minutes to chat with somebody, but then when we reached the crest, I would have to break off the conversation and return to my mobile solitary confinement. As for introspection, there was not a lot of opportunity. I had to pay so much more attention riding than walking, I couldn't even talk to myself. Either we were on the highway and I was gritting my teeth as the trucks roared past, or we were on a path, dodging sand or stones, tree roots or potholes. The worst part for me was when we passed a gaggle of pilgrims. We *bicigrinos* were a menace to the *peregrinos*, especially when the path narrowed. The hikers expected bikers to come in ones and twos, so when they heard our bells, they would step aside, see two of us go by, and then start to step back until they heard a third go by, at which point they would wait for the fourth, think that had to be the last, but then have to scamper out of the way once more for the fifth in the convoy. I felt like one of those jerks on a jet ski at the beach, sending his wake over all the swimmers.

Other moments were easier. We all liked the biking more when the path widened and you could see a long way ahead. At that point, it became almost enjoyable. After the slow progress of all that distance on foot, we loved eating up so many miles in a few minutes, and in that open country, being able to see for miles. Or imagining them, anyway, "seeing for miles" being a bit of poetic license in my case—I found biking sweaty enough work that

I often had to take my glasses off, which made the horizon more theoretical than real.

In retrospect, Cybèle had the worst of it. Usually, she brought up the rear so we wouldn't lose her if we had to stop. The only downside was that it wasn't good for her blood pressure: whenever one of us hit an unexpected stone or root, she saw us bounce, giving her a much clearer picture of all the dangers we were blithely pedaling through than the rest of us had.

Estella

Late that morning, just outside the town of Estella, I lost my enthusiasm for riding and the girls and Cybèle all passed me. Suddenly, the road turned to sand, and I slowed down even more. I tried to pedal faster to regain my momentum, but the sand just whirred out behind my rear wheel and I began to tip over slowly and gently, as if I had fallen asleep and decided to take a nap right there in the sand.

From the ground, I could hear two women I had just passed laughing. They were English.

"Are you okay?" one of the women asked.

"Fine, thanks ... That must have looked pretty funny," I said, as I pulled my left leg out from under my bike.

"Oh yes, hilahhhrious!" one of the women said, looking down at me. "Absolutely hilahhhrious!"

"Very, very funny," the other woman confirmed.[235]

We took our morning break in the central square. Cybèle sat looking at *Kapitán Pedales* but couldn't make sense of it, so she turned to the next table to confer with an American father and son who were also biking the Camino and also taking their morning break—the son in his 20s, the father in his late 50s.

I was initially well disposed toward the father, who reminded me of a law professor I call for a quote every few months, another big, blue-eyed man. They say coal miners can't get the coal out of their skin and I feel that's the case with professionals some-times—as if they can no longer shed the gray flannel. Even in his biking spandex, he retained a certain gravitas.

Cybèle asked if they knew the way out of town and if so, whether we could follow them when they were ready to leave, as our map didn't mark the way very clearly.

The pair couldn't think of any reason to turn down this pro bono assignment, but didn't seem happy to take it on either, and when we were on the road again, took just 10 minutes to lose us. When we reached the edge of town, they shot on ahead

---

235   It turns out that I was in good company—Estella has toppled a lot of people over the years. The town was the capital of the Carlist faction, a conservative group that fomented three civil wars in the 19th century, beginning in 1833, and did their part for tyranny in the 20th century too. The first time around, the Carlists wanted to replace the more liberal King Ferdinand with the conservative Don Carlos, who belonged to a different branch of the Bourbon family, and ever after, they kept trying to promote another scion of Carlos' line, hoping an old-style absolute monarchy would turn back the clock to the days before Napoleon's invasion. In the 20th century, Carlists were an important force in bringing Franco to power, but their allure has faded in the past few decades. In the last 40 years. Carlists have only managed to elect one supporter to the Senate, in 1977. The other time they made the news as in 2012, when a senator in the Basque regional parliament with Carlist sympathies, Inaki Anasagasti, proposed creating a Catalan-Basque-Navarese monarchy with Archduke Dominic of Austria, a claimant from the Hapsburg-Bourbon line, as its king.

down a steep gravel path and disappeared. "The path was literally straight down," Thea remembered. "We didn't even think of trying to ride down after them, and instead walked our bikes to the bottom and after that, decided to take the road for a bit."

The highway was smooth and more pleasant to ride on than the path, except when a truck roared by us every once in a while.

As we started up the next long hill, two young Italian guys all decked out in their Tour de France Lycra ciao'd us and zipped past, then geared down and started their long climb. They looked quite serious and strong but Thea, our skinny little girl, kept pedaling, and in the next few minutes, as the two huffed and puffed with Lance Armstrong-ish intensity, she casually passed them both.

It was one of my favorite moments of the whole trip, if not her whole childhood.

But it wasn't enough to convince the girls that we were having a good time. Later that day, Thea and Masha began to complain to Cybèle about the bikes. From what Cybèle told me, the conversation went like this:

"We hate this," Thea said, as they pushed their bikes up a hill.

"I know," Cybèle said.

"We really hate this," Thea said again.

"Why can't we quit?" Masha asked.

"Well, we've come all this way, and we just got the bikes yesterday—"

"So?" Masha asked. "We could return them—we just bought them yesterday."

"It would be a shame to give up now. We only have another 10 days, and Dad really wants to do the whole thing. And you would regret it if we stopped now."

"No, we wouldn't," Thea said.

"It will get easier," Cybèle said.

"You're not listening to us," Masha said.

"I am listening to you, I'm just not giving you the answer you want to hear."

"You're not listening to us," Masha said again.

"I am listening to you," Cybèle repeated, as she got back on her bike and pedaled off.

The next town, Viana, is famous for two things. First, Cesare Borgia, one of the infamous Italian Borgias, is buried here. Supposedly, his short buccaneering life inspired Niccolo Machiavelli to write *The Prince*. The illegitimate son of Pope Alexander VI, Borgia was only 31 when he was killed in an ambush here, while fighting Castile on behalf of the king of Navarre. Borgia's body was left naked in the street, except for a red tile that covered his genitals, but he was eventually buried in the local cathedral. His epitaph starts out

> Here lies in a little earth
> he who everyone feared,
> he who peace and war
> held in his hand.

More happily, Viana is also home of the massive Monasterio de Irache, which is famous among pilgrims for having not only a water tap, but next to it, a wine tap, sponsored by an adjacent vineyard. Cybèle wasn't interested but I welcomed the innovation. I think they should have these fountains every 10 kilometers or so.

At 2:30, we reached our destination, Los Arcos, an old town that used to mark the border between Castile and Navarre and changed hands between the two kingdoms a few times before

landing definitively in Castile. Just inside the city limits, people began calling out to us as we passed, as if we were old friends.

We noticed now that almost everyone in town—young, old, and in between—was dressed in white with a red scarf around their neck and often another red scarf as a belt, and they were all outside eating and drinking and dancing.

And definitely not telecommuting. While the rest of the family sat down to order a snack at the end of a long bench outside an incredibly crowded cafe, I went inside to see if I could get their Wi-Fi code, because I had an interview in 10 minutes. It was very busy inside too, and I felt ridiculous, as if I had wandered on stage during the first act of *Carmen* in bicycle pants, carrying a laptop. After a few minutes, I managed to flag down a waiter who gave me the Wi-Fi code, and then I went back outside and sat down at a lone empty table and tried to log on. No luck.

After trying various other tactics by phone but still not getting through, I eventually gave up, put the laptop back in its sleeve, slid the sleeve back to its usual place inside my backpack and the phone in the outside pocket, then went over to the long tables where the family was having a snack alongside 30 other Arcoans and ordered a melancholy beer. One missed call in 800 kilometers was not too bad a track record—I made mistakes like that at home at roughly the same frequency—but still, this felt pretty unprofessional. I felt crushed, guilty, and ridiculous. I couldn't even send a message to apologize. What was I doing here, anyway? What had I been thinking? *You're only doing this because you are crazy.*

Just then, the Arcosans broke in on my self-loathing fiesta. They were locking arms and leaning in unison backward and forward on the two long benches like rowers on an oddly shaped boat, and they wanted us to join in.

What that leaning backward and forward was about, I don't know, but it was fun. I have since learned that the Arcoans were celebrating a joint fiesta for St. Rocco (our old friend with the dog) and Mary—the Festival of Saint Rocco and the Assumption, the holy day that marks the ascension of Mary to Heaven. Every year, to celebrate the life of the ascetic animal lover and the expiration of the Virgin Mother of God, Arcoans spend a week or so eating, drinking, dancing, and going to bullfights.

The Assumption is an unusual holy day because it commemorates an event that isn't in the Bible or mentioned by any reputable source. In the 300s, the Church fathers had noted a plot hole in the Gospels—nobody mentions Mary's death— and this worried them. Did Mary die, like an ordinary woman? Or did they fail to mention it because she made her exit a different way? Around that time, a tradition of Mary's bodily assumption also started in the eastern part of the Roman Church, an event they called the Falling Asleep of the Blessed Virgin Mary. *The Book of Thomas*, a gospel that did not make the final cut of the New Testament, also mentions that Mary was taken bodily to heaven instead of being buried.[236] Another writer, Epiphanius, found an oblique reference in Revelation to a woman with a crown of 12 stars on her head, a red dragon, and a baby, but he doesn't sound entirely convinced:

> Perhaps this can be applied for her; I cannot decide for certain, and I am not saying that she remained immortal. But neither am I saying that she died.

None of this stopped the Church from celebrating the feast day, but it's theological tangles were problematic enough that the Vatican didn't get around to ratifying it as dogma until 1950, when Pius XII decreed that Mary had been assumed "body and soul" into heaven. However, he too stayed noncommittal on the question of whether she died first and then was taken, or was just taken.[237]

Snack scarfed, we checked into our hotel. The place had a late

---

236 In Thomas's version, she confirms her arrival in heaven by throwing her girdle down to the Apostles.

237 Nineteen-fifty seems to have been a good year for straddling questions. That year, Pius also published an encyclical that concluded that the theory of evolution does not contradict church teaching about the Creation, but didn't explain how they fit together.

1940s feel to it, though it was probably not that old—stylistically, the 40s lasted about 40 years in Spain—and this one came complete with a tough Bette Davis-ish peroxide blonde at the reception desk. No, she didn't have our reservation and no, they didn't have Wi-Fi, but yes, she did have room for us. We were lucky, given that it was the fiesta.

"Our room was huge but HIDEOUS," wrote Thea—a suite with Venetian blinds closed to keep out the bright white sun and walls painted a nauseous olive green I associate with Raymond Chandler and the Andrews Sisters. I loved it immediately.

After we cleaned ourselves up—which took awhile; being a bicigrino is a dirty business[238] —we went back out and found our way to the main square in the heart of town. Mass had just started in the cathedral, so we took advantage of the open door and peeped inside. The pews were mostly filled, and three-quarters of the congregation were dressed in white with red scarves. It was a very dramatic baroque church, with an interior that looked like a giant gold, silver, and baby blue Fabergé egg.[239]

Then we made our way out of the crowded church and out to the plaza, where we found a table and sat down for dinner. It was a beautiful early evening. As we sat watching the people saunter by, my phone rang: Hannah, Masha's best friend in Paris, wanted to see how she was doing. She was in the States this summer, visiting her grandmother in Baltimore. After a few minutes, Masha passed the phone to Thea, and Hannah passed the phone to her little sister Miley, who happened to be Thea's best friend.

Later, as we were ending our dinner, a procession began, led by three *papier-mâché* figures about nine feet high. One of the fig-

---

238 As Cybèle wrote, "We usually ended up covered with dust and grime and black oil stains on our legs and hands that we had to scrub off ... Showering took on more urgency and we usually showered right after we checked in." Having our own bathroom made the job easier at Los Arcos; showers in the hostels were more troublesome, particularly for the long-haired members of the team, "because the showers often were those button things that you had to push and it would slowly go back up—we had to push down at least five–six times."

239 They also have a Black Virgin, like the cathedral at Le Puy–en-Velay—or did, until she was "restored" to white in 1947.

ures was supposed to be Mary, judging by the crown and blue robe. Cybèle started taking pictures. As the procession passed us, she stood up suddenly and began following them down the street, camera in hand.

Mary and the Arcosans

After their mother ran off with the circus, Masha and Thea sat even glummer than before, now that they had heard all about their friends' glorious, lazy summer in Baltimore. *"Her life sounds so much better than mine,"* Thea wrote.

On our way back to the hotel, we picked up some churros for dessert from a snack wagon with a long zinc bar,[240] then stopped by an outdoor stage and watched some little kids do a dance routine in their party dresses. I was impressed by how happy and lively everybody seemed. With unemployment at a level where most countries would be on the verge of revolution, all 4,500 Arcoans seemed to be out having a good time. That takes character.

---

240   A fried-dough strip pastry the Spanish picked up from the Portuguese, who in turn may have copied the recipe from similar breakfast fritters they saw in China.

But my opinion of the town went downhill from there. When the first groups of singing Arcoans sauntered by under our window around midnight, I thought, how charming. But as the night wore on and I kept waking up every few minutes to energetic four-year-olds running races in the room above us and other groups of serenading Arcoans lingering on the corner, I began to turn into a very grumpy American. By two a.m., I was cursing the Spanish. By three, I wanted to go upstairs and chloroform the kids, and by four, when the last of the singers finally stopped, I was a good argument in favor of Europe's strict gun laws.

Cybèle, of course, slept through it. I envied her for that. Deafness is a nuisance generally, but to the hearing traveler, it can sometimes seem like a magic power.

August 15. Los Arcos to Najera, 58 km
In which Cybèle hurts an eye and the girls cheer up.

The next day was gray and cool. Exhausted from our long night, the girls and I were all in foul moods and stopped to argue every half hour or so, usually about whether we should take the path or the road that often ran parallel to it. Cybèle favored the path for purist reasons and because she had the crazy idea that not riding bicycles on the same road as eighteen-wheelers was somehow safer. Charlotte and I generally wanted to take the road, because the path was often bumpy and gravelly. We argued that all those bumps made the path the more dangerous option. Thea and Masha just hated us all.

Around noon, the mood lightened a bit. The path was nicely paved here, and we were riding alongside a stream, which added scenery and kept hills to a minimum. Nobody had anything to complain about. Best of all, we were a half hour from lunch, which would be in the next town, a biggish place called Logroño.

But just then a tiny piece of grit flew up into Cybèle's eye. She tried to ride with it but stopped after a few minutes, anxious in a way that she doesn't usually get.

First, she tilted her head up and asked me to take a look. I couldn't see anything. Then she lay down on the pavement and asked Charlotte to see if she could find something, but she couldn't see anything either (in addition to her role as family technologist, Charlotte was our designated emergency medical technician). Cybèle was so anxious though, there was no question of ignoring it—we would have to go to the emergency room.

This was unsettling for all of us, who thought of Cybèle as more or less indestructible. In preschool, the girls would all come home with crayon drawings of the family in which their mother was a tree and the rest of us little birds in her branches, and their attitudes had not changed much since.[241]

We crossed a long low bridge over the Ebro into Logroño and followed the signs to the hospital, which was just a block away on the main street. Unfortunately, the hospital was largely closed for the Assumption, and the one doctor we encountered, a cardiologist, recommended a clinic on the other side of town.

The doctor ordered a taxi. When the car arrived, we decided to split up – Cybèle and Masha would go to the clinic (because Masha had taken a little Spanish at school), while I stayed at the hospital with Charlotte, Thea, and the bikes.

It was cold and raining now. I sent Charlotte and Thea across the street to a hotel bar to have a hot chocolate and read their Kindles, while I manned a post in the hospital lobby. One of the disadvantages of biking was that we couldn't lock up the saddlebags, so I stood in the cold glass vestibule and watched the bikes and the rain, and worried about Cybèle's eye. No one likes eye trouble but for Cybèle the thought of losing her vision is terrifying. She has even asked me to kill her if she were ever to go blind.

A long hour later, Cybèle and Masha came back smiling. The doctor at the clinic hadn't found anything in her eye at first, but Cybèle insisted she could feel something. Masha, borrowing his special flashlight, saw a speck, and the doctor tweezed out a tiny metal shard on the underside of Cybèle's eyelid. He gave her some antibiotic drops, strict instructions not to drive or bike for the next couple hours, and sent the two on their way.

The rain had lifted now, and as we walked our bikes into the pedestrian street to look for lunch, the steady drizzle of grumpiness and contempt the girls had maintained the last two days let up too. Cybèle and I never figured out why; her theory was that they found it somehow comforting to see her vulnerable—not Simon Legree on a bicycle but just another person, maybe even

---

241 I remember having a number of arguments with the girls in which they insisted their mother was taller, though in fact I have about an inch on her technically if not morally. Even today, they —and some days we—still don't entirely believe me.

mortal. It felt like one of those optical illusions where you see a goblet or a girl but can't see both at once.

I think similar shifts can happen on a much larger scale occasionally, under the right circumstances. The Logroño witch trials, the biggest witch trials in history—are a case in point.

In 1609, reports started reaching the Inquisition in Madrid of a mass outbreak of witchcraft in Navarre and all over the Basque country. Near the coast, in villages where the men were often away at sea on fishing or whaling expeditions for months, the Devil seemed to have taken advantage of the man-less country to recruit new worshippers.

The Supremo, the Scotland Yard of the Inquisition, sent a team of inquisitors to investigate.

The inquisitors found evidence of witchcraft and brought several dozen people to trial in Logroño, the nearest big town. At the first trial, in 1610, they prosecuted several dozen women, children, and a few men, including priests accused of healing people through witchcraft. That trial ended with an *auto da fe*, the public penance of accused heretics and apostates, against 31 of the accused. A total of 11 or 12 were burned to death, and 5 more in abstentia, as they had died before the event and cheated the roaster.[242]

Not long after, rumors reached Madrid that the inquisitors had missed a spot, and the Supremo sent more inquisitors out to Zugarramurdi, the Salem of Basque witchcraft, to get to the bottom of it.

The leader of the mission, Alonso de Salazar Frías, a bright, hardworking, 46-year-old priest, and his assistants, persuaded nearly 2,000 people, including 1,384 children, to confess to having attended a witches' Sabbath, one of the night orgies where

---

242   It's worth noting that by European standards of the time, the Spanish Inquisition was usually not as bad as popularly supposed. For the most part, the Spanish favored one torture involving rope and another that's supposedly a lot like waterboarding. Stake for stake, according to Danish scholar Gustav Henningsen, an authority on the Logroño witchcraft trials, northern Europeans burned many more people.

witches supposedly worshipped the devil. After that, these 2,000 denounced 5,000 more. All in all, it was going splendidly.

Then one day, in the course of the inquisitors' confession-collection, an accused man started shouting. He was angry—his father had told him to confess although he had done nothing wrong. Salazar Frias didn't say anything and kept on collecting more confessions but wrote later that this outburst gave him some pause.

He kept his doubts to himself at first, as his fellow inquisitors were thoroughly convinced of the guilt of the accused. But when the trial began a year later, he spoke up:

> The real question is: are we to believe that witchcraft occurred in a given situation simply because of what the witches claim? No: it is clear that the witches are not to be believed, and the judges should not pass sentence on anyone unless the case can be proven with external and objective evidence sufficient to convince everyone who hears it. And who can accept the following: that a person can frequently fly through the air and travel a hundred leagues in an hour; that a woman can get through a space not big enough for a fly; that a person can make himself invisible that he can be in a river or the open sea and not get wet; or that he can be in bed at the sabbath at the same time... and that a witch can turn herself into any shape she fancies, be it housefly or raven? Indeed, these claims go beyond all human reason and may even pass the limits permitted by the Devil.

An account of his speech made it back to Madrid, and the Supremo—which had long had reservations about witch prosecutions—sided with him. In August 1614, the Inquisitor-General demanded that all the trials pending at Logroño be dismissed, and issued a new set of rules that made it tougher to convict someone of witchcraft. Since then, Spanish authorities have persecuted plenty of people (another motive for the dismissal, in fact, may be that the Inquisitors already had their hands full, rooting out Muslims and Jews) but never anyone else for witchcraft.[243]

The rest of the ride that day was uneventful. We skirted small lakes, vineyards, and a few suburbs, and then advanced through flat featureless kilometers that fortunately weren't hard for Cybèle to manage with her foggy eye.

Late in the afternoon, we reached Najera. The outskirts were dusty and uninteresting, like any other modern Spanish town, but nearer the older center, the buildings had more character, and the town started to look more promising.

We found our landlady in a seafood restaurant she ran with her family, and she led us across the street to their apartment building. The interior had white walls with white marble floors and a five-story atrium, all entirely new and apparently vacant, probably built during the boom years before the 2008–9 financial crisis. All that empty space made me think of the imaginary piazzas of De Chirico, the Italian painter, and feel as if we were walking through someone's dream (which in a way, we were—a real estate bust, unlike a crashed stock market, leaves a visible trace).

---

243   Unfortunately, Salazar Frías' logic didn't make it north of the Pyrenees. A number of northern European writers, including leading lawyers, argued that witchcraft was so dangerous that witch trials needed special exemptions from ordinary legal rules. "[T]hose who stuck to normal procedure or permitted themselves to doubt the reality of witchcraft were stigmatized as old-fashioned or even accused of sympathizing with the witches," Henningsen, the witchcraft scholar, has noted. Nor did the northern Europeans learn their lesson: the Salem, Massachusetts, witch trials took place three generations later, in the 1680s, about 500 years after John XXII had first classified witchcraft as a heresy.

But we modern people should not feel superior about this. Even today, people are still killed for practicing witchcraft in India, Saudi Arabia, and various parts of Africa. In Tanzania, about 500 older women are murdered each year after being accused of witchcraft —a sizable number given that car accidents kill about 700 Tanzanian women annually. Most of the world's witch persecution these days is Tanzanian-style freelance mayhem, but there are exceptions: don't pack your pointy black hat next time you visit Saudi Arabia, where the government still executes people occasionally for practicing witchcraft and sorcery. In 2011, a woman named Amina bint Abdel Halim Nassar was beheaded for possession of a number of books on sorcery, talismans, and bottles filled with mysterious potions.

And that's just witches proper. Add metaphorical witchhunts to the tally, and it's clear that we haven't made much progress at all. The moral, as Henningsen wrote in his introduction to a book on Salazar Frías and the Logroño trials, is that the impulse to root out witches never really goes away. "The European witch craze is now history, but it continually returns in a new and plausible disguise," wrote Henningsen. "We shall always need men with courage enough to tear away the mask."

In the evening, after we had cleaned up, we put on our flip-flops and went out to find dinner. We looked at the menu of the land-lady's seafood restaurant, then thought better of it once we saw the prices, and headed down toward the river.

The Ebro here was shallow, fast-moving, and white-capped, and looked more like a wide creek than a river. Across the bridge, we could see the old town, and not too far behind its red roofs a long wall of red cliffs.

Like Logroño, Nájera was place where rationality broke out un-expectedly. In the 1140s, although the Crusaders had already stomped all over the Near East and even taken Jerusalem, they had never learned anything about the people they were conquer-ing. As Dorothée Metlitzki writes in *The Matter of Araby in Medi-eval England*:

> The Crusaders were military men of action. If they were interest-ed in anything of the superior civilization of the Saracens, which it was their aim to destroy, it was in new techniques of siege and fortification, in military instruments, in trade, transportation, and the use of money ... whatever they learned from the Saracens was in spite of themselves.

Europe's depth of ignorance about the Arab world was stupen-dous, especially when it came to religion. "What scraps of in-formation about Islam Europeans possessed, usually centered about the figure of Mohammed, were utterly or in large part false," according to historian James Aloysius Kritzeck. Early in the Middle Ages, Europeans had thought that Mohammed was the god of the Muslims, but later, in the 12th century, the more prevalent view was that he was part of a pantheon. The *Song of Roland*, for instance, talks about Mohammed and the Qu'ran as two different gods. Other authorities held that Mohammed had been a heretical monk. Still others theorized that the Prophet had been an ambitious cardinal who, after his failure to be elect-ed pope, ran off to Arabia to start his own religion.

luny's abbot, Peter the Venerable, realized that Europeans were ignorant about the religion, and in 1142, decided to do something about it. Once the clergy understood Islam, he reasoned, they might have better luck converting people to Christianity, not "as our people often do, by arms, but by words; not by force, but by reason; not in hatred, but in love."[244]

As a first step, Peter commissioned translations of the Qu'ran and other important Muslim texts from Arabic to Latin. While on a pilgrimage to Santiago, he stopped at the monastery at Najera, where he met at least one of the two translators he wanted to hire for the job—two priests living in Pamplona, an Englishman named Robert of Ketton and a Slav, Herman the Dolomite.[245]

The two weren't interested in his project at first—their passion was translating Greek and Arab science from Arabic into Latin. Like the other leading Arabists of the day, Robert was, in Professor Metlitzki's words, "above all, a man of reason, fanatical only on request." But Peter was a persuasive fellow. As he wrote a colleague in France, he won the pair over in the end with a method that I happen to know still works with freelancers today—"entreaty and a high fee."

Robert and Herman had collaborated for some time. They had probably met in Toledo, or were introduced by people who had

---

244 This might sound self-evident but it wasn't at the time. Although people respected Peter personally—they started calling him the Venerable while he was still alive—less intellectual orders such as the Cistercians were growing more and more popular. The Cistercians were a kind of born-again group who considered the Cluniacs' interest in art and intellectual activity to be irrelevant. The Cistercians' abbot, Bernard of Clairvaux, told Peter, "You will find something far greater in the woods than in books. Stones and trees will teach you things which you cannot learn from the masters."

245 Or it may have been a debt-collection trip. Some scholars believe Peter's pilgrimage was a pretext to visit León and collect some money that the current king's grandfather, Alfonso VII, the king of Galicia, León, and Castile, had pledged to Cluny more than 40 years before—and which Peter really needed now, not only to complete their new grand church, but to recover from a failed hostile takeover by the prior, deposed abbot, who had sacked the abbey with an armed gang of men and women, then melted down the church's valuables to fund his ragtag band.

studied there, and were colleagues and good friends.[246]

The two had probably gone to Toledo because that's where the books were. How many volumes is not known, but given that the group of scholars known as the School of Toledo ultimately translated 1,500 manuscripts from Arabic and Hebrew at a time when Cluny's 1,800-volume library was the largest in France, the Toledo library must have been enormous. More importantly, it was an extraordinary collection that included modern Arab math and science, as well as Aristotle and other Greek classics that had been lost to the West for a millennium or more, and survived now only in Arabic.

The fact that the two men were from different countries, and neither of them Castilian, wasn't unusual. Translators in Toledo came from all over: Hugh of Santalla, Plato of Tivoli, Abraham bar-Hiyya of Barcelona, and Gerard of Cremona (and much later, Ibn Daud, Herman the German, Michael the Scot, and Rabbi Isaac ben Sad) all worked in Toledo.

Robert and Herman set to work, assisted by a Christian Arab named Muhammad and an unnamed Muslim. They worked on the Qu'ran for about a year, mostly in Pamplona. Where they got the Qu'ran is uncertain— Muslim religious law forbade its being touched by nonbelievers.[247]

It is fairly clear from Robert's letters to Peter that he did not have any sympathy for Islam, which he called the stagnant swamp of the Saracen sect, but Metlitzki attributes part of his attitude to "suppressed anger at having to spend his time on religious doctrine and theology instead of on what really concerned him—as-

---

246 We know this from Herman's dedication to Robert in his translation of Ptolemy's Planisphere in which he calls him "my sole, special, inseparable comrade in studies."

247 The work is considered so beautiful— the word of God dictated directly to Mohammad—that believers say it can't be translated. Even now, a Qu'ran in another language than Arabic is not considered a real Qu'ran, and title pages of translations are careful to describe it as an interpretation.

tronomical and mathematical science."[248]

The Toledo Collection, as Robert and Herman's translations for Peter became known, constituted the West's main window on Islam for the next 400 years; Martin Luther even published an edition in 1543. Modern scholars today say that the style isn't elegant, but it is accurate—as you might expect from translators of science.

Unfortunately, their work had roughly the same impact on Crusader Europe as intelligence about the enemy usually does when pitted against the stubbornly ignorant. Two years later, in 1146, Bernard, the leader of the anti-intellectual Cistercians, roused a huge crowd, whipping up what historian Christopher Brooke called "apocalyptic hopes and sadistic dreams" to launch the Second Crusade, which inspired attacks on Jews in southern Germany, pagan Slavs in eastern Germany, and eventually, a disastrous invasion of the Near East.[249]

We wandered the narrow streets of the old town looking for a place to eat and finally on a tiny street about three feet wide, found a tiny restaurant. Everything about the place was small: tiny tables, tiny plates, tiny glasses, and tiny prices (a seven-euro pilgrim special for four courses with wine). Even the owners were on the small side. As we ate, we talked to a couple

---

248   Once the pair finished the Islamic books, they went straight back to their secular projects. Among other things, Robert translated a mathematical work, Al-kitāb al-mukhtaṣar fī ḥisāb al-ğabr wa'l-muqābala (Compendious Book of Making Whole and Balancing), the book that introduced algebra to Europe, which as the ninth-century author Muḥammad ibn Mūsā al-Khwārizmī (whose name was latinized as Algoritmi) notes in his introduction, is pretty useful stuff

"in cases of inheritance, legacies, partition, law-suits, and trade, and in … .the measuring of lands, the digging of canals, geometrical computation, and other objects of various sorts and kinds …"

It starts out pretty well, as far as algebra textbooks go:

"When I considered what people generally want in calculating, I found that it always is a number."

249   The Second Crusade was a disaster. The Crusaders lost a number of battles and eventually, Jerusalem. Afterward, Louis VII's queen, Eleanor of Aquitaine, was so angry with her husband that they had to take separate boats back to France. Bernard apologized to the Pope for the debacle, but even this disaster didn't teach Christian Europeans their lesson. It took 150 more years before European knights gave up crusading in the Holy Land and focused their antisocial energies back on Europe.

at the next table—an old Spaniard with enviable posture and his younger wife. They were from Valencia, also bicigrinos, and spoke some English. When I met him again a day or two later as we pushed our bikes up a long hill, he told me he was 78.

After dinner we walked around the old town a little more and found a tortilla for Thea (our restaurant had had no vegetarian options) and then headed back across the river. On our way to our rooms, we passed by our landlady's seafood restaurant, where dinner was now in full swing. The windows were all steamed over but through the steam we could see various sea creatures waving a claw or a tentacle from their tanks as we passed.

August 16. Najera to Belorado, 43.6 km

In which we meet a chicken in a church.

*The chicken of
Santo Domingo de la Calzada*

Around noon the next day, we rolled into an old stone town, Santo Domingo de la Calzada, and stopped to visit its enormous gothic cathedral. It had the usual arches, the usual stations of the cross, the usual chapel paintings, the usual tomb for the local saint[250], but in one nave, in an elaborate baroque case, behind glass and bars, under a very bright light, a chicken.

An actual, *live* chicken.

For a few minutes, I stood dumbstruck, delighted with our random universe.

The chicken of Santo Domingo de la Calzada and his fancy coop commemorate the 14th century legend of the Hanged Innocent. Once upon a time, a family of German (or sometimes French, depending on the account you read) pilgrims stopped for the night in the town on their way to Santiago. The son of the couple caught the eye of the innkeeper's daughter, and she propositioned him. Unfortunately, the God-fearing youth resisted her advances, and in the morning, in revenge, she hid a silver cup in his pack and then accused him of theft. When the authorities searched his pack and found the cup, they had no choice but to hang the boy. The parents were sad, but as they had gone this far, they left him to face his doom, and continued on their pilgrimage.

A few weeks later, on their way back from Santiago, they passed

---

250 Santo Domingo de la Calzada (Saint Dominic of the Paved Road), the patron saint of Spanish civil engineers, an 11th-century monk who built a hospital, a bridge, and a new road for the pilgrims to Santiago.

through Santo Domingo de la Calzada again, and heard someone call from a tree. As Robert Southey (1774-1843), put it in his poem, "A Pilgrim to Compostella"[251]:

> Oh tale most marvellous to hear,
> Most marvellous to tell!
> Eight weeks had he been hanging there
> And yet was alive and well!

Their boy asked them to go into the town and get the mayor to cut him down. When the boy's parents came rushing into the mayor's house, Hizzonor was just sitting down to a nice chicken dinner. I'm sorry, the mayor said, but you're mistaken. Your boy's been hanged and there's no undoing it now. Why, he's about as alive as the chickens on this table. And at that moment, so the story goes, the roast chickens stood up, regrew their feathers, and

> Their heads saw their way to their bodies,
> In they came from the yard without check
> And each took its own proper station
> To the very great joy of the neck.

Of course, the mayor hurried out, cut down the boy, and the boy went home with his family. In commemoration of the miracle, the Calzadans have kept live chickens in their church for the last 500 years or so. Some authorities say these chickens are the descendants of the same chickens that reanimated on the mayor's table, but given the church used to do a good business in selling holy chicken feathers, I have my doubts.

After Calzada, we rode on through fields and rolling hills. It was getting hotter now, but not unpleasant. We were peddling hard enough though, that after awhile, my attention began to wander and suddenly, while riding along a flat narrow stretch with a cornfield on my left, I saw an old guy bicycling toward me.

---

251 Southey, once poet laureate of England, is now one of the lesser-known Romantic poets, remembered mostly for writing the original "Goldilocks and the Three Bears," introducing the words "autobiography" and "zombie" into English, and advising Charlotte Bronte against pursuing a career as a writer, which he said was no life for a woman.

Abuelo Har

He had blue eyes and a deeply tanned face and I only saw him for a second but could have sworn, after he passed, that I'd seen my grandfather, now long gone.

Harlan J. Walsh of 4916 NE Simpson St., Portland, Oregon, had turned up in my dreams a few times, but not like this. This was so unexpected and felt so real that it disturbed me afterwards, although at the time I tried to think of it as a cosmic thumbs-up.

The experience reminded me of the hallucinations soldiers sometimes report—I suppose fear, exhaustion, and disorientation must make it easy to think you see all kinds of things. The Greeks reported seeing gods all the time in battle, as did the Romans. In every era, soldiers under stress have seen strange things—and sometimes even the same things at the same time. In World War II, for instance, a group of 11 shipwrecked British sailors bobbing in the ocean for 65 hours swore they saw, individually and collectively, "an interesting range of sights, including ships, orange trees, dockyards, aircraft and a bar."

This is not just a military phenomenon: people often have memories of things that never happened to them. During the First World War, many British people believed an angel had appeared above a Belgian battlefield, a story later traced to a sermon by a minister who had misread a short story in the *London Evening News* as fact.[252]

Occasionally, too, I would add a third category of hallucination: fictitious non-events, like the Angel of Mons, that spark a series of actual hallucinations later.

---

252   Unfortunately for humanity, whether it's an angel over a battlefield or a self-rejuvenating chicken, the weird particular tends to stick. As Gabriel Garcia Marquez puts it, "If you say that there are elephants flying in the sky, people are not going to believe you. But if you say that there are four hundred and twenty-five elephants in the sky, people will probably believe you."

Something like that began—ostensibly— not very far from the cornfield where I saw Grandpa Har, in the village of Clavijo.

In 842, Alfonso II, the Christian king of Asturias, died. His nephew Ramiro I took over. Hoping to catch the inexperienced young king off guard, the Emir of Cordoba demanded the reinstatement of a traditional tribute of 100 virgins (50 nobles and 50 commoners), which Alfonso had refused to deliver during his reign. The young king likewise denied the emir his tribute and ordered his troops to prepare for battle. One medieval history recounted what happened next:

> Then the Saracens advanced in an exceeding great multitude: seeing that multitude, the army of King Ramiro betook itself to the place which is called Clavijo. And that same night the king (Ramiro) being doubtful whether he should fight, the blessed Santiago appeared to him, and comforted him, by assuring him of a certain victory over the Arabs the following day. And he arose with the break of day, and revealed what he had seen to his bishops and nobles, all of whom, thanking God for the vision, and being fortified by the apostle's promise, prepared for the combat.

As the battle began, soldiers saw Saint James on a white horse, slaying Moors right and left. Inspired by his sudden appearance, they shouted, "For God and Saint James! "and promptly slew 5,000 Moors. The battle was won and the legend of Saint James the Moor Slayer was born.

Throughout most of what was later remembered as the Reconquest, Santiago continued to do his part for Catholic Spain. By the 17th century, the Baroque poet Quevedo estimated—seriously, as near as I can tell—that Santiago had personally appeared in 4,700 decisive battles and killed "11,015,000 and some odd Moors."[253]

---

253 This sounds rather satirical to me, but Amerigo Castro, the Spanish historian and cultural critic, doesn't think so. He argues that Quevedo's decision to make a numerical defense shows that people at this time were midway between older magical thinking, in which the world was a mysterious place full of miracles, and modern Enlightenment thinking, which held that most things could either be proved or disproved. With respect to science, this middle path isn't very good. However, as far as literature goes, Castro argues, being able to believe and not believe at the same time is more or less perfect.

In the Americas too, Santiago kept galloping alongside the conquistadors: a number of cities in Mexico are called Matamoros (moor-slayer), and Matamoros remains a common surname throughout the Hispanic world. Nor has Santiago abandoned the Spanish in the 20th century: Franco often claimed that Santiago Matamoros had appeared to him the night before the Battle of Brunete, in 1937, a turning point in the civil war. Franco repaid the favor, by reinstating him as patron saint of Spain, sponsoring multiple archaeological searches for his bones in the church at Santiago de Compostela, and underwriting a contest for a book about the architectural heritage of the Camino de Santiago.[254]

Whether or not soldiers saw actually him later, there is an inconvenient fact about the Moor Slayer's debut: like the battle with the angel over Mons, the Battle of Clavijo never happened. Instead, around 1150, an imaginative canon at Compostela named Pedro Marcio concocted the Diploma of Ramiro I, a last will and testament for the ninth-century king that also introduced the story of the Battle of Clavijo.

The fact that a monk might make something like this up is not too surprising. One archival survey of 70 acts of the Asturian kings dated 718–910 classified 28 as definitely fake and 21 as possibly fake. Another survey of the cathedral at Santiago's archives found that out of 16 royal acts regarding the cathedral, 9 were either possibly or undoubtedly phony.

More remarkable, however, than the degree to which people believed in the battle is the fact that they believed what supposedly happened next: After the victory, Marcio wrote, King Ramiro was so grateful that he promised to give the cathedral at Santiago de Compostela a big annual donation of grain, wine, and a

---

254 The Left also tried to recruit Santiago, arguably with less success. During the Spanish Civil War, American prisoners held in San Pedro, the monastery outside Burgos where El Cid was once buried, liked to tease the guards that a Santiago Matamoros statue over the main gate whose sword hand had been cut off during an earlier rebellion in the 1830s was actually making a clenched-fist communist salute. Comrade Hemingway also tried to draft Matamoros for the Republican side, in heavily symbolic, deeply ironic guise. In *For Whom the Bell Tolls*, Santiago is the Christian name of the guerrilla leader they call El Sordo (the deaf one)—a brave, bowlegged cattle herdsman with a "hooked nose like an Indian's" who, dies on top of a mountain under an aerial bombardment—the Battle of Clavijo in reverse.

share of Moorish booty, forever and ever, amen.

Amazingly, the cathedral at Compostela was actually able to collect this annual pledge. In the 1200s and 1300s, only a few places near Santiago made the *Voto*, but after the conquest of Granada in 1492, Ferdinand and Isabella decided to make it a general requirement throughout Spain. On top of the annual taxes and church tithe, every farmer who owned two or more oxen had to send the cathedral half a *fanega* of wheat (four-fifths of a bushel —about 50 kg,—which might have amounted to as much as 10% of an acre's yield) or the equivalent value of his best crop if he didn't grow wheat. Only less-well-off farmers had to pay; cleverly, the writers of the vow had left the powerful feudal landlords exempt.

Many people fought this tax and several scholars proved beyond a doubt that the document had to be a forgery. In the late 16th century, some of the Voto's opponents brought a suit against the archbishop of Santiago. The protestors fought mostly with facts and once with a counter-forgery of their own and eventually, in 1628, after nearly 50 years of litigation, the judges in Madrid issued a ruling in their favor.

And yet nothing changed. Despite the court's decision, the king stood by his Moor-Slayer, and forced the peasants to keep on paying the *Voto* to the archbishop (including the Crown's modest commission for handling the collection). After the court decision, however, people hated the tax. "[I]n the eyes of most Spaniards from that time onwards it was a hateful and suspect thing," wrote historian T.D. Kendrick. Despite the disgruntlement, the Kingdom kept collecting the Voto off and on until 1834, when it was permanently abolished.

The real story behind what Edward Gibbon calls Saint James's "stupendous metamorphosis" from pilgrim to warrior does involve Muslim Spain, but in a different way than generally advertised—more in the nature of a counter-programming decision than a divine intervention.

In the 1080s, the kings of León had been able to make their

enormous bequests to the powerful monks of Cluny because military weakness in Muslim Spain had made it possible for León to force the many of the Muslim kings, the taifa, to pay enormous tributes. This went on until 1085, when Alfonso VI invaded Toledo and killed one of his golden *gansas*. After he took Toledo, other Muslim kings began to think they might be next, stopped paying their tribute, and sought help from the Almoravids, a fast-growing religious movement in North Africa.

The Almoravids obliged, but with a little too much enthusiasm for the taifas' comfort: the movement began to take control of parts of Muslim Spain, which made not only the Muslim kings but León and the Church nervous. With Cluny in trouble because León was in trouble, and León weaker after Yusuf ibn Tashfin, the Almoravid King, walloped Alfonso VI at the Battle of Sagrajas (1086), the pope eventually declared a holy war against the Infidel in Spain in 1123.

A decade later, Alfonso's son, Alfonso VII, began to ascribe his victories to the intercession of Saint James, and the connection between Saint James and battling "the Moor" began to grow. By 1150, with the ink barely dry on Pedro Marcia's story of the Battle of Clavijo, Santiago began to be treated as almost a counter-prophet to Mohammad. As the poet puts it in *Song of My Cid*: "The Moors shout: Mohammed! and the Christians: Santiago!"

Prior to this time, no one in the northern Christian kingdoms had felt any urgency to free their Christian brothers in Muslim Spain from the "Moorish yoke," because there usually was no yoke. Like the Jews, Christians in Muslim kingdoms were generally free to worship as they chose, provided they paid a tax for the privilege. Imagining Santiago locked in a struggle against the Infidel gave northern raids on Muslims a veneer of holiness, which the Church reinforced in the 1170s when Pope Alexander III chartered the Order of Santiago, a military-religious order of monks (the folks with the dagger-sword symbol) who were given the mission of protecting pilgrims and fighting the Infidel).

Whatever they were like on the battlefield, Santiago's military monks must have been good negotiators. They won a number of special rights, including the right to marry (provided they stayed away from their spouses during Advent, Lent, and a number of other holidays), and the right to keep everything they plundered from Muslim territory, even if it had once belonged to a Christian. It was only fair, wrote the pope, given the risks they had run. Women could also join, provided they were noble, but they were not allowed to fight.[255]

As for people's doubts about Santiago Matamoros, Church and State worked very hard to suppress them. As Gibbon puts it in *The Decline and Fall of the Roman Empire* (1789):

> The gravest historians ... celebrated [Saint James's] exploits; the miraculous shrine of Compostella displayed his power; and the sword of a military order, assisted by the terrors of the Inquisition, was sufficient to remove every objection of profane criticism.

We arrived at our hostel at around three, a nondescript place on the outskirts of Belorado, in that no man's land of overgrown ditches and billboards where in the United States, low-end motels and U-Haul franchises tend to go.

Thea and Charlotte sat out back on lounge chairs in the tiny yard, next to a tiny pool, and read their books. *"That's when I really got burned,"* Thea wrote *"but only on one side so I look like a soccer fan at Masha's new school—one half pink, the other white."*

That night, Cybèle made salad and scrambled eggs for dinner in the hostel's kitchen. After we cleaned up, I looked at an old newspaper clipping in Spanish that someone had pinned on a bulletin board, the story of an old guy who had made the Camino 37 times or some other extraordinary number.

---

255 After the final Moorish expulsion in 1614, the order was disbanded and reformed several times by the king. It still exists today, surviving in Spain as a small and hopefully harmless order of 35 aristocrats.

He wore a big black hat and looked a little like a Spanish Gabby Hayes.[256] [257]

Charlotte wrote, *"[w]e slept on bunk beds in a room that smelled like Vick's vapo rub. The beds had sheets but they were made out of jersey, which felt funny but at least we got to wash our sleeping bags."*

---

256 A character actor who usually played the grizzled sidekick in Westerns opposite John Wayne or some other dadburn young whippersnapper.

257 As I've thought about it more, I've started to wonder whether it's even possible to make a pilgrimage 37 times. After all, the whole idea of a pilgrimage is bound up with unfamiliarity: the dictionary says that the word "pilgrim" (peregrino in Spanish) is derived from the Latin, peregrinum (a stranger). Part of the reason a pilgrimage was considered a penance was that you had to endure the unpleasantness and danger of going somewhere nobody knew you. Did it count as a pilgrimage if he knew the Way that well, and liked it? That's assuming of course that he wasn't fibbing about the 37 times and hadn't added on a few trips to improve the story. Prime numbers are always a little suspect.

August 17. Belorado to Burgos, 46 km

In which we meet El Cid, Santiago Matamoros, Fat Fannie Freddie, and some gastronomic cannibals.

In the oak and chestnut forests east of Burgos, we saw signs that morning for a museum of prehistoric man in the Sierra de Atapuerca hills. Some of the oldest human remains ever discovered have been found here, bones from about 500,000 years ago that belonged to people who were around even before the Neanderthals.

Paleontologists haven't figured out a lot about these people, beyond the fact that you probably wouldn't want to introduce them to your family, particularly if your children are still on the tender side. At the Sima de los Huesos site, paleontologists have dug up the bones of 28 people, mostly teenagers and young adults. Six of the 28 bore marks that suggested they had been butchered and eaten: a three-year-old, a four-year-old, an 11-year-old, a 14-year old, and two 16- to 18-year-olds had been on the menu at different times. The fact that the marks on the bones were similar to

Burgos Cathedral

those found thrown in with other mammal bones found in the cave, including a break to make it easy to suck out the marrow, suggested to the paleo-pathologists that the six had all been eaten.

Cannibalism is not rare in the animal world, but it's usually either because the animals are starving or to show dominance. In this case, the researchers have deduced that the six people weren't eaten as part of a ritual, or because of starvation (the bones were tossed in the same pile as the bones of the other mammals the diners had eaten), but because the ancient people thought a little kid would hit the spot. It was a clear-cut case of "gastronomic cannibalism."[258]

We didn't stop, however. It was nearly lunchtime and we were feeling almost Pleistocene ourselves. I was also focused on getting to Burgos. I had seen the strange bristly white spires of its cathedral from the train on an earlier trip to Spain and wanted to make sure we got to see the church before everybody collapsed.

> "Going to Burgos wasn't bad but once we got there we had to bike through blocks and blocks of high-rise buildings and traffic and people," Thea wrote. "It was really funny because Masha was having a meltdown (that part wasn't funny) and Mom kept telling Dad to stop at the next place for lunch but Dad kept saying, `Oh no, that place looks so bad, we'll try the next place' for hours and hours. Finally we stopped at a schwarma place right by the cathedral."

Although it was hot that afternoon—almost burning—and the strangely shadeless main street seemed to go on forever, and Masha was on the verge of a nervous breakdown, I wouldn't stop. It's true that I didn't see a restaurant that looked at all good, but deep down, I was also afraid that once we stopped, we wouldn't be able to get everyone moving again, and I didn't want to miss my cathedral.

A rush of cold air met us at the church door refreshing as a miracle. The church itself was almost as beautiful as the air conditioning. It had been renovated recently, so instead of the dim corners and gray stone of most old cathedrals, the interior glowed in polished white limestone, like one of Washington DC's monuments. The girls' moods lifted suddenly—Masha, re-

---

258　Not far away, within a quiet hillside at La Pedraja, outside Burgos, the bodies of 135 people still rested, shot and flung into two mass graves by Franco's soldiers between July and November 1936. When the authorities finally got around to exhuming the graves in 2016, some people noted the irony that the government had found money to dig up the 500,000 year old cavemen at Atapuerca before unearthing the bodies of people who still had living relatives. (Then again, as there are about 120,000 bodies in mass graves like this all over Spain, it would be a much bigger job.)

It occurs to me that if you compare this 80-year-old mass grave to the Neolithic boneyard 10 kilometers away, it's hard to see any moral progress in a half-million years. Some people might see our modern aversion to cannibalism as a plus, but I suspect it just means we've gotten more wasteful.

vived by the cool air, even asked us for an audio guide.

I shouldn't have been surprised by the high-budget interior. Although Burgos "could hardly be called a real town until the mid-twelfth century," according to historian Maya Soifer Irish, pilgrim traffic and wool traders had put the town on the map, and politics kept it there, as Castilian power consolidated. First, it was an important city for the Kingdom of Castile, then Castile and Leon, and then Castile (incorporating Leon) and Aragon, and after the fall of Granada, the capital of Spain until Philip II moved the court to Madrid.

In addition to various Castilian monarchs, Spain's most famous medieval hero, Rodrigo Diaz, aka El Cid, is buried here.[259]

Born just outside of Burgos in 1043, El Cid had such a swash-buckling military career that Muslim Spaniards gave him the nickname *Sayyid*. This means "lord or master" in Arabic but I think would translate today into something more like "the Man." The Cid (as the name is usually spelled in Spanish) worked both for and against Christian kings, led various armies to glory all over Spain, and eventually won a kingdom of his own, the city-state of Valencia, backed by an army made up of both Muslim and Christian soldiers.

There are three episodes that people remember best from his career. First, he forced the king of Castile, Alfonso VI, to swear multiple times on the Bible that he did not murder his brother, El Cid's former boss, Sancho II, which Alfonso resented (part-ly because he may have done it). Second, he persuaded Doña Jimena to marry him even though he had killed her father, Diego Fernandez, the Count of Oviedo in a duel, because, really, it was the honorable thing to do, dear. And third, on his deathbed, and with his own kingdom under siege, he directed that his follow-ers stuff his corpse into his armor, mount him on his stalwart

---

259   The Spanish hero and his wife, Doña Jimena, were originally interred in the monastery of San Pedro de Cardeña, 10 kilometers outside Burgos, along with his horse, Babieca (in accordance with the Cid's wishes), but when Burgos' archbishop reinterred El Cid and his wife in 1921, he didn't bring along the bones of the white wonder stallion.

horse, Babieca, and send the two off on a final charge. Legend has it that seeing him on horseback led his men to take heart and the besieging army to take flight, and he won the battle *even though he was already dead!* What a guy.

The various books, operas, plays, and a Charlton Heston movie about the Cid all stem mostly from the 12th-century epic poem, the *Song of My Cid*, written at roughly the same time as the *Song of Roland*. If you look at a modern translation, you can see why the story might lend itself to 70 mm Technicolor Technirama. Here are a few lines from a translation into the American by Paul Blackman, on El Cid's expulsion from Burgos by his wicked king:

> They have to get a look at him,
> men and women both.
> Townsmen and their wives crowd the windows,
> tears in their eyes
> and in their mouths
> a single sentence:
>> "God, what a good vassal!
>> If only he had a worthy lord."

You get the idea.

Over time, pilgrim money, profits from the wool trade with Flanders, and Castilian political power, made the cathedral one of the most important in Spain. The current church is late gothic, erected in the 15th century, a masterpiece of Spanish Christianity that brought together a French architect (who was inspired by Bourges Cathedral, the buttresses of Notre Dame in Paris, and the window design of Sainte-Chapelle in Paris); a German architect named Johannes von Köln (or Hans de Colonia or Juan de Colonia to his Burgos friends) (who was responsible for the cathedral's bony spires and its florid-style gothic chapel); a Flemish artist who worked on the altarpiece, and a number of local sculptors and painters. All of it was supervised by the archbishop, Paul of Burgos, aka Solomon ha-Levi (as he was known until he converted from Judaism in 1391, at age 40), and his son Simon (who succeeded him as archbishop), and paid for in part by taxes on Burgos's large and prosperous Jewish community.[260]

The ha-Levis were unusual but Jews and Gentiles actually did live in close contact in Spain, at least among the middle and upper classes. Professional restrictions against the Jews were fairly limited until the 15th century. "As farmers (Yes! Jews could own land in Spain) artisans, merchants, shopkeepers, translators, royal advisers, physicians, tax-collectors, and yes, money lenders, Jews enjoyed a fairly free range of professions and economic pursuits," according to historian Teofilo F. Ruiz.[261] Professional restrictions depended on the particular locality. In Burgos, for instance, Jews were specifically prohibited from moneylending, as Christians had that business covered. Overall, Jews were largely tolerated in northern Spain, at least until Bishop Paul's time, when itinerant monks began to stir up the lower classes against the Jews.

In the Middle Ages, Spain was comprised of northern, Christian-led kingdoms that had Christian, Jewish, and Muslim subjects and Muslim-led kingdoms (mostly in the south) also had Muslim, Jewish, and Christian subjects. All three groups were considered part of the same society. In *The Song of El Cid*, for example, Spanish eternity is described as the period "while the people shall be of Moors and the Christian folk." The groups had not always liked each other but for the most part, they coexisted—Sharks and Jets on the plaza. Muslim and Christian leaders were for the most part equal-opportunity exploiters, forming alliances and fighting against each other not with some grand design of making Spain all Muslim or all Christian, but each for

---

260 Father and son converted but not the archbishop's wife. Sol-to-Paul's wife, Joanna, must have been a formidable women: she stayed faithful to Judaism until she died in 1420, when Paul had her buried in the Church of Saint Pablo.

261 (The enthusiastic parenthetical is Professor Ruiz's!)

his own advantage.[262]

Santiago Matamoros with Moros

Muslims are also represented in the cathedral. You can find them cowering under an enormous polychrome statue of Santiago Matamoros, an 18th-century Baroque sculpture installed about a hundred years after the Spanish Crown had crushed Islam in Spain.

Santiago Matamoros statues like these can be found in churches and monasteries all over Spain. In this particular rendition, the Moor-Slayer is brightly painted, which makes him look like a giant action figure. He sports a red cloak, a black tunic pinned closed by a scallop shell, and a hat with a scallop shell pinned to the brim, to make sure you don't confuse him with another saint. He has drawn his sword and sits on his white and black warhorse looking down at three Moors who have fallen and are a second or two away from being trampled and/or hacked to pieces.

Santiago has a distracted, slightly bored expression I have of-

---

262 This kind of cultural mixing was not unfamiliar to the Spanish or to anybody in Europe, for that matter. Today's monocultural states are to some extent a 20th century aberration As Tony Judt puts it in *Postwar: A History of Europe Since 1945*: "The continent of Europe was once an intricate, interwoven tapestry of overlapping languages, religions, communities and nations. Many of its cities...were truly multicultural societies *avant le mot*, where Catholics, Orthodox, Muslims, Jews and others lived in familiar juxtaposition." But between 1914 and 1945, "*that* Europe was smashed into the dust."

ten seen on sculptures of warrior saints and avenging angels. My theory is that it is a compromise between murderous rage, which isn't a particularly Christian emotion, and saintly benefi- cence, which doesn't go well with hand-to-hand smiting. Here, Santiago looks like he's holding a cue stick over a pool table instead of preparing to lop a man's head off. The Moors, on the other hand, seem quite invested in the moment.[263]

Fortunately, the Moors— who in a Matamoros statue are always placed under the hooves of Santiago's white or white and black charger—are about as real as the Moor Killer hovering above them. I don't mean that the Muslims that Christians fought for control of Iberia were imaginary, but that given for much of the Middle Ages, Spain was 75 percent Muslim and most people in Muslim Spain spoke Arabic as a first language, the image that we have of Moors as a dark, turbaned Other never really corre- sponded with reality.[264]

It's true that in the eighth century, the Iberian Peninsula was invaded by an army made up of a few Arabs and North Afri- can people who are often referred to even now as the Berbers— that is, the Barbarians (they themselves prefer *Amazighs*). Later, slaves imported from northern Europe and Byzantium became

---

[263] Goya makes fun of this expression in one of a series of paintings now in the collection of the Art Institute of Chicago, "The capture of the bandit El Maragato by Friar Pedro," based on a popular story of 1806 about a monk who turned the tables on a bandit.

El Maragato was a notorious highwayman, a muleteer who worked outside León. A murderer and a thief, he was eventually caught and sent to prison, but escaped, and went back to thievery. One day, he made the mistake of taking on one Friar Pedro, who managed to take his rifle away, shoot him in the rear before he could run off, and then tie him up.

My favorite of the five paintings is "Fray Pedro de Zaldivia hits the `Maragato' with the butt of the rifle," the red-cheeked friar wears the same, cool expression as Santiago Matamoros, while El Maragato has assumed the traditional position of the designated damned.

[264] Nor did this change immediately after Christian kings took over. Thirteenth-cen- tury Toledo, for example, was still culturally Arabic after the Castilians took charge: Christians still spoke Arabic on the street, in the market, and in the church. The Castilian royal family kept up with the latest in Andalusian fashion, often decorated with Arabic text, and in 1247, when Archbishop Rodrigo Jiménez de Rada died (the historian who exposed the Charlemagne story as a fraud), he was buried in chasubles decorated with Arabic calligraphy.

part of the mix as well. But the Moors were never a separate people ethnically. Even outside of Spain, the people that Europeans called Moors or Saracens shared a culture, not a genetic history. As Professor Metlitzki writes in her book on the influence of Arabic culture on English literature, *The Matter of Araby in Medieval England*:

> The people who contributed to the formation of what, in the Middle Ages, was known as "Saracen" culture were of the most varied ethnic origins. They were Greeks, Persians, Indians, Copts, Nestorians, Zorastrians, and Jews, whole populations living in a vast expanse of territories extending from the Indian Ocean to the Atlantic which the spread of Islam from the heart of the Arabian peninsula had engulfed with lightning speed. These indigenous peoples were the heirs of old and brilliant civilizations which had been consolidated in the Byzantine and Persian Empires. Yet under the influence of their Arab conquerors they were molded into a new cultural unity that expressed itself in a new Arabian way of life.

I understand the impulse to caricature your enemies—it's probably easier to kill people if you don't see them as people, and there was a fair amount of anti-Moorish propaganda from fairly early on.[265] But strangely, Matamoros sculptures like this one in Burgos became more popular many years *after* the destruction of Muslim Spain in the late 16th and early 17th centuries.

The statues were part of a larger campaign to recount the rise of Christian power in Spain as a manifest destiny rather than the long game of musical chairs it had actually been. Perhaps most importantly, by the time this statue was made, Spain had amassed a colossal global empire that stretched from Mexico to the Philippines, and the image of the Moor had come to stand not so much for Spanish Muslims as for any enemy, anywhere, who didn't believe in Catholicism, from Protestants in Europe,

---

265   Alfonxo X, King of Castile and Leon between 1252 and 1284, one of the more literary Spanish kings, writes a lot about Moors as ugly, savage, with long black beards, unlike the fair and handsome Christians— which is curious, given that historians give him relatively high marks for tolerance in his day job. The convention moved to England too, eventually, if in a somewhat subversive form. Some scholars have argued that in Shakespeare's *Othello*, where Othello is a black tragic hero, and the villain is named Iago, that is, James; in Shakespeare's day, Santiago was a stock villain's name, like Boris or Adolph. To make sure we get the point, Iago swears in Spanish and his confederate, Rodrigo, is the only other character in the play with a Spanish name.

to Aztecs in Mexico, to Muslims in Morocco.

With such a big world to conquer, Santiago's Moors stayed remarkably useful into the 19th century and even in the Spanish Civil War, when Franco's Falangists argued that the expulsion of the Moors and Jews "had not been completed, and these races had gone on to form the proletariat of modern Spain. The proletarian class was biologically inferior and racially susceptible to the `Oriental' doctrine of Marxism, a reference to Marx's Jewish descent," according to historian Paul Preston. Franco himself called the Civil War a crusade to rid "the Spanish race" of foreigners and foreign ideas promoted by a Masonic-Bolshevik-Jewish axis. Even after the war ended, this idea of inferior races remained important to his ideology: Franco titled a pseudonymous autobiography *Raza* (Race), kept the title in the 1942 movie version, and included the word in its partly de-fascified 1950 rerelease.[266]

The fascists' insistence on racial purity was curious on several counts, not least of which was that 20th-century Spain remained more of an ethnic paella than most European countries. In the 1930s as today, Spain was home to a variety of people who might carry Spanish passports but still consider themselves Basques, Catalan, or, like Franco himself, Galician, a people who were originally Celtic. Even now, around 25 percent of people with Spanish passports don't speak Spanish as their first language. The Caudillo's surname is itself evidence that a pure Spain was always wishful thinking: Franco is a popular surname among Sephardic Jews and in the Middle Ages referred to anybody from north of the Pyrenees.

Despite the absurdity, Franco's lie about the racial nature of the struggle worked. When mythology goes full gallop against truth,

---

266   In the 1950 rerelease, Franco cut six minutes of fascist salutes and anti-American diatribes and changed the title to *Espíritu d'una raza* (The Spirit of the Race). It was part of a larger effort to repackage himself not as an anti-American fascist hoping at some level to avenge Spain's defeat in the 1898 Spanish American War, but as a reliable Cold War ally who had stood his ground against the Reds.

mythology can win— especially if backed by an army.[267] It took between 250,000 and a million deaths and plenty of censorship, but a generation of Spanish children "grew up believing that the war had been fought by Spaniards against foreigners."

Assuming, of course, they were listening. In our experience, kids can be hard to impress:

> "'*In the Church we had the most BORING audioguides ever!*" Thea wrote. "*The Church weighs 10,000 kg. Bla Bla Bla.*'"

Burgos had charmed me so far, but probably not for the same reasons it had appealed to Franco, who made it his provisional capital during the civil war. In addition to whatever strategic advantages it offered, Burgos was a deeply conservative town and home to a number of important symbols from Spain's glory years, including the cathedral.[268]

This mattered not only because it fit in with Franco's dream of making Spain great again, but also because the generalissimo needed all the gravitas he could muster. First, his party was never very popular (in the general election of 1936, the Falange won less than 1 percent of the vote). Second, he didn't cut a very impressive figure. At 5 foot, 3 1/2 inches, Franco was shorter than Mussolini, Hitler, Stalin, and even Napoleon. One historian of the regime, Stanley G. Payne, noted that Franco's "squat, roundish figure, ill-fitting uniforms, moist hands, timid manner,

---

267   Ironically, 40,000 Moroccan soldiers from the Spanish protectorate of Morocco constituted the core of Franco's original fighting force. They had been told that the Republicans were "people without God," that is, nonbelievers.

268   The Burgos clergy were firm supporters of Franco. When the Nationalists announced their provisional government in Burgos on July 25, 1936, church bells rang out all over the city, creating a din so loud that one public official described it as "a titanic symphony, a continuous clashing of metal invading the whole life of the city," according to historian Mark Lawrence.

high-pitched voice, and tendency to waddle a bit as he walked were an enemy cartoonist's delight and the target of sarcasm even among a few of his senior generals and cabinet members." One of those insiders called Franco *Paca la culona* behind his back, which Payne translates as "Fat fanny Francie".

Francisco Franco, aka "Fat Fanny Francie"

But Franco compensated as best he could. Unlike most 20th century dictators, Franco had a keen love of religious pomp—whenever he entered a church, he entered under a canopy, like the old Spanish kings—and may have even been a genuine Catholic. His eldest niece later insisted, with some understatement, that "his faith was genuine and by no means a mask of accommodation, even though his way of understanding the Gospel might leave a good deal to be desired."

Beyond the Church, Franco tried to associate himself with Spanish tradition in other ways as well, such as getting his propagandists to liken him to El Cid, and arranging for the sponsorship of a 1961 Hollywood movie of the same name that starred Charlton Heston, Sophia Loren, and a cast of thousands. *The New York Times* reviewer described it as a movie where "all the men are men, and all the women are Sophia Loren."

It's a pretty good movie in an over-the-top, Hestonish way. Just like the Burgos cathedral, *El Cid* the movie was the product of an unlikely multicultural collaboration involving the Caudillo, looking to restore Spanish glory and the country's international reputation; a Hollywood producer named Samuel Bronston (ne Bronstein—a Russian Jewish immigrant, distant relative of Lev Davidovitch Brontstein, aka Leon Trotsky), drawn to Spain by its low production costs; an American industrialist (Pierre DuPont III) who backed Brontson; Ben Barzman, a Canadian-American screenwriter who had been blacklisted by Hollywood for not naming names to Sen. Joseph McCarthy; and 1,700 mounted

Spanish soldiers and 500 mounted Madrid police, lent by Franco as extras, who were paid $2 a day if they brought their own horse.[269]

The result was a three-hour, 10,000-costume Super Technirama epic "as big as Ben Hur if not bigger," as Bronston's publicist put it, designed to function both as propaganda for Franco and as propaganda for racial equality, a cause of Heston's—a $6 million investment that earned $20 million at the box office (about $172 million today). President Kennedy was a big fan—he screened it three times at the White House.[270]

Later, we pedaled back up the now shady main street until we reached our stop, a dark and smoky budget hotel that someone with a sense of humor had named the Hostal Hilton. After cleaning up and then flopping for a few hours, we went out to look for dinner. We didn't see anything promising near the Hilton but eventually found a Tex-Mex place on a square where we ate outside and watched the people. There was a young and lively crowd out that night, tattoed waitresses, plenty of salsa music, and bright lights. I hadn't seen Charlotte quite so happy for a few weeks.

---

269   Bronston met Franco while scouting for locations for an earlier film, a biopic of John Paul Jones, the founder of the American Navy. Chester Nimitz, the World War II admiral and a technical advisor on the project, introduced them. The Caudillo and the man who would be a movie mogul had a few things in common. Besides being short and in love with movies, they were also both very insecure—Franco, desperate that he and Spain not be treated as pariahs abroad; and Bronston, equally desperate to get away from his impoverished childhood as an uneducated Jewish refugee by remaking himself into a Hollywood giant. Like Franco, Bronston did whatever it took to reach his goal, including hobnobbing with anti-Semitic fascists and trying to convince Pope John XXIII that he was Catholic. (That was partly to get the Church's thumbs-up for his life of Jesus. That picture was directed by Nicholas Ray, who made *Rebel without a Cause*—critics said the title should have been not *King of Kings* but *I was a Teenage Jesus*). Between deals, he spent long periods of his life tortured and alone, "living by imagination, sheer will and the relentless hunt of bankable properties," as his son wrote.

270   Despite Bronston's value to Franco as a propagandist, their collaboration ended a few years later with Bronston's spectacular bankruptcy, which had followed the box office failure of The Fall of the Roman Empire, another lavish production, for which Bronston built a full-scale Roman Forum outside Madrid.

Overspending on historical details was Brontson's Achilles' heel. "I want every scene to be real," he said during the production of El Cid, "not just look real." After the bankruptcy, he never quite pulled his career together again. One of his last pitches was for a life of Queen Isabella, which would have starred Glenda Jackson. The script left out the part about the expulsion of the Jews.

August 18. Burgos to Boadilla del Camino, 67.6 km

In which I'm nearly turned into Benburger.

In the morning, after our *cafés con leche*, we headed out of town through the *paseo* along the river. A quarter mile on, the cool green paseo ended and the suburbs began, and then the suburbs ended and we began to pedal through the kind of dry and golden country you probably think of when you think of Spain.

The Camino here was a wide, dead-straight collection of ruts that ran between wheat fields, usually near a freeway, then once in a while through a village, until it narrowed and turned left on a gravel road that twisted dramatically up a steep hill for a kilometer or two, like the path to a volcano sacrifice.

Downtown Hontanas

It took a long time to get to the top because the 12 percent grade was too steep for us to pedal. Pushing the bikes wasn't easy, especially loaded down with the portbaggages.

When we finally reached the top, we stopped for a minute to read the graffiti on the wall of a shelter, where pilgrims had left messages for friends on scraps of paper and taped them with bits of blister bandages.

Back on their bikes, the girls zoomed ahead straight down the hill, but when my turn came, I hesitated—the road down looked awfully steep and rocky. I kept looking down, while Cybèle waited patiently for me to move, until I started getting disgusted with myself. Even then, I waited. Maybe I could walk it down—

In the end, gravity made the decision for me.

As I flew over the loose rocks down the mountain, nearly tumbling over the handlebars, it occurred to me that I had made a serious and probably uncorrectable mistake. On the one hand, stopping would be dangerous, maybe impossible. On the other, going on didn't look very promising either, as the road ahead (or rather, directly below me) appeared to be a dry waterfall of stones and pilgrim femurs.

The instant the grade eased a bit, I stopped, amazed that I hadn't somersaulted all the way down the mountain. For the next 50 meters, I walked the bike, and then when the road flattened out a little more, climbed back on and bounced the rest of the way to the bottom, surprised I wasn't dead.[271]

Then we were back in the wheat fields again.

Aside from the occasional close call, there were advantages to the Spanish Camino. One was that it was much harder to get lost than in France. Often, the path ran in a wide rut through open fields, and at regular intervals, we would see an official

---

271 This was only one of several close calls we had. Once, Masha was pedaling along a gravel path that ran high over a busy highway when her tires lost their grip and she fell over, but fortunately, the grass on the embankment was long and she was able to grab it before she went sailing down into the traffic. One morning, Charlotte ran into a pole. Another time, outside one small town, the road turned but Thea didn't and went instead head over heels over her handlebars and into another, busier road, but again fortunately, nobody was coming just then. None of these episodes were traumatic enough at the time that anybody even made a note of them in a journal, and in fact, only Cybèle remembers them in detail. In retrospect, however, we were very, very lucky.

blue and gold Camino highway sign, and between those signs, yellow arrows painted sloppily or stenciled on a wall or a stone in whichever direction we were supposed to head next. We loved the yellow arrows, which were big and impossible to misinterpret. Unlike the French trail markings where white-red-red means one thing and red-white-red might mean something else entirely, and often with no direction indicated, the yellow arrow always dealt a clear and unambiguous commandment to Go.

Not that it was appreciably tougher in the old days. The early pilgrim guides talk a lot about the hardships the pilgrims faced, and how they had to steer by the Milky Way to reach Santiago de Compostela, but I think they exaggerate. When it comes to assessing their own hardships, Christians tend to leave their thumb on the scale. Even in the Middle Ages, getting to Santiago must have taken about the same level of navigational skill as staying on Interstate 80. Pilgrims followed Roman roads through France, over the Pyrenees, to Pamplona, and then made a right.

That day, just outside the old town of Castrojeriz, we passed a short length of Roman road that had been restored, and after that, a long rough line of paving stones that the legionaires hadn't maintained for quite a while— a remnant of what had been a 10,000-kilometer network all over Spain.

In Spain and all over the empire, the Romans built their roads in more or less the same way: legionnaires, slaves, or unfortunate locals would dig a trench at least three meters wide and roughly two meters deep, fill the trench with a meter of stones and sand, then cover it with gravel and tamp it down flat. At this point, they would either declare victory and move to the next section or cover the surface with flagstones, which were arched in the middle so water would run off. Next, they would lay paths of packed gravel for pedestrians on both sides of the road, and every three to five meters, two stone blocks. The blocks kept the wheeled traffic from veering into the footpath and gave people riding mules or horses a stepstool for mounting or dismounting. Roughly every 50 kilometers, they would build a station or a town where travelers and their animals could stay the night.

And most of it was as straight as they could make it, either for speed or just because of that peculiar love of the right angle that authoritarians often have.

A little later, we passed a ruin of a building that had been a palace built by Pedro the Cruel of Castile in the 12th century, and rebuilt as a hospital for pilgrims by the presumably kinder monks of the Order of San Antonio in the 14th for the care and feeding of pilgrims. They also specialized in curing Saint Anthony's Fire (ergotism), a disease caused by eating rye grain contaminated by the ergot fungus. Ergot "contains a chemical that makes the sufferer go berserk and causes gangrene of the hands and feet...victims had the sensation of being burned at the stake, before their fingers, toes, hands and feet dropped off,"[272] Two arches still span the old road like a medieval drive-in.

Other than occasional monuments like the Roman road and the old drive-in, it was hot, dreary country. Being able to whizz through all that superfluous space felt good. On the other hand, I was still finding biking hard, lonely, and sometimes irritating work—and it was about to get worse.

The first time I blew a tire, we were passing a spot in the dry neart-desert where the highway department had erected a concrete picnic table shaded by a concrete awning, as if they knew we were coming.

No problem, I thought. I would take the tire off, pull out the canister of goo the bike guys at Decathlon had sold me, spray a little Hole-Be-Gone, and off we'd go. In no time at all, we took the wheel off the bike, pulled the tire off, and pulled out the flaccid inner tube. Cybèle, Charlotte, and I squeezed the tube here and there until we felt a tiny puff of air, sprayed the goo on the hole, shoved the inner tube back in the tire, and took turns pumping until we were purple in the face—and decided we needed to try

---

272   The last big outbreak was in France in 1951, when 200 of the 4000 people in the village of Pont Saint Esprit went mad simultaneously after eating some bad rye bread. "They had hallucinations, writhed in agony in their beds, vomited, ran crazily in the streets and suffered terrible burning sensations in their limbs," according to one medical writer.

it again.

We took the inner tube out once more, resprayed the hole, then tucked it back into the tire and pumped—but again, nothing. Whatever the white foam did, it did not repair inner tubes.

Masha and Thea, meanwhile, had retreated into the shade of the picnic shelter and stretched out flat like hot cats on the square of cool concrete. *"Mom and Charlotte kept arguing about how to fix it—I just sat and read my Kindle while eating Cheezy Whatsits (in Spain they are called Riscettos)," * Thea wrote.

Tired girls

Charlotte proposed trying to put a new inner tube into the tire before pumping—she had watched a video about it at Decathlon while the rest of us were still trying on bicycle shorts. Cybèle, on the other hand, had changed a few tires when she was a kid, and now remembered something about pumping up the new spare inner tube, then stuffing it into the tire. Charlotte, however, pointed out that once the inner tube was full, it would be very hard to squeeze inside. I stayed neutral.

I don't remember who was right in the end, but I do remember that Charlotte became sputtering mad at our obtuseness at one point, too angry and frustrated to speak, in that special zone we've all visited on the far side of profanity but just short of murder.

Forty minutes later, we were back on the road. Around 5 o'clock, we reached Boadilla del Camino, a brown dusty farm town sur-

rounded by brown dusty country. The little town looked picturesque, but not promising. It had a big church with an enormous
stork's nest on the roof, like a lot of the churches we passed in
Castile; an empty piazza ringed by mustard-colored buildings
with cracked walls and sagging tile roofs; a construction site
where some kind of building seemed to be going on; and in the
center of the piazza, a four-meter-high column that looked at
first like a memorial but on closer inspection turned out to be a
fancy whipping post, the Rollo de Justicia. The authorities had
once meted out punishments there a few centuries ago, back
when the town was big enough to support miscreants.

But when we walked through the gate of our hostel, we found
a deep green lawn with trees and a little pool, and backpackers lounging around who looked like they'd found the Big Rock
Candy Mountains, the Depression hobos' promised land:

> *Where the boxcars all are empty*
> *And the sun shines every day*
> *And the birds and the bees*
> *And the cigarette trees*
> *The lemonade springs*
> *Where the bluebird sings*
> *In the Big Rock Candy Mountains.*

At dinner that night our host seated us with a family of six Belgians, who were also *bicigrinos*. The parents, Jean and Gert, were
roughly our age—serious bespectacled people who had bicycled
from Vézelay in central France the past few weeks with their
teenage kids, two girls and two boys. I mentioned that we were
finding biking much harder than walking. There was so much
more to worry about—panniers and tires and gears and brakes
and remembering to lock them up whenever you stopped.

The Belgians smiled but hardly knew what we were talking
about—they were practically two-wheeled centaurs. They had
bicycled a lot around Belgium as a family, and the parents had
biked the Camino before, on their honeymoon.

We compared notes about how our kids had liked the trip so far.
Cybèle said we had had to push the girls to do it, but hoped that

someday they would remember the nicer moments fondly. Jean said this had not been a problem for them—they had taken a vote about whether to make the trip.[273]

I mentioned we had seen only one other family on bikes: a blond couple pulling a blond toddler in a tagalong trailer. They were Swiss, judging by the flag that billowed near the child's ear. Jean said he had seen them too and talked to them. "What did they tell the kid?" I asked, imagining how impossible it would have been to keep our toddlers happy in that little trailer hour after hour.

"They didn't tell her anything," he said. "They decided it would just lead to questions about when they were going to get there. They let her think they were just people who biked."

Cybèle and I found the Belgians encouraging. We had seen a few families here and there, but most of them walked for a few days or a week at most, and no one had tried to tackle the whole thing with a pack of adolescents. The fact that the Belgian kids didn't seem the worse for wear and like our girls even looked conspicuously hale reassured us too —Jean and I could have started a support group for the trials of fathers with unusually good-looking children. Maybe we weren't engaged in some eccentric act of child abuse after all.

Dinner was good, but I didn't like the guy who ran the place. He was a youngish man in a stocking cap who seemed to have modeled himself on Che Guevara and offset his jokes to the girls with veiled hostility toward Cybèle and me—I guess for pushing our girls to go on the trip, or being middle-aged, or being American—or all of the above.

After dinner, the girls went and borrowed my computer and watched *Romancing the Stone* again, this time with the Belgian kids on the grass out in the backyard. Those kids hadn't seen a movie in a month, and all of them but Thea stayed outside even

273 In fact, their kids told our kids later that they hadn't voted. My guess is that there was a vote but if I had seen my father look forward to this trip as much as Jean evidently had, I don't think I would have had the nerve to vote no either.

after it turned chilly and dark.

On a downstairs landing later that night to check my email, I heard one side of a video conversation a fellow middle-aged American was trying to have with someone back home, shouting into the camera on his phone to compensate for the weak connection. He was DOING PRETTY WELL. They had seen a lot of interesting things. THE PEOPLE WERE NICE. MOSTLY. HOW'S BONNIE? UH HUH. I'M SURE SORRY I MISSED HER BIRTHDAY. I was sure sorry he had missed it too. I have no doubt he was a nice guy who led an exemplary life, but for a minute or two, as he kept shouting (Do other people shout as much as Americans or do I just notice it more?), I suddenly felt a little sympathy for Che.

August 19. Boadilla del Camino to Sahagún, 62.9 km

In which various good deeds are done.

"As usual we were the last people up. Charlotte was sick and we ate black cookies and hot chocolate. Today we biked by a canal— we had to go slowly so Charlotte didn't hurt herself," Thea wrote.

Midmorning, as we biked down a gravel road next to a steamy green canal, a car crunched up behind us and then alongside me, and the driver rolled down her window. I stopped. A young woman was behind the wheel. As I got off my bike, Che from the hostel reached across the driver's seat and handed me a bundle of blue passports: Cybèle had been distracted that morning, looking after Charlotte, I had been dazed as usual, and we had left them behind in the safe in our room.

I felt very grateful, thanked Che, and silently took back all the bad things I had thought about him. But then he said I should give the girl some money for gas, and I reconsidered my reconsideration. Yes, they had done us a huge favor, but the ill-humored sneer that accompanied the hint that made me think my original instinct had been right.

"Oh, of course," I said, and after a little maneuvering, fished my wallet out of my backpack, and took out a bill. "Is that enough?" I asked.

The Comandante scowled but nodded in the affirmative, reached across his friend's face, snatched the 20 out of my hand, and then told her to drive.

They pulled on ahead, alongside Cybèle (I was in my usual mid-morning slump and she could not help but pass me again.), and tried to say something to her about whether she was missing something. She didn't know what they were talking about either, so after evidently not getting the response he wanted, they made a U-turn in the wide rutted road and rattled off down the rutted lane, dust billowing behind them.

And the day ground on.

"After lunch at about three," Thea wrote. *"Dad popped his tire again (surprise, surprise). This time we just sat on the side of the trail under a 'tree' (basically a stick in the ground) and Masha and I planned our perfect government/town (it was kind of totalitarian but in a good way)."*

A scarecrow taking a break outside Sahagun

Midafternoon we reached our destination: Sahagún, another dusty village but a little better known place than Boadilla del Camino. There had once been an important Cluniac monastery here, and it was the hometown of two well-known churchmen, Saint John of Sahagún and Bernardino de Sahagún, who between them exemplify some of the best and worst impulses of the Spanish Church.

Saint John was a 15th-century friar and priest famous for a special power to read hearts. His sermons inspired people to take action—sometimes to blurt out their sins and reform; sometimes to try to kill him. Once in Salamanca, after preaching on the evils of extravagant dress, John was attacked in the street by a group of (presumably) fashionable women, who threw stones at him until the authorities made them stop.

I like the sound of the other local hero better. Bernardino de Sahagún didn't make saint, but he doesn't seem to have had any stones thrown at him either. He was born in the town in 1499, and after studying at the university in Salamanca, became a Franciscan missionary to New Spain—that is, Mexico. He arrived in 1524, just three years after Cortés.

Bernardino founded the first university in the Americas, learned Nahuatl, the Aztec language, and spent 60 years studying and writing what amounts to an encyclopedia about the native cultures. He goes into such detail—he even recruited indigenous artists to paint pictures of their customs and costumes—that he has been called the first anthropologist.

As part of that work, he wrote the first history of the Spanish Conquest from the Aztec point of view, and clearly saw it as a catastrophe, concluding that by the end

> No semblance of what they had formerly been remained. Thus they are held to be barbarians and a people of little worth, yet in truth, in matters of culture, they are a step ahead of many nations that presume to be civilized.

Our hostel tonight, like the Rock Candy Mountains of the night before, was also behind high walls, but the interior courtyard here was no oasis but clean-swept concrete and tile, like a well-run gas station, and set up especially for *bicigrinos*. The proprietor had worked on the Spanish theme a bit more too: terra cotta roof, plaster lion guarding the gate, and a big cast iron sign that said "Albergue" with a cut-out of a scallop shell dangling beneath it Shell Oil-style but upside down.

In the yard, we saw six silver bicycles, parked all in a row. The Belgians again! Trust the big families to find the cheapest places.

Inside the big bunkroom, I found Jean, and told him about our tire troubles. He offered to help me try to figure it out. We went out into the courtyard and he told his son to fill up a big outdoor sink with some water, which the boy did right away.

I admired the way he said it and the way his son responded. Jean hadn't said it in a mean way and his son didn't respond resentfully, but there was a military crispness to the exchange that made me think maybe I had done the dad business all wrong.

The kid—a redhead around 17—pumped up one of our punctured inner tubes, then Cybèle and I watched him hold it a few inches under water, then another few inches under water, and another, until we saw bubbles dribbling up out of a small hole in the rubber.

"There," Jean said, "there's the hole."

His son took out their patching kit and patched it with glue and a little rubber square. They gave me a few of the patches and I bought Jean a beer. I was grateful, and not only for the help; I admired their restraint in not pointing out how stupid we had been not to learn how to do this earlier.

Dinner was jolly, served by a heavy-set proprietor who kept bobbing in and out of the room with more wine.

Eating with Jean and Gert that night, I tried to collect more reassurances that the Camino was a good thing to do with kids. Jean mentioned that the Belgian government sometimes gives juvenile delinquents and minor criminals the option of making a pilgrimage to Santiago in lieu of jail time. Apparently it works well, he said, but I have not been able to find more detail about this not cruel but definitely unusual punishment.

However, as much as Jean was enjoying the trip, he seemed a little sad tonight. He had that vaguely disappointed quality of a well-mannered kid at Christmas who has opened all his presents but keeps sneaking looks under the tree to see if there is one he missed. He had reached that point in his holiday when he had started thinking about going back to work and he wasn't looking forward to it. He worked for a big computer company in high-end sales, and he liked it less and less. The company's motto had once been "Think" but his new boss now just said, "Do," which really summed it up for him.

After dinner, Cybèle, Gert, and I strolled around the town. Gert was a geography teacher, and like all teachers in August, dreading September.

The streets were quiet and almost deserted. When we turned around to walk home, we passed through a newer part of town, a modern subdivision. Most of the houses were dark. It was summer, after all, and sensible people were on actual vacations, cooling off in the mountains or swimming in the sea.

But our girls had a good time that night. *"All the kids (including me even though I am wise beyond my years) went to watch Die Hard,"* Thea wrote.

August 20. Sahagún to León, 64 km.

Wherein I meet the Swiss Killer again.

Tomorrow Cybèle had scheduled a Day of Rest, our last before Santiago. We would be in León, a big city, in a proper hotel with cotton sheets and a private bathroom, and after all the hostels, we were looking forward to it immensely.

The biking stayed easy all morning, except in the outskirts of the city, where we had to cross two expressways via immense pedestrian bridges that looked like gigantic green hamster runs.

The only points of interest in the outskirts were houses built into the sides of hills. These turned out to be *bodegas*—caves that people have traditionally used to store wine, cure meat, and cool off in the summer time—but that afternoon, were all shut tight as tombs.

Bodegas outside León

León started out as a supremely unimportant place 2,000 years ago that gradually worked its way up to a semi-important place around the end of the first millennium.

The city was founded as a camp for Augustus's Victorious Sixth Legion, the Legio sexta vitrix, in 29 BC, and became the permanent base of the Twins' Seventh Legion, the *Legio septima Gemina* (named for Romulus and Remus, the twin founders of Rome) in 74 AD. One measure of how little anybody thought of the city is that its original name, *Legio,* just meant Legion, which is a bit like naming your truck stop "Truck." Particularly when you think that the other major northern towns had names like Caesar-Augustus (Zaragoza) or Pompeiopolis (Pamplona), it doesn't suggest anyone had high hopes for León.

And they were right. For nearly a thousand years, the town didn't make much of a mark, either under the Visigoths or the Muslims. It wasn't until the Christians took it back in the 10th century, by which time the name had eroded from Legio to León, that the town began to take on some significance as the capital of the Christian Kingdom of León.

If Cybèle and I had been alone, we probably would have gone to the hotel first to drop off the bikes and then go back out, but we knew that the girls would be hard to move once we checked into the hotel, so instead, we decided to bike straight to the cathedral, and visit in shifts. Cybèle and the girls went inside first, while I stayed out in the plaza and stood guard.

This wasn't entirely altruistic. I had seen a lot of cathedrals at this point and this one looked less impressive to me than the Burgos cathedral—a bit blockier somehow—though both of them are supposedly based on the same plan as the cathedral at Rheims, and the guidebooks all raved about the stained glass.

Plus, I was enjoying watching the people come and go on the wide piazza.

As I stood waiting, I looked up at the sky, which had turned an apocalyptic yellow-orange.

Then, before I could think more about what that might mean—assuming it wasn't actually the end of the world—a young woman who looked somehow familiar stepped out of the crowd. The Swiss killer!—our friend from the French Camino, now out of her hiking gear and in a summer dress. I said hello. It took her a second before she placed me.

Amazingly, not only was she still hiking, but she had kept up with us— she had to have been covering 40 km a day!— and in fact, had arrived in León a few hours earlier than we had! I forced a smile, feeling suddenly self-conscious in front of my fat mountain bike with the granny seat, and in my diaper-ish bicycle pants. In two minutes, I went from feeling like a lean cross-country cyclist to being a sunburned codger.

After she sauntered on—off the trail, she evidently shifted to a lower gear—I saw Gert, the Belgians' mother, and then the rest of the Belgians coming out of the cathedral. They looked at the sky too.

"It's a forest fire," Gert explained. "We saw some flames on the way here."[274]

"If the fire spreads, we aren't sure yet if we are going to be able to keep going tomorrow," added Jean.

The parents looked anxious; the kids, not so much, as bits of ash fell around us like gray snowflakes.

---

274   In the summer of 2012, Spain had its worst fires in almost 20 years—over 1,400 square kilometers (550 square miles), which authorities blamed in part on unusually wet winters that had encouraged the growth of underbrush, and a major decline in the sheep population, which had fallen by more than a quarter in the prior four years. More brush minus sheep plus hot temperatures minus forest rangers (the government cut back on forest management after the financial crisis) equals more forest fires.

August 21. León, 0 km

Welcome to the Hotel Santiago, such a lovely place...

"*REST DAY!!*" wrote Thea. "*This morning we woke up at like 10:00 and went down for breakfast. They had really good food and Charlotte drank about two liters of coffee.*"

After the bunkhouse in Sahagún with its open dormitory and vinyl mattresses like plus-size car seats, our hotel in León felt positively luxurious. It was an old building with yellow walls, high ceilings, and lots of dark wood antiques, decorated in a Hollywood-Spanish, Man of La Mancha style.

Spain does much less of this style of decorating now that the Franco years are behind it, but when the country was trying to pull itself together after the civil war, the government saw tourist kitsch like this as a strategic commodity. In a 1953 competition for ideas on how to promote Spain to tourists, one contestant wrote:

> the tourist wants amenities and ease of travel, comfort in hotels, good food at the restaurant, better wine, and espanolads [a usually derogatory term for any cliché of Spanishness]: bulls, dance, Flamenco, singing, Gypsies ... We must resign ourselves, where tourism is concerned, to being a country of pandereta [tambourines].

Even before the war, the country had tried fairly hard to cash in on its *espanolads*. In 1928, King Alfonso XIII converted a number of old castles and monasteries into posh hotels. Later, after the civil war, Franco added many more monuments to the chain, including several along the Camino de Santiago.

One of the grandest of the *Paradores de Turismo de España*, as the government-owned chain is called, is the five-star Hostal de San Marcos in León, the former clubhouse of the old Order of Santiago, a pile so impressive that during the Renaissance, members supposedly boasted that their palace was as fine as the king's in Madrid.

The Hostal was built long after the Order's crusading days, in the first half of the 16th century, when the Order had evolved into an aristocratic honor society, like an Order of the Garter (Velasquez, for example, was a member). Commissioned by Ferdinand, Isabella's other half, to replace the Order's collapsing medieval home, the Hostal is considered one of the best examples of the Plateresque (in the manner of a silversmith), a style of carved stonework that covers a building's entire exterior with intricate raised reliefs. If you can imagine a waffle iron a city block long that incorporates a clock tower, a church covered with scallop shells, scenes from Spanish history, and an unusually buff Santiago Matamoros, you have a fair picture of the San Marcos façade.[275]

We visited the Hostal late that morning. The San Marcos is pretty nice still—we walked through the majestic, red-carpeted halls before being quickly shooed out. The Parador people have done the old palace up up in an Eloise of the Park Plaza-meets-Velasquez style that we mostly liked. Something about combining luxury with monasticism seemed odd to me, but perhaps this does capture the true spirit of the original lodgers, who were, after all, basically just pirates with a purpose.

Over the years, the palace has hosted some famous guests. In 1639, after a lifetime of making enemies, the ornery, hard-drinking Francisco de Quevedo, a member of the Order of Santiago and one of Spain's literary heavyweights, was locked up here on unspecified charges, left to rot for three and a half years, and then just as mysteriously released. Even then, nobody bothered to explain why they had arrested him—the government just said

---

275 Actually, it's not Santiago – it's Saint Isadore, whose tomb is inside the complex—in a Matamoros pose. To liven things up, saints in Spain occasionally traded poses and outfits. Besides being confusing, the effect is also a little unsettling, like seeing Lucy in Charlie Brown's shirt.

they had locked him up "for a serious reason."[276]

During the civil war too, the palace had many distinguished involuntary visitors, among them León's most famous modern writer, Victoriano Crémer. He wrote a fictionalized account of the experience in his 1981 novel, *The Book of San Marco*, in which he recalled how he and his fellow inmates began each day at 6 a.m. with 600 seconds in the central courtyard, during which time they had to wash their utensils, drink as much water as they could from the horse trough, run to the filthy latrines, and get back to their cells before the guards and militiamen came into the courtyard, swinging their rifles like maces.

During the war, you didn't have to be a writer or even particularly political to win a stay at the San Marcos. In Crémer's time, the San Marcos was a much less exclusive club than in Quevedo's. From July 1936 to 1940, up to 6,700 men were imprisoned there—nearly 16,000 in all. Many didn't survive: 791 were shot and 1563 "walked" out of the prison ("paseado"), which generally meant being taken to the country and shot. Another 598 disappeared.

When it came to picking their enemies, the Fascists tended to be fairly ecumenical:

> If you had taken part in any movement that wasn't purely Spanish, whether it was vegetarianism, learning Esperanto, teaching in a Montessori school, or joining a Rotary club, you were immediately suspect. Just wearing a red necktie could be considered a sign of Communist leanings and cause for arrest. In León, one

---

276 Quevedo is not the jolliest. One of his most famous poems, "¡Ah de la vida...!" (Hello, Life) begins:

> Hello there, life! Is there no-one answering me?
> Come back those past years that I have lived!

One of the more surprising people influenced by Quevedo was William Carlos Williams. Williams (who was part Puerto Rican and spoke fluent Spanish) loved Quevedo, and with his mother even translated a novel once attributed to him. Like Williams, Quevedo was a minimalist who worked "to attain a surface simplicity that was actually charged with subtle, unexpected encodings of wit," as the critic Julio Marzan puts it, and Marzan argues he gave Williams an important model for his own work. Marzan makes the case that the flat haiku-ish tone Williams developed, which we generally associate with American modernism, is actually something he picked up from the Baroque master by counting syllables rather than stresses. Who knew so much depended on a red-nosed poet?

man was denounced by an informer for having attended a lecture on Darwin's theory of evolution and asked questions that sounded knowledgeable. He was shot...

Other victims were simply poor. On the whole, the fascists "regarded the Spanish proletariat in the same way as they did the Moroccan, as an inferior race that had to be subjugated by sudden, uncompromising violence," as the historian Paul Preston puts it.

Once the civil war was over and all possible scores settled, you would think the Fascists would want to put this episode behind them as quickly as possible, but that didn't happen with the San Marco, which Franco & Co. didn't get around to converting into a parador until the 1960s. Why it took

The San Marco

so long, I'm not sure. It may just take a lot of scrubbing to convert a prison and torture chamber into a 220-plus-room luxury hotel. Even then, they reportedly weren't able to sand all the prisoners' carved initials off the cloister walls. We didn't see any of those initials on our quick stroll around the building, but then again nobody pointed them out.[277]

---

277   Little information about this is available in English yet beyond a few newspaper stories about outraged travelers who tried to post information about the San Marcos' history on Tripadvisor and Booking.com but had their posts blocked by the booking agencies when their comments snagged trip wires intended to block hate speech. "Never forget" may be the best motto, but if you're trying to fill rooms and sell tapas, "Try not to remember" seems to be the rule. To be fair, however, the Parador people are trying to be more open about San Marcos' past now than when we were there. Their website now mentions that the hotel was a concentration camp during the civil war, and in 2013, the hotel hosted a conference by a local group, AERLE (Association of Studies on Repression in León) to present its new book on San Marcos, *El Campo de Concentración desconocido* (*The Unknown Concentration Camp*).

August 22. León to Santa Catalina de Somoza, 60 km

In which Santiago almost meets his match.

The next day we were back on the road.

We didn't make very good time that day. First, we started late—no one wanted to skip the hotel's nice breakfast. Then, the suburbs went on forever. The yellow arrows were also sloppier here, and less reliable—one even led us off the trail to a shop. And to top everything off, I had another flat—I now led the family 3-0:

"Dad's tire popped again so we only got to Astorga for lunch at like 4:00," Thea wrote. "When we got there we went to a bar that turned out to be really expensive. They charged us 7.00 for a plate of chips. Anyway we were all in really bad moods."

After our potato chip feast, we left our bikes in the hotel bar's courtyard and walked across the street to the big brick cathedral. The cathedral had a nave with a ceiling upholstered in brightly painted angels' heads that look like little buttons, and a remarkable Baroque bas-relief in the entrance of an angry Jesus chasing the money changers out of the temple. By now, we were used to seeing Matamoros slaying Moors, but we had not seen this scene in a Spanish church before, which included a larger-than-life relief of Jesus swinging a cat o' nine tails over his shoulder, raining punishment on a bunch of cowering Jews.[278]

Like the Santiago Matamoros action figures, this scene was sculpted in the 17th century, long after the people being per-

---

278 Ironically, the original money changers in the Temple were also part of a pilgrimage: they sold special Holy Shekels used to pay Temple fees to the hunderds of thousands of pilgrims who would travel to Jerusalem from all over Palestine and beyond to take part in one of the great feast days.

secuted had been banished—nearly 200 years after the expulsion of the Jews in 1492.[279]

The anti-Semitic virus arrived relatively late in Spain. The first serious outbreak came in June 1391, when an archdeacon inspired a mob in Seville to burn down a Jewish neighborhood to punish them for some imaginary crimes. From there, the destruction spread all over Andalusia, Valencia, Aragon, Catalonia, and the Balearic Islands. These pogroms were destructive and violent enough—in Castile, around 25,000 of the 200,000 Jews died or ran

Now the other cheek--

away—that many of the Jews who remained converted to Christianity. In Castile, about half of the 200,000 Jews became Christian. In the end, the kingdom had 100,000 Jewish *conversos* (converts) and 75,000 practicing Jews.

But paranoia is a gift that keeps on giving, and in 1412, fearing that the Jews would tempt the conversos to return to their old faith, Queen Catherine of Lancaster, an Englishwoman who had become the ruler of Castile after the death of her husband, Henry III, ordered Jews to wear a distinctive yellow garment and live in ghettos that were to be locked at night. Jews were not allowed to eat dinner with Christian friends, employ Christian servants or practice a variety of professions—all measures intended to thwart relationships with Christians.

279   I am assuming the money changers are supposed to be Jewish not because of any distinctive features but because the stereotype of Jews and Conversos as being all merchants and money changers was a big part of the anti-Semitic literature at this time, in such books as the wildly popular Sentinel against the Jews stationed in the Tower of the Church of God, written by a Franciscan Friar named Francisco de Torrejoncillo and published in 1674.

By the mid-1400s, the attitudes and rules about Jewish-Christian contact relaxed once more, but the fraternization between conversos and Jews began to worry some of the people who now called themselves Old Christians. Some Old Christians, feeling threatened by the rising New Christians, began to claim, sometimes with justification, that the conversos weren't the genuine article. They invented a new term of abuse for the New Christians, *marranos* (swine) and started thinking that Old Christian blood could be made impure by intermarriage with the New.[280]

Eventually, these lingering fears led Pope Sixtus IV to authorize Ferdinand and Isabella to appoint inquisitors to interrogate conversos and ferret out any backsliders. As tends to be the case with a dutiful investigative body invested with absolute power, the inquisitors found what they had been asked to find. Between 1485 and 1501, over 2,000 conversos were burnt at the stake, many under the watchful eye of Tomás de Torquemada, the Grand Inquisitor.

Torquemada, a clergyman whose grandparents may have been Jewish, was supposedly one of the key people who convinced Isabella and Ferdinand that they needed to expel the Jews. The monarchs themselves weren't anti-Semitic (after all, Ferdinand's mother was part Jewish, according to Castro) or particularly bloodthirsty (Isabella didn't even like bullfights) but several factors may have persuaded them that Torquemada was right.[281]

Constantinople had fallen to Muslims 40 years before, and the Turks were making inroads in North Africa. Muslim pirates conducted regular raids, and the government worried that the Muslims and the Jews would undermine the Most Catholic kingdom.

---

280 In 1449, Toledo had its first pogrom against conversos, which the government followed up with a law restricting anyone with Jewish ancestry from becoming a public official, encouraging the permanent isolation of Jews and conversos alike. Candidates seeking admission to religious orders or important positions in the Church began to be required to prove they had no Jewish ancestors.

281 The other big event of that year, 1492, may have also involved a converso: there is some evidence that Christopher Columbus had a Jewish background and may have had some Jewish crew members. They sailed west in August 1492, the same month as the Jews were ferried out of Spain. Simon Wiesenthal, the Nazi hunter, wrote a book about it.

Ironically, Isabella and Ferdinand's conquest of Granada in 1492 and the repression of the conversos, rather than ease their anxieties, made them even more anxious that the Muslims might rebel. To top off these concerns, an idea had also filtered down from north of the Pyrenees that the stability of a country depended on religious and ethnic homogeneity.

Beyond all those political considerations, the Most Catholic Monarchs seem to have been persuaded that expelling the Jews who would not convert was also the right thing to do for religious reasons.[282]

One Jewish scholar predicted, correctly, that the expulsion of the Jews wouldn't end the troubles of the conversos. "The Gentiles will always revile them, plot against them and falsely accuse them in matters of faith; they will always suspect them as judaizers, especially in our time, when the smoke of the *autos de fe* has risen towards the sky in all the realms of Spain," wrote Isaac Arama.

The later drama with the Muslims played out in a similar way, but at a faster and bloodier pace. No sooner had the Catholic Monarchs given Muslim Spaniards the choice of baptism or the sword than the powers that be started to worry that the conversions the threat had inspired weren't sincere. Nor did baptism turn Muslim Spaniards into standard-issue Castillians in other respects, as the Catholic Monarchs seem to have imagined it would. For one thing, the Moriscos ("little Moors," as the Old Christians called the converts) still spoke Arabic. Many also still behaved and dressed differently than Christian Spaniards.[283] Fearful of an uprising, the Inquisition began investigating informants' tips that neighbors had been engaged in such notoriously Muslim behavior as washing their hair or eating couscous—and when that did not cool down the paranoia, eventually resorted

---

282   The ignorant mob usually gets the bad press it deserves, but I think we often go too easy on ignorant rulers.

283   Spanish Muslim men sometimes wore turbans and caftans or dressed like Christian Spaniards. The women wore pantaloons, bright colors, henna tattoos, and a lot of jewelry. As is usually the case when it comes to sizing up the Other, Christian observers believed the Muslim women to be sex-obsessed and well, kind of hot.

to increasingly vicious repression.[284]

Later in the century, Philip II tried to make all these cultural differences illegal, but his attempt to ban Arabic and almost everything Arabic- and Muslim-related triggered a violent uprising and guerrilla war in Granada, and eventually, the deaths of and expulsion of thousands of Arabic-speaking Spaniards.

The intolerance in the court and the cathedral doesn't seem to have extended to the street. In fact, from the 14th century onward, the Spanish Church seems to have had to work hard to keep up the animus against Jews and Muslims—directly through the Inquisition and the genealogy obsession and more indirectly through the Santiago Matamoros cult. As Matthew Carr writes in *Blood & Faith: The Purging of Muslim Spain 1492-1614*:

> The Church might prohibit Christians from buying meat from Muslim butchers, but such meat was sometimes cheaper, and Christians bought it anyway. Muslim builders and craftsmen built churches and cathedrals, and Muslim and Jewish doctors tended Christian patients. Muslim gambled and got drunk with Chris-

---

284 But people kept resisting. One of the more imaginative counter-punches occurred in Granada, the old capital of Muslim Spain (Al Andalus), a few years before the final expulsions.

In 1588, a mysterious box was discovered in the minaret of an old mosque (Torre Turpiana) in Granada that was being demolished to make way for the new cathedral. The inventory included a handkerchief that supposedly belonged to the Virgin Mary, a bone of Saint Stephen the Apostle, and most importantly, a parchment in Latin, Arabic and Castillian that seemed to prove that Christianity had been in Granada much longer than anyone had previously believed.

A few years after this event, between 1595 and 1599, several more mysterious manuscripts, the so-called Lead Books of Sacromonte, were discovered in a cave in the hill of Valparaiso, near Granada, all of which offered various proofs that Arabs and Jews were part of God's plan. Some of the books were supposedly written by the first bishop of Granada, Saint Cecilio, and his brother Saint Tesifón. Another recorded the sayings of Mary. The largely Arabic text made the case that Arabs were excellent people, religiously speaking. The book on Mary included a dialogue between Peter and Mary in which Mary prophesizes that Allah had planned a special role for the Arabs in the Last Days on account of their knowledge of Arabic, which she describes as the best language in the world, as superior as the sun is over the stars. Like other false relics and chronicles that were turning up at the time, the motive behind the Lead Books (which are now believed to have been created by a Jesuit who was possibly from a converso family), was to invent a past for Spain that included "Arabs who were liberated from Islam, and Jews who were freed from responsibility for the death of Christ...", according to Mercedes Garcia-Arenal Rodriquez and Fernando Rodriguez Mediano.

Amazingly, thanks to the pride of the local church and the excitement of the country generally at finding these relics, it took 83 years before the Church ruled that the documents were forged.

tians in taverns. They worked alongside each other in the fields and sometimes in the urban workplace.[285]

Even in 1486, six years before the expulsion of the Jews and the final defeat of Granada, the last remnant of *Al Andalus*, many Christians, Muslims, and Jews were still living together fairly peaceably, just as they had for hundreds of years.

Some surviving records suggest that a number of people remained tolerant even after the Muslims and Jews were expelled. In the 1620s, a woman of Muslim origin believed that "the Muslim can be saved in his faith as the Jew can in his." One Christian peasant believed that "everyone can find salvation in his own faith," while another told the inquisitors that "Jews who observe their law can be saved."

This attitude was widespread, historian Henry Kamen writes, "and could be found in every corner of Spain and every inlet of the Mediterranean, so much so that we can almost regard it as a commonplace of rural philosophy in southern Europe." Other peasants were skeptical of religion altogether, or at least Christianity. "I care nothing for the gospels," said a resident of Cuenca in 1490. Another said, "I swear to God it's a fraud, from the pope to the cope!"[286]

Many upper-class people also opposed what we would now call Spain's ethnic cleansing —the expulsion of the Jews in the 1490s, the suppression of Arabic culture in the 1500s, and the cruel and bloody expulsion of the Moors (Moriscos) in 1609– 1614. Catholic aristocrats had often oppressed and exploited Jews and Muslims in all the usual ways, but they generally made money off them too, which fostered some degree of loyalty. (One proverb had it that "he who has a Moor has gold.") When the repressions began in earnest, many landlords tried to stop the

---

285   In 1322 and 1323, church councils in Valadolid and Toledo complained that Christians, Jews, and Muslims kept attending each other's marriages and funerals, and that Christian women were inviting their Jewish and Muslim friends to Mass. As late as 1486, Ferdinand had to order the Christians in the town of Tortosa to stop allowing Muslims to use their church for their services.

286   The silk mantel priests often wore.

government from harassing *their* Jews and *their* Moors.

As is often the case with a crime, the impulse to justify it didn't end when the last boat left. The bas-relief of Jesus chasing the money changers that we were looking at now had been executed more than a hundred years after any Jews lived on Astorga's Jew Street, long after the expulsions, as if the Church desperately wanted to convince somebody of something. Cybèle said it reminded her of the Confederate statues in the American South, which were mostly erected long after the Civil War was over.[287]

Another sign that not everybody was thrilled with the Jewish and Muslim expulsions is that just a few years later, Santiago almost lost his job to the granddaughter of a converted Jew.

In the 1620s, although he was still winning victories in the Americas and now in Asia, back in Spain, the Moor Killer had started to seem old fashioned to many Spaniards, who argued that Spain now needed a patron saint with a different skill set, as the corporate people would say now—a better secretary of Hispanic affairs in Heaven, to paraphrase Amerigo Castro.

One name that came up on everyone's short list was Teresa of Avila, according to Castro:

> There was much to be said in support of this imaginative idea.
> Teresa was Spanish; she belonged to modern times; she had been
> personally known to many people still alive; she understood the
> current politics and social problems of Spain; she had brilliant
> administrative ability and a good business head. She had been
> affectionately kind-hearted; she could laugh; she could tease and
> scold. And she was greatly loved. Images and pictures of her were
> to be seen almost everywhere, both in churches and private houses.

---

287   Nor did their semi-final solution put an end to Spanish racial anxieties. Instead, the length of time a family had been Christian became a key status question, and people would even be categorized as one-quarter or one-eighth New Christian, for example. That led to an overlap between religious and racial identities that would plague Spain well into the 19th century and then fester again under Franco in the 20th, with far-reaching consequences for the culture. Castro claims that fear of the Inquisition stunted Spanish intellectual life to such a degree that "not to think or learn or read" became habitual for Spaniards who faced the "sadism and lust for plunder of those of the Holy Office." Even today, the Order of Santiago, for example, is open only to a practicing Catholic who descends from two generations of legitimate forbears and has no non-Christian ancestors.

Not only had Teresa been an effective reformer of the Carmelite order, but it was accepted as fact that she had gotten Philip II sprung from the torments of Purgatory in only a week, which seems to have been a celestial record. Supporters argued that, as a woman, she would be a more persuasive advocate for the Spanish than Santiago. God would have to grant her petitions or "Christ himself would blush with shame to see her denied."

In addition to the gender advantage, Teresa was quite eloquent— her autobiography is said to be the most widely read classic in Spain after *Don Quixote*[288] —and people felt they knew her, from her books and from her good works.

Teresa was born in Avila in 1515. Her paternal grandfather had run into troubles with the Inquisition at one point for allegedly returning to Judaism, but her father had assimilated more successfully. Teresa herself was ambitiously Catholic from an early age. At 7, she ran away from home with her little brother Rodrigo seeking martyrdom among the Moors, but an uncle spotted the two kids outside the town walls and brought them home.

Later, as a Carmelite nun, Teresa became a renowned mystic. She did not practice "calm me down so I don't quit my day job" meditation, but something much more dramatic. During one of these encounters, people even reported seeing her levitate. At times, her descriptions of these states read more like *Fifty Shades of Jesus* than a typical devotional work. For instance, in one of her visions, an angel drove the fiery point of a golden lance repeatedly through her heart, "The pain was so great, that it made me moan; and yet so surpassing was the sweetness of this excessive pain, that I could not wish to be rid of it..."[289]

When she died in 1582, Teresa was already one of Spain's most famous writers, and after her death, her fame continued to grow.

---

288 I haven't read it yet but it does start out promisingly:

If I had not been so wicked, the possession of devout and God-fearing parents, together with the favour of God's grace, would have been enough to make me good.

289 This isn't an original observation, by the way; take a look sometime at Bernini's aptly titled Saint Teresa in Ecstasy.

In 1614, the pope beatified her,[290] and her order, the Barefoot Carmelites, nominated her to become the co-patron saint of Spain. Philip III liked the idea too, and in 1618, he made it official. Once Pope Gregory XV had made her a full saint in 1622, and the next pope, Urban VIII, had named her a second patron saint of Spain, her elevation should have been complete.

But it wasn't. Although Philip's and Urban's pronouncements were both careful to say Teresa's promotion did not mean any loss of status or power for Santiago (or an end to the Voto, which was threatened in this same period) many Santiago partisans— who were particularly numerous in the Church hierarchy—were outraged. For several years after the decree, a battle raged between pro-Santiago and the pro-Teresa factions in the court and Church. On the one side was a group that tended to be suspicious of conversos generally, and on the other, a group of supporters that included many conversos, who had provided financial support to her order from the beginning.

The poet Quevedo was among those who didn't think much of the decision to elevate Teresa. How could you go on pleading for Santiago's help after you've asked him to hand his sword to Saint Teresa? And wouldn't this make the other saints anxious, particularly as sainthood often ran in families? For instance, wouldn't Saint Eugenio, patron of Toledo, worry that his nephew Saint Ildofonso might go after his job? Or Saint Isidore, patron of Seville, feel threatened by his older brother, Saint Leander?

Other Santiago supporters feared that the Spanish had annoyed their Son of Thunder (one of the saint's nicknames), who was known for his bad temper. After all, terrible things had started happening around the time the Barefoot Carmelites began their campaign to promote Teresa to patroness—earthquakes, floods, treasure ships sunk, and battles lost. And who knew how Teresa felt about the appointment? Maybe she was annoyed too. Maybe, instead of gaining a second patron, the Spanish had acciden-

---

290   Beatified is one step away from canonization. You are not quite a saint yet, but you're on your way—a two-star general, say. Technically, it represents public recognition by the pope that you are in heaven and now have the capacity to intercede on behalf of individuals.

tally enraged two powerful saints.

Under pressure from the Spanish Church hierarchy and the Order of Santiago, Philip III's son Philip IV asked the pope to reconsider. In 1630, bowing to the royal will, Urban VIII decreed that Teresa needed to be accepted as a patron saint only in localities where she had already been elected to the post. In the end, despite what the people and even the king had wanted, Teresa maintained her official status as co-patron only among the Carmelites, while the bishops all stuck by Santiago.

Saint Teresa says more tears are shed over answered prayers than unanswered prayers, and I think that may be the case with the restoration of Santiago as Spain's supreme patron saint.

The bishops' preservation of Santiago—and not incidentally, the Voto that went along with it—helped them to hang onto their possessions much longer than in many parts of Europe. At its peak, the Church owned 20 percent of Spain's arable land and produced 25 percent of its agricultural products. The government only began confiscating the church's land in the 18th century and broke the Voto in the 19th century.[291]

This meant that medieval glory wasn't a distant memory to the Spanish Church in the 20th century. Even in the 1920s and 1930s, Franco wasn't the only Spaniard who spent a lot of time

---

291   Of course, it almost goes without saying that the poor peasants who had worked the church lands went right on plowing—but now for the larger landowners to whom the government had auctioned off the monastic estates. The Voto finally ended, however, in 1834, during the regency of Maria Cristina. Even then, two bishops protested, although many people knew the practice was based on a fraud. The bishop of Barcelona argued that the archbishop of Santiago needed the money to support a variety of good works, while the bishop of Cordoba made the interesting and, to an American ear, familiar claim that the reasons the Voto had started didn't matter now because it had been the law for such a long time.

daydreaming about the good old days. Years before Franco came to power, the clergy already tended to see any politics that might further erode Church privileges as the devil's work, as this 1929 catechism suggests:

> Q. What kind of sin is liberalism?
>
> A. A very serious sin against the faith.
>
> Q. Is it licit for a Catholic to call himself liberal?
>
> A. No, sir.
>
> Q. May Catholics approve of liberalism in whole or in part, taking the name of 'Catholic-liberals'?
>
> A. No, sir, because Catholics may not approve in whole or in part of what the Church has condemned.
>
> Q. What kind of sin is it to vote for a liberal at elections?
>
> A. Usually a mortal sin.

I suspect the Church's grievance over its lost possessions also reinforced its tendency to view any disagreement as an ethnic and religious dispute. For example, when relations between striking coal miners north of Astorga and the government turned violent in the early 1930s, the Church blamed the strife on people who were not "pure" Catholic Spaniards. During a serious strike in the province of Asturias in October 1934, Juan Bautista Luis y Pérez, the bishop of Oviedo, charged in a pastoral letter that the strike of 20–30,000 miners had been "organized by the Jews and Freemasons."[292]

Nor when the full civil war broke out two years later did the Church mince words about what had to be done. Communism was a gangrene that needed to be cauterized "without compas-

---

292 These attitudes seem to have been quite deep-seated in the Spanish Church. Around this time too, a Jesuit magazine published a translation of the *Protocols of the Elders of Zion*, the notorious, fraudulent Russian document that purported to be the Jewish plan for global domination. But to be fair, the Spanish Jesuits weren't alone. In the late 1920s, Henry Ford printed 500,000 copies of the Protocols and only toned down the anti-Semitism in his newspaper, *The Dearborn Independent*, after a group of Hollywood studio heads threatened to start running pictures of car crashes in every newsreel.

sion and if necessary mutilate all that is not purely Catholic and Spanish," wrote Father J. M. Remesal, S.J.

The Francoists also pushed hard for that old-time religion. Antonio Vallejo-Nagera, head of psychiatric services for Franco's armies, even thought they needed to bring back the Inquisition. "The blood of the inquisitors flows in our veins and inquisitorial chromosomes are in our paternal and maternal genes ... Those who wish can label us reactionaries ... Nothing will halt our impulse to resurrect the Tribunal of the Holy Inquisition."

Logically enough, defenders of the Spanish Republic saw the Spanish Church as a reactionary institution in league with Franco. When the war began, Republican mobs attacked the Church in all kinds of ways. A number of towns named after saints changed their name; for a time, San Fulgencia del Segura became Ukrania del Segura. Some revolutionaries wouldn't say "adios" because of the "Dio" in the word. Churches were burned, relics ransacked. In Lepe, Andalusia, rioters took a statue of the Virgin and "pulled out her eyes, stripped off her clothes and jewels, shot her, chopped her into pieces and threw these into the river."

And they did much worse: In a violent frenzy during the first two months of the civil war, people killed 3,400 clerics, and by the end of the war, 4,184 clergy in total, including 12 bishops, 2,365 monks, and 283 nuns.

Francoists blamed Marxists and the ever-useful international Jewish conspiracy for the anticlericalism but in fact, hatred of the Church was a deep-rooted tradition. A collection of Castilian proverbs published in 1627—the year before the court concluded that the *Voto de Santiago* was a fraud—included 300 proverbs about the clergy, almost all of them hostile: "To have a clean home, build no dovecotes and avoid priests"; "a priest without children is a priest without testicles"; "the love of a nun is the same thing as a fart."

Historians have proposed several causes for the depth of anticlerical rage. Perhaps the biggest is that the social contract had always tended to run in one direction, according to historian

Sanie Eleanor Holguin:

> The Church controlled the educational system, but the "policy of
> the religious orders in the early nineteenth century had been to
> prevent the poor from learning to read"; their fervent antiliberal-
> ism isolated middle-class Spaniards from the teachings available
> in the rest of western Europe. The Spanish church rejected any
> ideas associated with Enlightenment education and seriously dis-
> couraged importing any of the scientific and educational trends
> that were then emanating from northern and western Europe.

As late as 1930, roughly 30 percent of Spaniards still did not
know how to read. By contrast, in France, since the 1890s, that
figure had been less than 10 percent.

Deepening the working class's alienation even more was the fact
that many had very little contact with priests, particularly in the
southern part of the country and in urban working class neigh-
borhoods. Churches were state funded during this period, and
the government had been slow to open new parishes in poorer
places where the population had grown. State subsidies to the
Church had also shrunk, which served to make the church even
more distant. It also didn't help that the bishops were highly
educated aristocrats who had little in common with the priests,
most of whom had only a high school education.

By the 1890s, churches were usually empty—in some places,
only 5 percent of the people went to Mass and most died without a last confession. Ordinary people saw the local priest as little more than "a public functionary who collects from his parish-
ioners for conducting baptisms, marriages, and funerals." One
official report talked about a priest who spent his days alone in
his rectory—"not even the devil called ... no one ever appeared
even by mistake."

Yet although people did not know them well, the clergy remained
very visible— conspicuous strangers who lived apart from the
community and dressed distinctively, a combination that made
them easy to find and easy to scapegoat: "Cassock we see, cassock we kill."

During the civil war, the attackers sometimes spared rich land-owners but seldom priests. Ordinary priests were comparative strangers who had little to bargain with, as the state paid them less than the minimum wage for a factory worker, and Republicans do not seem to have thought of them as much more than parasites. One investigator found that, when asking who had been killed in the terror, witnesses would often list the victims in their community and then add in a matter-of-fact way, "Er—oh yes! The priest as well."

Often, the anticlericalism doesn't even seem to have been personal. The historian Julio de la Cueva recounts a reminiscence of one revolutionary who killed his own parish priest:

> "I killed, among others, Father Domingo, at Alcaniz."
> "Dear me! And why did you kill him?'
> "It's quite simple. Because he was a priest."
> "But then, did Father Domingo meddle in politics or have personal enemies?"
> "No sir, Father Domingo was a very good man. But we had to kill all the priests."

Persecution of the Church ended with the fall of the Spanish Republic, of course, but other kinds of religious tolerance took a few more decades to arrive in Spain. In 1967, a law granting religious liberty went into effect, and in 1968, the Franco regime repealed the 1492 Edict of Expulsion of the Jews. But even under democracy, relations with Jews have not always been easy. In 1986 (the same year Spain established diplomatic relations with Israel), 46 percent of Spaniards rated Jews unfavorably. Today, that's fallen to 19 percent, about average for Europe. Unfavorable views of Muslims stand at 42 percent.

August 23. Santa Catalina de Somoza to Villa-franca del Bierzo, 56 km

"E ultreïa, E susseïa!"
— Old French pilgrim greeting (roughly, "Upward, farther!")

We started early.

Cybèle had warned me that it would be a hard day. Before we left the hostel, she showed me *Kapitan Pedales*'s helpful elevation map, which had been more or less flat the past four or five stages but today looked like the Manhattan skyline. Santa Catalina de Somoza means "Saint Catalina Under-the-Mountains," and we had to get up and over these obstacles to get to Galicia, a climb of about 1,000 meters.

I didn't like the look of that but I was glad that we were almost in Galicia. This meant that we were getting close—260 kilometers to go, to be precise — and I couldn't wait to get off the bike, particularly after my latest flat tire. Collectively, we were getting better at bicycling, but I had fallen toward the back of the class, and Cybèle had compounded my humiliation by insisting that she take one of my panniers, reasoning that maybe it was the combined weight of the bags plus my backpack plus me that my tires couldn't withstand.

We were heading into wilder country now. You could even see it on the map in the names of the towns we would be passing through: Rabanal (Field of Radishes); Cruz de Fierro (Iron Cross); El Acebo (the Holly); Ponferrada (Iron Bridge); Molinaseca (Dry Mill); Villafranca del Bierzo (Foreignerstown of the Bierzo); O Cebreiro (The Wild Donkey); Triacastela (Three Castles); Portomarin (Sailor's Bay); Melide (the Farm of Mellitus); and Lavacolla (Wash Your Ass), the last stop before Santiago de Compostela.

The first few hours were flat and civilized— it was a beautiful morning! — but then we began a slow and steady climb. As we pedaled, we left the fields behind and moved up into fir trees and dry scrub. There was a bit of haze but the smoke from the forest fire was mostly gone now, and you could see all the way from our highway, the LE-141, to some fairly distant hills.

Further up, we came to the village of Rabanal, which looks like an ordinary Spanish village set on a 20-degree angle. After Rabanal, the landscape began to get colder, steeper, and foggy. As the Cycling Pilgrim notes with some understatement, "it is *seriously* <u>uphill for the 11km or so from Rabanal</u> ..."

We kept pedaling for as long as we could, but every other kilometer or so everyone but Thea would give up and walk for a little while. "Hard-going, wearisome mountains," is how Picaud describes the Serra de Ancares in the original pilgrim's guide, and it's still true.

In the old days, we might have hired a Maragato and his mule train to help us. The Maragatos lived in the region around Astorga (including Santa Catalina) and specialized in driving mules between Galicia and points east – León to begin with, but eventually as far as Madrid. For the most part, they hauled dried fish, wine, and sometimes gold dust from Galicia and returned from the plains bearing sausages and ham. They held that franchise for at least 400 years, until the railroads came in, and once you've tried pedaling up those hills, it's easy to see why they didn't have much competition.

Although Maragotos had a reputation for being honest and trustworthy, they were still considered one of the Cursed Peoples (*Pueblos Maleditas*) – a category that included the Cagots (Agotes),[293] the Xuetes of Majorca, the Vaqueiros of Alzada, the Mercheros, the Gypsies (Roma), Muslims, and of course Jews – groups who for one reason or another didn't quite fit into Ferdinand and Isabella's vision of a united, homogenous and Catholic Spain.

The Maragatos are an interesting group in that like the Cagots it's hard to figure out what people found so different about them.

---

293 The French untouchables we met earlier, outside Montréal-du-Ger.

They are Catholic. They speak the same Spanish dialect that is spoken all over the province of León. They look like other northern Spaniards (though this didn't stop nineteenth century scientists from measuring their skulls). Physically, their main distinction seems to be their unusual traditional dress – the men wear black suits with colorful vests, and the women wear a similar

Rabanal

outfit, but with chunky metal jewelry.[294] They have some special customs, too, including the highly suspect habit of eating their soup for the second course instead of the first.[295]

Yet for hundreds of years, Castilian Spain has struggled to place them. Celt? Visigoth? Moor? In the eighteenth century, a monk tried to prove they were Berbers. In the nineteenth century, someone else insisted they were Jews. Nor have people still quite given up. Geneticists have proven only negatives — they don't seem to be Basque or Galician or North African. Their name is now believed to go back to Mercator, or Merchant, but that's related to their muleteering. Who they were and where they were from before they settled in eastern León, nobody knows. The truth seems to be more along the lines of what one slightly exasperated Maragato told a reporter in 2003, "There have been too many myths about us," he said. "We are like any other Spaniards."[296]

In the end, the more important mystery may not be the ancestry of the Maragatos as why the idea of them and their fellow "Cursed Peoples" bothered the Castilians so much.

Freud argues that aggression is such a part of human nature that the only way we can love each other in the aggregate is by finding a common enemy to despise – and whatever it takes, we'll

---

294 John Adams, the American founding father, was unimpressed with the Maragatos. In 1779, after his ship sprang a leak and had to land on the Spanish coast, he passed through Astorga on his trip overland to reach his diplomatic job in Paris. He liked Astorga but had a mixed opinion of the people: "Found clean beds and no fleas for the first time in Spain. Walked twice around the city... saw numbers of the Mauregato women, as fine as squaws, and a great deal more nasty; crucifixes, beads and chains, ear-rings and finger-rings, in silver, brass, glass etc. about their necks, etc."

295 After the railroad opened in 1860 and the mule trains ended, many Maragatos emigrated to León and Madrid or to Patagonia. Under Franco, they were treated as harmless, colorful holdovers from the old days – like Navajos selling trinkets in Monument Valley, say — and made money as a human tourist attraction. Only three or four thousand live in the region now, which is still known as the Maragatería. Today the few who are left seem to be cashing in on eco-tourism.

296 The only substantively distinctive thing about the Maragato culture is that back in their muleteering days, the women worked the fields while their men went off hauling and trading, a division of labor that made them much richer than the ordinary peasant. One anthropologist has noted that as with most of the Cursed Peoples, "they were considered sinful for their profit-making mentalities and great spatial mobility."

find one. Get rid of religion and nationality, he says, and people will fight over personal possessions. Get rid of possessions, they will fight over sexual loyalty. Liberate desire and who knows what they'll find to fight over, but there will be something, he concludes. Or as Stephan Zweig puts it, "each new era uncovers a fresh group of unhappy persons upon whom to empty the vials of collective hatred...some comparatively small and weak group are made targets for the annihilative energies latent in so many of us."[297]

But it may not be so random. At least along the Camino, I kept discovering that intolerance has always tended to be a pretty good business, at least for a little while. Whether you're talking about the elimination of the mentally ill or the Jews in World War II, the forced conversion of the Huguenots, the crushing of the Cathars in the Midi, the stigmatization of the Cagots, the expulsion of the Jews and the Muslims from Spain, the elimination of communists and priests in the civil war, or the discrimination against the Maragatos, in almost every case, somebody stood to make money on their repression. I suspect when you get down to it intolerance is just a specialized class of theft.

Late that morning, near the timberline, just as the highway broke out of the forest and began hugging its way along a fogged-in cliff, we stopped at a place that looked like a ski-lodge. Cars, campers, motorcycles and trailers stretched out along the highway to either side of the lone building.

The girls were happy to get a hot chocolate and warm up inside for a little while, even though the place was crowded, chock-full of shivering pilgrims in ponchos as well as ordinary tourists who had pulled over to stop for a coffee before they drove over

---

297   A Jewish Austrian writer who basically died of a broken heart in Brazil in 1942.

the pass. It felt very festive – everyone was glad to be inside the steamy lodge and out of the damp cold wind.

After our break, we bundled ourselves back in our fleeces and windbreakers, then walked our bikes through the blind turns of the winding, foggy pass. Sometimes, far below, you could see the trail where the pilgrims were climbing single file, like a mule train in bright polar fleece. At least we weren't doing that, I thought.

Not too much farther along, the road straightened out and we could get back on our bikes. A few minutes later we reached the iron cross that marks the highest point of the Camino, 1520 meters. Thousands of pilgrims have stacked rocks here and over time it has grown into something like a model of a mountain on top of a mountain. A bunch of pilgrims had stopped to take pictures of each other but as there wasn't much else there besides the rock piles, cold, and fog we didn't stay long.

Then we started downhill. We probably should have heeded the instructions of *The Cycling Pilgrim*, who in his cautionary notes about this segment warns:

> 1. from this high point to Molinaseca, and especially after El Acebo the road descends almost 1000m in about 12km. It is very steep in places, with blind hairpin bends. Make sure your brakes are in good order and avoid overheating the rims by stopping every 2-3km to check them...2. take care through the village of El Acebo – especially in wet weather. The tarmac changes to concrete at the entrance to the village with large cobblestones, and the central herringbone gutter has 'ribs' about 2m apart on either side. The surface may also be strewn with straw and dung. If in doubt – better dismount. The tarmac starts again at the end of

the village near a monument to a German pilgrim cyclist who was killed here.

We passed the hamlet of Manjarin, a cluster of souvenir stands, which maybe because of the fog reminded me of the more disreputable junkyard/saltwater taffy/live bait emporia I grew up with back in Oregon that you always hoped were fronts for some illicit business because the licit one couldn't possibly be working.

One blink later Manjarin was behind us and the highway narrowed and began winding down the mountain. The road wasn't all that steep at first, and wove downward between boulders, which with the blooming mauve heather and the fog gave the mountain the look of a Japanese garden. Then the grade started to get steeper.

Further down the hill, the white path of the Camino proper darted in and out every few hundred yards, until we came to a sign that said, in English and in Spanish

> *Pendientes Fuertes — en 15 km Circule con Precaucion*
> *Attention cylists – Outstanding Strong in 15 km*
> *Circulate with Caution*

and then a long straight hill, where we circulated cautiously, and a more substantial stone village called El Acebo.

At that point, the road began to open out into an even longer straight downward drop where you could see way down the side of the mountain toward what looked at first like other roads, but which I realized after another turn was our own road, slaloming down and down again.

Every once in a while, we could see long files of hiking pilgrims far below us, heading up or down. How the Church had talked people into doing this for a thousand years was hard to imagine.

In fact, it didn't quite: enthusiasm for the Camino tapered off during the Reformation, when Protestantism and war reduced the stream of foreign pilgrims. By the time the travel writer Richard Ford visited Santiago in the 1840s, he found that when it came to the pilgrimage, "[t]he carcass remains, but the spirit is fled." Tourists and religious people would visit the cathedral, but by 1900, only a few pilgrims would show up in Santiago every year, and it stayed that way up through the Civil War.

After the war ended, the Fascists saw an opportunity. From the days of Alfonso VI in the 11th century, the pilgrimage had always been an important symbol of the monarchy, and Franco saw some political advantages in bringing it back to life. In 1943, a Holy Year, specially chartered trains took Falange, military, and youth groups to Santiago. Over 140,000 people made the trip. In 1948, the next Holy Year,[298] half a million people visited, many of them for an August 28, 1948 jamboree organized by a right-wing group called Spanish Youth Catholic Action (JEAC) who persuaded 70,000 "Pilgrim Scouts," mostly young men, to come from all over Spain and Latin America and converge on Santiago de Compostela. These were modern *peregrinos*, however. Almost all the 1948 pilgrims reached the city by motorized transportation, with two exceptions that attracted some news coverage: a group of 288 cavalry soldiers who made the trip on horseback, stopping to pay their respects at Santiago's old imaginary stomping grounds, Clavijo, and a smaller phalanx of 120 university students, members of the Sindicato Espanol Universitario, a Falangist students' union. The students, all dressed in Falangist-blue uniforms, marched from Roncesvalles to Santiago in 33 days, backed by a large and presumably motorized support team that carried their meals and tents. The boys in blue walked the whole way, except for a little 300-kilometer stretch between Burgos and Ponferrada, where they took the train.

The rebooted pilgrimage was a hit. The director of another fascist organization said he had not heard of the pilgrimage before that expedition but was now very interested. "It is something very athletic, very Spanish, and St. James is very fascist," he said.

---

298   In 1122, Pope Calixtus II granted an indulgence to everyone who visited Santiago's shrine in any year when the Feast of Saint James, July 26, falls on a Sunday. This happens every 6,5,6, and then 11 years.

Despite its popularity, the 1948 event would be the last big pilgrimage year under Franco.[299] The Caudillo would visit Santiago again, in 1954, the next Holy Year, to give a sermon about Spain's crusading spirit and to show off his crash-renovation of Queen Isabella's old pilgrim hospital on the cathedral plaza[300] – but even with the power of the state and the Church behind him, he never did manage to revive the pilgrimage. Throughout his regime and a few years beyond it, the Camino de Santiago remained about as lively as the Oregon Trail: In 1978, the cathedral at Santiago awarded the Compostela diploma to 13 pilgrims.

A few kilometers on, we were in Molinaseca, another small town, notable mostly for a seven-arched bridge that the Romans built and several others have since rebuilt over the last two millennia, and then on to the small city of Ponferrada, an old mining town – initially gold, and more recently, coal.

We stopped for a few minutes in one of the city's main plazas, which is across from a restored Templar castle. As we drank our Cokes and admired the castle, the Italian bikers Thea had passed a few days before strolled by. "Ah!" said the guy who spoke the most English. "How is the happy family?" and we grimaced at each other. I don't think he had forgiven Thea for passing him on that hill.

It's a nice castle, with a moat, a drawbridge, battlements, the whole nine yards – 9.5 on the Errol Flynn scale, eminently swashbucklable -- but looking at it exasperated G.G. King, the intrepid

---

299   The 1948 event did have a major impact on Spain, however, in that the amount of foreign currency the Holy Year visitors brought in, aided in part by the decision to provide some stereotypically Spanish pastimes, such as bullfighting, to the mix (although bullfighting was never part of Galician culture), led the government to realize that foreign tourism could be big business for Spain.

300   The year before, he had ordered the hospital renovated as a luxury hotel, a whim that kept 2000 men busy for 11 months.

Bryn Mawr professor, who found it exasperating that we know so little about the Templars. Even answers to simple questions like, why had they ended up with this particular castle? don't have clear answers. Ostensibly, the Templars were here to guard pilgrims, but they were such serious financiers, I suspect the real reason may have had less to do with the Camino than the gold in the hills around Ponferrada, the same reason the Romans had built the seven-arched bridge: access to Las Medulas, the Romans' biggest gold mine.

We didn't get to Las Medulas – it's about 30 kilometers away from Ponferrada — but I remember seeing a bit of its red-orange length near the horizon. It's supposed to be very beautiful up close, and in pictures looks a bit like the red canyon country in Arizona or Utah. After 17 or 18 centuries, the scarred hills have worn away into a manmade natural wonder impressive enough that UNESCO named it a World Heritage Site in 1997, over the objections of Thai, German, and Finnish delegates who thought environmental destruction shouldn't be rewarded.

The main pit covers 1,879 hectares, enough room to store seven Central Parks with a little space left over. It's the largest hole ever dug without power equipment. Romans didn't have explosives or even sufficient manpower to do this much damage on their own, but they found a way to do it with a low-tech fracking technique: first, cut shafts into a mountain, then flood the shafts with huge quantities of water brought in by aqueduct. Eventually, the shafts would fill and the mountain would explode, blasting an avalanche a few kilometers long. When the mud settled, tens of thousands of men would pick over the tailings and take them to the smelter.

The smelter they used to separate the gold from the ore was also a vast, dirty operation. Hydrologists analyzing core samples of ancient ice in Greenland have found traces of lead and copper from Las Medulas. Europe would not see worse air pollution until the Industrial Revolution 1,700 years later.

Archaeologists estimate the Roman miners destroyed about 300 million tons of earth this way in order to extract 90 tons of gold, leaving the land so weakened that landslides and floods remain a problem today. Pliny the Elder, Rome's most famous naturalist, visited the site in 74 AD, and said the hills "look as if they have been half-eaten by giants."

> The mountains are bored with corridors and galleries made by lamplight with a duration that is used to measure the shifts. For months, the miners cannot see the sunlight and many of them die inside the tunnels. This type of mine has been given the name of *ruina montium*...How dangerous we have made the Earth!

At five or six, we wobbled in to Villafranca del Bierzo, yet another of the string of towns that grew up along the Camino francés. Cluny founded a monastery here in 1070, and as I mentioned earlier, other foreigners moved in after the monks. We noticed that something of the sort seems to be happening again now: a surprising number of former English, French, and German pilgrims have opened hostels and pensions in these little towns, evidently having enjoyed their pilgrimage so much they never wanted to go home or rather decided that they *were* home. As Cybèle's friend Caroline said when they got back from their four days on the Camino, "the Camino isn't a hike, it's a subculture."

I could understand that. Some of the places were kind of cozy: our hostel that night was -- a big hobbitty place built in stone and wood, its courtyard full to bursting with young backpackers. We were late and they had given our beds away in the bunkrooms but the hostess offered us a trailer in the middle of the courtyard. Not the kind of trailer that people drive to the beach and camp out in but one of those mobile sheds that contractors use to store their tools and lunch boxes. It had a missing step, six bunks, one window, and one light bulb and although it was stuffy and the girls didn't like the look of it, it was better than nothing – which was the only other option on offer that night.

Later, they sat all 40 or so of us down in a big dining room along two long wooden tables. Only three parts of the dinner have stayed with me: first, that the old man who owned the place – a Galician, I think -- had everyone hold hands for a prayer before dinner began; second, the big bowls of a delicious Galician chicken and chick pea soup, *caldo gallego*; and third, a very red-faced wino who kept lurching across the table to reach for the wine pitcher.

Something about the soup and the drunk's enthusiasm made me think of the episode in *Don Quixote* in which Sancho runs across six German pilgrims, or rather, five German pilgrims and a Morisco from his village now living in Augsburg. Ricote, the exiled shopkeeper, greets Sancho as his dear friend, his good neighbor, and his brother. He explains that he is disguised as a pilgrim in order to sneak back home to dig up a treasure he left behind in their village when he had to leave Spain.

At one point, the real pilgrims, the fake pilgrim, and Sancho all settle down for a picnic, when

> all at once, the whole squadron together raised their arms, and bottles aloft, and joining mouth to mouth, with their eyes fixed on the firmament, they seemed to take aim at heaven. In this manner, shaking their heads from side to side in token of the satisfaction they received, they continued a good while in the act of transfusing the contents of the bottles into their own bellies.

After four similarly sacramental chugs, they empty their bottles, and

> From time to time, each pilgrim in his turn shook hands with Sancho, saying, "Spaniard or German, all one, goot companion." To which compliment Sancho replied, "Good companion, by the Lord!' and [burst] out into a fit of laughter which lasted a whole hour...

August 24. Villafranca del Bierzo to Triacastela, 47.3 km

An account of the priest who resurrected the Camino.

In the morning, we pedaled first downhill through the town and then across a pretty, old bridge and out along a highway. After a few miles, we veered off to the right, up into the hills, following the signs and the occasional yellow arrow up and up and up a narrow but still paved road.

I was in a good mood: it was a sunny morning, we were getting close to the end, and to top it all off, midway through the morning, halfway up the first big hill, something wonderful happened: Thea had a flat tire! This wasn't wonderful for her or for us really, but her bad luck made me feel as if my tire curse had been lifted, or at the very least, that maybe the problem hadn't been me.

Farther up, we left the woods for some steep bare hills and muddy pastures. At one point, we had to stop and wait for a herd of cows to amble by, which they eventually did, but with a grumpier air than the flatland cows we were used to meeting.

A cow pursues Charlotte

The country was getting greener every mile now, and then we rounded one more bend and suddenly we were in Galicia, which looks more like Ireland or Brittany than Spain and feels like another country, as it easily might have been with a different roll of the dynastic dice.

I think the role of chance in life is often underrated. I know I have often thought about how slight changes in how things went would have changed everything for me —What if I had not sent a change of address post card to that gorgeous deaf artist my roommate Marc played bridge with when we moved from Avenue B to 11th Street? What if the Risk Waters group had hired me in 2001 and I had been covering their risk management conference at Windows on the World in the World Trade Center on September 11? To make matters even more frightening, it's not just our own actions that frame our destinies. We live in a world where every minute, the great if-then of life keeps changing, and Cleopatra's nose attracts or does not attract somebody who may or may not be Mark Antony.

One case in point: the fact that we were pedaling this morning through the Galician mountains, and that there were so many people on the trail near us, was due in large part to the reaction of one small boy to a school fieldtrip to the village of O Cebreiro in the mid-1940s.

It was cold and misty when we reached O Cebreiro.[301] The village of 154 people has the look of a place that is always cold and misty, and I imagine it was like that when a little Galician boy named Elias Valina Sampadero visited the half-ruined village on a school fieldtrip from nearby Sarria in the late 1940s.

As Elias and the others were shown around the old stone buildings and the old stone church, a guide told the students the strange and bloody story of the miracle of the Holy Grail of Cebreiro.

In the early 14th century, a French monk was celebrating the

---

301 From *o ezebro,* "the wild donkey," in Galician and old Portuguese. The word shares the same etymology as zebra.

Mass on a very stormy Sunday. The weather was so bad that only one person, a peasant named Barxamaior, showed up. Suddenly, as the monk said the Mass, the bread turned into actual bleeding flesh, and the wine turned to blood. The priest was so overwhelmed by the shocking miracle he fainted and died in the peasant's arms, soon to be followed by the peasant. Both were buried in the church, where the bloody relics are still preserved in reliquaries presented by Ferdinand and Isabella.[302]

Don Elias's nephew Jose Valinas, believes that his uncle decided then and there that he wanted to become the parish priest of the village, "a place so far from everything but so close to the world," because the whole world had passed through there, on its way to Santiago de Compostela.[303]

Most little boys move from one dream to another, but Elias stuck to his: he became a priest, got himself assigned to the parish of this tiny village, and in his spare time wrote a multivolume dissertation on the history of the Camino at the University of Salamanca.

The dissertation won a prize, and Don Elias was asked to join a national council of scholars. This membership made it possible for him to raise money to restore the village of O Cebreiro, including nine *pallozas*, the Galicians' ancient thatched, stone igloos,[304] and then the old pilgrim's hostel, and the church.

Jose, who now runs a gift shop in O Cebreiro, recalls his uncle as "a person of small stature, 1.68 meters (5 foot 5), thin but very wiry and extremely energetic." He would be up at seven in the morning, helping workman move stones for the rebuilding of the hostel or out working in the fields, do his priest's work

---

302 Pope Innocent VIII and Alexander VI both certified the miracle, and it was further ratified in some versions of the King Arthur stories, as Sir Galahad makes a mysterious pilgrimage here too. The libretto of Wagner's strange and punishingly dreary opera Parsifal has a relationship to it as well, as does *Monty Python and the Holy Grail*.

303 I got most of this from Don Valinas' nephew, Jose Valinas, in a written interview, with the help of Jessamyn Jackson of Cambridge, Mass.

304 No one is sure when the style of building developed but it is said to date all the way back to the region's Celtic days.

during the day, and then at night, after everyone else went to bed, study until three or four in the morning.

Today, the village bustles with tourists and pilgrims, but Jose, who was born in the village in 1970, remembers when only a handful of pilgrims would come through every year. When they did, his uncle would invite them to dinner and give them a spot to sleep near the fire of the living room of the Hospederia that he had restored with his sister, Jose's mother.

When Jose was about 10, his uncle embarked on another quest, to write a hiker's guide to the Camino, something that had not been done before. Whenever he was home from boarding school, Jose remembers, they would go out and review one more section of the Way. Elias would carry only a small bag of clothes on these expeditions, the draft of his guidebook, so he could add notes, and his camera. For their meals, they would buy something in the supermarket and eat it en route, without stopping. "At night we slept in a hostel in a double room or in a priest's house and he would wash my socks because I was too tired," he remembers.

The next day, they would do it all over again—get up at six, eat a quick breakfast, and then walk all morning, checking where they were against an old itinerary. "The Way at that time was almost nonexistent," Jose recalls. "[W]e had to take a car to check sections, write and draw, point out where there was a fountain or a tree to take it as a reference in the guide."

They also carried cans of yellow paint and brushes with them, painting big arrows to make it easier for the next pilgrims. Jose says he and Elias chose the color of the arrow together. "We liked it and it looked very good at sunrise and sunset," Jose recalls. Rumors that they stole the paint from the highway department were not true. "We would buy the paint in O Cebreiro and carry it along the Camino with us."

Once, his uncle gave him a job that only Jose could do: paint yellow arrows on the French side of the Roncesvalles Pass. Spain hadn't joined the European Union yet and Elias worried that the French gendarmes might give him problems, given the concerns at the time about Basque terrorism.

Jose wasn't Don Elias's only helper. One summer, Jose says, some college students volunteered to help him with the trail, and over a meal, he asked one especially enthusiastic boy to start an association of friends of the Camino in Galicia. The student agreed but forgot about it and was very surprised when Elias showed up at his dorm a few months later to ask him how the project was coming along.[305]

As more people began hiking the trail, Don Elias helped coordinate the creation of associations for the Camino de Santiago all across northern Spain, and even met groups in France and Germany interested in restoring their own sections.

After his uncle died unexpectedly in 1989 at 61, Jose kept on working on the trail, where he would occasionally run into people who remembered his uncle. Once, he said, while working on a new edition of Elias's guide, his car got stuck in a river. "The man who helped us get the car out of the river told us, `The only time I had to take out another car out of the river was for a man who was crazy, said he was a priest and was making a guide of the Camino.'"

Today, there is a small monument to Father Elias near his church—a bespectacled bronze head that sticks out of a scallop shell-embossed block of granite. It's an odd sculpture that looks, appropriately enough, like a bust crossed with a Camino highway marker—but that doesn't much matter. The real monument to the man that nearby bronze tablet describes as "curate of O Cebreiro and first among the pilgrims," was in that snug little cafe that morning, where we were surrounded by a crowd of other shivering pilgrims, drinking coffee to try to warm themselves up, and the thousands of others on the trail behind us, all the way back to Saint-Jean-Pied-de-Port, Vezeley, Arles, and Le Puy en Velay, France, and even Munich and Vienna, and the thousands of others on the trail ahead of us, following the yel-

---

305 Eventually, the student became a professor, also focused on the Camino, and wrote his own guides.

low arrows to Santiago— the 192,000 who would receive their diploma in 2012, and the thousands who have followed us since then, a number that now exceeds 300,000 in a normal year. [306]

On the other side of O Cebreiro, we began a long drop—600 meters, from 1,337 to 753 meters' elevation. Before taking the plunge at one of the crests, I was reminded of the end of the first *Star Wars* movie, just before the rebels blow up the Death Star, when the pilots are trying to get up the nerve to make the big dive.

"I'm getting that 'I'm going in, Porkins,' feeling," I told the girls.

"Or in your case," Thea said, "'I, Porkins, am going in.'"

It was a nice long ride down, particularly if you had the advantage of ballast. Cybèle hated these long, steep drops—she always rode behind all of us, where she could see the girls wobbling in the wind, and me, without my glasses, flying down the hill—and knew there were reasonable odds that one of us might end up either somersaulting into the ditch, if we were lucky, or halfway down the mountain, if we were not.

But these hills didn't scare me, for some reason, I'm not sure why. It wasn't that I hadn't noticed plenty of markers for expired perigrinos and, I suppose, bicigrinos, by the side of the road. I had also not forgotten about Leen's friend with his 67 operations. But maybe because I was so glad not to be pushing my way up the hill or just for the sheer exhilaration, I enjoyed those long whizzing flights. It belonged to that category of experiences I remember having more of when I was younger —a stupid thing

---

306 If you have any pull at the Vatican, you might mention Father Elias. Given that Domingo de Calzada earned his saint-stripes just for building a bridge and a hospital, I would think bringing the whole Camino back might be worth at least a beatification.

to do that would have been an almost equally stupid thing to miss.[307]

Later in the afternoon, it started to rain, not the kind of torrent you can duck out of for a few minutes until it passes but a persistent soak that seemed likely to continue all day long, and did.

We reached Triacastela around four, wet and tired.

Once we had checked in and dried off, I checked my email and found a message from an editor that made me jump:

```
Ben, Just checking in. I need from you:
Estimate of final word counts for Kumar and
Lessard, as well as number of infographics
(i.e., exhibits that contain graphics, as
opposed to text tables) in each.
ETA for each.
How's it going? If something's the matter,
let me know.
Best,
Martha
```

By now, I felt beyond tired, almost bruised. I'd never tried to juggle work and travel to such extremes before, and the gears of the editorial machine were starting to smoke and spark.

There was no working cash machine in town that day, so dinner ended up being a little mingy. I had another bowl of Caldo Gallego, which I also liked. I have tried to make it several times since then, without much luck—maybe because I forgot to add the 50-kilometer bike ride.

---

307 If you think about it, however, we have this all wrong. As you get older, you should actually be less risk averse, given that you have less time to lose.

August 25. Triacastela to Portomarin, 50.7 km
In which we near the end.

I was glad to leave Triacastela, which despite the promising name no longer has even *una castela*. It's a cute little town—mostly green and white and wet that day, and judging by the general dankness, maybe every day—but our hostel that night had cold concrete walls that seemed to bring the dampness inside. Our housemates included a nice young guy from Taiwan who didn't speak much English, and an American woman from Madrid who unfortunately did. It is possible we caught her on an off day or she caught us, but for whatever reason a faint air of superiority clung to her like bad perfume. The place also had a poor kitchen—one pot, one burner, and a sign limiting use to particular hours, although only eight or nine people were staying there.

Most of the day the road was relatively flat, with views of well-tended fields in every direction.

Midmorning, we passed Saria, the starting point for many walkers because it's 100 kilometers from Santiago—you get full pilgrim credit if you start from there. Several school buses were unloading troops of school kids, especially middle schoolers, about to start their walk.

A paved road ran right alongside the gravel path, so we would weave back and forth between the road and the trail, depending on how smooth and busy the trail looked. The ups and downs were gentle so we made good time, particularly when we hit another long drop.

At one point in the midafternoon, we were slowed down by a part of the path covered with tree roots, and as we walked our bikes around them, I heard coming up behind us, and steadily gaining, a familiar click, click, click—

The Swiss Killer! The young woman was still marching along, and not only that, passing us again—even though we had been on bicycles now for nearly two weeks!

"Amazing!" I said

"How are you doing?" Cybèle asked.

"Good," she said, with a curl in her lip that may have been a smile.

"Maybe we'll see you in Santiago?" I asked.

"Maybe, but I'm going on to Finisterre," she said, glancing backward as she passed.

Finisterre!—the end of the world—the ocean. Some of the guidebooks claimed this was where the ancient, pre-Christian pilgrimage ended, and now people were bringing that section back too, making the Atlantic the end of their hike rather than Santiago de Compostela. I thought of the ocean and the sun setting straight into the sea, just like being back home in Oregon. That would be a great way to end it all right. I made a mental note to discuss it later with Cybèle. [308]

Then we crossed a river, the rio Miño, and soon we were in the town of Portomarin. The Miño looked tidal at Portomarin— muddy and full of seaweed—but the water level must have just been way down, because it runs south to Portugal, about 300 km. away. [309]

---

308 The guidebooks all mention this connection between the Celts and Finisterre but I have not actually found any evidence of one. Given there were no imaginative monks involved in the creation of this pilgrimage, I was inclined initially to give its boosters the benefit of the doubt. However, after a look at a book on the invention of the Finisterre pilgrimage (Heritage, Pilgrimage and the Camino to Finisterre: Walking to the End of the Earth, edited by Cristina Sánchez-Carretero), it seems clear to me that Galicians have not lost their touch for storytelling. In the mid-90s, at roughly the same time as scientists cloned Dolly the sheep, tourism promoters for the towns on the rocky Coast of Death (another recent marketing invention) essentially cloned the Santiago pilgrimage, adding a route from Santiago to the towns of Finisterre or Muxia on the coast, including the system of stamps and passports, and the awarding of a diploma. The Church would have nothing to do with this invention—locally, the Finisterre walk is sometimes called the Camino of the Athiests. But even without the Church's help, the pilgrims came up with their own rituals to mark the end of the pilgrimage—the burning of their old clothes or objects they had carried with them (a practice now banned), a swim in the sea, and contemplation of a sunset. Celts or no Celts, the modern Finisterre walk has turned into a real pilgrimage for the tens of thousands of people who now make this hike every year.

309 Appropriately enough for pilgrims, the word "Miño" goes back thousands of years, to the Indo-European root for "walk," or "go."

Portomarin used to be right on the banks of the Miño but was relocated to higher ground in 1963 when the government dammed the river. The more architecturally significant buildings were disassembled brick by brick and rebuilt higher and further back, behind the high cliff that marked the new river bank, but something about the result seemed odd, like a drawing where the perspective is slightly out of whack.

At the heart of the square, some distance apart from the other buildings, stood the church of San Xoán (Saint John), a fortress-like building that used to belong to the Order of Saint John of Jerusalem, a military order like the Order of Santiago, also known as the Knights Hospitaller. It's an austere bunker that has about as much grace as a castle built of granite Legos. The church was prettier inside—mostly gray stone and an austere whitewash, and only one other visitor, a nun who sat with her legs up on a bench near the sacristy, making herself at home. I guess membership has its privileges, as American Express used to say.

The town used to be a fishing village before the dams killed most of the fish, but it's worked out in the end because these days Portomariners are doing well as fishers of men—the town was packed with pilgrims. Most of the hotels were full and we were worried, because I had forgotten to make a reservation.

Fortunately, we found a hostel that still had space. From the entrance, it didn't look very big but once we were inside we realized we had walked in on the top floor of a tall building built on the side of a cliff, like a troopship that had berthed in the harbor, which had hundreds of bunks and enough facilities to care for a small army of Christian soldiers, with room left over for five infidels.

August 26. Portomarin to Melide, 44.7 km
Wherein I discover a new favorite food.

The crowds in Portomarin made it hard to imagine that the modern Camino was so new, and harder still to think that it had begun in the 1980s, just a few years after Franco's death, at a time when many younger Spaniards were giddily, gleefully secular.[310] Given the close ties of the Church to the old regime, the odds of a medieval pilgrimage with strong fascist and racist associations making a comeback would seem fairly low.

But somehow it happened: since the mid-1980s, the number of pilgrims heading to Camino de Santiago has grown continually, and have now reached proportions not seen on the trail for centuries.

Why the Camino has struck such a strong chord again is an interesting question. Beyond the crucial pull of Father Elias and his yellow arrows, a number of other forces seem to have been at work.

Perhaps the biggest thing is that many pilgrims came home feeling that they had done something that had some significance. One anthropologist says that many people seem to find the Camino a transformative experience, whether or not they are religious. "Pilgrim 2.0," as Lucrezia Lopez at the University of Santiago de Compostela calls today's pilgrims, get something out of the walk but not necessarily something Catholic. Out of 63 Italian pilgrim diaries published on the Internet she studied, only 12 said they made the walk for religious reasons. Post-pilgrimage, the parts they enjoyed most was a sense of a freer way of life with no commitments, no constraints, and no frenetic

---

310   One case in point: in 1983, at about the same time as Don Elias was painting his arrows, Pedro Almodóvar, the filmmaker, was performing in Madrid in a punk transvestite duo, Almodovar and McNamara. Their 1983 hit "Yes, I'm going to be a mom," included the lyrics "I'll have a baby ... I'll dress him as a woman ... I'll call him Lucifer."

rhythms. Some saw it as a special life experience (17) that taught them new ways of looking at the world (16).[311]

On the other hand, pilgrimages are something that people have always liked to do. For instance, scholars have catalogued 24 different kinds of pilgrimages that people undertook in classical and Christian Rome.

The impulse is strong enough that pilgrimages have sometimes even jumped religions. Arabians, for example, have been making a pilgrimage to a temple known as the Kaaba (the Cube), since the third century BCE, which Muhammad reinvented it as an Islamic ritual.

In the 1500s in Mexico, a popular pilgrimage grew up very quickly to a shrine for Saint Anne, the Virgin Mary's mother. The Aztecs described this as a pilgrimage to Toci (Nahuatl for "our grandmother"), and although Bernard of Sahagun, the Aztec ethnologist and missionary, acknowledged that they were technically correct—Saint Anne was Jesus's grandmother—he suspected they were observing their old religion under a new name.

In the end, however, why pilgrimages are so universal remains a mystery. As G.G. King puts it in *The Way of Saint James*, "The known facts of geography, though edifying, cannot ... tell why, though religions come and go, men set their feet eternally toward a certain hilltop, there to lift up their hearts. *Sursum corda!* [Lift up your hearts!] The attitude is old as humanity, the emotion is strong as death."

Or it may just be the walking itself that people like. Walking meditations have a long history, and walking generally also tends to get good press.

It's natural, I suppose, to try to see your compulsions as vir-

---

311 I think a lot of this comes down to a feeling along the lines of something I read recently by the Buddhist monk Thich Nhat Hanh:

People usually consider walking on water or in thin air to be a miracle. But I think the real miracle is not to walk either on water or in thin air, but to walk on the Earth. Every day we are engaged in a miracle that we don't even recognize...

tues, but some of the great walkers have considered walking to be a primal state of being, maybe even a primal religion. Thoreau imagined an old chivalric order of walkers errant, "a sort of fourth estate outside of Church and State and People." The English travel writer Bruce Chatwin thought about writing a book called *The Anatomy of Restlessness*, the central thesis of which would be that

> in becoming human, man had acquired, together with his straight legs and striding walk, a migratory 'drive' or instinct to walk long distances through the seasons; that this 'drive' was inseparable from his central nervous system; and, that, when warped in conditions of settlement, it found outlets in violence, greed, status-seeking or a mania for the new. This would explain why mobile societies such as the gypsies were egalitarian, thing-free and resistant to change; also why, to re-establish the harmony of the First State, all the great teachers - Buddha, Lao-tse, St Francis - had set the perpetual pilgrimage at the heart of their message and told their disciples, literally, to follow The Way.

Chatwin may have been onto something here: a few scientists have noted that this tendency to wander does seem to be distinctly human. Tosquelles, the radical psychiatrist of Saint-Alban certainly thought so. "Man is a guy who goes from one space to another," he said. "He cannot stay in the same space all the time. That is to say that man is always a pilgrim, a type who goes elsewhere." And it's true that our nearest cousins don't go in for migration, as a rule—for the most part, monkeys only stir themselves in search of sex or food. Plenty of people have had the good sense to stay at home rather than sell their farm to go see someone else's, as Shakespeare puts it, but the fact remains that of the more than 100 species of primate in nature today, all are territorial and never migrate.

Except for us.[312]

---

312 I emailed E.O. Wilson, the great socio-biologist, and asked him whether pilgrimages might have a biological basis. He sent me the following generous note, which I'm including because I think it could be used as a model of well-mannered deflection:

Dear Mr. Voyles,

You make a very good point. I hope you will continue research on this important subject.

Warmest,
Edward O. Wilson

As we neared Melide, at a narrow bridge where we had to get off our bikes and walk, we met another family, a father with three girls roughly the age of ours. They were from Madrid, and the father spoke some English. He was separated from his wife, and for several years now, he had taken their daughters out to bike different sections of the Camino every summer. This year they were going to finish, and he seemed sad about that.

"When you get to Melide, you should get some *pulpo*," he advised, as we got back on our bikes.

So we did.

Melide, it turns out, is the pulpo (octopus) capital of Galicia, which is saying something, because octopus may be more popular in Galicia than anywhere else this side of Japan.

Traditionally, the Galician coast has been a paradise for octopi and octopus eaters. One anthropologist believes that the Galicians have been eating octopus since prehistoric times, but this seems to be mostly a guess, as "the octopus has no bones and leaves very little in the way of archaeological remains." Historians do know for sure, however, that it has been that way a long time: as early as the fifteenth century, peasants often paid their tithes and rents in dried octopus. In 1752, a census of the town of San Xoan de Arcos recorded 102 heads of family in the village— 48 laborers, 39 tanners, 19 cobblers, and nine octopus vendors. *Pulpo* is still very popular, but to keep up with the demand, Galicia must now import about 24,000 tons of the 30,000 tons of octopus it consumes every year, drawing from the catch of 24 different countries.

I'm not sure why Melide became the octopus capital—the town is an hour's drive from the sea—but judging by the number of pulpo-related signs, its position is secure.

A man stood at the door of every *pulpería* (octopus-eria), snipping off the tentacles with scissors, as if he were chopping up some fat pink carrots into a pot, and then stirring the little rounds with salt, olive oil, and sweet and spicy paprika. Normally, I'm not a fan of octopus—there is something too anatomical about it to my taste—but barbecued pulpo is about as good as it gets.[313]

After lunch, we went first to our hostel, which was again large and crowded, and then wandered around the town. Melide is a nice place, a more substantial town than we had seen for the past few days. As G.G. King noted, "Most of these villages, strung along the Way literally, as minnows are strung on a willow switch, have no streets but the main road, only foul alley-ways on either side, climbing up or winding down. But Melide is built like a miniature city, with streets and squares and convents, many church-es, and outlying chapels."

Melide was bustling with street markets and people out walking. It felt like a carnival, and the girls' excitement about finishing and the prospect of back-to-school shopping raised the collective mood too. On one of the main streets, we ran into a familiar face—our friend the gangly French woman we had last seen outside Cahors. Her feet were bandaged now and she was evidently in a fair amount of pain—like the Swiss Killer, she must have been walking at least 40 kilometers a day—but

---

313   To make polbo *á feira*—Galician fair-style octopus —you take one octopus, then dip its tentacles three times in a copper cauldron of boiling water, until the tentacles start to curl. Next, let the tentacles boil for up to 90 minutes until they aren't rubbery, take the cauldron off the fire and let it stew for 20 minutes.

Trim the tentacles, toss with salt, olive oil, and paprika. Serve on wooden plates and bread with little barbecued green peppers. By tradition, you're not supposed to serve water. A young Galician red wine is generally advised.

she was still smiling as much as ever. She couldn't believe it was almost over, she said, looking dazed and wistful.

We didn't spend much time with her—the guy she was with, an older American with suspiciously bright blond hair, looked the other way while we talked, his expression distinctly unfriendly.[314]

After we left our friend but before we went for a second round of pulpo, we passed a group of people who were sitting down at an outdoor café to celebrate a wedding. Next to them on the small plaza, an older couple, evidently the duo Nebraska, to judge by the sign behind them—a singer in a glittery dress, dark-dyed hair, and plenty of makeup, and a keyboard player—were testing microphones and setting up an outdoor dance floor.

---

314 Something similar had happened in a restaurant the night before, when we met a table of older American women; Cybèle and I concluded that for some people, seeing a family on the Camino sucks the romance right out of the adventure. If an American family can do it, you might as well have gone to Disney World.

August 27. Melide to Santiago de Compostela, 55.9 km

"My tale is doon; we been almost at towne." Chaucer

It was foggy in the morning, and the path was wider than before and better paved. We passed more clergy on the trail now, including many nuns in white, which helped give the whole scene an eerie quality, like one of those low budget, time travel pictures where the hero bicycles into a fog and comes out 500 years earlier. *Pray, Sirrah, whence cometh ye and whither ye goest on yon clockwork steed?*

"One day away from Santiago," Cybèle wrote, *"I feel both sad and relieved—sad that our summer is almost over and relieved that we are still alive and that we were able to do what we wanted to do. The girls are in a good mood now that they see the end and they are much more comfortable on the bikes and don't have a fit every time they see a major hill. They really understand that most uphills mean a downhill."*

Besides the uphills and downhills, the other truism that struck us as profound was that no two days were the same. Just when we thought we had figured it all out, there would be a new development—something new would break down, something new would happen, or we would see something that we could not possibly have predicted. In the end, it's a "chicken in a church" world.

We started to realize too, particularly now that we were on this busier part of the Way and every few kilometers passed a monument to a prematurely expired pilgrim, that there were all kinds of ways you could get hurt, or even die doing this. There could be a rock in the road, a hill that was just a little too steep, a car zooming unseen from around a corner—which is probably just as true at home, mile for mile, but we felt it more on bikes.

At the same time, we also began to think there is more kindness in the world than generally acknowledged. People often went out of their way for us: the farmer's wife who got up early to make pancakes for the girls for breakfast; the hostel manager who gave Charlotte and Thea her lavender oil to keep off the mosquitos; Frodo, who warned us against biking down the mountain path; and our Belgian friends, who initiated us into the mysteries of tire changing.

Since then, on the long reading pilgrimage about the Camino that I took once we got back, I learned another, darker lesson as well. Medieval people, as we have seen, treated saints' relics as something powerful, like a smidgen of plutonium. While it's easy to laugh at that now, viewed from a slightly different angle, I think they were right: in the end, myths should be handled with care. Whether they lead you to turn against communists or  Cathars, priests or Muslims, Protestants, "witches," Jews, or the insane, getting you to go along with the pogrom requires that you first believe in an "Us" and a "Them," when the truth of the matter is that we are all *perigrini*—"strangers"—bound not necessarily on *the* Way but on *a* way—and you should be very wary of anyone who insists otherwise.[315]

A few miles from Santiago we passed a place with a stream called Lavacolla (literally, "wash your ass"[316]) in which, the 12th century guide hinted, "French pilgrims, out of respect for the Apostle,

---

315 I think often of a mentally disabled man I interviewed in Middletown in my newspaper days, who was trying to set up a support group for people with similar challenges. I began, "So, as a mentally retarded person, would you say that—"

"Stop," he said, raising a finger, "we don't like that word."

"What would you prefer?" I asked.

"People who are a little slow in the learning department," he said.

He had a point, and the more I thought about it, the better the point got. The only problem with his description is that I think it actually covers all of us one way or another.

316 This point is disputed. Some scholars argue that the root of the streams name comes either from the word for testicles (*colae*) or neck (*cuello*), or washing clothes (*lava e colle*). The hint, however, remains the same.

wash not only their private parts but, stripping off their clothes, clean all the dirt from their bodies." [317]

Not being all that dirty, at least compared to the old-time pilgrims, we skipped our dip, and started pedaling down the last hill before Santiago, which we could now see five or six kilometers in the distance—city, cathedral, and all.

For me, the adventure ended about halfway down that hill, on a bumpy path between a ditch and a cyclone fence. As we passed the landing strip of the Santiago airport, a big plane roared in over our heads, the first we had seen up close in two months. For a second, the jet seemed to hang in the air above us, strange, white, and huge. In two days, we would be on that same plane heading the other direction, but right now, it looked as unreal to me as a flying saucer.

On the other side of the airport, we came to a succession of industrial buildings and car dealerships, and the Way became surprisingly rough and badly marked, as if Santiago wanted to give his pilgrims a final challenge.

After some bumbling through the traffic we reached the old town, where we went from being a little lost to extremely lost. The city was busy, filled with tourist shops and a lot of posters of a very grizzled Tom Jones, the old British pop star, who was performing in town that night. There were signs to the cathedral here and there, but the streets were narrow and crowded and the buildings tall enough that we couldn't see the church at all until we finally came out on the plaza. I saw a long Renaissance building in front of us—which I recognized from the guidebook as the royal hospital that Ferdinand and Isabella had built and Franco had restored as a hotel—and on our right, the old pockmarked cathedral and its forest of steeples.

317　Apparently not everyone, however: I have read but not been able to confirm that the practical reason for the famous giant incense burner in the cathedral at Santiago was not just to bless the pilgrims but to fumigate them.

Santiago!

Afterword

In which we learn to live without yellow arrows.

It was fairly late by this time, so we didn't go into the church right then, but went instead to look for our hotel. The hotel was about as hard to find as the cathedral had been, located just out of the old town, on the fifth and sixth floors of a nondescript, modern building. Having just a few floors of a building is a common thing for two-star hotels in cramped old European towns, but it also felt odd to me just then, as if the hotel was also not quite real.

I often had that sensation of unreality over the next few days. Even after we had rolled the bicycles into the UPS office to ship them home, picked up Masha's passport that our friend Linda had sent there for us, and stopped for a haircut so I could feel respectable again, I still felt as if the real world were out on the trail, and the city more or less fake. It's a feeling that still comes and goes for me even now, like the rosacea I developed that summer that in some moods gives me a look of permanent pink surprise.

As we walked through the front door of the hotel, Charlotte noticed six silver bicycles parked under the stairs in the landing. The Belgians! It had to be. In a city of 95,000 plus who knew how many tourists, we had ended up in the same hotel. The woman at the desk said yes, the bicycles did belong to a big Belgian family, so later that night I called their room, spoke to Jean, and we agreed to meet for breakfast in the morning.

Outside, the rain was falling hard, and Tom Jones would soon be giving his concert. Before we went to bed, I showed the girls a few of his videos on YouTube, singing "It's not unusual" over and over again for five decades. It's not unusual to have a hard time getting old, but to do it as a pop star must be hell, particularly if your signature step is a hip wiggle that over the years has slowed and stiffened to a rheumatic stitch. But then again, there must have been a lot of British pensioners in Spain who remembered Jones in his prime, so maybe the stadium concert in the rain that night wasn't as sad as I imagined.

Coming Attractions

We met Jean in the morning with two of his kids. Gert and the rest had already left for Antwerp, so the eight of us walked up the fresh-washed street to an old tin-ceilinged cafe for churros and coffee. They were out of their bicycle clothes now as well, and we all had the unsettled look of people recently discharged from an institution. Jean seemed to have made his peace with the trip being over.

We talked about the religious side of the pilgrimage, and he mentioned that his brother was a priest. Personally, he said, Catholicism was something in the background that he didn't think too much about, but was somehow still a little there.

I was still no Catholic, despite our pilgrimage, but right then, I envied him for that sense of assurance. I still remembered how nice it was, in the past, to have a bit of cosmological scaffolding overhead.

After an hour or so we said our goodbyes.

Our second order of business was to go to the cathedral and get our Compostela, the certificate that said we had completed our pilgrimage.

For some reason, I really wanted to do this, and kept reminding Cybèle about it. I'm not sure why, given that, as I mentioned, I still had not turned Catholic again. Maybe I just wanted to cross the official finish line, or to be able to prove that we had really done it—really covered all 1,500 kilometers. But as I think about it now, I wonder if I also just wanted to stay a pilgrim a little longer. I have spent so much of my life barely explicable to anybody, including myself, that I think I had enjoyed being part of a herd for a little while, following one yellow arrow after the other.

When we got to the square, we found a long line of pilgrims at the pilgrim office next to the cathedral waiting to get their *credencial*. Two kinds of diplomas are distributed: one for the true religious pilgrims, which is in Latin; and another for heathens, which just says you have done it. I felt a little torn about this but my greed for the fancy diploma won out, and I decided I would say I had made a religious pilgrimage, and advised the rest of my gang what I had read.

At the counter, a friendly old Englishman looked at our pilgrim passports, which were now covered in stamp after stamp. He chatted with us a little, passed us on to another desk, where they filled out our paperwork, and then handed us our diplomas—four in brown with a Latin inscription, and one more like a school participation award, set in a cartoony font (14-point Comic Sans), for Thea, who had been honest.

Outside the office, I looked at my brown diploma for a second— it had an engraving of Jesus with a walking stick at the top, a stamp and a scallop shell at the bottom, and in between a paragraph of Latin and my name—and then gathered it up with the other four diplomas and slid them into my backpack behind the computer. Thea was annoyed that hers was different, but soon forgot about it. I don't think any of us have looked at them since, though I have looked at the pilgrim passports and the row after row of stamps a few times. That part of the pilgrimage, anyway, had been real.

Next, we went into the cathedral, which was crowded that morning. Professor King imagined that, "In the great years, and at the height of the season, this church must have been—God forgive me!—rather like Coney Island." There would have been

> immense crowds tramping through and everything had to be shown to them, and everything explained, so that those on the outskirts could hear, and offerings had to be accepted and if necessary stimulated, and the sacraments of penance and the Mass somehow put through, with the perpetual lisping rustle at confessionals and the perpetual tinkle of sacring bells at minor altars....[318]

> The pilgrims [would have] pushed about stupidly in the dark, and asked each other where one went for the certificate of confession, and where one went for the certificate of communion, and how much money to have ready for each, in the exact change, because of the crowding.[319]

Inside the cathedral, we passed a statue of Santiago Matamoros on horseback, his sword still raised high, smiting three and a half Moors now coyly hidden behind some plastic shrubberies, and then made our way around the rest of the dark old church.

---

318 In the old days, there would also have been guides to add to the confusion. Art historian Conrad Rudolph notes that guides had been part of traveling since the Greeks, without any break, and most major churches had guides for visitors in the Middle Ages. In the 14th century, the Franciscans even offered walking tours in multiple languages to pilgrims in Jerusalem. The quality would vary wildly—in every era, people have complained about overly imaginative tour guides—but some churches posted sheets of parchment with information to set them straight, or rather, to give them the official story.

319 Even in modern times, visitors to the church have often been on the wild side. King, who visited in 1920, complained that the women in the church were very rough, which she attributed to their being abused by their husbands. "In consequence, they unite the strength of a man to the irresponsibility of a child. At Compostela, in the church, they would go through a crowd like rowdy small boys, by sheer strength of shoving with muscular elbows and trampling with heavy shoes."

After we finished our visit at the cathedral, we told the girls they could get a souvenir if they wanted one but only Thea took us up on the offer.[320]

On our last night in Santiago, we stopped at a bakery and bought a *torte de Santiago*, a delicious almond cake covered in powdered sugar except for a stenciled cutout of the dagger-cross, a local

---

320   Thea was pleased with the little silver scallop shell necklace she found and wore it happily. It had been a good trip for her, though she never admitted it. All the fresh air and exercise agreed with her and seemed to make her (like me) less moody than back home during the year. She felt proud of herself too, as she should have—not many 11-year-olds could have done what she had done, keeping up with the rest of us every step of the way. This mood lasted a few weeks, until Miley and her other friends convinced her that the trip sounded like a horrible and stupid way to spend a summer, and the locket disappeared into a drawer. (Thea has a different version:

> First, the souvenir was not offered on the spot —it had been agreed before leaving Paris that I would get a special necklace for participating (I remember this because at 11 years old, the legalities of my greed were very important). Secondly, it didn't disappear into a drawer because of bullying—I did think the trip was lame at the time but I was very willing to ignore that out of mercenary interest— the chain broke...)

In any case, she didn't lose the scallop. Just last year she put it on a new chain, along with a few other things.

As for the other girls, Charlotte still thinks the Camino was a waste of time, although over the next few years, she did join us on other family endurance contests, even when she reached an age when she might have made other choices, and a few years ago did make a long bicycle trip up the Elbe voluntarily with a friend. Masha has actually talked about walking the Camino again, this time with her friends. It's not an adventure if you do it with your parents, she says. I think she may be right about that, at least if the parents are halfway conscientious; after all, as a kid, you're on a package tour, which is almost guaranteed to be a little boring. That isn't true if you're nominally in charge—there were several moments on the trip when Cybèle and I thought afterward we really might have died—but as long as you're a kid in the family, you don't feel that anxiety, whatever happens. That's the parents' problem.

Cybèle and I missed the Camino a lot after we got back, and still think seriously of turning nomad. Buried here in my papers, I miss carrying everything I need on my back. I miss the hills, the churches, and the sunflowers. I miss being outside, and the feeling of physical tiredness at the end of the day. I miss the people we met too, and even now, I sometimes think I see them on the street. Jean and I emailed a few times, and he invited us once to Easter in Antwerp, but we never worked out the logistics.

specialty we planned to bring to our friends in Madrid the next day.

In the crowded moonlit main street on our way back to the hotel, we ran once more into the Italian bicyclists.

"Ah," sneered the one who spoke the most English, "the happy family!"

We forced a chuckle and went on our way, but the phrase "happy family" gnawed at me. Of course, at some level, we would always be a family, but we would be taking Masha to boarding school in three days, and over time, if all went according to plan, the girls would just be visitors who turn up in the apartment from time to time, and our life as a family mostly a memory. The adjective was even more problematic. Had we been happy? Like our summer, there had been more good days than bad, and we had been very lucky, but happy? What did that even mean, when you got down to it?

This wasn't quite the way I had imagined our adventure would end—with me just one more sunburned tourist shuffling back to our hotel with a torte de Santiago. Really, the way we *should* have done it was to push on to Finisterre, to the Atlantic, like the Swiss Killer. An orange sunset! A windy cliff! Father and mother, nodding sagely on the shore of the Western sea. The daughters, now tougher and wiser. The whole family, together to the last, casting a cold eye on the face of eternity! Now that would have had some style to it.

"I've been looking at the map," I had told Cybèle, at our last coffee break before we reached Santiago. "It's just 80 kilometers to Finisterre. There's a small mountain range, but—"

"Next time," Cybèle said.

Acknowledgements, bibliography, and further notes

I want to thank my readers, particularly Don Durfee of Reuters and Washington, DC, Brenden Gammill of Berlin, Germany, Pamela Grundy of Charlotte, NC; Jessamyn Jackson of Cambridge, Mass.(who gave me the idea of the 18th Century titles); the intrepid Bill Nagler of Farmington, Conn. (who slogged through it twice!); my academic guardian angels, Dean Robert and Professor Robin Stacey of the University of Washington; my parents, Jim and Shirley Voyles of Sunriver, Oregon; my daughters, Masha, Charlotte, and Thea, and above all, my tireless co-maniac pal, Cybèle Troyan, who was with me every step of what turned out to be a very long trip.

I also want to thank our traveling companions on the first part of this trip, our fellow pilgrims, and the people who took care of us along the way. My descriptions of what we saw as well as our occasional disagreements were intended to give the reader a feeling of what it's actually like to be on a long slog like the Camino, not to hurt anybody's feelings. My nonfiction-writing teacher, John Hersey, said that a journalist needed to be fair to himself, his subjects, and his readers, and I tried to do that.

Helena de Felipe of the Universidad de Alcala was also extremely helpful in explaining several aspects of medieval Spain, and Ramsay MacMullen, professor emeritus at Yale, offered good advice on understanding the transition from paganism to Christianity. Given that I researched this book without ever setting foot in a library, I also owe a tremendous debt to Archive.org, Amazon, ABE books, Google, JSTOR.org, and (although it was not always a reliable friend) Wikipedia. And finally, I would like to thank Vladimir Cerić of Belgrade, the most patient book designer in the world.

I have tried to keep names and terms as simple as possible—for example, by sticking to one name for something even though in practice it may have more: the Camino de Santiago is usually called the *chemin de Compostelle* in France and sometimes

the *Camino francés* in Spain. The language of southern France is sometimes called Occitan but I've stuck to the more familiar Provençal. The crusade against the Cathars is also often called the Albigensian Crusade—after Albi, a center of Cathar life. Historians these days usually call Muslim Spain *Al-Andalus*, but for clarity's sake I stuck to Muslim Spain.

A number of other names have been changed to protect the innocent, as they used to say on *Dragnet*.

I've committed many acts of journalism, and for better and worse, the work doesn't train you to be very exacting bibliographically. However, I have tried to note the major sources I've leaned on, and I list them here mostly in order of appearance.

The major guides—*The Way of Saint James*, Allison Raju (Cicerone); *Miam-Miam, Dodo* (Les Editions du Vieux Crayon)—I consider more as characters than references—and for *Don Quixote* I usually use Smollett's translation.

The other title that comes up a lot is the *Codex Calixtinus*, a five-volume collection, including the first guide for pilgrims, which was written, or at least compiled, in 1139–1145 (see August 11 for more details). I didn't have a favorite edition.

Of the modern books I used, the one that made the most impression was Georgiana Goddard King's *Way of Saint James* (1923). King was a pioneering Bryn Mawr art historian who wrote about several journeys she made alone, in part by donkey, between Toulouse and Santiago from 1911 to 1921. "[A] female Indiana Jones, dressed in culottes, wearing a pith helmet, and brandishing an umbrella" who believed that "`[t]he only way to know anything is to go and look.'" (Chance, Jane, ed., *Women Medievalists and the Academy* (University of Wisconsin, 2005). King is an enthusiastic and intrepid guide.

Another worth noting, but also worth warning about, is Walter Starkie's *The Road to Santiago - Pilgrims of St. James* (John Murrays, 1957), an early book about the modern pilgrimage. A professor of Spanish literature, Starkie has interesting insights but he's not terribly reliable. A fascist sympathizer and a lover of gypsies—a difficult combination to sustain, if you think about it—Starkie made me a little uneasy. An actor who knew him, Michael MacLiammoir, wrote

> ... with Don Gypsy Starkie of Trinity College, Lansdowne Road, and the Albaicin, everything is possible, everything is improbable, everything is majestically unreal. Would he produce a bottle of the wine of Samothrace from his wallet, or a pack of cards painted with the images of Fate and Change and Adventure from his pocket, or a rabbit from his hat, or merely a sheaf of Cooke's travel cheques? (Damian Keane, *Ireland and the Problem of Information* [Penn State Press, 2014]).

Finally, I took a lot from Richard Fletcher's book on Diego Gelmirez, the wily archbishop of Santiago: *Saint James's Catapult: The Life and Times of Diego Gelmirez of Santiago de Compostela* (Clarendon, 1984).

All mistakes are my own, of course. My readers did their best.

With the exception of two drawings by Thea and Charlotte, the illustrations are mine, and drawn in pencil, ink, and watercolor pencil, then spruced up a bit in Photoshop. Most are from photographs taken by Cybèle.

Most of the book is set in Old Iowa.

Preface

Borde, Andrew. *The Fyrst Boke of the Introduction of Knowledge* (Early English Text Society, 1870).

Chaucer, Geoffrey, "A Voyage to Compostella," Harvard's Geoffrey Chaucer Website, Chaucer.fas.harvard.edu.

July 7. Le Puy en Velay: Notre-Dame du Puy

Adams, Henry. *Mont-Saint-Michel and Chartres* (Constable, 1936).

Ahmad, Fikri. *Art roman du Puy et les influences islamiques* (Leroux, 1934).

Bavon-Tollet, Jacqueline. *Le Puy-en-Velay et la révolution française, 1789-1799* (Universite de Saint-Etienne, 1982).

Campbell, Joseph. *The Masks of God: Primitive Mythology* (Penguin, 2000).

Ettinghausen, Richard, et al. *Islamic Art and Architecture* 650-1250: 2nd Edition, (Yale, 2003).

Mandet, Francisque, *Notre-Dame du Puy: légende, archéologie* (1860).

Moss, L.W. and Cappannari, S.C. "The Black Madonna", The Scientific Monthly, Vol. 76, No. 6 (Jun., 1953), pp. 319-324.

Taine, H.A. "Napoleon's Views of Religion," The North American Review, Vol. 152, No. 414 (May, 1891), pp. 567-58.

July 8. Le Puy en Velay to Saint-Privat-d'Alliers: Saint-Roch

Boccaccio, Giovanni. *The Decameron* (Delphi Classics, 2017).

Karkov, Catherine E. *The Art of Anglo-Saxon England* (Boydell, 2011).

Ortega, Jessica. "Pestilence and prayer saints and the art of the plague in Italy from 1370 – 1600," https://stars.library.ucf.edu/

honorstheses1990-2015/1367.

de Voragine, Jacobus. *The Golden Legend or Lives of the Saints,* Englished by William Caxton in 1483 (IntraText edition 2007).

Zielinski, Sarah. "Plague Pandemic May Have Been Driven by Climate, Not Rats," Smithsonianmag.com, Feb. 23, 2015.

July 9. Saint-Privat-d'Alliers to Saugues: Beasts of Gévaudan

Greene, Jeffrey. *The Golden –Bristled Boar: Last Ferocious Beast of the Forest,* (University of Virginia Press, 2011), quoting Jean Lavollee, a French boar authority.

Hemingway, Ernest. *Hemingway on Hunting* (Simon and Schuster, 2011).

"Wild boars run amok," *The Local.fr* (https://www.thelocal.fr/20180827/french-farmers-furious-as-wild-boars-run-amok)

Taake, Karl-Hans. *Solving the Mystery of the 18th-Century Killer "Beast of Gévaudan",* National Geographic.com, 9/27/16.

Taake, Karl-Hans. *The Gévaudan Tragedy: The Disastrous Campaign of a Deported 'Beast'* (Kindle, 2015).

Wright, Nicholas. *Knights and Peasants: The Hundred Years War in the French Countryside (Warfare in History)* (Boydell 2000).

July 11. Chapelle Saint-Roch to Aumont-Aubrac: The revolutionary hospital of Saint-Albans

Faupin, Sabine. "Auguste Forestier's unbroken wanderlust," *Epidemiology and Psychiatric Sciences,* Vol. 26, Issue 3, June 2017, pp. 228-230.

Favereau, Eric et Artières, Philippe. "Une Aventure de Fous," a five-part series about *François* Tosquelles and Saint-Albans,

437

Libération, 29/7/2016.

Auguste Forestiere entry,Art Brut Collection abcd, Montreuil, France.(https://abcd-artbrut.net/en/collection-en/forestier-Auguste)

Meyers, Todd. Jean Oury and Clinique de La Borde: A Conversation with Camille Robcis.(http://somatosphere.net/2014/06/jean-oury-and-clinique-de-la-borde-a-conversation-with-camille-robcis.html)

Robcis, Camille. "François Tosquelles and the Psychiatric Revolution in Postwar France," *Constellations*, Vol. 23, Issue 2 (June 2016), pp. 212-222.

Robcis, Camille. Interview with historian Camille Robcis:Hidden Persuaders: Institutional Psychotherapy in France: An Interview with Camille Robcis (BBC.ac.uk, 28 Sept. 2016)

(http://www.bbk.ac.uk/hiddenpersuaders/blog/robcis-interview)

Sauvargnargues, Anne, trans. Bankstone, Samantha. Deleuze and Art,(Bloomsbury Academic, 2013).

July 12. Aumont-Aubrac to Nasbinals: Aubrac

Moulin, Annie. *Peasantry and Society in France Since 1789* (Cambridge University Press, 1991).

Bessière, Jacinthe. "Local Development and Heritage: Traditional Food and Cuisine as Tourist Attractions in Rural Areas, Sociologia Ruralis, Vol. 38, Issue 1, April 1998, pp. 21-3.

Mendras, Henri and Cole, Alistair. *Social Change in Modern France: Towards a Cultural Anthropology of the Fifth Republic* (Cambridge University Press, 1988).

July 13. Nasbinals to Saint-Chely-d'Aubrac: Chez Germaine

"Saint-Chély-d'Aubrac. Chez Germaine: passage oblige!"La Depeche, 18 May 2010.

July 14. Saint-Chely d'Aubrac to Espalion: Spires, petanque, decapitation

Larson, Frances. Severed: *A History of Heads Lost and Heads Found* (Liveright, 2015).

Navrot, Jacques. "La Boule Integrale," (http://lyon.monplaisir. free.fr/Sauvegarde%20ancien%20siteBoule_Integrale.htm)

Interview with Dylan Rocher (http://www.codesport.fr/actualites/autres/pétanque/article/dylan-rocher-la-releve-assure#. XX8IxyVS-V4)

"Dylan Rocher pétanque on a quand meme la pression de gagner," *Le Parisien*, 26-12-2018.

July 15. Espalion to Golinhac: The D'Estaings

Henley, Jon. "A genuine chateau seals Giscard's noble destiny," The Guardian (17 Feb. 2005).

Valance, Georges. VGE, Une Vie (Flammarion, 2011).

July 16. Golinhac to Conques: Monky business

Adrian R. Bell and Richard S. Dale, "The Medieval Pilgrimage Business," Enterprise & Society, vol 12, no. 3, September 2011.

Kinstedt, Paul. *Cheese and Culture: A History of Cheese and its Place in Western Civilization* (Chelsea Green, 2013).

Foucault, Michel. *Discipline and Punish: The Birth of the Prison*, trans. by Alan Sheridan (Vintage, 1995).

Geary, Patrick J. *Furta Sacra: Thefts of Relics in the Central Middle*

Ages (Princeton University Press, 1978).

Pacioli, Luca. *Cripps, Jeremy. Particularis de Computis et Scripturis 1494 Fra Luca Pacioli: A contemporary interpretation*, pdf. (Pacioli Society, 1994).

July 17. Conques: Saint Foy

Sheingorn, Pamela, ed. and trans. *The Book of Sainte Foy*. (U. Penn. Press, 1995).

July 18. Conques - Livinhac le Haut: Bridges

Bottenberg, Ray. *Bridges of the Oregon Coast* (Arcadia, 2006)

Child, Julia with Prud-homme, Alex. *My Life in France* (Knopf, 2006).

July 21. Cajarc to Limogne en Quercy: Francoise Sagan

Hughes, Robert. *The Spectacle of Skill* (Knopf 2015).

Sagan, Françoise. *Et tout ma sympathie*, second edition (Editions Stock 2014).

Quoirez, Jacques and Grudet, Claude. *«Allô oui» ou les Mémoires de Madame Claude* (FeniXX, 2015).

July 23. Mas de Vers – Cahors: John XXII

Albe, Edmond. *Hugues Géraud, évêque de Cahors: L'affaire des poisons et des envoûtements en 1317* (Creative Media Partners, 2018; originally published in 1904).

Bailey, Michael D. *Fearful Spirits, Reasoned Follies: The Boundaries of Superstition in Late Medieval Europe* (Cornell University Press, 2013).

The Bank of the Pope, Or, The Sacred Taxes of the Chancery, and of the Penitentiary, of Rome, as Established by Pope John XXII in 1316, and published by Pope Leo X in 1514 (Barrett & Jones, 1846).

Boureau, Alain. *Satan the Heretic: The Birth of Demonology in the Medieval West* (University of Chicago, 2013).

Collard, Franck. *The Crime of Poison in the Middle Ages* (Praeger 2008).

Groom, Veronica J. *The trial of Hugues Geraud: City, church and papacy at the turn of the fourteenth century*, University of Exeter thesis 2001 (downloaded from EThOS).

Houlbrook, Ceti and Armitrage, Nathalie., eds. *The Materiality of Magic* (Oxbow Books, 2015).

Rollo-Koster, Joëlle. *Avignon and Its Papacy, 1309–1417: Popes, Institutions, and Society,* (Rowman and Littlefield 2008).

Sanders, Michael. *Families of the Vine* (Random House, 2001).

Schmidt, Muhammad Wolfgang G.A. *"And on this Rock I Will Build My Church: A New Edition of Philip Schaff's History of the Christian Church,"* 1049-1517 (Disserta Verlag 2017).

Schwarz, Hans. *The Christian Church: Biblical Origin, Historical Transformation, and Potential for the Future* (Fortress 2000).

Thorpe, Adam. *Notes from the Cévennes* (Bloomsbury, 2018).

Trivellato, Francesca. *The Promise and Peril of Credit: What a Forgotten Legend about Jews and Finance Tells Us About the Making of European Commercial Society* (Princeton University Press, 2019).

Weakland, John E. "Administrative and Fiscal Centralization under Pope John XXII, 1316-1334", Catholic Historical Review 54 (1968).

Weakland, John E. "John XXII before his pontificate: 1244-1316:

Jacques Duèse and his family," *Archivum Historiae Pontificiae*, Vol. 10 (1972), pp. 161-185 (25 pages).

July 24. Cahors to Montcuq: The Cathars

Barber, Malcolm. *The Cathars: Dualist Heretics in Languedoc in the High Middle Ages* (Pearson, 2000).

Boswell, John. Christianity, Social Tolerance, and Homosexuality (University of Chicago, 1981).

Lambert, Malcolm D. *The Cathars* (Blackwell, 2003).

Léglu, Catherine, Rist, Rebecca, and Taylor, Claire, eds. *The Cathars and the Albigensian Crusade: A Sourcebook* (Routledge, 2014).

Marvin, Laurence W. *The Occitan War: A Military and Political History of the Albigensian Crusade, 1209-1218* (Cambridge University Press, 2008).

Puylaurens, William of. *The Chronicle of William of Puylaurens: The Albigensian Crusade and Its Aftermath* (Boydell 2003).

Shirley, Janet, trans. *The Song of the Cathar Wars: A History of the Albigensian Crusade (Crusade Texts in Translation)* (Routledge, 2000).

Taylor, Claire. *Heresy, Crusade and Inquisition in Medieval Quercy* (Boydell & Brewer, 2011). (For the Simone Weil quote.)

Taylor, Claire. *Heresy in Medieval France: Dualism in Aquitaine and the Agenais, 1000-1249* (Royal Historical Society Studies in History, 2011).

July 25. Montcuq to Moissac: Saving the Jewish scouts

"F. Boulet: Moissac a sauvé autant de juifs que le Chambon," *La Depeche*, 24/08/2014(https://www.ladepeche.fr/article/2014/08/24/1938742-f-boulet-moissac-sauve-autant-juifs-chambon.html).

Braswell, Sean. *When the US turned away 20,000 Jewish children fleeing Nazi Germany.* (https://www.ozy.com/flashback/when-the-u-s-turned-away-20000-jewish-children-fleeing-nazi-germany/79700)

"The Flood of the Century in Southwest France, 3-4 March 1930," https://vanessafrance.wordpress.com/2015/03/03/the-flood-(o(f-the-century-in-southwest-france-3-4-march-1930).

Hirsch, Jean-Raphaël, *«Réveille-toi Papa, c'est fini»* (Albin-Michel, 2014)

Les Inondations de 1930 à Moissac (Version longue) (https://www.youtube.com/watch?v=QaIgK2R41oA).

Lewertowski, Catherine. *Les enfants de Moissac: 1939-1945* (Flammarion, 2009).

July 26. Moissac to Saint-Antoine: Quills and Handwriting

Blake, William, "Ah! Sun-Flower."

Daybell, James. *The Material Letter in Early Modern England: Manuscript Letters and the Culture and Practices of Letter-Writing, 1512-1635* (Palgrave MacMillan, 2012).

Labalette, Francoise and Raoul, Yann, "Current uses and markets of the French Sunflower production" (Onidol and Sofiproteol, white paper from isasunflower.org, undated).

Nuseed.com, "History of the Sunflower" (nuseed.com, undated).

McCulloch, J.R. *McCulloch's Commercial Dictionary* (Longman, Brown,1832).

Santoy PhD., Claude PhD. *The ABCs of Handwriting Analysis* (Da Capo, 2005).

Wong, Frederick. *The Complete Calligrapher, Frederick Wong* (Dover, 1999).

July 27. Saint-Antoine to Lectoure: Cybele

Alvar Ezquerra, Jaime. *Romanising Oriental Gods: Myth, Salvation, and Ethics in the Cults of Cybele, Isis and Mithras* (Brill, 2008).

Benko, Stephen. *The Virgin Goddess: Studies in the Pagan and Christian Roots of Mariology* (Brill,1993).

Boreaud, Philippe. *Mother of the Gods: From Cybele to the Virgin Mary* (Johns Hopkins University Press, 2004).

Gibbon, Edward. *The History of the Decline and Fall of the Roman Empire* (Project Gutenberg, 1776).

Lane, Eugene N., ed. Cybele, *Attis and Related Cults: Essays in Memory of M.J. Vermaseren* (Brill, 2015).

MacMullen, Ramsay. *Christianity and Paganism in the Fourth to Eighth Centuries* (Yale University Press, 1999).

Rebillard, Eric and Rupke, Jorg, eds. *Group Identity and Religious Individuality in Late Antiquity* (Catholic University of America Press, 2015).

Tripolitis, Antonia. *Religions of the Hellenistic-Roman Age* (Eeerdmans, 2002).

Williams, Craig A. *Roman Homosexuality: Second Edition* (Oxford, 2010)

July 28. Lectoure to Castelnau-sur-Auvignon: D'Artagnan and Gers

Dumas, Alexandre. *The Three Musketeers* (First Avenue Editions, 2017).

July 29. Castelnau-sur-l'Auvignon to Montreal du Gers

Defoe, Daniel. *The Life and Surprising Adventures of Robinson Crusoe of York, Mariner; Who Lived Eight-and-Twenty years, All Alone, on an Uninhabited Island, Near the Mouth of the Great River Oroonoque; with an account of his travels round three parts of the globe, written by himself*

(Reprint - Limbird, 1833).

Médan, Léopold. "Une traversée des Pyrénées à la fin du XVIIe siècle: Robinson en Gascogne." *Revue de Gascogne*, 1910, p. 385-419.

Thomas, Sean. "The last untouchable in Europe." The Independent (28 July 2008).

July 30. Montreal du Gers to La Hanque

"Qui-sont les Nouveaux Immigres qui vivent en France?" *Sud Ouest.fr* (https://www.sudouest.fr/2014/11/28/qui-sont-les-nouveaux-immigres-qui-vivent-en-france-1751452-705.php)

August 2. L'Air sur L'Adour to Pimbo

Brillat-Savarin, Jean Anthelme. *The Physiology of Taste or Meditations on Transcendental Gastronomy*, 1825, MFK Fisher trans. 1949 (Vintage, 2011).

Melville, Herman. *Moby Dick or The White Whale* (St. Botolph, 1922)

August 5. Le Sauvelade to Navarrenx: Henri Le Febvre

Elden, Stuart. *Understanding Henri LeFebvre* (Bloomsbury 2004), quoting Manuel Castells.

Le Febvre, Henri. *The Critique of Ordinary Life*, vols. 1,2,3 (Verso, 2014).

Wolfe, Michael. *Walled Towns and the Shaping of Medieval France: From the Medieval to the Early Modern Era* (Palgrave MacMillan, 2009).

August 6. Navarrenx to Chateau de Joantho: Jeanne d'Albret

Bryson, David. *Queen Jeanne and the Promised Land* (Brill 1999).

Jeanne d'Albret, edited and translated by Kathleen M. Llewellyn. *Letters from the Queen of Navarre with an Ample Declaration* (Iter, 2016).

Smiles, Samuel. *The Huguenots in France.* (Cambridge, 2015).

August 7. Joantho to Ostabat-Asme: Basques

Anonymous. *The Pilgrim's Guide to Santiago de Compostela* (ca. 1140), from the Codex Calixtinus.

Aske, Jon. Basque. Basque proverbs. (https://www.buber.net/Basque/Euskara/proverb.php)

Kurlansky, Mark. *The Basque History of the World* (Penguin, 2001).

August 10. Bayonne to Saint-Jean-Pied-de-Port; Saint Jean to Burgete: Roland

Anonymous. *History of the Life of Charlemagne and Roland: Codex Calixtinus.*

DiVanna, Isabel. "Politicizing national literature: the scholarly debate around La chanson de Roland in the nineteenth century," *Historical Research*, Vol. 84, Issue 223, February 2011, pp. 109–134.

August 11. Burguete to Larrasoaña

Cox, Ian, ed., *The Scallop: Studies of a shell and its influences on humankind* (Shell Transport and Trading Company, 1957), a commemorative book for Shell Oil's diamond jubilee.

Kyle, Chris. American Sniper: *The Autobiography of the Most Lethal Sniper in U.S. Military History* (Harper Collins, 2013).

August 12. Larrasoaña to Pamplona: Hemingway

Hemingway, Ernest. *The Sun Also Rises* (Scribner, 2016; originally published 1926).

King, David. "Hemingway, Catholicism, and his struggle to find meaning," Georgia Bulletin (https://georgiabulletin.org/commentary/2016/11/hemingway-catholicism-struggle-find-meaning).

Williams, John, Stones, Alison, eds.,*The Codex Calixtinus and the Shrine of St. James* (Gunter Narr Verlag, 1992).

August 13. Pamplona to Puente La Reina

Castro, Américo. *The Spaniards: An Introduction to their History* (University of California Press, 1985).

Judt, Tony. *Postwar: A history of Europe since 1945* (Penguin, 2005).

August 14. Puente La Reina to Los Arcos: The Assumption Fiesta

Porter, Arthur Kinglake. *Romanesque Sculpture of the Pilgrimage Roads* (Hacker Art Books, 1966, reprint from 1923).

Whitehead, Nadia. "People would rather be electrically shocked that left alone with their thoughts." Science (July 3, 2014).

August 15. Los Arcos to Najera: Witch trials

Gilitz, David M., Davidson, Linda Kay, *The Pilgrimage Road to Santiago: The Complete Cultural Handbook* (Macmillan, 2000)

Henninsen, Gustav. *The Witches' Advocate: Basque Witchcraft and the Spanish Inquisition (1609-1614)* (University of Nevada, 1980).

Keitt, Andrew W., *Inventing the Sacred: Imposture, Inquisition, And the Boundaries of the Supernatural in Golden Age Spain* (Brill, 2002).

Southey, Robert. *The Poetical Works of Robert Southey: Collected by Himself*, Vol. 7 (Longman, 1838)

Najera: Peter's Quran

While researching this I ran into a a book, *The Matter of Araby in Medieval England* (New Haven, 1976), written by an old friend, a professor I adored, Dorothee Metlitzki, a brave and slightly mad lady who tried and largely failed to teach me the Bible in English literature at Yale. She was a quadruple émigré – from Russia to Germany to England to Israel to the USA – who had a deep belief that literature was more than a parlor game and a capacity for moral outrage I admired. One case in point: I remember visiting her once at her home in Hamden during the Iran-Contra hearings, and hearing her say, "The one good thing about Russia is that in Russia, all these men would have been shot."

Kritzick, James Aloysius. *Peter the Venerable and Islam* (Princeton University Press, 1964)

Abu 'Abdallah Muhamad ibn Musa al-Kharizmi; ed. and translated by Rosen, Frederic Originally the *Compendious Book on Calculation by Completion and Balancing, republished as The Algebra of Mohammed Ben Musa* (Oriental Translation Fund, 1831).

August 16. Najera to Belorado

Bennassar, Bartolomé. *The Spanish Character: Attitudes and Mentalities from the Sixteenth to the Nineteenth Century,* trans. by Benjamin Keen (University of California Press, 1979).

Eby, Cecil D. *Comrades and Commissars: The Lincoln Battallion in the Spanish Civil War* (Pennsylvania State University, 2007).

Farina, William. *Saint James the Greater in History, Art and Culture* (McFarland, 2018).

Kendrick, T.D. *Saint James in Spain* (Methuen, 1960).

Wreglesworth, John. "The Chronicle of Alfonso III and its significance for the historiography of the Asturian Kingdom 718-910 AD: A critical study of the content, purpose and theme of a late

9th century historical text," (University of Leeds PhD dissertation, 1995).

August 17. Belorado to Burgos

Blackburn, Paul, trans. *The Poem of the Cid* (University of Oklahoma Press, 1998).

Hourihane, Colum. *The Grove Encyclopedia of Medieval Art and Architecture*, Vol. 2. (Grove, 2012).

Ingram, Kevin. *Converso Non-Conformism in Early Modern Spain - Bad Blood and Faith from Alonso de Cartagena to Diego Velázquez* (Palgrave Macmillan, 2014)

Irish, Maya Sifer. *Jews and Christians in Medieval Castile* (CUA Press, 2016).

Lawrence, Mark. *The Spanish Civil Wars: A Comparative History of the First Carlist War and the Conflict of the 1830s* (Bloomsbury Academic, 2017).

Martin, Mel. *The Magnificent Showman: The Films of Samuel Bronston* (Bear Manor, 2007)

Payne G., Stanley and Palacios, Jesús. *Franco: A Personal and Political Biography* (University of Wisconsin, 2014).

Purkis, William G. and Gabriele, Matthew, *The Charlemagne Legend in Medieval Latin Texts* (Brewer, 2016)

Ruiz, Teofilo F., *Spanish Society 1348-1700* (Taylor & Francis, 2017).

Soyer, Francois. *Popularizing Anti-Semitism in Early Modern Spain and its Empire: Francisco de Torrejoncillo and the Centinela contra Judíos (1674)*. (Brill: 2014)

August 18. Burgos to Boadilla del Camino

"Cuts blamed for deaths caused by devastating Spanish wild-fires," Guardian (Aug. 22, 2012).

"St Anthony's Fire – Ergotism," Medicinenet.com

Soyer, Francois, *Popularizing Anti-Semitism in Early Modern Spain and its Empire: Francisco de Torrejoncillo and the Centinela contra Judíos* (Brill, 2014).

August 19. Boadilla del Camino to Sahagún

León-Portilla, Miguel. *Bernardino de Sahagún: First Anthropologist* (University of Oklahoma Press, 2012).

August 20. Sahagún to León

Bond, Sarah E. "Sacrificial Lambs: Livestock, book costs, and the premodern parchment trade," personal blog. [https://sara-hemilybond.com/2016/04/04/sacrificial-lambs-livestock-book-costs-and-the-premodern-parchment-trade]

Castro, 424-425.

Hodgett, Gerald A.J. *A Social and Economic History of Medieval Europe* (Routledge, 2006).

Kamen, Henry. *The Spanish Inquisition: A Historical Revision* (Phoenix Giant, 1997),p.8.

O' Callaghan, Joseph. *A History of Medieval Spain* (Cornell University Press, 1975).

August 21. León: Welcome to the Hotel Santiago

Crémer, Victoriano. *El Libro de San Marcos* (Nebrija 1981)

Digby Wyatt, Matthew. *Architect's Note-book in Spain* (Lectour, 2020, originally published 1872).

Fernandez-Jalvo, Yolanda, et al. *Human cannibalism in the Ear-*

ly *Pleistocene of Europe (Gran Dolina, Sierra de Atapuerca, Burgos, Spain)*, The Natural History Museum, Journal of Human Evolution (1999) 37, 591–622.

Hochschild, Adam. *Spain in Our Hearts: Americans in the Spanish Civil War.* (Houghton Mifflin Harcourt, 2016), p 32.

Lawrence, Mark. *The Spanish Civil Wars: A Comparative History of the First Carlist War and the Conflict of the 1930s* (Bloomsbury, 2017).

Marzan, Julio. *The Spanish American Roots of William Carlos Williams* (University of Texas Press, 1994).

Moreno-Luzón, Javier and Núñez Seixas, Xosé M. *Metaphors of Spain: Representations of Spanish National Identity in the Twentieth Century*, edited by Javier(Berghahn, 2017), p. 249.

Preston, Paul. *The Spanish Holocaust: Inquisition and Extermination in Twentieth-Century Spain* (HarperPress, 2012).

Wikipedia article, Convento de San Marcos (León), sourced to ÁLVAREZ OBLANCA, Wenceslao; SERRANO, secundino (2009). La Guerra Civil en León.

August 22. Leon to Santa Catalina de Somoza

Carr, Matthew. *Blood & Faith: The Purging of Muslim Spain* (Hurst, 2017).

De la Cueva, Julio. "Religious Persecution, Anticlerical Tradition, and Revolution: On Atrocities against the Clergy during the Spanish Civil War." Journal of Contemporary History, vol. 33., No. 3 (July 1998), pp 355-369.

Dykema, Peter A., and Oberman, Heiko Augustinius, eds. *Anticlericalism: in late medieval and early modern Europe* (Brill, 1993), p.239, quoting Bartolome Bennassar.

Holguin, Sandie Eleanor. *Creating Spaniards: Culture and National Identity in Republican Spain* (University of Wisconsin Press, 2002).

Ingram, Kevin. *Converso Non-Conformism in Early Modern Spain: Bad*

Blood and Faith from Alonso de Cartagena to Diego Velázquez (Springer, 2018).

Johnson, Paul. *History of the Jews* (Phoenix, 2013), p. 116.

Kendrick, T.D. *Saint James in Spain* (Methuen, 1960).

Lannon, Frances. "The Social-Political Role of the Spanish Church – A Case Study," *Journal of Contemporary History*, Vol. 14, No. 2 (Apr., 1979), pp. 193-210.

Lieberman, Sima. *The Contemporary Spanish Economy: A Historical Perspective* (Routledge, 2005).

Rodriquez, Garcia-Arenal Mercedes, and Mediano, Fernando Rodriguez. *The Orient in Spain: Converted Muslims, the Forged Lead Books of Granada, and the Rise of Orientalism* (Brill 2013).

Teresa of Ávila, *The Life of St. Teresa of Avila by Herself*, trans. J. Cohen (Penguin, 2004).

August 23. Santa Catalina de Somoza to Molinaseca

Adams, John. *The Works of John Adams*, vol 3: Diary, essays, autobiography (Little, Brown, 1865).

Freud, Sigmund, trans. by Gregory C. Richter *Civilization and its Discontents* (Broadview 2016).

González, Pablo Alonso. "Race and ethnicity in the construction of the nationa in Spain: the case of the Maragatos," Ethnic and Racial Studies, Sept. 2015.

Zweig, Stephen, quoted in Carr.

August 24. Villafranca del Bierzo to Triacastela

Nabhan-Warren, Kristy. *The Cursillo Movement in America: Catholics, Protestants, & Fourth-Day Spirituality* (University of North Carolina, 2013).

Meades, Jonathan. "From bombs to Benidorm: how fascism disfigured the face of Spain," *Guardian* (26 Aug. 2019).

Pack, Sasha D. "Revival of the Pilgrimage to Santiago de Compostela: The Politics of Religious, National, and European Patrimony, 1879-1988," *The Journal of Modern History*, Vol 82., No. 2, June 2010, pp. 335-367.

Sampadero, Jose. All quotations from Jose Sampadero are from an interview by email translated with the help of Jess Jackson.

Sánchez-Carretero, Cristina, ed. Heritage, *Pilgrimage and the Camino to Finisterre: Walking to the End of the World* (Springer 2015).

Oficina del Peregrino, Santiago. Statistics (https://oficinadelperegrino.com/en/statistics).

Sanchez y Sanchez, Samuel, ed. *The Camino de Santiago in the 21st Century* (Routledge, 2017).

August 25. Portomarin to Melide

Chatwin, Bruce. *The Anatomy of Restlessness: Selected Writings 1969-1989* (Penguin, 1997).

Hanh, Thich Nhat. *At Home in the World: Stories and Essential Teachings from a Monk's Life* (Parallax, 2019).

Picq, Pascal. "Homo, the great migrating ape," 14 June 2015, Colloquia on the Archaeology of Migrations. (https://www.inrap.fr/en/homo-great-migrating-ape-12774)

Schweld, Richard, *Octopus* (Reaktion 2013)."

"No hay pulpo gallego para tanta 'pulpeira,'" *El Pais* (26 Dec. 2017).

August 26. Melide to Santiago de Compostela

Rudolph, Conrad. "The Tour Guide in the Middle Ages: Guide

Culture and the Mediation of Public Art," *Art Bulletin* 100 (2018) pp. 36-67.

Bennett Voyles is a business writer who lives in Berlin. He is working now on a book about a walk he made from Berlin to Rome with his wife, Cybèle Troyan, in the fall of 2018. The working title is *Andjiamo, Schatzi! or A Ramble to Rome, Being an account of a 1,500 kilometer walk through Germany, Switzerland, Lichtenstein, and Italy by two escapees of an empty nest.*

Index

Chapter subject index

Places index

Printed in Great Britain
by Amazon

29654175R00270